Penguin Books

WE WERE THERE

Dr John Barrett is a reader in history at La Trobe University in Victoria. His book *That Better Country* (Melbourne University Press, 1966) examined religious facets of Australian colonial life, while *Falling In* (Hale & Iremonger, 1979) looked at Australia's first conscription scheme in the early twentieth century. By the accident of birth in January 1931 he has never been a soldier, not even a peacetime national serviceman. But he cannot forget seeing his brother go into the RAAF in 1940, or his father join the Second AIF twenty-five years after he had joined the First.

WE WERE THERE

AUSTRALIAN SOLDIERS OF WORLD WAR II

JOHN BARRETT

Penguin Books

Penguin Books Australia Ltd,
487 Maroondah Highway, P.O. Box 257
Ringwood, Victoria 3134, Australia
Penguin Books Ltd,
Harmondsworth, Middlesex, England
Viking Penguin Inc.,
40 West 23rd Street, New York, N.Y. 10010, U.S.A.
Penguin Books (Canada) Limited,
2801 John Street, Markham, Ontario, Canada L3R 1B4
Penguin Books (N.Z.) Ltd,
182–190 Wairau Road, Auckland 10, New Zealand

First published 1987 by Viking

Published with corrections in Penguin, 1988

Copyright © John Barrett, 1987

Typeset in Bembo by Abb-typesetting Pty Ltd,
Collingwood, Victoria
Offset from the Viking edition
Made and printed in Australia by
The Book Printer, Maryborough, Victoria 3464

CIP

Barrett, John, 1931–   .
We were there: Australian soldiers of World War II.

Includes index.
ISBN 0 14 011145 X (pbk.)

1. World War, 1939–1945 – Personal narratives,
Australian. I. Title.

940.54'81'94

CONTENTS

NX163469, Lieutenant R. B. Joyce, in August 1945

AUTHOR'S DEDICATION

Professor Roger Bilbrough Joyce had long been working on a biography of Sir Samuel Griffith. When it seemed that it might soon be completed, I wandered into his room at La Trobe University one day and asked, 'What are you going to do when you've finished old Griffith?' He looked up with his impish grin and said frankly, 'I don't know.'

I tossed him an idea, and developed it sketchily. 'How about coming in with me on a book that lets Australian soldiers of World War II talk about themselves? We could give them a questionnaire . . .' Intentness replaced the grin on his face. 'Yes,' he said, 'all right.' He was a man of quick decisions. It had taken perhaps five minutes.

The sequel took several years, but Roger Joyce built up great enthusiasm for the project. When *Samuel Walker Griffith* was published at last, and the bulky questionnaires were in, he set to work on coding their contents. He was one among others in that job, but he did more than his share – having unusual powers of speed and concentration. He was relaxing in a game of pennant squash when his heart gave out. Very suddenly Roger Joyce was dead at the age of sixty, but he had lived his own way to the end, punching vigorous activity into his minutes and wanting always to achieve more.

This may not be the book he would have liked to see. His repeated cry was, 'There are dozens of books that could come out of this marvellous stuff. I don't know how we can do justice to it.' He was right. It was not easy to see or agree on the best way. In the end he had no hand in the writing, but he did much towards making this book possible.

It is therefore dedicated to Roger Joyce, who was once NX163469, as well as to all men, living or dead, who served as Australian soldiers in World War II.

A RECONNOITRE

Who lay where? Australians look for comrades' graves, North Africa, late 1942

1 • SNAPSHOTS

Old soldiers often have photographs, neat in an album or dog-eared in a drawer. They have mental snapshots too. Lasting impressions, big moments, odd trivia, the whole wide range of war . . .

Waiting to attack Tobruk, 1941. I remember exactly when I started to smoke: 0400 hours, 21 April 1941. We had filed up into position, spread out and lain down in the desert. In the bitter cold we put our groundsheets around us and waited for the guns to open up. I was one day short of my eighteenth birthday. The peerless night sky was ablaze with stars, and I must have been whimpering to myself – I know I was wondering if I would ever see tomorrow's night sky – because the soldier on my right shuffled up and said, 'Come on, son. Have a drag.' We put a groundsheet over our heads. He rolled a cigarette, licked it, cupped his hands and lit it, then thrust it into my mouth. I will never forget his kindness. Between spluttering and trying to smoke, I forgot my self-pity. I've been smoking ever since, and I used to notice on leave that you could always tell an infantryman; he would have nicotine stains on the palm of his hands from constantly cupping his cigarette. We were expert at hiding the glow of a cigarette tip, because to show a light was to get shot at, or reap abuse from the sergeant and one's mates [Roland Marsh].

Flinders Street, Melbourne, 5 September 1939. A good question, why did I join the army. One thing was being sick of being used up at a few bob a week. Another chap and I were working the orchards at Doncaster. Tucker pretty rough. Boss – well! We decided to push our bikes down to Melbourne. He was 25, me 19. Lined up to the window. The bloke said, 'How old?' Twenty, I said. 'You'll have to get your old man's consent.' Right-o. Round the corner, borrowed a pen, put the father's name on it. Little did they know I never even knew my father. The boss at the fruit place, soon as he was told we had both volunteered for the AIF, the bastard he sacked us. October 19th received a letter to report to the drill hall, Hawthorn [VX5416 – the army number of the man concerned].

Australian family, between the wars. I was born in 1916 and my father enlisted in that year and served in France in 1917–18. Afterwards he went farming under the returned soldiers settlement scheme in a rather undeveloped area. We grew up closely associated with the Returned Soldiers League activities in the Memorial Hall, and we knew well the Anthem and the shape of our flag, the meaning of Anzac and Armistice Day, and the sacrifices made by those young men of the First World War. The farm was too small to support our large family – there were ten of us children – and the depressed economic years made it worse. I commenced to earn outside at 15. I was nearly 24, and a head stockman, when I enlisted, and three of my four brothers also enlisted – one aged 21 and two others while still under 18. My father was an invalid pensioner by then, and all of us had left the farm [R. J. Anson].

Sydney, 1940. A lot of men made great financial sacrifices in joining. Also, I admired those with wives and families. I do not recall one man saying he was glad to get away from home. If a marriage was shaky there were less dangerous ways of breaking it up. I'll never forget the farewells before we boarded troopships for the Middle East. There were normal banners saying 'Good luck' and 'Goodbye Joe', and some ferries were booked out by relatives for circling the ships, but many men were pretty upset by other banners: 'Five-bob-a-day murderers.' A lot of the public wouldn't have leaked on the AIF then if it had been on fire ['Tom'].

Australian army camp, 1940. As a sergeant, I put two men on a charge for answering back. The CO sentenced them to 28 days hard labour, which was out of all proportion. From then on I dealt with whatever (rare) trouble occurred without reference to the CO. I would put the name of the offender once, twice, even up to four times in my 'black book', and the name was crossed out once for every extra or unpleasant duty given to, and performed by, the offender. This system worked exceptionally well. Names were *seen* to be entered, and *seen* to be crossed out [William John].

2/7th Field Ambulance, 1940–41. The men under my command gave me a nickname. Even quite serious offenders I never sent away, but fined 28 days pay. So they called me Colonel February [L. E. Le Souëf].

Indian Ocean, 25 April 1940. Anzac Day. Convoy at sea. The British battleship HMS *Ramillies* steamed through the ships, band playing Waltzing Matilda, signal flags flying message 'Welcome to New Anzacs' (or words to that effect). Most inspiring, but prompting a little doubt that we would be worthy of the name [VX876].

North Africa, December 1940. We were making some attempt to dig in. We'd got one trench about four feet at one end and eighteen inches at the other, and seven or eight of us were standing around when some planes flew over the hill above Salum. We had decided they were ours returning from a raid when Chica Newman suddenly said, 'Something fell out of one of those planes.' They weren't ours, and the something was bombs. The site of the bombing was a safe distance away, but the planes continued their run in our general direction. In panic we all dived into the trench, such as it was. From the bottom of the pack Curly Quinn complained 'Haven't got me tin hat', to which someone in the top layer replied, 'Bloody bad luck for us if *you* need your helmet, Curly' [NX4320].

North Africa, 1941. The first shelling we experienced outside Bardia convinced all ranks that slit trenches and gun pits were not a bad idea after all. Lieutenant J. A. R. K. Strong (later Major) inquired what the bloody hell those Ities were doing, the careless bastards had almost hit him. As I crouched in a very shallow hole with him, he said loudly to me, 'Is that you shaking, Sar-major?' 'Yes, sir.' 'No, it's me. Christ, I'm a frightened officer.' Laughter from all. For the remainder of the war this great officer did or said something outrageous whenever things were bad, thus relieving the strain [VX876].

Lebanon, 1941. Mount Taubel is situated outside Tripoli, and the 9th Division spent some months there, building fortifications. After the desert, Mount Taubel was a paradise. Beyond it a huge mountain rises over 12 000 feet, with the hollows of the foothills obscured by a vivid purple haze, while mountain streams sparkle in the sun. Where the mountain proper emerges from the hills, and the orchards give way to bushes, a sheer red rock-face stretches a thousand feet to the snowline but is often covered in cloud. One afternoon I was watching this when the sun's rays broke through a cleft in the clouds to shine full onto the red rock of that tremendous cliff. The whole was transformed into a magnificent glowing ruby set into the mountainside. I stood spellbound until, too soon, the clouds rolled over. In the midst of war and the litany of battle, the tranquil moments, the unexpected and the beautiful, are long remembered [NX27474].

Middle East leave, 1940–42. This is not intended for polite eyes, but it was the war. 'Rev on one and coast home on the other' was a vulgar sex-game played on our occasional one-day leaves to Tel Aviv or some other place. The minimum number of men performing was three plus the race starter himself, and the winner was the one who could keep it up the longest. Each Arab girl was paid 5s for her services, and would select her initial jockey. Everyone in their birthday suits, the men's tools at the slope, the starter would call 'Go.' No slacking allowed. Then the starter would call 'Change', and every man would have to uncouple and move to the next girl. Many men failed with the first filly, but I could often win by concentrating on football, fishing, manoeuvres – anything except what I was doing – and split the stakes with the starter [NX5872].

What amount of sex could anyone have on 3s a day? (I could have got 6s a day, but I made 3s allowance to my mother.) I never did give sex much thought; the older men said, you leave that until you go home [T. C. Birch].

As a married man with a strict Protestant upbringing, my experiences in Sister Street, Alexandria, were confined to voyeurism – and on one horrifying occasion we made a dash for the street where two of our number were physically sick in the gutter from what we had merely *seen*. Hygiene was also a factor. As a medical unit, we supervised the army-approved brothel in Aleppo and it surprised me, the numbers and types of men who patronised it. I knew because all who went to the brothel were checked in and out by the army, and their numbers recorded to ensure that all precautions against VD were taken. If VD was contracted and there was no record of your number in the book, it was regarded as a self-inflicted wound, and pay was stopped. I have no means of knowing, of course, whether the men went to look or act [SX9054].

Western Australia, 1942 . . . 1943 . . . 1944 . . . I am sorry, but I cannot answer any questions about my army life, and for these reasons. I was married with a family, and over thirty, when I enlisted in the AIF and was posted to the Armoured Division. Sent to Western Australia, I began 3½ years of my life that I have since endeavoured to erase from my mind just because I was kept there all the time. [A complex of decisions and changing circumstances resulted in hundreds of men in the armoured corps being trained and retrained, but never sent into action.] I became an NCO in that magnificent yet frustrated division. I was claimed by another unit, but my application for transfer was rejected; as an NCO I was 'key personnel', but if I returned to the ranks my application could be favourably considered. I returned to the lowest rank possible, that of driver. Still no transfer. Many others tried to transfer out of the division, and some gained their wish, but I was kept there until discharged at the end of the war, embittered. Then to find I was a member of the AIF but not entitled to join the RSL [because of no service overseas or in a designated war zone] . . . I am not proud of my army service, nor do I want to take part in any associated activities. As a result of those years I suffered permanent mental and physical disability [from a reply by one whose name is now a household word in Australia and beyond].

Greece, Anzac Day and the day after, 1941. They spent the day hiding off the beach at Kalamata, these veterans of Libya and Greece. They had smashed up their trucks to make them useless to the enemy, and so awaited night and the coming of the *Costa Rica.* The former liner from the South American run duly arrived to be packed with men, the machine-gunners among them mounting their guns. The Stukas [German dive bombers] found the ship at dawn. They did not do well; some were shot down by the machine-guns and no bomb hit the target; but the planes kept coming. Throughout that chaotic day the men in the saloons were entertained by one soldier who sat like a virtuoso at the grand piano replaying the songs the soldiers loved. I've never known who he was, but every time the klaxons warned of another attack, the pianist broke into 'And the captain's name was Captain Brown, and he played his ukulele as the ship went down'. Gilded mirrors reflected filthy, weary young men, and through the racket cheers rose and music tinkled. It was the last bomb from the last Stuka that hit the stern of the *Costa Rica*, which sank so comfortably that the men on board got safely off [A. I. Allan].

Getting off the Costa Rica, *26 April 1941*. It wasn't actually a direct hit that opened up the *Costa Rica*, but a near miss. She stopped and heeled over somewhat. We lined up and stood about, waiting for whatever was to happen, and I regretted not having learnt to do more than dog paddle. A couple of boats were launched but I think the list was too great to get others away, so we continued to stand around. Then the British destroyers came back and manoeuvred close enough to hold the ships together with grappling hooks. 'Jump, lads,' the crew kept shouting, and we jumped onto the rising and falling deck of a destroyer. I often think of that fine Mediterranean day, and that bizarre scene. I still think of those sailors from the *Defender*, *Hereward* and *Hero*, all sunk soon after. Every time I hear some idiot loudly revealing his racial prejudice against 'Pommies', my mind goes back to that day [V. H. Lloyd].

Tel el Eisa (Hill of Jesus), 1942. It's early Sunday morning. On the right, 'D' Company is being given the *Afrika Korps* benediction of shells. Men are still seen approaching the rendezvous for Mass, so some of 'C' Company are allowed to move off too, being told to keep well dispersed 'just in case'. They pass the ruins of the railway station, negotiate a minefield and arrive. Confessions are heard, and the Mass begins. At the time of the Consecration comes an ominous roar – experienced ears calculate about thirty bombers escorted by fighters. Father Byrne's congregation can clearly be seen from the air, and his own white vestments shine like a beacon against the desert. Close by are disused dugouts. Eyes turn to them. A stir runs through the men. A mild rebuke from the chaplain, and the only men moving are those beginning to receive the Blessed Eucharist. Engines whine. Bombs scream. Anti-aircraft guns explode. The earth heaves into shock waves. Prayer becomes very earnest, but no man looks where the bombs fall. Father Byrne might be celebrating Mass in a quiet church in his native Ireland. His congregation belongs to the faithful. Faith of our fathers. Faith of the blessed martyrs. Protestants and scoffers will be sparing them glances. Show the faith. Peace returns, suddenly. The Mass too is over. Is it God's miracle that the little flock is untouched? Do the pilots see what is happening and sheer away, and is that a miracle? Who knows? But the Catholics disperse to field positions with triumph in their hearts [NX27474].

North Africa and Italy, July–December 1942. We sappers cleared gaps in the minefield and barbed wire, but no vehicles appeared to be guided through, and no one relieved us, so we decided to go ahead and join the infantry on Ruin Ridge. About 2.30 a.m. a runner came in saying that the Germans had encircled us. Orders were not to fight our way out, but wait for the tanks. The only ones that came rolling up were German, so about 9.30 a.m. our surrender took place. Before the officers were taken to a different camp, the CO said he was sorry that he had let us down, to which we replied, 'It wasn't your fault, sir.' Then into Italian hands and on to Benghazi. A protest when an Aborigine was ordered to join black African troops bound for a coloureds camp. 'He is a black man, and yet you want him to stay with you,' shrugged the Italian colonel. 'So be it.' From Benghazi to Italy, narrowly missing being torpedoed on the way, luckier than the hundreds of POWs drowned when their transport was sunk near us. March through Brindisi, where posters on the walls showed soldiers in our uniform cast in the ugly man roles, yet there was much weeping among the crowds as we passed. In Bari our officers were our neighbours and they showed great kindness by throwing some of their food to us over the wire compounds. (Under the Geneva Convention they received the same as the officers of the detaining power.) Christmas came, and we each received a cash present donated by our officers in their camp.

Comment by Kiwi friend: 'You Australians certainly look after each other' [F.A.J.].

Greenacre, NSW, 1982. I started to write the attached on the way home from England on the SS *Mauretania* in July 1945, left off, and when I picked it up again thought what the hell, no one will believe it, so did not bother writing any more. It may be of some interest.

At the start of 1945, after well over three years as prisoners of war in Germany, we were roused at 2 a.m. and unceremoniously – helped along by rifle butts – urged out on to the road. The Russians were beginning to break through, so we would march across Germany in mid-winter. At Schulitz we met former colleagues who gave us what little bread they could spare, not knowing that within 48 hours they would crave for it themselves. POWs, displaced persons, slave labourers, Jewish women branded on the forehead – all forced to stagger along day after day until they dropped, fingers falling off from frostbite, great sores that soap and water would have prevented . . . Hunger pains wracking our bodies from the inside and the elements seeking to tear our rags from us outside . . . Does God still look after us? Men dropping and being carried by mates too weak to help themselves. 'Macca' whispering in my ear – or maybe shouting, 'Get up, you bloody fool' – and lugging me along, sobbing in his throat . . . Day followed day, night followed night. A blizzard . . . I woke to find that some chaps had got on to some Red Cross parcels and – your friends of yesterday – were wolfishly eating and not offering you any. That day I hated men of my own nation . . . Ten days on we had a break. We were put into a German barracks evacuated because of the speed of the Russian advance, and we found some bread and cigars. On a stove was a pot of hot soup for the guards and, as no one was around, we took it – and twenty men had their first decent meal for almost two weeks. Soon there was a burst of shooting, and we were told that three Frenchmen had been shot for stealing the soup. We hastily washed our dixies, but we didn't care. Death was as much a part of the day's march as was the snow we stumbled through. We were losing our sense of values . . . A week past and we – the walking dead, passing through scenes of brutal horror – were shut in barns. A waggon loaded with hot potatoes was driven into the farmyard for pigs, and men broke from the barns, ignoring shots and clubbings until the guards gave up and stood watching six hundred men fighting in a foot of slush for food for pigs (yes, 'English' pigs, as the Jerry said later). Men turned to animals not so much because they were hungry as because they knew that hunger was sapping at their will, so they were afraid to let any chance of a feed pass. They will go back to civilian life, go to work with the paper tucked under their arm, and a little badge showing they are returned soldiers. I shall see them and smile, and they will smile back at me. In my mind's eye I will always see them grabbing for another man's rations . . . [S.A.R.B.].

North Africa, February 1941. The hardest thing I had to do was to take part in the retreat known as the Benghazi Derby. At one stage of it I was sent out on a patrol, moving out miles behind the retiring army. When we rejoined the company I sat on a heap of rubble, bearded, dirty, unable to remember when I had last eaten, had a drink of water, or slept. I was done. A little Italian girl about three years old came and put her hand on my knee, leant forward and looked anxiously up into my face with large dark eyes. Warmed by the little mite's concern, I put out my hand and lightly teased her curls. Suddenly she was snatched away by her mother, who gave me a look of disgust and hate. I was the enemy, and I felt it more then than when I was being shot at. I was hurt, but it helped me appreciate the state of mind of civilians in occupied territory [J. W. Quinn].

Singapore, February 1942. A little Chinese boy clung to me throughout an air raid. When it ended he hugged and kissed me, then shook my hand and wandered off down the road. That made me feel as big and strong as the Sydney Harbour Bridge [C. J. Weir].

New Guinea, 1942. At Isurava a party of our wounded from the 39th Militia Battalion were going south when Colonel Honner sent a runner to say that the battalion was in trouble, and anyone who could get back the three miles was needed. The *battalion* was in trouble, so twenty-seven out of thirty went back. The three who didn't were minus a foot, had a bullet in the throat, and a forearm blown off. We never did it for God, King, Country – forget that. We did it because the 39th expected it of us [J.W.B.].

New Guinea, 1943. Plodding through mud up to the knees for days on end, with a 25 lb pack plus weapons and ammunition, made me curse the war in no uncertain terms. Then one day I heard a soldier behind me praying, 'Dear God, help me pick *up* me feet. *I'll* put the bastards *down*' [SX20848].

Indian Ocean, 1943. Returning with the 9th Division, the last to come back from the Middle East, I was on the *Niew Amsterdam*. Two hundred miles off the Western Australian coast we smelt the smoke of fires in the eucalypts. Tough as we thought we were, there were few without tears in their eyes. We were going to make it. We were bloody going to make it! This is April 1983, and I have tears in my eyes again. Maybe that's what it means to be an Australian, mate [NX31016].

Ross, Tasmania, 30 June 1944. Dear Captain Fleming, it is very hard for me to find words . . . I most sincerely appreciate all the kind things you said about my late husband's qualities, as all I have left is his memory . . . The fact that Bruce and I were only married nine months when I received the news of his death makes it very hard for me to realise that I am, in such a short space of time, a widow and now a mother. I have a son, whom I called Bruce after his Daddy . . . Words cannot express my thanks . . . to each and every one of you for your kindness. I am, yours sincerely, Frances [from a letter kept for forty years by A. J. Barry, the mate of Bruce, who was drowned while on patrol in Dutch New Guinea].

Cowra, NSW, August 1944. I was on the staff of a camp filled with new recruits on the night of the mass breakout of Japanese from the nearby POW camp. The troops were ordered to patrol their own camp. Someone in authority got to thinking: these recruits had not yet fired a rifle. So the order went out for all rifles to be taken from the guards. Someone in authority got to doing some more thinking: these recruits had not yet had bayonet training. So the order went out for the bayonets to be taken from them. There they were – patrolling the night with empty scabbards only [M.R.T.].

Labuan Island, 1945. Food in the tropics was, even by army standards, unbelievably bad. Midday. Line up with your rusted dixie. A sawyer (copper) is bubbling with hot lunch: bully beef with curry powder added, and sultanas floating in the scum on top – bloated and brown like turds. Temperature and humidity around ninety. In New Guinea they had powdered eggs – inedible; dehydrated spuds – like the starch Mum used to stiffen the shirt collars in; tropical butter – you could *pour* it onto the army biscuits; and I vaguely recall some kind of tinned bacon. God, it's a wonder a man's stomach lasted the war out, let alone these peacetime years [NX31016].

Japanese POW camps, 1942–45. We doctors kept detailed records. Are they just pigeonholed? No textbook has told of the effects of prolonged, untreated malaria, dysentery, malnutrition, beri beri, pellagra and other vitamin deficiencies occurring simultaneously in the same patient, who still had to work hard under unrelenting stress. There has been no controlled experiment? My medical colleagues should not be so ignorant, and my POW colleagues should have their claims recognised. We POWs were the victims of a vast experiment. We are the result [I. L. Duncan].

Borneo, 1945. I took up the evening meal, ammunition and so on to a forward party near the Manggar Kechil River just on dusk. A lad of about 18 years was crying while his sergeant was insisting, in a compassionate way, that the boy would have to go out to repair the signal wire from the forward patrol. (It had been cut by the Japs – who often did this, and then lay in wait for the unfortunate signaller sent to repair it.) The sergeant was explaining to the young sig. that it was his turn to go, and if someone else was sent in the lad's place, and he copped it, neither of them would ever be able to forgive themselves. It was a pitiful sight. It upset me, and I didn't linger there any longer than necessary. I prayed that he would be okay [QX6794].

Soldier, 1940–45, discharged at war's end. I feel that the war broke my confidence by showing me how frightened I was – something I might never have known otherwise. I have strong feelings about this. A wound to the ego may carry no visible sign, but can be enormously damaging to the whole of life. It can't in any normal way be got out of the system. I saw two instances of self-inflicted wounds, and often wonder how the men involved faced up to themselves. I also saw instances of men who were overjoyed to receive 'homers' – wounds just bad enough to get them out of it. Not all that different, perhaps, from those with SIW – but a significant difference in mental attitude afterwards [WX7927].

Soldier, 1939–43, discharged because of wounds. The act of killing a human being was stressful in a way I did not understand, but it had severe and lasting effects. On the other hand, it pushed me into a search for peace, and I do believe I have developed a very important appreciation of family relationships and of love. Perhaps if I had not had the experience of suffering, I would not have the things I value most. There always seems to be a plus with every minus, and not always a minus with every plus [NX7971].

A handful of snapshots from the 1939–45 men, fadeless prints of a generation and their war; some reluctantly produced, but all taken by men who were there.

2 • 'TYPICAL ACADEMIC BULLSHIT'

After forty years, several thousand men who had been in the Australian army during World War II suddenly began to write about themselves as young men and soldiers. They came up with the 'snapshots', and they poured out a great deal more material – much more than could be contained in one volume. They did it for the simple reason that they were asked to tell their stories.

Behind the asking and the response lay other reasons no less important for also being simple. All history is in part determined, and in the larger part endured, by ordinary people. Mostly they record little about themselves. They are full of experience, rich in memories, and they know in their hearts what they really believe – then they die with too little of it spoken. Later generations are left to speculate on what the ordinary dead once felt and thought.

By the early 1980s all surviving members of Australia's 1939–45 army were at least beginning to grow old. They were in their late fifties, their sixties, seventies . . . Most of them would never produce a personal record of their youth, their war and its effects – their part in making history. It seemed a good idea to give them a way to do it, and encourage them to participate in the writing of better history, as once they had participated in what might have been – paradoxically – a war for a better world.

Through 1982–84 an appeal was made. Would males who served in the army answer a questionnaire about themselves? It would cover their early lives, and the experiences and ideas

To their surprise, some respondents would see themselves in a history book

they had when they were joining and serving. It would also give them a chance to comment on their immediate postwar years and the later effects of war on them. The questionnaire was to be posted to them, answered at their leisure and returned by mail again. The call was made in country and city newspapers throughout Australia, and in the publications of sporting bodies, churches, automobile associations, trade unions, businesses, ex-service and unit associations – anywhere and everywhere that space was given. A great many editors were extraordinarily helpful in that regard. *People* magazine did its best by placing the paragraph next to a picture of a shapely girl, with the ambiguous headline 'Your historian needs you' – but only ex-soldiers replied. Radio publicity worked badly, and television was never used, but the print medium drew a good response. So did an invitation on the questionnaire to give the names of others who might be approached; hundreds of men were dobbed in by 'mates', and they usually took it well since it was very close to what the army had often called 'volunteering'. Assurances sometimes had to be given that there were no angles, political or otherwise, behind this 'army project'. La Trobe University gave its general support, with extra money coming from the government's Australian Research Grants Scheme, but what underlay the work was the plain conviction that more should be recorded about ordinary people by ordinary people – whether they were soldiers from one war or members of any other group in war or peace.

Those who responded to the invitation to put their memories on paper appreciated what they were about. They were a
perishable item, often made more vulnerable by ailments
traceable to war. 'Hurry up with the job,' said respondent Ivor
White with touching directness, 'us chaps are dropping off the
perch every day.' More poetically, F. R. Tyler wrote, 'Your
pens are full of ink, make haste'. They themselves wanted to
know what other ordinary soldiers, looking back, would say.
They wanted to be properly recognised for what they had
been, good and bad, so they took their unexpected opportunity
to say how they saw it. Often they put in enormous labour,
and were clearly impressed by the plea to be completely frank.
They were protected by as much confidentiality as they
desired, and sometimes preferred to be identified only by initials, army number, nickname or nom de plume. Poorly educated and essentially simple men some of them were, yet wise
enough to see the main point: they should be heard and recorded more than they had been. They were not much given
to writing about what was deeply personal – but, hang it, it
was true: as ordinary men they were part of the people, and it
is the people who help make history, who suffer in the wars
made for them, who give life and take it away, who lay life
down and go on living.

Respondents faced up to a very long questionnaire. It asked
something like 180 questions and invited answers as extended
as each man liked to make them – an invitation many men
took up with overwhelming readiness. Others groaned under
the burden. In days more coy than the 1980s a sweetheart, or
perhaps a devil of a little brother, might print on the back of
that special envelope the letters SWALK – it was Sealed With
a Loving Kiss. One respondent, wearied by question after
question, struggled through most of them and then adapted
the lovers' acronym to his own different mood: on the back of
the return envelope he scrawled, 'Sealed with a loving *kick*'.
He may stand easy in the knowledge that in their turn the
originators of the questions had to struggle through answer
after answer thousands of times.

A former major, with a distinguished career in wartime North Africa, would give no answers. As an old man in his eighties, he returned a blank questionnaire with the comment, 'Typical academic bullshit'. He was approached again on the grounds that of course the project would fail if men like him would not co-operate, whereas his answers would enable the inclusion of more than academic bullshit. He did not rise to the bait, but contented himself with complaints that Australia was now a corrupt society with no ethical standards, and that the project could have no historical value since answers would only come from the 12 to 15 per cent of the army who were literate – a comment that successfully hooked some resentful men when it was quoted in the press, a few of them being angry enough to suggest, as a gross libel, that illiteracy might be preventing the old boy from doing the questionnaire himself.

All the same, the major had a point about the literacy and the bullshit. 'One of the fellows had partly completed the questionnaire,' wrote NX4320, 'but found the form of some questions hard. He did not continue, and he knew of one other who had also given up. I found some difficulty myself, principally with questions on political, industrial and civil matters. While overseas we had little exposure to them.' So the questionnaire was sometimes sealed with a loving kick or thrown into the waste-paper basket. In one case it was returned with only the first page filled in by a man who described his prewar occupations as 'Delivering milk. 18 months in a Boys Home. Worked in a plant nursery and coal mine till I enlisted in August 1941'. On the cover he had written, 'Sorry too difficult'. If, despite the major, there are people in Australia who are still interested in a moral of some sort, and they happen to be devising a questionnaire, there is one for them here: keep it simple.

Even so, more than half of the questionnaires sent to named individuals were returned completed, and a total of 3700 men qualified as respondents. Spelling and grammatical errors were of no account; much more impressive was the capacity of so many men to give vivid descriptions in limited space, often achieving artless art. As they got into the swing of it, respondents sometimes opened up so much that they explored their own subconscious minds. 'Is there a chance,' asked ex-Corporal Bowman, who had joined up when he was seventeen and in his fifties was on a 35 per cent disability pension – 'Is there a chance that I could have a copy of what I've written? I've told more there than I have ever told anyone else – Repatriation Department, doctors and even myself.' A few men died with their questionnaires partly completed, and the documents were forwarded by relatives. 'I want to send this in,' wrote a widow, 'because my husband was so interested in your project.'

So they mostly tried to do the right thing, and it was not uncommon for the less literate to do as well as any, and much better than some who had every educational advantage. When they have been reported in these pages, their misspellings and odd construction of sentences have been retained, usually without remark, wherever they seemed important in describing the men or making a point. At other times errors have been put right. Nearly all the longer 'direct quotations' were reconstructed, in fact. Great care was taken not to misrepresent any opinion, of course, but scattered comments were sometimes brought together, statements were shortened and even rearranged for greater clarity, and most quotations were shaped up in the interests of easy reading. It was no more than the respondents deserved. They were remarkably adept at making pithy points and telling a good story, but few of them were professional writers and many were just jotting down answers as they occurred to them. Like all writers, they benefited from editing that streamlined without distortion.

To edit freely – and shock the purists for whom quotation must be *exact* – was a risk cheerfully undertaken. What of the risks associated with the 'sampling'? How good a cross-section of the army were the 3700 respondents? 'As an old statistician,' wrote Mick Sheehan, who was a public servant after the war,

'I am always concerned when people have to use the results of limited samples.' He meant that, forty years on, it was impossible to get a group of respondents so representative of the wartime army that they reflected it perfectly, and also that a more reliable sample might be attainable by a method more statistically sophisticated (and even more time-consuming and expensive) than the rough-and-ready one used. He was right to sound a warning and point to various biases: the reliance on men who *volunteered* to reply (what sorts of men did and did not?); those who meant well but failed to finish the questionnaire; the diversity of the army and of men still reacting differently – being willing or quite unwilling – when asked to pick up a pen . . .

NX65735, born in 1919, pointed to some kinds of men who do not answer questionnaires, or not so often:

Most countrymen of my generation never attended high school – there were none available – and have a complex when it comes to writing letters. Then there was the kind of man, quite common, who ended up sleeping under newspapers on the Harbour Bridge stairways . . . or as hermits in small isolated hamlets . . .

Another infantryman, Maurice Melvaine, underlined that point – not so far removed from the old major's exaggerated claim. It would be impossible, he said, to get sufficient numbers of those for whom life had always been very hard, so few of them had survived the war or many years after it, or would be able to write about it. There were nine men in his section before the Owen Stanleys campaign, in which four were killed and three wounded. One man did not go into action, and only one man came out of it more or less fit – and he died twenty years back.

A few widows, loyal and still grieving, tried to answer on behalf of their husbands, but it could not really be done. Only the men themselves could have spoken. Various respondents pointed out that, in some ways, the questionnaire was at least forty years too late. Sometimes it was not death but bitterness that lost men as potential respondents. A questionnaire was returned unanswered, with a covering note:

A friend of mine often claims that the main problem facing Australia today is that it has too many professors. After looking at your questionnaire, maybe he's right. My army service was shortened by a gunshot wound in the skull in November 1942. This occurred in Papua New Guinea. I had near-misses in Greece and Syria, where a bullet through my steel helmet grazed my head. I don't think my army service had any lasting effect on me.

A Queenslander considered his army service to have been five wasted years, though he and his volunteer mates could only blame themselves, unlike the national servicemen conscripted for Vietnam – against which the Returned Services League raised no objection: 'Your army project is only another way of glorifying war.' An early enlister from New South Wales found that he was agonising over the questions too much to do them: 'It's not laziness or failure to respond to a worthy cause, but rather a mental tiredness which emerges in some other areas as well. How does the joke go? I used to think I was indecisive but now I'm not sure.' A Tasmanian ex-prisoner of war would not answer:

While in agony in those rotten prison camps I visualised a world police force . . . but alas! Man is his own worst enemy. I could write many pages, but why? The small dark clouds are already bursting around the world, and the large dark clouds are gathering, and we are in exactly the same if not worse position than we were in 1939. I am concerned and I worry, but I'm too old and experienced to relate my ideas to the new generation and have them accepted, so I liken my time to a writing in the sand.

Another man, from Queensland, found 'many of the questions quite objectionable . . . Most of my teenage buddies and some of my older friends and relatives were among those who never returned. My father-in-law died at age 54 from injuries received while on active service. Sorry, but this is one period of my life that I have no wish to relive'. Men thus torn by grief and burdened with despair do not answer long question-naires, and no one blames them – though they help to muck up neat academic samples.

So the respondents did *not* form a random sample in the true statistical sense, and the percentages of them falling into var-ious categories should *not* be applied to the army as a whole. Nevertheless those who responded were still so large and div-erse a group that they can be useful indicators and signposts. Their commentary on other men, including the under-repre-sented, can be very illuminating. Even weaknesses in the method were not always absolute. Hundreds of respondents were not so much volunteers as men pushed into replying by pressure from dobbers and unit associations. Scores of men who had given up, or might have done so, were persuaded to try again by follow-up letters. Questionnaires were often left partly unanswered but still returned with valuable infor-mation on them. There were numerous men of limited schooling who might have had a complex about writing but who still sweated out full answers; some were helped by friends and relatives. If there were men who found the attempt too painful, there were respondents like L. J. Blake who sent in full answers except for a part where the thought of describing a beach landing, and other horror, left him silent and still for two distressed hours. In finally declaring 'I do not want to write about it', he came close to saying it all. Certainly he represented those for whom to remember was to suffer.

In spite of the fate of the men in his section, Maurice Mel-vaine survived the Owen Stanleys and answered a question-naire, and so did his corporal. Intelligent – and later educated – enough to give very good answers indeed, Melvaine still be-longed to those who had always struggled for a living as young fellows, and he powerfully represented them. There were a lot of others from the same mob, perhaps not sufficient statistically, but enough to point in the right direction anyone who would understand the wartime army. Other groups of men less likely to respond, such as those who emerged from the war as alcoholics, also produced their spokesmen, for a few from most types had found a chance, a cure, a determination, some encouragement – whatever was needed – to enable them to write for their kind.

Only a few Aborigines responded, but at least they emerged as a reminder that they served, and had formed no privileged caste in society or army. 'Dick' and VX61245 remained privates and 'Mil' managed, in Japan, to be made a lance-corporal in the British Commonwealth Occupation Force. Their average standard of education had been around the end of primary school, and two of them claimed a partial trade-training. (In those ways they were like a lot of white men.) 'Dick' was 21 years old, and Church of England, when he went into the army 'to be with the gang'. His father lived and worked on a reserve, his mother had been a nurse, and his brother an Anzac. 'Dick' had been doing 'pick and shovel, road and street work, and a lot more'. The 16-year-old 'Mil' – his father a stockman and his mother formerly a mail sorter – had been on a farm and, in the matter of religion, accepted 'only Aboriginal beliefs and lores'. He enlisted, he said, 'to help save my country from invasion by the Japanese and others', as many of his relations had done in more wars than one. VX61245, aged 20, had been brought up in an orphanage, where he had been made to attend church (he did not say which one). He had worked on a farm, but had been out of work for six months, and he joined up, he said, 'because the country needed me'. He liked the companionship of the army, and most disliked the cooking. What 'Dick' hated most was the time when he and others unjustly 'got CB [confined to barracks] for 14 days over 1 man, drunk, making a row. We all got off. The hole unit stood up and got us off'. His company commander, indignant at the sentence, marched the company of 'Albury's Own' (the 2/23rd Battalion) to 'the big boys' and threatened that they would all go on strike. 'That's our we got off.'

Most Aborigines who were asked to reply did not do so: too

much academic bullshit. Yet from those who did answer – and there were several more – a little light breaks through. Aborigines were in the army (including irregular units on remote coasts and islands); some won medals for gallantry, and the odd man received a commission – but they were not running the army. They loved and served their country, but they were not running that, either. They and other important groups that were statistically *under*-represented among respondents were still *represented*. Readers with some knowledge of Australian society, or just alert to the clues provided by a few examples, will thus be prompted to make mental allowances for, or inquire further into, the groups that did not come out statistically right but did come through.

Even as a limited sample, the respondents are positive indicators of some facts about Australia's wartime army. If poorly educated men are least likely to answer a written questionnaire, and if most respondents had only primary or minimal secondary schooling, it is obvious that modest formal education was one characteristic of the army. If very few of the respondents had, as soldiers, a highly developed interest in political questions, it is clear that such was the case with most soldiers, aged under 21 years and voteless as many of them were on enlistment. A much less reliable indicator is the percentage of respondents who were unemployed when they joined up. The matter is discussed in its proper place (which happens to be Chapter 5), and here only two things need to be said. First, the respondents certainly under-represented the unemployed; but, secondly, they were useful reminders that only a small minority of Australian males were out of work in 1939. Popular fancy often has the 6th Division – the first raised for overseas service in World War II – *filled* with the unemployed. Did somebody mention bullshit? Granted that too few of the jobless showed up among respondents, granted that there was much *under*employment on top of *un*employment, and granted that precision is impossible, it is still most likely that a greater number of men gave up jobs – even jobs that were paying well – to join the 6th Division in 1939.

Some of the really old soldiers still smart under the charge
that they were the unemployed – a word that may imply
unemployable. During the gathering of material for this
book, the writer attended a reunion of the 2/2nd Field Regiment in Melbourne. One man said, 'Well, I went into the
army because I was unemployed.' Three or four others looked
wearily at each other and immediately started to speak. 'I
didn't.' 'Me, neither.' 'I gave up £5 a week to join the army on
six bob a day.' Between the four or five of them they were
probably beginning to get the proportions about right. A cynical social critic standing by muttered another comment: 'I
suppose most of us, whether we knew it or not, were economic
conscripts.' At any rate, whatever the limits to the respondents
as a sample, their signposting is likely to take us much nearer
to the army as a whole than false rumour ever would.

Some respondents did not trust any statistics, however
impeccable they were claimed to be; they believed that the
unique was likely to be more important than the average, and
that very little that was most important could ever be quan-
tified. Others just found statistics dull, and dared a faint hope
that they would eventually see something readable rather than
statistical. They could all be heard sympathetically, yet the
uses of statistics and the value of a well-balanced group should
not be dismissed so curtly. To take the simplest example, it is
going to be repeatedly said that there were, say, 40 per cent of
the respondents in one category, 30 per cent in the next, and 20
per cent in the third. (And it will often have to be taken for
granted that the remaining 10 per cent did not answer, left it
unclear or were oddball.) Such figures should not be seen as
boring. They should be welcomed as being much more helpful than the vagueness of terms like 'a few', 'some', 'others',
'many', and 'a significant number'.

Certain figures also indicate the strengths and weakness of
the respondents as a sample. Ideally they should have been
represented in proportion to the young male population of the
various states and territories. In fact New South Wales, at 38
per cent, and Western Australia, at 9 per cent, were about right

for the time, and the most significant variations were that Queensland was down (10 per cent instead of 14) and Victoria was up (33 per cent instead of 28). It might say something about the Scots and Irish, but there were too many Presbyterians (15 per cent instead of 10) and too few Catholics (15 per cent instead of 21). The Anglicans (members of the Church of England) were either over-represented, at 45 per cent instead of 39 per cent, or about right if a proportion of those not answering in the censuses are assumed to have been Anglican. Other religious groups were represented in something like their due proportions, although the tiny Jewish minority was up and the small Lutheran minority down. A big difference came in the proportion of respondents who declared that they had no religion: 3.5 per cent of them, compared with 0.3 in the census. But these were men saying what the real situation was at the time, not earnest parents filling out a respectable census form in the 1930s.

As the men continue to describe themselves throughout this study, other breakdowns will be given on their party allegiances, their occupations and education, their self-perceptions in class terms (or, in many cases, their lack of them) and so on. Different readers will come to diverse conclusions on the respondents as a good, reasonable, or bad cross-section of the army recruits. But, at worst, whatever the distortions, they are a recognisably Australian group; they do not seem to come from some other society in which 60 per cent are Catholic, and they are not drawn 50 per cent – or 1 per cent – from Queensland. In that sort of way the group is not too disappointing, given that the net was simply flung wide to catch whoever would swim into it, and only limited correctives were attempted, as in trying to swell the ranks of Queensland Catholics and reduce the excessive proportion of Victorian Presbyterians.

In other ways the sampling was far less successful. As is explained in the following chapter, the Australian army was divided in two, between an overseas force and a home-defence force – the Militia. Soldiers often began in the Militia and later transferred to the other, the Australian Imperial Force, and it was so among respondents. Many men, however, were militiamen throughout the war, and far too few of them answered the questionnaire. The respondents were overwhelmingly AIF, or Militia plus AIF. Similarly, men who served only in base areas in Australia were hard to convince that they and their war years were worth describing. Either their time in the army had not meant much to them, or they thought that the 'army project' would be only interested in heroes.

Their reluctance helps to explain the oversupply of Returned Services League members among respondents. Perhaps only one-third of all eligible men are actually members of the RSL, but almost two-thirds of respondents belonged to it. They were not always keen, or even active, and sometimes they were very critical – the president of a Queensland sub-branch expected to be expelled, and 'Little Sav' remained a communist – but they were still members. It all reflected old problems, about men who are 'joiners' and those who are not, and about men who will write about their war – not necessarily boastfully or even comfortably – and those who will not talk at all. Still, once more, the under-represented did find their spokesmen. The corporal of Maurice Melvaine's ill-fated section in the Owen Stanleys had never been a member of an ex-service association. He had loved army life in some ways, but other aspects of it still gnawed at him:

To this day I am troubled by the fact that I had to shoot and kill human beings. I charge our politicians with failure to do their chosen duty in finding peaceful solutions. Also, the loss to Australia of all those fine young men . . . What a waste! I still refuse to march on Anzac Day because so many people wish to glorify war.

But he saw the questionnaire for what it was: a chance to put his point of view. The pity was that his brother would not answer (and has been quoted among those who refused), and too many other men who would not join an ex-service association also failed to take part in the survey. After all, most of the respondents hated war too, but answered the questionnaire in order to explain – partly to themselves – why they had done what they felt they had to do.

The project relied on long-term memory, and some people have doubts about the reliability of that. (There are so many critics of everything it is a wonder that others still dare to attempt any kind of historical reconstruction.) NX65735 complained about the questionnaire being sent out years too late. 'I have now forgotten much important information,' he said. He then went on to scrawl page after page of valuable material. 'It is libellous,' he warned, 'and can't be used in its present form, but I've used men's names for accuracy.' There was little doubt about its essential truth. Fundamentally reliable was most respondents' recall of what had been important to them and filled their days, whether it was of making a living before the war or surviving during it – or of what had turned their dreams into nightmares ever since.

There were some unreliable replies. There was the case of the very old man who had served in both world wars and kept mixing the two up – but profound insight was there too. A former prisoner of war on Ambon asserted that some men died as the result of experimental injections given them by the Japanese. This persistent claim has never been proved – or finally disproved, for that matter. However, no Japanese was charged with that particular offence at the War Crimes Trials. The matter was investigated but Lieutenant-Colonel E. C. Palmer, of the 2/10th Australian Field Ambulance, was inclined to believe the Japanese claim that they were – with Australian and Dutch approval – testing the potency of stocks of typhoid vaccine. Right or wrong, Palmer's verdict was officially accepted: 'I do not see how any harm could have come . . . from an experiment such as the one described.'*

* Richard Glenister, as a postgraduate student at La Trobe University, unearthed the relevant document in the Australian Archives, Canberra: CRS A471, item 81709, pt 4 (exhibit 132).

In another case, a respondent told a story in great detail, and stuck to it when questioned, about the 17th Brigade going on strike in Ceylon during 1942 over the flooded state of their perimeter and a refusal to allow them to move to higher ground. As a result, the 16th Brigade was brought up in full battle order to subdue the 17th, but the good sense of the men prevailed over the stupidity of the officers, and no harm was done in the end. Certain sceptics associated with the project said, 'Check'. The ever helpful Curator, Written Records, at the Australian War Memorial, M. G. Piggott, found nothing in any of the relevant unit war diaries. Some appropriate individuals and battalion associations were written to, and over a dozen of them replied after discussing the claim with mates and members, and all dismissed it as a 'furphy'. Since some of them were signallers in constant touch with both brigades, they reckoned that they would have known all about that, if it had happened. So the startling revelation had to be set aside as not proven, although the respondent will be angered by its rejection.

Long-term memory can be better than short-term. Though it is hard to credit, particularly by anyone who has seen the questionnaire, two men had sufficiently poor recent memories to ask for it twice and complete it twice. (They were quite unlike another respondent who was accidentally sent a second questionnaire and smartly returned it with the remark, 'I have already done this thing once, and have no intention of doing it again.') Yet the double answers hung together well enough, showing nothing much wrong with recollection of events long past. Most doubt lay over respondents when they were repeating what they had once been told, not what they knew at first hand. 'Charlie' was told that in Bougainville a militiaman was advised to transfer to the AIF if he wanted the 'high honour' he was being considered for. The man did transfer, and was awarded the Victoria Cross. The trouble with that story was that only two VCs were won by Australians in Bougainville: Corporal R. R. Rattey won his almost three years after his transfer to the AIF, and Corporal

F. J. Partridge won the medal as a militiaman, which he remained throughout the war.

A respondent who had suffered some nervous disorder ever since being a POW, and who readily admitted to vagueness about many details, had his answers vetted by his wife of many years. From what he had said over that time, and her own wide experience as a World War II corporal, she thought it still had the ring of truth. The exclusion from the survey of that corporal herself, along with all members of the women's services, the nurses, the airmen and the seamen, is much regretted – by many respondents as well as the project staff – but limited time and resources dictated the restricted scope. All those excluded, not forgetting war-workers and wartime housewives, deserve similar attention. The only question is, will they all get it soon enough? Those lives and recollections can also be likened to 'a writing in the sand'.

Some men aided their memories by consulting letters and diaries. J.F.B. wrote:

I am sorry for delay in completing the questionnaire. I have all my letters I wrote home during the war and also diaries I kept of various campaigns, and I read them through to try for any information . . . The problem at this time and distance from events is what one thought then and not now. I was surprised at events in my letters that now I have no recollection of. (This is not so of events in action.) I have no recollection of my return from Borneo to Melbourne.

Many men were similarly aware of the dangers (what they thought then, not now; what they mixed up or forgot) and tried to test – or restrain, or remind – themselves in various ways. Before the end of the questionnaire they often corrected their first statements, making them more accurate or better balanced. Sometimes they had afterthoughts and wrote again. There were men who would not do the questionnaire at all because, they apologised, they could not remember sufficiently well and would rather exclude themselves than get it wrong. There were 3700 respondents to be used as checks against each other, and other sources to be referred to when necessary. Men do not usually forget the kind of upbringing they had, or the kind of war they experienced, or what was instinctive behaviour to them, or big jolts to their thinking. That is what could be most confidently relied on.

In a paper delivered in 1984 to an AWM history conference, Tim Bowden reported that he and his fellow investigator of World War II servicemen, Hank Nelson, had found that men often got figures wrong – the number of casualties or a date – but usually recalled events much more satisfactorily and 'at times with astonishing veracity'. On the whole, respondents' answers were similarly impressive in their honesty, their hesitancy over some things and certainty over others. To historians' sharpened instincts, and after occasional checking against other sources, nearly all the respondents seemed to be real men truly describing themselves and no longer trying to pretend, to themselves or others, that they had been what they had not been. 'Suit yourselves whether you use my name or not,' wrote Ray Aitken, formerly of the 2/2nd Commando Squadron and the Far Eastern Liaison Office (an intelligence unit for psychological warfare), 'at 68 I'm too old to tell lies or care what people think.' There were ways in which the questionnaire was *not* forty years too late, but came at about the best time . . .

There is no need to worry overmuch about memory's tricks. (Those who say that memory is the historian's least reliable source usually try to justify their fears by appealing to something they remember.) Big things, and odd little things, are often indelibly – and sharply – impressed when the mind is young, and too much concern about the limitations of memory may simply verge on the paranoiac. A South Australian ex-corporal nicknamed 'Kyogi' put it this way: 'Some of the answers must surely be highly subjective – but then, who else but the serviceman, thinking back, could answer any better?'

No one will believe all that the respondents claimed. Nobody could do so, since some claims, some experiences, flatly contradicted each other and attitudes must vary as men do. In organising the material the main aim was to display the range of opinion and variety of experience, and to group them in the proportions in which they occurred *among the respondents*. How much they applied to the whole army, others are welcome to conjecture or more scientifically calculate.

When it seemed most appropriate, some background details have been supplied about the men being quoted. They were not meant to clog the story with irrelevance, but to help readers gauge what kinds – and what different kinds – of men might be inclined to think or do this or that. Sometimes a tentative conclusion is drawn in the text; at other times that has been left for readers to do, if they feel like it.

Being quoted might gratify some respondents – and their sterling effort deserves every reasonable reward. Some will not care one way or the other. Others will be hurt by not being singled out, but they should be disappointed rather than hurt. All the answers on every questionnaire were read, each answer was put into some category or other, and nearly all were useful. Many answers were also coded as 'quotable' – and that best of research assistants, Dr Nancy Renfree, used to say, 'It's with constant mental apologies to the men that I don't mark more answers as quotable, but we can't publish them all.' Indeed we could not. What is more, after – say – 386 quotable answers to one question had been fed into the computer, it might have been asked to regurgitate only a random sample of fifty names from among them. It is sadly possible that some of the best of all answers did not reappear, and were not recalled by human memory – which, it must be admitted, can be battered by an information barrage into something less than reliable. Unquoted respondents should do the fashionable thing and blame the computer, not themselves, the coders or, least of all, the writer.

There will be critics who pour scorn on this book because it took its final shape in a university but is not a 'proper' academic treatment. The judgement depends on the point of view, and not everyone believes that academic work must always be confined to endless correlations, tests of statistical significance, texts no ordinary person can read, and masses of learned footnotes, some of them in foreign languages. Other people, and they are the ones who matter here, might say with relief as they read on, 'But this is hardly academic bullshit at all.' It was never meant to be. It was always intended to be a compilation of the experiences and attitudes of some Australian soldiers, described – with a little help – by the men themselves.

3 • ONE ARMY, TWO ARMIES

At the outbreak of war in September 1939 the Australian army consisted of a tiny permanent force of under three thousand men and, for home defence only, the volunteer Citizen Military Forces, or Militia, of eighty thousand part-time members. In the preceding twelve months, fears about the inadequacy of Australia's defence had led to a recruiting drive for the Militia, and over half of that eighty thousand men had joined in response. Being only 'hobby' soldiers, many of them relatively new to training and indifferently equipped, a lot were poorly prepared for war. Consequently, soon after war began, some militiamen were compulsorily called up for three months of continuous training, and their numbers were bolstered by the conscription of unmarried men who turned 21 in the year ending 30 June 1940. Within two years, single men and childless married men aged between 18 and 35 years were liable to be conscripted for home defence, and many of them were called up. With a proportion of the previously volunteer Militia compelled to go into camp, and an increasing number of other men required to join up for wartime service, the first effect of World War II on the Militia was to make it mainly a compulsorily enlisted force. Nevertheless it always contained a good number of volunteers of one sort or another: prewar members who stayed with it, lads who were too young – and lacked parental permission – to go overseas but had come forward on their own initiative, men who offered themselves for the army but found that recruitment for a newly established 'overseas' force was temporarily suspended, and those who would fight for Australia but not England, or made some other compromise between no service and unqualified service abroad.

In 1939 the government began to raise that special force of volunteers for service overseas, the Second Australian Imperial Force (AIF), successor to the First AIF raised for World War I in 1914–18. Some of the Second AIF personnel came from the permanent force and also from the Militia, who thus volunteered to change their role from the direct defence of Australia to that of defending the empire and its allies wherever required; but insufficient men became available from those sources. Since it was not desirable to excessively deplete Australia's home defence or its workforce in essential industries, many militiamen were retained as such, and others were classified as exempt from military service because of their civilian occupations. Married men were actively discouraged from enlisting, and many found that the pulls of home and high pay were strong anyway. So, for various reasons, amid official confusion and conflicting aims, volunteering from the Militia was not particularly strong in 1939. Three-quarters of the AIF division raised at the beginning of the war came from outside the Militia, mostly from young men (then aged from 20 to 34 years) with no military experience and whose work did not place them in an exempt category. A minority of these men had little or no work to leave.

So the Australian army – which was finally to absorb a grand total of 700 000 men – was divided into two distinct forces. There was the AIF, all volunteers, willing to go anywhere, and widely regarded as the elite. And there was the initially larger part of the army, the 'new' Militia, increasingly conscripted, described as vital for home defence, yet rather shabbily treated and frequently looked down on as second-rate. Since the 'home' to be defended by the Militia included the territories of Papua New Guinea, the soldiers encountered there by the Japanese in 1942 were often militiamen. But in the early years of the war the Militia was severely handicapped. From 1939 it had lacked equipment, often being without rifles for basic training. Many militia-men were in camp for only a few months and then returned to civilian life until recalled in the next year. There was a high turnover of personnel as men transferred to the AIF, other fighting services or essential services in industry. The Militia was long denied privileges enjoyed by the AIF, such as tax relief, free postage, a deferred-pay system to promote savings, and 'wet' canteens for the purchase of alcoholic drinks. The minimum age of entry into the Militia being 18, militiamen were often particularly young. (The minimum for the AIF was lowered to 19 after a time, and only later to 18 – still with the consent of parents and on the understanding that the recruit would not be sent overseas before his nineteenth birth-day. There were plenty of lies and forgeries, of course.) While the war remained far from 'home' the militiamen were sneered at as 'Koalas' (not to be exported or shot) or 'Chocos' (chocolate soldiers who melted in the heat), and were con-sidered to be unwilling and unreliable, particularly by some of the AIF. All such attitudes and facts had to be surmounted, and the Militia had to be deeply involved in active service, before the army could be brought to its peak. Much was eventually overcome. Regulations that discriminated against the Militia were changed, and relations between Militia and AIF improved as both forces shared the hard campaigns in Papua New Guinea. The area in which the home-defence force could serve was somewhat widened in 1943, and anyway, so many Militia units voluntarily transferred to the AIF that the balance between the two forces altered. Early in 1943, pris-oners of war excluded, the ratio of AIF to Militia was 1:2, but it had become 3:1 by the end of the war. An unhappy dis-tinction was being blurred.

Back in 1939, however, the Second AIF was marked off as a very special force indeed, although the first army division raised for it reflected existing army organisation in its ordinal number: it was dubbed the 6th Division. There had been five

infantry divisions in the First AIF and the citizen force had
maintained the same organisation between the wars, so that
there were already five skeletal divisions of Militia at the
outbreak of war. Therefore the Second AIF formed a 6th
Division.

But what was an infantry division? It was basically centred
on a headquarters staff and three brigades of infantry (fighters
on foot, using small arms). The numbering of the brigades also
carried on from where the Militia left off, so that the first
Second AIF brigade was the 16th. Each brigade consisted of
three battalions, and a battalion at full strength might amount
to 800 riflemen and support troops. (Numbers could vary
markedly. The respondent P. R. Wellington, who was 'battalion postman' for the 2/19th, said that in July 1940 its
strength was 1000 officers and men – 520 riflemen and 480
specialists; and respondent J.W.B. spoke of 1500 militiamen
in the 39th Battalion in October 1941.) Attached to the core of
'infantry' brigades could be at least as many support troops
again in 'divisional units' of armour, artillery, engineers, signals, service corps, medical corps, police and others. In total, a
division usually amounted to some 14 000 men – although the
6th Division originally had 16 500.

The new overseas force did not surrender so much to the
existing army organisation when it came to ordinal numbers
for the battalions. In World War I, for instance, New South
Wales had produced a 1st Infantry Battalion as part of the
First AIF, and it produced a 2/1st for the Second AIF. The
prefix '2' marked that battalion off from both the original 1st,
in the First AIF, and the continuing Militia battalion known
as the 1st. To take another example, any Australian infantry
battalion described as the 9th was raised in Queensland, but a
description of the Milne Bay battle that refers to the 2/9th
Battalion and the 9th Battalion is thereby distinguishing
between two different battalions, the one AIF and the other
Militia. Similarly, the letters before each individual soldier's
number indicated both his state of origin and whether he was a
member of the AIF or the Militia. 'N' meant New South Wales

Left: *Coping with snow in Syria, New Year's Day 1942*

Below: *Part of the 6th Division in England in October 1940. From left, Peter Bowen (killed in New Guinea, at Buna, in 1942), Geoff Williams, 'Sandy' Blight and D. L. Whittington*

Bottom: *Greece, North Africa and the Middle East*

and Militia, but 'NX' meant New South Wales and AIF; 'V' was for Victoria and Militia, whereas 'VX' stood for Victoria and AIF – and so on around the states.

So the 6th Division, raised from all over Australia but with every man having an 'X' in his number, organised into battalions preceded by a '2' and further combined into three infantry brigades, or attached to headquarters or some divisional unit, prepared to leave Australia. It sailed early in 1940, two brigades going to Palestine and one to England.

During 1940, as the Australian government decided to enlarge the AIF and found that the fall of France in June vastly increased the number of Australians volunteering for service abroad, three more AIF divisions – the 7th, 8th and 9th – were initiated. The 7th and 8th were established in logical order, but it was not a case of the last volunteers forming the 9th Division. For the actual formation of the 9th, in Palestine early in 1941, the army shuffled and reshuffled its units. The 9th was to be formed around those original 6th Division men who had gone to England initially, but they were soon switched to the 7th Division, which had to transfer two of its brigades to the 9th. Pride was hurt by these changes, and men were resentful, yet those with the truest grounds for complaint were the raw reinforcements of the 8th Division: most of them were bound for captivity in Japanese hands.

In North Africa, in January 1941, the 6th Division went into battle against the Italians as part of an Allied force that captured towns like Bardia, Tobruk and Benghazi. Then the 6th was withdrawn to take part in a hopeless attempt to defend Greece and Crete against a German invasion in which the enemy's command of the air was complete. After a short, savage campaign, most of the Allied forces were withdrawn, but some five thousand Australians were captured. Having by this time (mid-1941) also lost nearly two thousand killed and many wounded, the 6th Division was sadly reduced, yet still supplied a brigade for the Syrian campaign. Reinforced and rebuilt, it was brought back early in 1942 to help meet the new threat from the Japanese.

The 7th Division, on the whole, was luckier than the 6th in what it had to do. Admittedly, its 18th Brigade had a difficult role as part of the defence of Tobruk from April 1941, but in mid-1941 the rest of the 7th, with support from the 6th, fought against the Vichy French (collaborators with Germany) in Syria and Lebanon. It was no picnic – 1500 Australians were wounded or killed in five weeks – but the campaign was successful and the losses comparatively light. The 7th, complete with the brigade that had been evacuated from Tobruk, returned from the Middle East early in 1942, along with the 6th Division.

The 9th Division had been committed to action in North Africa to enable the 6th to go to Greece. A reduced Allied force in North Africa soon came under strong German attack, and the Allies were driven back towards Egypt. Some of them, however, remained in the port of Tobruk, totally cut off by German forces on the land side, and maintaining only a dangerous access from the sea. Yet these Rats of Tobruk, a mixed force but at first mainly Australian (parts of the 7th and 9th Divisions), held off all German attempts to take the town. The siege began in April 1941 and held out for eight months until the Germans gave up and withdrew. Only one Australian unit, the 9th Division's 2/13th Battalion, saw that final triumph, for the rest had been gradually withdrawn and replaced by other troops, but the Australians had done much to make the achievement possible. Six months later, in June 1942, another Allied garrison in Tobruk did not fare so well: a massive German attempt to take and hold the whole region of Cyrenaica and north-western Egypt came close to success, and this time Tobruk was surrendered. By then, however, the British were almost ready to start rolling back the German and Italian forces once and for all. Australia's 9th Division, refreshed and refitted after a stay in Syria, was brought into Egypt to take part in the campaign and, between July and October 1942, covered itself in glory for its share in the battles associated with Ruweisat Ridge and El Alamein, which began the clearing of the enemy from North Africa. Proud, if

*El Alamein railway station,
July–August 1942*

battered (having suffered six thousand casualties – killed, wounded and POW – in a few months), the 9th Division finally reached Australia again in February 1943.

Meanwhile, what had happened to the 8th Division? Two of its brigades had been sent to Malaya during 1941, and received reinforcements – many of them almost totally untrained – early in 1942, the war with Japan having broken out in December. Nothing prevailed against the Japanese at that time. Some of the Australians, among others, gave stiff resistance to the invaders of Malaya, but they and their allies were quickly overrun and Singapore was surrendered to the Japanese in February 1942. So the bulk of the 8th Division and associated units, over fifteen thousand Australians in all, became prisoners of the Japanese for the rest of the war. The 1800 Australians who died in the Malayan campaign were often luckier than those who were later to die as prisoners (close to 8000 from 23 000 Australians of all units and services in Japanese hands, compared with 264 deaths among about 8600 Australian prisoners of the Germans and Italians). The remaining brigade of the 8th Division had been dispersed battalion by battalion to garrison south-west Pacific islands such as Ambon ('Gull Force'), Timor ('Sparrow Force') and New Britain, where they in their turn opposed the advancing Japanese until they were mainly killed (in battle or by execution) or held as prisoners of war, although some were successfully withdrawn – and the 2/2nd Independent Company, part of

withdrawn – and the 2/2nd Independent Company, part of 'Sparrow Force', harassed the Japanese on Timor throughout 1942 before being evacuated. So the overwhelming power of the initial Japanese thrust swept virtually a whole AIF division off the battlefields and into their own terrible war as prisoners.

Some of the Australians returning from the Middle East, notably the 2/3rd Machine Gun Battalion and the 2/2nd Pioneer Battalion, with other corps units, were disembarked in Java to serve as 'Blackforce' in February 1942. After joining British and Dutch allies in a vain effort to contain the Japanese surge, nearly three thousand of these Australians also went into the POW bag. Here and elsewhere in the islands the Japanese seemed to be as invincible as ever. Then, in May 1942, in the naval and air battle of the Coral Sea, an American and Australian force compelled a Japanese invasion fleet to turn away from Port Moresby, in Papua, and retire to New Britain. During the following month the US navy had such a success in the battle of Midway – far away to the north-east – that the Japanese lost their superiority at sea. The tide was at last beginning to turn.

Land forces in Papua New Guinea were soon to achieve other important victories. The Australian 2/5th Independent Company and the New Guinea Volunteer Rifles (as 'Kanga Force') engaged the Japanese in the Lae–Salamaua area. In addition, as the Japanese moved overland from Buna, along the faint and frightful Kokoda Trail, they were engaged by a mixed Papuan force and the Australian 39th and 53rd Battalions – units of Militia made up of very young troops, neither well trained nor well equipped. Things did not go well with them at first (how well had they gone for AIF units pitted against the Japanese up to this time?), but soon – right there on the Kokoda Trail – the 39th established a proud reputation. The 53rd got a bad name that tended to stick, probably undeservedly; they have been strongly defended by F. M. Budden in *That Mob* and, as the 55th/53rd Battalion, with a good record of service behind them, eventually became

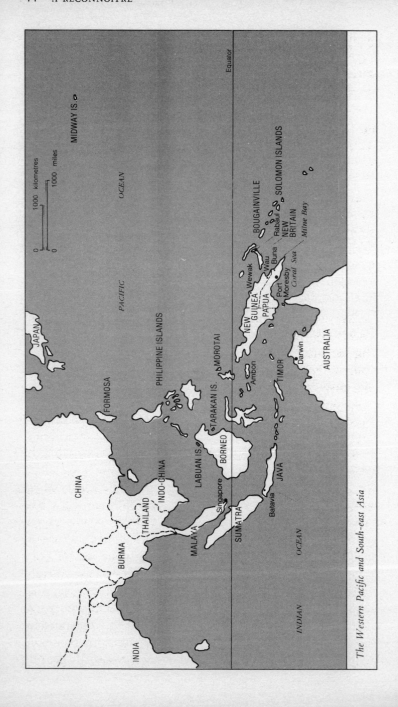

The Western Pacific and South-east Asia

of Papua, in August 1942, that an important clear-cut victory was won against the Japanese – the first that invader had suffered on land in the whole course of the war. With crucial Royal Australian Air Force support, the rest was done by the 7th Militia Brigade and a brigade of the returned 7th Division, AIF. At Milne Bay the raw Militia units – the 25th and 61st Battalions saw most action – may not have had the edge on two AIF battalions, the 2/9th and 2/12th, but the militiamen did better than the third AIF battalion, the 2/10th Battalion, which had behind it an excellent campaign record in Tobruk and later was to do well again in the islands, but rather came to grief at Milne Bay. The AIF and Militia were not very different in capacity; far greater differences were produced by the state of the enemy and their own varying circumstances of training, equipment, fitness, support, leadership, experience – and plain luck. At any rate, it was Militia and AIF (with RAAF) together that won this historic land victory, which cheered the hearts of all soldiers everywhere who were fighting the Japanese, and which closed off one intended Japanese route to Port Moresby. The Kokoda Trail then seemed to be the only way still open to the Japanese, but another combination of militiamen and men from the 6th and 7th Divisions, AIF, finally closed that route too. Port Moresby was saved before the end of 1942.

American troops had by that time joined the Australians in New Guinea (there were some American engineers at the Milne Bay battle), and all were engaged in savage fighting against the Japanese beachheads. By the end of January 1943 the enemy was beaten in the Buna–Gona region, having lost probably ten thousand dead, but the Papua New Guinea campaign to that point had also killed more than two thousand Australians and hundreds of Americans. On through 1943 and well into 1944 the battles to reclaim New Guinea continued. Gradually, at heavy cost, the Japanese were subdued by American and Australian troops, augmented by the 9th Division back from the Middle East, and all vitally assisted by naval and air force support – such as the sinking by Allied aircraft of

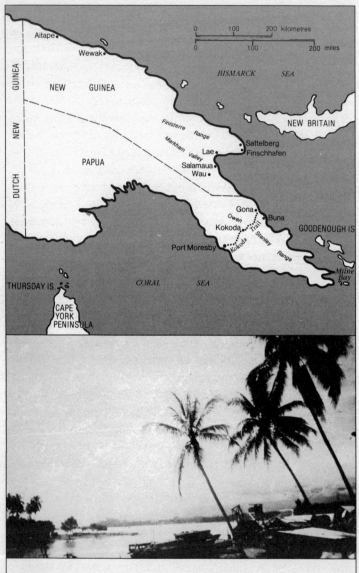

Top: *Papua New Guinea*

Above: *'Portion of my outfit in the Lae area, 1944', wrote G. R. W. Carter. 'Romantic looking, isn't it?'*

eight Japanese troopships attempting to reinforce New Guinea in March 1943. By mid-1944 the Allies had almost won back Papua New Guinea.

From then until the war ended in August 1945, the Australian army was engaged in lesser roles: the final clearing of New Guinea, and campaigns in the Solomon Islands (Bougainville), New Britain and Borneo that steadily reduced the Japanese garrisons and confined them to limited areas. The enemy was by far the heavier loser, but there were – and remain – doubts about the necessity for those campaigns, which together cost over a thousand Australian lives. Could not the Japanese have been simply blockaded and bypassed? At any rate, Japan surrendered after the dropping of the atomic bombs. Australians helped to oversee the surrender; those of the POWs who survived came home; and some Australian troops went to Japan as part of the British Commonwealth Occupation Force, even supplying its commander-in-chief.

So bald a summary probably distorts the Australian army's role, and certainly omits too much. The commanders are missing, along with a great variety of branches and directorates and special units and service, the garrisons of Ceylon, the Australian New Guinea Administrative Unit, the men (including Aboriginal trackers) in the North Australia Observer Unit who patrolled remote areas, the Farm Company that in July 1942 harvested 100 000 lb of tomatoes in Western Australia, the instructors in the RAAF School of Army Co-operation, the army's role in war crime trials, the armoured divisions held back in Australia until many of their men – good men – felt bitterly wasted . . . On and on the list of omissions could run, but all that is possible is an apology to those who go unmentioned. They include nearly 36 000 women who served in the army: the nurses, a number of whom lost their lives in awful circumstances, and the Australian Women's Army Service, with some members on duty in Papua New Guinea by 1945. Yet even a truncated version of the story cannot hide the extensive service of Australian troops.

GROWING UP

*With trousers to grow into during hard times, a future member of the
Second AIF poses at the Booleroo Centre (SA) High School in 1930*

4 • FAMILY, FUN AND FAITH

Meet Jack Ralla before he became an Australian soldier. There were many rather like him.

As a child I was devoted to my parents, especially my father. He worked hard and long hours, often up at 4 a.m. and not finishing until 11 or 12 at night. I used to help him all I could; somehow I was able to use my initiative and instinctively knew what was needed of me. At school I worked hard and finally topped the class in grade 7, even though I missed school every Monday because I had an exemption to help my father on market mornings in the purchase of fruit and vegetables, loading and unloading the old 1 ton T-model Ford. We used to travel 200 miles every weekend.

There were ten of us kids, and I was fourth to last, born New Year's Day 1918. Boy Scouts was introduced to our town when I was about 11 years old, and I became a troop leader, and loved the bush patrols and camping out. I went to Sunday School (Methodist), but I only tolerated that. We used to have woodwork at school, and I gained a certificate on completing 36 models. During the holidays I made a Coolgardie safe to keep our food cool at home, the only one we ever had. Living close to the River Murray, I became a good swimmer before I was ten, and could swim over and back across the Murray with ease. Also, we often ran five miles out of town and back again, for the fun of it. A mate and I used to set rabbit traps, and sell rabbits for threepence each around the town; and we used to have a good vegetable patch that I helped weed and plant and water, so I could sell something from it if I wanted money for sweets, or pictures, or fetes.

Later I used to love the country dances every Saturday night, especially the lavish suppers – sponge cakes, cream puffs and sandwiches. I worked on fruit blocks for four years, and then took over my father's business when he died in 1939. War came and the petrol shortage made my business impossible. I was single, and volunteered for the air force as a driver, but the time went on and I got no notice to report. I missed my old mates who had enlisted, and the casualty lists made me think I should be helping them, so I welcomed my call-up for Militia service early in 1941, when I was 23. Very soon I transferred to the AIF.

Origin and family influences

Like Jack Ralla, most respondents belonged to the generation born in the years 1914 to 1924, and 60 per cent of them joined the army when they were between 18 and 23 years old. Some were even under 18 – Ralla was really quite elderly – so the accent was on youth, on those who had barely grown up. They had known many sorts of boyhood, and none could be called typical, but there were certain common characteristics.

For one thing, they were *Australian* boyhoods. An ace in the pack was E. J. L. Taylor, who claimed that his mother – still alive in 1982, aged 97 years, after bearing fifteen children – was the oldest living descendant of the earliest free settlers, and a third generation from the first white child born in Australia. Taylor himself was born on his parents' property out from Pallamallawa (NSW), went to the public school at Moree and, still in the state of his birth, was doing farm work at Narrabri when called up, aged 19, in 1940. Yet Taylor's ace was trumped by the men like 'Mil', 'Dick' and VX61245, who were Aborigines.

Fewer than one man in ten had been born overseas (mostly in the United Kingdom), and nearly all the immigrants had lived in Australia for ten or twenty years when war was declared. NX45311, for instance, had come from England in 1929, aged 11 and assisted by the Barnardo organisation for

Recruits at Woodside (SA) in November 1939. Jacki Burgess (top right) was of Aboriginal and Chinese descent. Tom Mahon (bottom right) died at Buna in 1942

destitute children; he had married and was dairy-farming at enlistment. A. J. Moreno had arrived independently as an 18-year-old Englishman in 1928, the son of his father's mistress, but he had been turned into an Australian: farmhand, station worker, cane-cutter, banana-grower and taxi-driver. Doug Taylor was about 4 years old when he arrived from the United Kingdom with his parents in 1921; he went into the army 'to look at the other side of the world', and came out of it convinced at the end that Australia was 'a great place to live in'.

The respondents came from all over Australia and do not seem, on the whole, to have done much moving from the states in which they were born. Mostly they enlisted from the state of their birth, and they quite frequently appreciated the unexpected opportunity to travel in Australia. F. K. Abbott, an 18-year-old carpenter from Western Australia, got his 'chance to see other Australian cities, up to then only names'. John Routley was 22 years old and a pharmacist's assistant when he enlisted in Launceston. He said, 'As I was a Tasmanian I only knew mainland Australia by name'. C. H. Allison, 21 and a

Many soldiers saw more of their own land than they had ever expected to see before the war. Whether they travelled in comfort is another matter. The 18th Australian Line Section sets out in 1942 to go from Coen (Qld) to Darwin (NT), via Mount Isa

worker on a New South Wales dairy farm, had 'never been able to travel Australia before'; and L.H.F., a storeman from Sydney aged 19, soon found he was in 'Brisbane, Townsville and a few other places' that he 'would not have seen otherwise'. The army also burst narrow confines of a different sort: Evan Foster, a city worker until becoming a soldier at 19, said that his short leaves from camps in rural Australia opened his eyes to 'the problems of the country people'.

One in three of the men had grown up in a large family of five or more children, and a mere 6 per cent had been an only child. Family bonds were close and warm for many of them. Coming in the middle of a family of ten children, WX28144 had started work in retail drapery when 15 years old, and from his weekly wage of 15s in 1930 the family was readily given 12s 6d. He had married by the time he enlisted and, while 'it was always difficult to say goodbye to a loving wife and near relations', their protection was much on his mind. Furthermore, the experience of family co-operation helped him adapt easily to group life in the army. R. F. Emonson, on the other hand, arriving well down a line of eleven children, 'resented parents for having more children than they could look after'.

His father was in turn a miner, forestry officer and SP bookie, but apparently earned little at any job. Emonson could only recall 'being hungry all the time as a child', and he bitterly regretted being forced to leave school early to help the family. In 1942, at 16, he got into the Militia, where his domestic background did nothing to help, but his boxing ability did (after the war he boxed professionally under the name of Ron Ford).

Being older or younger in the family had no discernible effect on a man's joining up, and neither did having only brothers or only sisters; respondents joined older members of the family already in the services just as often as they went to protect younger members still at home, and often there was no sequence of that kind at all. VX77113 was the oldest of thirteen children. He was married with two children of his own, and had a farm in the Mallee, when he joined up in 1942 at the age of 35 years, and already five of his nine younger brothers were serving in the army. All six men went overseas, and all returned. The army was often a family affair. Though very reluctant to leave his new wife in Sydney, G.R. went into the army to be with his triplet brothers. There were four Cotterell brothers from the Queensland station country in the 2/9th Battalion, and four Sherry brothers left Ballarat for service in the Middle East. All seven boys in N. J. R. Cook's Melbourne family served, along with a brother-in-law; two became POWs, and one was badly knocked around in Japanese hands, but all eight men survived the war.

Yet one sad sequence was common enough: men going to *replace* a brother. 'A Queensland Countryman', aged 25, was working on the family grazing property as part-owner when his youngest brother was killed in action in 1942. Feeling that his folk 'could carry on without hardship', and that the family 'should still be in it', he promptly enlisted. When S.E.'s older (and only) brother was killed at Tobruk in 1941, he left his boot-trade apprenticeship for the AIF at 18.

Increasingly sisters also got into the act. W. J. Warriner was born at Hamilton (Vic.) and – true to the common pattern –

Stages in the lives of two brothers from a Melbourne suburb: Fred and Dick Loughhead as youngsters; Dick as a teenage hunter near Omeo; Fred as a Boy Scout

enlisted in Melbourne. Nor was there anything unfamiliar in the fact that his brother joined up and so did his father, who had previously served with the First AIF. The new development was that two of his sisters became servicewomen. A young woman too was part of the tragedy that befell a family from a Victorian farming area. As VX9418 recalled, there were five children. Two boys were killed serving with the 17th Brigade, a third died in a bombing run over Germany, and the fourth boy was lost in a naval encounter. The only girl, a nursing sister, was butchered by the Japanese in the Bullwinkel episode – 'a whole family wiped out'.

When the respondents enlisted, their parents were mostly alive and living together, although death had taken one parent from nearly a quarter of these recruits, and both parents from some more. Divorced parents were uncommon (3 per cent), but S.E. had his family destroyed by the parting of his parents about the time his only brother was killed in action. Also among the few were the father and mother of VX21749, who had been divorced back in 1924. Their son's comment was that it was hard to grow up 'in a narrow-minded town when one's parents had broken up', and he did not meet his father again until 1940 – when a young soldier somehow ran across a foreman on the docks, loading ammunition. But odd things did happen. A son of long-separated English parents, David Cambridge set eyes on his father for the first time in ten years on the troopship *Otranto*: they were both in uniform, going to the Middle East.

Of the respondents' fathers, about one-quarter were pensioners (sometimes from World War I), retired, unknown or dead. Almost one-quarter were in white-collar or managerial positions, and over one-quarter were blue-collar workers. Farmers or graziers made up a somewhat low 13 per cent (perhaps reflecting the retention of some men on the land), while 6 per cent were professional men, 1 per cent had private means, and between 2 per cent and 3 per cent were themselves in the armed forces. Of those of the fathers (2 per cent) who were unemployed and seeking work, some were in the white-

collar category, but twice as many were blue-collar men. Of
the whole group, under 18 per cent were 'employers' of
labour, mostly of from one to four hands (and sometimes
seemingly as managers rather than owners), but almost 4 per
cent employed ten or more workers.

Women old enough to have a son in the army were overwhelmingly engaged in home duties, if the mothers of this
group are anything to go by. With 79 per cent at home, and 13
per cent dead, on pensions or unknown, only 8 per cent were
engaged in paid work outside the home – and even then it was
sometimes in the family business. Yet these working women
are worth noticing because they can too easily be forgotten
among their more numerous sisters. Some mothers who were
included in the home duties category must also have played a
crucial role on the business side of the farm or other family
concern, and the proportion of working women was doubtless
higher in some of the classes under-represented among the
respondents. But what of those who were here defined as
working? Professional women were almost equalled in number by domestic workers, and together they amounted to 62
per cent of the income-earners. Shop assistants slightly outnumbered factory workers, and together they were 32 per cent
of the group. Office workers were well down, being only 5
per cent of those who got a pay packet. A few mothers, very
few, were actively looking for work but had found none, and
there were some in miscellaneous categories – such as running
a farm.

Working widows included the mothers of A. A. J. Vane,
NX48913 and J.M.: a trained nurse, a tailoress engaged on
army work, and the second in command of the New South
Wales Women Police. When the father of 'A Victorian
Plumber' died, his mother, who had never before worked for
wages, 'was lucky enough to land a job as a cook in a small cafe
in the city' – *lucky* enough . . . The father of F.S.J.I. had been
'savaged by unemployment', so the mother took in boarders,
let rooms to a dentist and acted as his nurse, and also looked
after a newly born granddaughter whose mother had died.

NX16411 was one of seven children whose father 'never worked' – virtually unemployable? – and whose mother did washing and ironing. R.C.B.'s parents had a large guest house. F. M. Orr's father was unemployed but his mother ran a boarding house as 'a slave to sixty meat-workers'. T. O'Connell's father served in the army in both world wars, and his mother was a munitions worker. W.R.M.'s mother was obliged by manpower regulations to work as a clothing machinist soon after he enlisted; she had never worked before, and her husband was schoolteaching. A. K. Thompson's mother and stepfather (fifteen children between them) had a stall in Prahran market. D. W. Callaghan's mother was a schoolteacher, John Cockroft's a journalist, H.E.S.'s a fortune-teller, and J. D. T. Daniels's the 'principal boy' in a Sydney theatre. The mother of S. Brahatis – a schoolteacher before her marriage, and whose husband had given up or lost his mixed business – *cleaned* theatres.

Fewer than one respondent in a hundred had been a state ward, or knew nothing of either parent, but some harsh childhoods emerged. NX119826 could not recall his father, but did know his mother. An illiterate girl, she left her country home because her father was violent, and went to Sydney where she had a de facto relationship with a Greek, which also ended in violence. At a very young age the boy who was to become NX119826 was placed in a children's home, where he finally became desperately ill. His grandfather – who had refused to allow the child's erring mother to return – had died by that time, and NX119826 went to live with his grandmother. He was 'tolerated as well as a bastard could be at the time', although he was not *told* that he was illegitimate until after the war. He began to rebel against discipline and, aged 11, was sent off to his mother's one-room-plus-balcony in Redfern, where he was mainly in the care of the landlady (at an extra charge) while his mother worked long hours in a canteen. He attended school, and even a Methodist church, but he was drifting towards 'a life of crime'. He was naive and lonely, at once neglected and bullied, essentially lacking a base and moving in a couldn't-care-less way with a Redfern corner gang; it was company that 'knew how to take advantage' of people like him. He was saved from this fate by his army call-up, although it did not perform instant miracles. He had no objection to going into the army because, by 1942, he had been 'saturated' with propaganda, and was 'very nationalistic, although in general had never been outside of Sydney'.

F. F. Fenn had been very far from Sydney. His childhood, as he recognised, could have been a good deal worse than it was; but in some ways it was bad enough. He was the son of a white man (who was later prominent in the South Australian pastoral industry) and an Aboriginal woman – the mother unknown to Fenn, but presumably employed on Dalhousie Springs cattle station, north of Oodnadatta. At 5 years of age Fenn was sent to the Methodist Children's Homes at Magill, and at 14 he went into the workforce. He had no close relations with his father, only occasional 'friendly' contacts, but he was grateful because his father could have done so much less for him. He joined up at 23 – the year was 1939 – 'mainly for adventure', and he chose the army as the service in which he thought he had 'a greater chance of being accepted'. He had very early learnt the difficulties of that: there was not only his father's 'reason to have him played low-key', but also his first job with a waterworks gang, which started with the foreman asking the men if they would be willing to work alongside of a part-Aboriginal. To their credit, they were; but it was only in the army that he found the full acceptance he was looking for. He earned it too: he was once written up in the press for saving men's lives, although he was awarded no medal for valour, and he declined the promotion that was offered.

Appalling childhoods were *not* typical of the respondents: there were a great many like Jack Ralla and WX28144, poor but happy – and quite a number not even poor. Yet the tragic cases have to be fully taken into account. A. E. Denny's was another one. He did not know his mother. She walked out forever when Denny, her seventh child, was ten months old. She had come to the end of her tether with a husband who was drunk and violent whenever he was home in Parramatta, which mercifully was not as often as it might have been, since Denny senior was a skilled bullock-driver, and often away. He gave neither wife nor children much encouragement. Illiterate himself, he did not believe in education for his kids. When he died, his youngest child was 13 years old, a boy simply left to fend for himself with neither mother nor father, and with none of his brothers or sisters able to take him in, since they were all married and struggling 'to make two ends meet'. Out to whatever work he could find went young Denny in 1936, and into the Militia – an eager conscript – in 1942. It made him feel he 'was somebody needed, and trained to do a job'.

Yet even a hard life could be lifted onto a new plane by the coming of love. The mother of VX5416 died not long after his birth, and his father placed all the family in an institution. But, at 3 years of age, the future VX5416 and one brother were taken into the kind home of Mr and Mrs Dobson, a hard-working couple who were share-farming at Koroit. The little boy soon loved them both, and to the town the fostered lads became known as 'the Dobson boys'. From about 8 years of age VX5416 saw 'hundreds of men walking the roads and offering to work just for a feed or a packet of tobacco. They were mainly rough looking, but honest'. He watched them and, to some extent, modelled himself on them. At 14, with a limited education and no trades in the town, he went onto a farm at 5s a week with keep, for work from daylight to dark, and was soon to carry a swag himself. Yet it was the Dobsons, and their relatives who accepted him as part of the family, and the local people generally – 'rough and tough Irish Scotch, so kind to an orphan' – who gave him 'a life to begin; otherwise God knows where and how I would have finished up'. VX5416 knew almost nothing about his own father, but Mr Dobson was his 'Dad', and Mrs Dobson his 'best loved friend'. When she died in 1937 it was 'sort of the end of the world' and – though he always kept in touch with the Dobsons – VX5416 wandered from job to job until he enlisted in 1939.

So much for the exceptions: the state wards, the boys from broken homes and those who became drifters. In their youth most respondents were rather state-bound Australian boys. They usually came from seemingly stable homes, often reasonably happy ones. In those homes there had mostly been other children, and often quite a lot of children. Being frequently very young themselves when they joined the army, respondents had usually not begun families of their own; in fact, 85 per cent of these recruits were single, and very few of them were even engaged to be married.

Filling their leisure hours

Girls, indeed, went notably unmentioned when respondents listed their particular interests as youths: only 7 per cent included girls. Well, certain things are just taken for granted; except by the badly deprived, food was not usually mentioned either, yet young men are normally obsessed with it. Nor could girls be claimed as a 'hobby' by the many respondents who were shy and short of opportunities. Both the interest and the inexperience frequently emerged in later comments on sex and the soldier, and a few mentioned these handicaps when reporting their pre-army interests.

One man in ten claimed that, in those difficult days of the late 1930s, he had no time to spare for hobbies, but had to keep his mind on getting a living. Most of the group, however, had some leisure, and they tended to enjoy it out of doors. Cycling and motorbikes, walking and horses were often listed. Certainly three-quarters of the respondents went camping-hunting-riding and fishing-swimming-boating, or keenly followed organised sport, or actively played it – and half of the whole group were competitive players. Membership of sporting teams was therefore very common; in addition, about one man in five belonged to the Boy Scouts, the Militia, a church youth group or something of the kind. A quarter of the group belonged to three or more leisure-time organisations

*When this smart Melburnian became the standard Tobruk Rat,
his wife sent him a hairnet*

(particularly sporting teams), but at least another quarter belonged to none – so the proportion of loners was large enough to be significant.

Manual hobbies such as mechanics or woodwork were a major interest for 14 per cent, reading for 13 per cent, and performing music or engaging in drama for 8 per cent. The young men were not so often involved in such hobbies as stamp-collecting, wireless, photography, first aid, chess or poetry – although all appeared; and very few had an impressive range of interests. Only one man in twenty was seriously committed to studying in his own time to improve his qualifications, although some consciously tried in a general way – such as reading – to keep learning.

On the other hand, a mere 12 per cent bothered to include such entertainments as pictures and dances as a main interest, although those diversions were probably another thing often taken for granted. Almost none of the respondents centred their relaxation around drinking and gambling: 79 per cent, in fact, were either teetotallers or very light drinkers at enlistment, and 92 per cent never gambled or had only the occasional flutter. In these matters the youthfulness of the group was a significant factor. Take one of these young men and he would most likely spend his happiest hours in playing (or

perhaps just following) some sport, or in getting out into the
open. He probably lacked the money, facilities or intellectual
stimulation to do much else.

But let the men themselves flesh out the statistics on
leisure.

> Sport generally, mainly cricket and Australian rules football;
> and I was in the Militia [D. M. Gooch].
> Surfing, Scouts, cricket, reading ['Slim'].
> Cricket and football clubs [R. L. Maddison].
> Cricket, football, tennis, surfing, reading [C. E. Lemaire].
> Reading, shooting, fishing, swimming [VX133911].
> Football, tennis, cricket, choral society, Church of England
> younger set [J.F.].
> Outdoor sports, hunting, fishing, football, carpentry, boating,
> Militia [A. Fraser].
> Model aeroplanes, bike riding, hiking, camping and fishing.
> These last interests saved our lives in the years ahead when we
> had to do professionally what we had previously done as a
> hobby. We could hardly have had a better background for the
> jungle. I belonged to no clubs or societies; these were depressed
> times, and I had no money for that sort of thing ['The Gink', of
> Sydney - and the bush].
> There was very little of a sofisticated nature in the way of
> entertainment, study of the arts, etc., for the young to partici-
> pate in, and contact with knowledgeable people and persuits
> was very limited. Because of the lack of chance to meet people
> of the higher learning bracket - the social environment which
> most of the rural young experienced - I think most of us were
> glad of the chance to enlist, apart from loyalty to the cause and a
> desire to serve our country. Here for the first time was a chance
> to associate with people from the cities and other areas within
> Australia, and perhaps most of all the chance to visit some of
> the places overseas that our parents had told us about [VX50978,
> who left school at 13 to work on farms and road construc-
> tion].

Two of those respondents mentioned the volunteer, prewar
Militia as a major interest, and there was a keenness for it
apparent among a small proportion of the group. Yet there
were many others who did not number its activities among
the things they took particular pleasure in. NX15930, as one
example, was interested in 'tennis, jazz, dancing, reading and
bushwalking', but – for unexplained reasons – 'avoided membership of organised groups'. Yet he joined the Militia in 1938
because he believed he 'had a duty to do'. Was army training
in many cases what one *should* do, rather than what one *wanted*
to do? NX15930 remained interestingly mixed in his reactions as he moved through the Militia into AIF service: he
approached it 'enthusiastically', yet disliked 'the discipline of
routines'; he valued 'the friendships made', and he became a
sergeant, but he also developed an 'anxiety neurosis in North
Queensland' although – or because? – he had seen active service in the Middle East. NX15930 might be just his own
individual case; but the prewar Militia was not always seen by
its members as a personally preferred interest.

The poverty or limited means that continued to affect a fair
proportion of the population was quite often apparent in what
respondents could or could not do in their youth, and in how
they did it. Among the poor were found many of the
loners.

> My father was dead and my mother a waitress. I had three
> young sisters, so I left home at 14 and became a station hand and
> kangaroo shooter until I went into the army at 17. My main
> hobby was staying alive and getting enough to eat [J. D. Buck-
> land].
> At 18 I'd been bumming around Australia for two years. Main
> interest was where my next meal came from [QX1558].
> I was under 18, and a trainee telegraphist with the PMG on 30s a
> week, out of which I had to pay board, so my interests were
> economical ones like viewing shipping and art galleries [R. L.
> Williamson].

My parents were hit by the depression, and I was living away
from home, earning 18s 3d a week with a butcher and paying
10s for room rent – leaving 14d a day for all other expenses. I
walked two miles to work for a 5 a.m. start and a 68-hour week,
and lived mostly on baker's buns and oatmeal – one three-course
meal on Fridays. So I (1) tried to stay alive, and (2) collected
stamps by gathering discarded envelopes and wrappings behind
warehouses and business premises – a no-cost hobby. As a boy
back home I'd gone shooting and fishing at night for food, and
this had made me too tired to concentrate at school, where
antagonism developed between the headmaster and me – plenty
of canings – and I only progressed to fourth grade. But later I
read a lot: Holy Bible to Boccaccio, Plato and Bacon . . . [A. E.
Few].
Football and tennis, fishing and hunting – to eat, as well as for
sport [R.J.C.].
Bike riding, model making, shooting and cricket – but, as an
apprentice survey draftsman, I couldn't afford to belong to a
cricket club ['Jab'].

Such men were very different from P. N. McArthur – 'upper-
class' and son of a gynaecologist – who was married, working
on the land and 'too busy making a living' to indulge in hobbies, yet did belong to local golf and tennis clubs and the
Melbourne Cricket Club, and who squeezed in the Militia too,
when 'war seemed imminent and learning how to be a soldier
was a good idea'. Learn he apparently did: his record includes
a Mention in Despatches in Syria – 'doing as I was told;
nothing special' – and the rank of captain in 1944.
   There were not many in McArthur's upper-class category,
and there were few who shared – or had the same level of
success – in the great interests of some other respondents.
Slum abolition was one of the concerns of T. S. Butterworth, a
25-year-old trade instructor with a youth employment
scheme. Charity work in the slums was the more immediate,
stop-gap enthusiasm of VX56661, 27 years old, and a bank
clerk who was also a singer, Freemason, badminton and tennis

A Rugby car bought by one of the more fortunate young men for £20 in 1937: 'We thought war was inevitable, so we lived it up a bit.'

player, reader and bushwalker. S. Y. Bissett (6 ft 1 in tall, and nearly 14 st) and B. J. Porter (just over 5 ft 5 in and 10 st) were in the Australian Rugby Union team that arrived in England the day before war broke out; not being allowed to enlist there, they returned to Australia to do so. C. K. Hart owned his own motorboat before he was 21, but it was not a case of the silver spoon all the way. He left school just before turning 14 and worked for five years on his father's farm, after which the property was sold. The father became a spec. builder on the outskirts of Sydney, and young Hart went to a butter factory:

I was not particularly keen to become a factory worker, but options were few in 1936. I decided I would secure all my trade certificates and prove myself to my employer, so it was head down and arse up. I discovered that after five years on the farm I could not express myself, so I did many hours composition writing.

VX3511, with the rare experience of having been to Oxford University and the Sorbonne, was also unique in having 'eighteenth century artefacts' among his more conventional hobbies of surfing and horses. 'Flip' included the relatively uncommon interests of photography, membership of a young people's club whose object was to raise money to help 'old diggers', and 'aviation' – from modelling planes to visiting Mascot regularly. The last was not so unusual, and would have been even more widespread among those who went into the RAAF – as 'Flip' tried to do. The irony was that his RAAF entry examination revealed that he suffered from acrophobia, an abnormal fear of being at a great height. QX21388, aged 26, was a Freemason, member of a debating society and secretary of a service stations association, but his main preoccupation was studying to improve his limited education and develop his business acumen, so that he could make a success of his life and overcome the family poverty caused by his father's philandering. Starting as a bowser boy in 1930, he was assistant manager of a car and farm machinery firm in a provincial city by 1939. It was his dedicated study in his own time that put him among a minority.

C. J. Butwell, worker in a sawmill and Anglican lay reader, played cricket and rugby, and had 'a passion for politics' – which was another unusual interest among this group of men. At an early age Butwell had become the effective head of a large family when his father deserted it. He was a member of the Australian Workers Union, had been strongly influenced by two men – the one a socialist and the other a communist – and his passion was 'to see Labor elected and the Tory party banished forever'. There were others too who, one way or another, were vitally concerned with politics. E. O. Bloomfield, whose father 'disappeared' before his son was born, was a labourer in a small printery, and a communist. His interests were 'politics, swimming, dancing, walking and card games', and it was a hatred of fascism that led him – aged 25 – to enlist in 1941, after Germany attacked Russia. VX77113, a devout Catholic, was interested in 'all types of sport and politics', and had stood for Country Party pre-selection before enlistment. R.C.B. joined a library in 1934, when he was about 15, and thought he 'must have read every copy of *Hansard*, especially speeches on defence and foreign affairs' before he was called up – late because of poor eyesight – in 1942. He was not *impressed* by federal politicians generally, but he favoured the

United Australia Party because of Labor's poor prewar record on defence. So a few people with a keen, informed interest in politics appeared among the respondents, but they were never more than a tiny handful among thousands who had no such interest.

Other minorities were the 'girls' group and the 'drinking' few. NX25011 fell into one of those categories: 'Motor cycle racing, surfing, and I must add drinking beer in pubs mostly.' H.M.W. put himself in both groups. A small-tools worker and 19 years old, he belonged to no organisation and had only two major preoccupations: 'girls and grog', both of which he pursued further during army service. L. A. Hintz, a machine operator aged 17, had a wider range of hobbies: 'Horses, tennis, shooting, hunting, concert group (Western singing, ballads), sheilas, sheilas and more sheilas. Belonged to small-town girl-hunters group (not violent).' The motorboat owner C. K. Hart had interests beyond the boat and hard work: fishing, shooting, playing football and tennis, being trombonist in a brass band and drummer in a dance band, singing, amateur theatricals, concert parties, 'and of course girls; was constantly in love from the age of 12 (a late starter) and still am at 64 (quite a stayer)'. R. R. Vial was a bank clerk and part-time university student in 1939. (In twenty-seven days of that year he moved from private to lieutenant in the AIF, having had Militia training; and within the next four years he had reached the rank of lieutenant-colonel, with a DSO won in Greece along the way.) On entry to the AIF his interests were 'Scouts, skiing, golf, fishing, a steady girlfriend (in about that order)'; he did not specify whether the order was ascending or descending. The 20-year-old A. R. Forder, who rose to lance-sergeant, was more consciously guarded about his priorities: 'Animal husbandry, Church of England choir, cricket team, dramatic society, girls, sex, further education – not necessarily in that order.'

Closer to the general run of respondents, who were mostly silent on girls, were two men respectively aged about 17 and 20 years at the time. Their interests were:

Picnicking at the River Murray, but dressed with great propriety, in 1939. The man on the left remained in his reserved occupation (the railways), but the other two went into the army. The young woman seated between the two men later married an AIF sergeant

Cycling. Looking (wistfully) at girls. Home carpentry. Young Men's Christian Association, though a fairly nominal Presbyterian [VX100383].

Anglican church (very pro-God, although I was querying things after being introduced to Charles Darwin in 1938); the social life of the church (my club) and its choir; starting to listen critically to music (ABC); model-making (aircraft and ships); long walks solo; thinking about girls, but never went out with one. Weird adolescence! Perhaps lack of sisters generated my subsequent adoration, and intense fear, of girls [W. J. Cameron; towards the end of the war, he joined the Communist Party – the only political group that seemed to have the answers].

There were also the few who had crossed the Rubicon. J.V.A. took an interest in bushwalking, geology and music, but his first 'hobby' was his marriage. For H. E. Copping it was mainly a case of 'getting married life going – we had a little girl, a new small home, a garden to be made'; but there were also the Baptist church and the city library – 'learning to learn'.

SX9054 was a bank officer who somehow found time to get married amid a great deal of other activity. In his home town of Booleroo Centre he had played tennis for the town team, and then for the Catholic team, as well as joining the Catholic dramatic society. Going to Adelaide, he had easily moved over to the Cheltenham Congregational church's Brotherhood (secretary and treasurer), tennis team and dramatic society (producer and director). Back in the country, at Berri, he captained the town tennis team (premiers 1938–39), was in the Winkie Golf Club team, captained the Berri Methodist footballers, held high office in the Methodist Order of Knights and Young People's Club (drama, vaudeville, sports, debating), played in the Methodist table tennis team, and joined a preaching band that went to outlying farms. He was also treasurer of the local branch of the Henry George League. When he joined the AIF in 1940, Berri must have missed him.

N180258 was involved in so much at the age of 29 that he had 'no hobbies as such'. A single man, he made himself responsible for his aged parents, and was 'an office bearer in many Catholic church groups, as well as playing in district associations for tennis and cricket'. He was a member of 'two committees registered to raise money for public charities – one an orphanage, the other a services auxiliary', and he 'assisted in arranging housing, care and nursing for young, unmarried mothers-to-be'. On top of that, N180258 'managed the largest fresh fish agency in Australia, and promoted and managed the largest firm in the Commonwealth for the importing and distributing of frozen fish and lobsters'. He considered 'the nature and importance' of this business, when combined with his other commitments, sufficient grounds for an appeal against his conscription in 1941. He lost the appeal.

Very different from that reluctant conscript was J. W. H.
Atkinson, who was in the AIF as a volunteer at 20. Yet in one
respect he was like N180258, and others noted in passing: he
had a church connection.

The roles of religion

Atkinson had left school at 13 to work for no wages on his
parents' bush selection, and they went to the Presbyterian
church because they 'had always gone, and believed it made
for better living'. What is more, there was 'no other social life'
for them. E. M. Wilson went out to work at 14. All his
childhood he had gone with his family to the Church of
England, where they had dances and basketball, and after
church the Wilsons had supper, 'mostly toast and dripping
(beaut)'. But once he started to work, although he 'always
believed', Ernie stopped attending church. R. G. Kappler, a
married labourer and aged 27, was also an Anglican, and he
'always had a strong belief in God and the Bible teachings, but
lack of money and good clothes were a handicap in the days
before the war', so he went rarely to church. N. K. D.
McGrath, clerk and storeman in a butter factory, lived in
small towns of fewer than one hundred people, where it was
customary to attend church – the Church of England in his
case. 'Much of the social life was directly or indirectly connected with the church. There was a sort of "clan" feeling
which induced most people to gather together whenever possible.' So he accepted the church 'as part of normal routine'.
E. J. L. Taylor attended the Anglican service once a month in
the church on his father's grazing property: 'Church was like
a family gathering, as all close farmers attended.' What was
more, Taylor 'believed in religion then'.

In such ways religion touched the lives of many young
Australians. Some religious affiliation at that time was
claimed by 96 per cent of respondents, although about half of
them rarely or never attended church. The surprise lies in the

Methodist boys at South Broken Hill (NSW) off on an outing about 1935, with bikes that are notably basic. Some of these lads became servicemen, and their minister – J. C. Barrett, on extreme left – an army chaplain

half who claimed to have been church attenders, either going 'once or twice a month' (23 per cent) or 'frequently and regularly' (28 per cent) – and this was from a group in which Catholics, often good churchgoers, fell below their real proportion in the community. The claims were probably inflated by an uncertain number – the exact position was not always clear – who *had been* regular attenders (while at school, perhaps) but had already fallen away by the time they enlisted. Even so, on top of weddings and funerals, a considerable level of churchgoing was part of the background of half of this group.

In the decision to attend church, often or infrequently, by far the largest single factor was the young man's personal inclination; but family pressure – or loyalty – was the next-strongest influence, and mere habit was quite significant. Despite the examples of social activity drawing people to church, comparatively few respondents gave that attraction as the *main* reason for their connection with a congregation, or even mentioned it at all. And social *pressure* – in the sense of respectability and securing jobs – was felt by even fewer. By World War II, the community at large did not make a youth attend church, but his family – or boarding school or orphanage – might do so.

Attending church was one thing, but what of attitudes to religion? Of the known Catholics, well over half (57 per cent) claimed to have been personally devout, but the same claim was made by only about one-third of those clearly identified as 'other Christian', so a Protestant background was more likely to have produced the strong rejecters of religion, the uncomfortably sceptical, the shallowly conventional, or the purely nominal adherents. About 9 per cent of respondents said that they were 'seriously religious', or at least 'believers', without going to church. Add them to the 'devout' church-goers of all denominations (32 per cent of the entire group), allow also *some* acceptance among the neither particularly committed nor very sceptical churchgoers (15 per cent), and those with positive attitudes to religion might again have made up half of the respondents. So, according to this group, an Australian boyhood in the 1920s and 1930s was as likely as not to have produced a 'favourable' attitude to religion, even if only one youth in three was a 'devout churchgoer'.

Some of the respondents thought that the war weakened the role of religion in community life. D.R.W. was a keen Anglican at 20, believing that 'Christianity was the only true religion'. His own faith was made 'probably stronger' by the time he was discharged after infantry service in the Middle East and the Pacific, but he blamed the war for a worsening of people's general behaviour and a drop in moral standards. J. P. Kenneally was a sincere Catholic whose Irish birth gave him no empire loyalty, but whose love of Australia led him to join the AIF when Japan threatened his new land. He gave up his job as a wharf labourer, which was well paid and exempted him from military service, because of a sense of duty to the country. Neither the war nor anything that had since happened weakened Kenneally's own faith, but he did think that the war 'greatly reduced the influence of religion on the lives of people'. A. G. Willcox, a young bookbinder, was completely 'undenominational' yet a 'believer in God' and he 'tried to act as was expected of a good-living young man', going to one church or another once or twice a month. He thought later that 'after the war fever left the nation, church attendances dropped'.

T. A. Klingberg, a Methodist, felt that 'war fever' was one way in which social pressure was applied to encourage church attendance. He enlisted at 18 in 1943, and well remembered the 'calls to pray for the end of the war, for the wounded, etc., which were quite common by 1943; so propaganda was a substantial social pressure'. He was also under some parental constraint to go to church, although he had 'no great conviction – perhaps God existed – but distrusted Roman Catholics, due to family ideas about them'. R.W.B. recognised that habit and family expectations, as well as his own personal devotion, played their part in his regular and frequent church attendance; in fact he was 'rather smug about the superiority of Presbyterianism over lesser denominations' – and it was not only the Scottish tradition and the Covenanters: he also thought it had something to do with 'middle-class solidarity'. Thus he pointed to a social force that must have had some effect, and possibly more influence than youths often realised. It was this young man, so well aware of status, who was soon to deplore chaplains in the army who 'forgot that Christ was a carpenter'.

Pressures, of course, can be counterproductive. NX171583 was at an Anglican school right up to the time he joined the army, and he remained stubbornly unconfirmed even though the school had made him a regular chapel attender 'under threat of severe disciplinary punishment'. At the end all he could say was that religion was 'good for other people'. C.B.P. had finished his Anglican education years before he went into the army (he was a 29-year-old grazier). Because he had been made to attend 'three chapels a day' at school, his attitude to religion on enlistment was 'nil – had a gutful of it and, apart from church parades during the war, have never been in a church since'.

Sometimes, although it was the luck of the draw, orphanages could achieve more than private schools. 'The Brigadier' (he was actually a private, but the commander of his brigade bore the same name) was a farm and station worker who had found religion 'appealing' from his days in a Methodist orphanage in Queensland – 'basically as a standard of behaviour' – and attended church as often as possible, which was once a month on the dairy farms and twice a year on a station 62 miles from a town. (It was a remote spot, and World War II was two months old before 'The Brigadier' read about it in a newspaper; there was no wireless.) But he steadfastly stood by his beliefs:

Mustering camps and shearing sheds always produced that person who disliked a bible-basher and wowser. Whether it was pure stubbornness on my part, or something due to a basic Christian education, I don't know, but right was right and wrong was wrong. I did receive some black eyes and scars from time to time because I wouldn't be put down.

The part-Aboriginal F. F. Fenn was one more country worker grateful for the faith he learnt in another Methodist home for children.

Among the Aborigines, 'Dick' was in the habit of attending the Church of England, since he 'liked it very much'. VX61245 merely reported that he had gone to church at his orphanage because 'attending was the rule' there, but he added nothing more. And 'Mil' (it may be recalled) specifically rejected Christianity; he classed himself as 'Aboriginal Spiritual'. Non-Christians could have their problems: a Jewish family in a small town, commented WX4637, could only give home instruction to the children, and could not regularly worship in a congregation. Allen Lapin was Jewish, although he had become agnostic, and he faced an acute problem when the Germans captured him in Crete: probably no Jew had ever been converted to Presbyterianism more quickly.

Many men made simple declarations of faith. R. T. Klaebe, in the carpentry trade at 27, was a committed Anglican: 'I was a believer and took an active part in church life.' QX62468, an aircraft engineer of 18 years, was a keen Baptist who 'believed religion to be a necessary part of life, and that Christ died to free men from sin'. R.J.McA., brought up on a grazing property but a machinery salesman at 25, said that his continued attendance at a Methodist church was 'the product of a strong family religious background'. The 19-year-old telephonist J.J.L. wrote: 'My life was based on the teachings of my church. The whole family were practising Catholics.' To 34-year-old A. N. Richardson, a truckdriver, his Methodist faith 'was very dear, having been brought up in a Christian home, and being married to a Christian girl'. After many and varied jobs, E. J. Smith had ended up as a maintenance fitter. He was 26 years old, married, and very serious about religion, yet he could not correlate what was preached in Presbyterian and Methodist churches with what he read in the Bible, so he was still 'searching for the truth'. (By 1982 he was a Christadelphian – 'Eureka!')

Some respondents elaborated on what religion meant to them. J. M. Eddy, an apprentice tailor, was a Baptist who had experienced 'a deep and genuine conversion' at the age of 12 years. Another assurance was given him when he was 20: 'God gave me a promise before I enlisted: "You shall not die, but live and declare the works of the Lord" (Psalm 118:17). I was always aware of a Presence, invisible but real, overshadowing me throughout the war . . .' His war years included three and a half as a POW, part of them on the Burma railway. He was confirmed in the things 'that matter most: a generous spirit, straight dealing, self-restraint . . .' He stopped thinking of men as simply good or bad, finding that they 'could be bad, even very bad, but they could also be very good – giving themselves for the sake of their mates'.

R. J. Anson found his faith through the ministry of Anglicans to the people of the outback:

My parents were Presbyterian, but we lived in an isolated place in south-west Queensland, so I was baptised C. of E. in 1916 by the Bush

Not premiers that season, but ripening for war service – St Teresa's (North Essendon, Vic.) Catholic Young Men's Society football team, 1935

Brotherhood. It was one tiny ray of light each time a Bush Brother caught up with us, and the good Book was most times our only daily reading material. The Bush Brothers were no-nonsense men of religion, down-to-earth types, and they spread their Christian joy to all creeds. Due to their ministry I was far better able than many to appreciate the Holy Land when we reached it. Throughout the war, in and out of action, I carried *The Good Gospel according to St John*, a church booklet that I read much. Our Roman Catholic battalion padre was like the Brothers, and I often sneaked into his services, after the important rituals, to hear his point of view. Wonderful man was old Fr Byrne of the 2/17th. I always believed that all men were entitled to the creed of their choosing.

The creed of E. M. Waddington and H. R. Liston was that of the Christian Brethren. Though bound by no dogma, the Brethren had a strong pacifist element among them and so might find the question of war service a difficult one. For Liston it was not so. He had come to Australia from Scotland as a small boy, and at 25 years of age was a qualified tradesman; but he had spent two terms at the Melbourne Bible Institute, having 'made a personal commitment to serve the Lord Jesus and make him known to others – without being fanatical about it'. He spoke of no religious problem over his service as a commando in the islands. For Waddington, however, it was 'a very, very hard point'. He was 40 years old, a commercial flower-grower, and his faith was his 'way of life, taken seriously', making him an open-air preacher and a Sunday school teacher. Some of the Brethren thought that he should not enlist at all, and he himself felt that he could not carry arms, yet the protection of his wife and children was uppermost in his mind, and he 'could not bear to think what would happen if Japs got in and were let loose'. So he volunteered for the Militia in a field ambulance unit, and later served in a camp hospital – although he finally joined an advanced ammunition depot. He remarked on a common tendency 'to make religion look silly, but the real thing is a practical help to people in need'.

Religious problems over involvement in war took various forms. Douglas McPherson came from a Seventh Day Adventist family; as such he might be a non-combatant but was forbidden to take life – which could be rough on a soldier. But McPherson also had an extended family, which posed for him the conundrum of 'how to be brave like Uncle Bert in World War I and yet be pure like Jesus'. He decided for Uncle Bert and served in an armoured regiment and an infantry battalion. He thought, in fact, that the best qualities for a soldier might be 'ignorance, prejudice and xenophobia', whereas the worst soldier might indeed be 'a sincere Protestant Christian'. Other respondents who spoke of religious difficulties about war and killing included the sensitive Baptist QX62468, who was deeply disturbed on his own account, and the Jewish agnostic Allen Lapin, who thought that army chaplains 'all had difficulty in reconciling the existence of God and war'. David Cambridge had maintained frequent attendance at Catholic churches, despite a hard and wandering life before the war, yet he was worried: 'I was devoted to my faith, but disillusioned with priests in big cars while parishioners starved, and the Church's pre-occupation with desecrated buildings in the Spanish civil war while ignoring human suffering.'

Some men found problems where others saw none. The clerk William John arrived in Australia from Wales when a few months old, and at 17 was happily going fairly often to an Anglican church, from personal conviction about as much as family persuasion. His was 'an inculcated attitude that one had a duty to God and to one's neighbours, and to look after one's body ("formed in the image of God")'. But NX42618, by contrast, no longer attended church. Certainly he was much older and tougher than John, and had been unemployed, 'on the track', a wood-machinist, a first-aid attendant and, in prewar New Guinea, a medical assistant; but that was not why he did not go to church. The reason was that, as a child, he had suffered under a Presbyterianism 'typical of the day and age: a God of reward and punishment; a God of fear, not love; a God who did not give peace of mind – rather the reverse, especially in formative sexual years when playing with one's tossle was a straight ticket to hell'.

There were plenty of recruits who had 'never thought about religion', or 'had no contact with it', or in some other briefly dismissive way said that religion had never been part of their lives, although they still gave themselves a denominational label. There were those too who did not bother about churchgoing, but prayed every night of their lives – 'and sometimes during the day, in a crisis' – like H.M.G., who was working-class, a townsman, a professional musician and nominal Anglican. Some skipped both church and prayer, yet were tolerant of it all in others. K. G. Wilson was a shop assistant and smallish in build; when he joined a commando unit in which there was another Wilson, nicknamed 'Horse', he was promptly dubbed 'Pony'. More to the point, 'Pony' had had a rather tenuous connection with a Protestant church because of its football team, but on religion and church he was just 'open minded, not caring about going personally, but for those who did – it was their prerogative'. The factory worker R.J.C. 'didn't have any strong religious convictions one way or the other – but some *elderly* people had very strong opinions about religion'.

QX17835 was different again. He did many things: work

that had taken him, a junior public servant, through a pastoral job to mining; leisure activities that ranged from boxing and surf life-saving to sketching and writing poetry. One thing he did not do was attend his Methodist church, and that was because, while he believed in 'a God and Christianity', he had 'no patience with religious dogma'. A. A. Clavan showed a sense of humour, but his poor, hardworking country background did not include much schooling: 'When told in Singapore that we had capitulated, I had to ask a mate what the word meant; I thought it was some sort of attack we were going to do.' Nor had Clavan had a religious training, although he was officially Church of England: 'No reason to believe in it: two brothers killed in a car accident when I was about 2 years old; Dad and Mum never went.' No later experience changed anything for him. He thought God existed, but the church was 'just another big business', its priests often hypocritical. Clavan continued to live by his own rules.

More basically sceptical was T. D. Cross who, at 30, was a married man with two children, and an employee of the Perpetual Trustee Company. The death of an older brother in World War I, 'in spite of sincere prayers', had turned young Cross into both a religious sceptic and a convinced pacifist. Hitler – 'so evil that he should be opposed in every way possible' – changed Cross's mind again, and he enlisted; but war service only made him 'more doubtful about God than ever'. Another respondent, 'South African Immigrant', arrived in Australia in 1935 and was unusual in several ways: as a migrant, a recent migrant, a migrant from a country other than Great Britain, and also as an only child. He was not, however, alone in being a sceptical (or hopeful) searcher among the churches, which he decided were:

a hiding place for gullible, gutless people. I was curious and poked around the various religions, attended their meetings, joined them in their bowings, bleatings and chantings, and tried to find what they got out of it. But, like Omar Khayyam, 'evermore came out by the

same door as in I went'. Just couldn't find anything. Described myself
as a realist, an agnostic.

R.B.Y. was a communist rejecter of religion. At 30 he was a
shipping clerk still recovering from a difficult childhood. He
had never known his father, and he wished the same had been
true of his stepfather – an ex-British army WO, a 'bastard' of a
man who put him down constantly and gave his mother a bad
time before her accidental death when R.B.Y. was aged 13.
R.B.Y. 'wasn't interested one tiny bit' in religion:

When I was about 12, a wicked old man gave me a copy of *The
Martyrdom of Man*, by Winwood Reade [a nineteenth-century free-
thinker]. 'This'll educate you, Bob,' he said. It changed my whole
life, and I still have my old Thinker's Library edition. My cousins
used to tell me about the old fellow with the beard, sitting 'up there',
putting crosses against wicked people's names, but even as a child I
was a doubter.

The army, however, liked men to nominate a religious
denomination for the purposes of church parades and burials.
W.G.B. found that out when enlisting in Melbourne in 1939.
He was a 20-year-old greenkeeper, studying at night with a
helpful headmaster in an attempt to get into the police force,
and he was an atheist: 'But on my enlistment form I was not
permitted to write "atheist". I was compelled to nominate a
religion, so I opted for RC, the religion of my family.' Doug
Baker, a foundry hand, was surprised when he fronted up to a
recruiting office at Toowoomba early in 1940:

The bloke behind the desk took my form, looked at it and then
asked:
    'What age is that you've put down?'
    'Twenty.'
    'That's too young for the AIF without parental consent. You have
to be twenty-one. We'll fill out another form.'

The pen scratched on a new sheet for a while. Then the bloke spoke again.

'What religion?'

'None.'

'You've *got* to have a religion. Ours is a *Christian* army. I'll put down C. of E.'

But I had been conned. I found out that there were at least two non-Christians in my unit.

5 • LEARNING AND WORKING

Whether or not Australia was a Christian country, fewer than 30 per cent of the respondents received even part of their education at church schools. How many had been given a reasonable education anywhere?

VX66546 was among the 21 per cent of these men whose schooling had not gone beyond primary level.

Education had a rather low priority among us. I was a child of the Depression, and our family (seven children) was hard put to survive on the 16 acre fruit block, without thinking of higher education. In any case, the only secondary school was ten miles away – too far. Only a small percentage of the children who went through primary in my time thought about higher education.

Where did education get you anyway?

About half of the respondents rated schooling highly, and 16 per cent expressed deep regret at not having been able to go on to the level of education they would have liked. There was also a proportion who were far luckier than the normal Australian: those who had begun or finished degree or diploma studies formed 13 per cent of the group, which was at least double the community average in the 1930s. Despite that bias, a low level of formal education among this generation of soldiers was apparent.

Even education at a private or church school (13 per cent

A South Australian school band in 1929. By 1945 all but two of the boys in the back row had served with the Second AIF, and the smaller boy next to the drummer had been a high-ranking RAAF officer

Catholic, 10 per cent Anglican and 5 per cent Presbyterian or Methodist) had not necessarily meant a high level, since many boys did not stay long, and the school might have been run merely by a small-town convent. In fact, on top of the 21 per cent who went no further than primary grades, and the few who had been to no school, another 41 per cent had only 'some' secondary education – a year or two beyond primary school until they were about 14 years old. Even the 22 per cent who claimed to have 'completed' their secondary schooling had probably gained no more than a junior certificate in many cases, and only 2 per cent had ended their secondary education at the highest possible secondary level (although some of the tertiary-educated would also have passed through it). At the time, one in three of these men had no regrets about their minimal formal schooling – they put a low value on it. Sometimes it was life in the army that made men realise that education had its uses. Certainly, among respondents, almost two-thirds of the commissioned officers came from the higher educated ('completed secondary' or above).

That connection between education and promotion in the army was recognised by respondents, but their reactions varied. A.D.C., an ex-jackeroo and clerk with minimal secondary schooling, merely remarked that 'educational qualifications enabled easier access to commissioned rank'; his own highest rank was that of sergeant with a machine-gun battalion. NX101784 had part of a diploma in accountancy, and had attended state and Catholic schools, as well as a business college. He served with a tank battalion and a port operations company, rising to lance-sergeant; his comment was tart: 'A greater public school old-boy's tie certainly helped a man into technical and officer training.' 'A Queensland Countryman' found he could not advance very far in the artillery because of his limited schooling, something he came to regret. D. G. Bourne did more about the problem. He had left school at 14 to work in orchards and always wished his education had been better. In the army he started a course in agriculture with the Army Education Service and, when he found that his mathematics was inadequate for the tank gunnery course, took maths through an international correspondence school: 'So actually I was studying tank gunnery in the daytime, and agriculture and mathematics at night. I doubt if I'd pass as the typical digger, as some didn't learn anything in their spare time. I also swotted up Morse Code for a wireless operator's job.' He made the grade, saw action on Tarakan Island and in North Borneo – and suffered mentally and physically from that service for forty years.

The highly educated VX3511 (Oxford and the Sorbonne) and the better-educated-than-usual N180258 ('completed secondary', plus part of an accountancy diploma) both considered that, in a World War II infantry battalion, formal schooling was not important for the men. It was 'necessary for officers, but did not necessarily contribute soldierly qualities', and 'all an infantryman required was a modicum of common sense; a strong, mobile and work-oriented frame; and a fanatical will to survive'. 'Irishman' agreed with them. He had been on holiday from Eire when war broke out, and enlisted because of his disgust at Germany's attack on neighbouring countries. He served with transport units in the Middle East and the islands, and had some secondary schooling and a little training as a law clerk behind him, but he said that education 'was not much good when you were in the sights of the enemy's gun – and that was how one lived, just from day to day'.

Yet there were respondents who argued the opposite case. Some were influenced by the area in which they served or by the specialist units they joined, and were not speaking of the fighting infantry. L. A. Day, who had to leave school early to earn a living, and at that time thought education unimportant anyway, gave up his job as a messenger boy to sneak into the Militia before he was 16 years old. He transferred to the AIF, but served only in Australia with the 35th Fortress Engineers and the 5th Australian Air Liaison Unit. From that perspective he thought that 'an educated background' made the best soldier and the opposite produced the worst. R. R. Edwards, a junior clerk with limited schooling, who served in the Pacific with units ranging from HQ signals to the Special Wireless Group, thought as Day did: a decent education was most helpful. Men like 'Charlie', however, did not necessarily exclude infantrymen from those who could benefit from a good education. He was one of those with a 'completed' secondary schooling, although to his mind the urgency of the war situation (he joined up in 1942, aged 17) quite suppressed any appreciation of education. While serving, he thought a lot about the educated and the uneducated in his many units – infantry, combat intelligence, commando and others – in New Guinea and the Solomons, and he decided that 'those with secondary education seemed to survive better in battle conditions, but the least educated coped more easily with poor living conditions and bad food'. He thought that the many Militia NCOs with a good education were far better to be with on fighting patrols than a lot of junior officers who had less education but were promoted because they were AIF, and officially preferred on those grounds.

What sort of education, trade skills and training were needed to overhaul tanks at Maitland, NSW? Tend the wounded (including Germans) at El Alamein? Repair boats and barges at Hertzog Lagoon, Lae?

VX66546, that soldier from the fruit block who had been forced to leave primary school for casual farm work, was nonetheless intelligent. Reflecting on his service in the Pacific, he considered the effectiveness of soldiers from the angle of the whole army team:

The unemployed, the unskilled and those from poor circumstances tended to go into combat units, and it is in this area that Australians earned their reputation as good soldiers. We have to remember, though, it needed a number of men in support to sustain one man in the front line, so it is hard to say who made the most effective soldier. It depends on what is meant by 'effective'.

Men like V. A. Hill could also see various sides to the question. English-born, Hill grew up on a soldier-settler farm in the Riverina and could not attend school beyond primary level because of isolation. He did some correspondence lessons to Grade 8, but was working at 13 years of age. The army gave him mixed feelings, not so much about the intrinsic uses of formal education as about unrealistic emphasis on it. Natural ability, he thought, was too often disregarded in favour of mere 'qualifications'. 'The need for them in today's modern forces can be appreciated,' he wrote, 'but at that time – when we had little else other than physical strength, raw courage and ability to depend on – the waving of a scrap of paper was rather useless. The combination of *both*, of course, produced the supreme leader.' Hill served with infantry battalions in the Middle East and the Pacific – and he did finally become a lieutenant. A. A. J. Vane arrived at the same conclusion as Hill. On the death of his father, Vane had to leave school after taking the Intermediate Certificate, and he went into an insurance office and then joined the army as 'a rather stupid young man'. He learnt much during training and service with both the North Australia Observer Unit (horses and black trackers and loneliness in remote territory) and also the 1st Australian Corps Signals in Morotai and North Borneo. He became a corporal – a section leader. But was he as adequate as

he might have been with a better education? Vane thought
that two things together made the outstanding section leader:
'It was the trained *and* educated section leader who was the best
soldier, on whom battle success depended and from whom
future officers could be chosen.'

E. M. Wilson swung the balance back with the comment,
'Education handy, but not really necessary; a King's Scout
most times would leave an academic for dead'. He served with
the 5th Battalion (Victorian Scottish Regiment) and the Australian New Guinea Administrative Unit, and became a
WO II. Entirely indifferent to education was VX4494, a private with the 2/6th Battalion, who had not even finished
primary school: 'some had education, some didn't – that was
life.' His father was bankrupted in 1929 and the family moved
to the country to eke out an existence: 'I was a big lad and in
those hard times it was a tough job to feed and clothe a person.
An exemption from school was granted and, aged 13, I happily
went out to work in an orchard. Wages £1 for a 48-hour
week.' For the 'Redfern bastard' NX119826, a gunner or sapper with heavy anti-aircraft and other units, talk of education
was not altogether appropriate, he felt: 'The emphasis on education and the facilities for it were just not so great in those
days.' R. E. Bridge, whose father was dead, who had an 'end-
of-depression youth', and for whom the 'Hollywood movies
were a fairy-land of glamour and mystery', had no thoughts
on education then. Schooling to the age of 14 was 'considered
ample for the majority' and he followed the trend, being at
work in Sydney at 14. He was a driver with the Service Corps,
then a late and reluctant corporal; but by the end of the war,
and later as a successful public servant, Bridge had come to
value education. WX35961 (a gunner with heavy artillery,
and then a private in the 28th Infantry Battalion) came out of
the army 'embarrassed about a lack of education; I tried to
study, but couldn't concentrate, and I thought I couldn't
learn'. And for a long time he had great difficulty in settling
to anything. Before the war he had held to a clear-cut view, as
an electrician's assistant and the son of a sheet-metal worker:

Wep (W. E. Pidgeon) drew a picture of Private Maurice Melvaine, DCM, in 1944. Much later Wep was discarding sketches while talking to a cleaner in the Daily Telegraph *office. She snatched up one of the discards and exclaimed, 'But that's my nephew!' Wep presented it to her*

'Education was for those who didn't have the guts to do hard work.'

Another of the men who at that time put a low estimate on schooling was Maurice Melvaine. He left school early, in difficult times, and – like his father, who had to move from one temporary job to whatever else came up – young Melvaine worked with orchardists and a bee farmer, dug potatoes, picked fruit, went sucker-bashing (clearing regrowth) and prospecting for gold, and was 'banker man' (worker at the 'face' or 'bank') in a granite quarry. He improved his education in the sense of becoming a freethinker after 'enough geological experience to know that Genesis was utter rubbish', but in general he was 'too busy learning first hand about facts to think about education'. In the army, serving with the 2/3rd Battalion, he remained a private – 'refusing promotion under military rules'; anyway, his country background fitted him best for roles like forward scout, and he won the Distinguished Conduct Medal with a bayonet in Syria in 1941. Yet in later life Melvaine insisted that Australians needed to learn that their future depended 'utterly on good brains educated in the latest technology – and, let's hope, aware of social obligations. Away with the damned caste system that pervaded Australia in the 1930s and 1940s'.

A number of those who had to cope with the system in the 1930s did not feel that schooling was valued within it. L. W. Piper, who 'prized education highly', became a baker's assistant after primary school. His father could not afford to send him to high school in a larger town and, anyway, 'There was an attitude in small NSW towns of looking down on someone who wished to advance himself'. (He did, however, advance: after the war he was for a time the artist for the Ginger Meggs comic strip.) C. R. Thompson had gone on to some secondary education, but that did not help him – or others known to him – when it came to getting work in the depression. He was 14 in 1932 and was unemployed for a year, later moving into jobs in the vehicle-building industry, at a garage, with a bootmaker and in the railways; but his schooling was still not recognised. K. R. Battye also put education at a discount because employers did so. Although his much older brother had passed all subjects for a secondary certificate, it did not save him from being sacked by his metal firm at 19 to make way for a junior. Battye was well aware that the lower paid juniors were often favoured when it came to employment, so – with his father on the relief work provided for the unemployed – he left school early to go on an assembly line in a wireless factory, the first of a series of short-term jobs. The money was needed at home more than a schoolboy was.

NX43929, however, was well aware that big advantages could flow from education, although he had all too little of it. He went only to a small Catholic primary school in the country: 'I knew nothing else other than the RC religion, and it was flogged into me breakfast, dinner and tea, and into the night.' He fell out with his devout father over the family's giving all the money the dairy farm produced to the church, and he left home at 13 years. He knew what it would mean for the likes of him:

If you had no education you walked all the way. I worked on dairy farms for some of the worst people you could find in the country for 5s and 7s 6d per week and keep. Keep? Our breakfast was one egg

At Sydney's Taronga Park in December 1938, Keith Battye, Vince Campbell and Keith Hughes little knew how much farther afield they would soon go as servicemen

between two boys. Lunch was a handfull of proons. At night we had boiled pumpkin and potatoes, a limited quanity. The paper came three times a week; it cost twopence and we were charged a penny each for reading the headlines bringing it home. Three of us milked by hand 80 cows morning and evening, and worked hard in the paddock with a bush hook during the day. For the benefit of people who did not live in that age, I put these things down. I worked 17 hours a day . . . I slept in barns with fleas, rats, you name it. Why wouldn't anyone want to join the army? It couldn't be worse . . . Politicians are again making a mess of the best country in the world. It is a disgraceful set up to see young people once more out of work right from school. Sir, I hope what I've answered may be of some help. I am not the most Intellegent Bloke about by any means but I still help the Digger where I can.

So he went into the army and, walking all the way, was a private in the 2/1st Machine Gun Battalion in the Middle East and the Pacific. His answers, however, were much more than 'of some help'.

If it was harder for the poorly educated to win a commission in the army, it was far from impossible. One man who managed it was VX9418, serving with the 2/7th and 2/8th Battalions. The eldest in a family of eight children, he had had only primary schooling before taking on hard physical labour in the malting industry. For a time he tried commercial travelling, but was beaten by the depression and returned to his former work. Nevertheless he was keen on self-education:

I tried to absorb as much knowledge as I could by attending the Workers Extension Association lectures and by reading in the Melbourne Public Library. I went to various churches and religions, and rationalist and freethinker lectures, to see if there was any real answer to life's wonderful great mystery – without finding the answer. I remember too that there was on sale – for one penny – in a left-wing bookshop the Baron Tanaka memorial to the Japanese emperor; it outlined the subsequent drive by the Japanese through South-east Asia and towards Australia, and it had been published after Communist agents had obtained a copy. The establishment in Australia, England and the USA denied its authenticity, but later changed their tune.

QX7328 was another from the minority of the lower educated group who reached commissioned rank. He had had a minimal secondary schooling before farm and bush work, but had always had a 'very high regard for education – the higher the standard the better', so was eager to take whatever opportunities came his way.

E. R. and L. A. Exell were twin brothers, two of a deceased hairdresser's eight children. They had only primary education, and became farm labourers. Neither brother was promoted, either in Australia during the war or, in Len's case, in Japan during the occupation. Yet Ern valued the schooling he had been given because 'there were soldiers who could not read or write'.

The illiterates

Gavin Long, in *The Final Campaigns*, p. 85, reported the finding of the Army Education Service in 1943 that about 4 per cent of Australian soldiers were illiterate. Respondent A. E. McIntyre recalled that thirty-three illiterates were identified among approximately three thousand men in the 4th Ar-

At his one-teacher school in 1949 a former prisoner of war in the steamy heat of Singapore was under snow in a cold part of New South Wales. Perhaps his habit of writing letters for illiterate soldiers helped him as he coped with forty-one children from Years 1 to 9 in a single room

moured Brigade in 1943 – about 1 per cent. They were mostly from the outback, and the Catholic padre conducted a voluntary class for them, at which they made 'spectacular progress' in three months, all of them gaining a good basic command of reading and writing. (With amphibious operations pending, all non-swimmers were also put through a course, and McIntyre recalled no drownings in all the action that followed. Other troops were not so fortunate; drownings were quite frequent and so were respondents' comments on fear among non-swimmers and the difficulties caused for all by the lack of that ability.)

NX65735 described some of the illiterates he knew. He himself had been educated at country and Sydney suburban schools, gaining his Qualifying Certificate in 1930 (though never remembering being advised by anyone on whether he should try for the 'Bursary' exam), going on to a technical school, but leaving at 14. Later, however, he got his Intermediate Certificate at evening classes. Son of a letter-sorter, NX65735 realised the value in education for himself, and was an apprentice lithographic artist at enlistment. After the war he became a schoolteacher, and the illiterates in his 2/18th Battalion must have sensed his potential:

A married man told me he was illiterate, and would I write his letters home? He was only one of many – all of whom, for some reason, he seemed to know. He said that in the country he had never been near enough to a school to go. (I don't know the illiteracy rate in city battalions.) His wife used to read him cowboy stories in bed. The things he wanted me to write to her were astonishing, and he had an unusual turn of phrase. He once said, 'Tell Molly that when I get home she'll think she's been hit in the crutch with a plate of porridge.' Unfortunately he never did reach home; he died on the Burma railway.

The majority of the men in the army didn't read. 'Reading is a waste of time', I was once indignantly informed. The men's needs were simple; as they expressed it, 'Grub, grog and growl'.

Billy Hull was an illiterate with whom D. J. Lee enlisted at Prahran in 1939, and for whom Lee memorised the eye test, which Hull in turn memorised (no mean feats of intelligence) before fronting up. Another mate helped Hull over other hurdles, and he was worth helping because on Crete he won the Distinguished Conduct Medal. What's more, either during or just after army service he learnt to read and write, and ended up as a building inspector. (As it happened, Hull was not a respondent and therefore did not personally demonstrate his delayed literacy.)

An example of near-illiteracy turned up among the completed questionnaires. A South Australian fisherman did his best to describe and complain about a number of potentially significant things, but his answers were mostly incomprehensible, so poor was his English expression. Much less handicapped, and much to be admired for his very successful completion of the long and involved questionnaire, was QX11548. A stockman's son, he became a stockman himself and – apart from war service – remained one all his working life. He had only four months at a school, and the rest of his

*A far cry from the spic and span tank workshops at Maitland, this
workshop in northern Australia in 1941 made the 2/11th Field
Company, Royal Australian Engineers, self-supporting and gave
useful trade-training to many men*

education (he reached fourth grade) was through correspondence lessons supplemented by visits from itinerant teachers
two or three times a year. He wished he could have had more
education, and was grateful to the army for making him
'more than just a bushy'; he also had the intelligence to see the
value of recording ordinary men's experiences, as well as the
courage to take up his own pen.

The educational pattern among respondents had a parallel
in their formal professional or trade certification. About
60 per cent of the men could claim nothing of the kind,
whether completed or started. Professionally qualified men
made up 5 per cent, and those with some professional training
8 per cent. Fully qualified and partly qualified tradesmen
amounted to 8 per cent and almost 15 per cent respectively.
Some 2 or 3 per cent put themselves into a miscellaneous
category – 'piano teacher', 'permanent army artilleryman',

'competent transport driver', 'private study towards second mate's ticket' – and not one of those skills, not even the pian-ist's, was out of place in army life. One of the respondents was H. B. S. Gullett, and in his book *Not as a Duty Only* (p. 47) he illustrated the point. His 2/6th Battalion was travelling by train in Greece at night:

After one prolonged stop, Major Rowan came along waking us all up and asking if anyone could drive a steam train because it seemed the civilian drivers had disappeared. As always happens in an AIF bat-talion, a couple of men came forward and they must have known their business for soon we were off again. No one was surprised. It would have been the same if he had asked for camel drivers or water diviners.

Indeed, in spite of the high proportion of respondents with no formally certificated skills, there was a very handy mix in the group, with over one-third fully or partly 'qualified' and many other men with skills that never win diplomas but help to win campaigns, or survive them.

In and out of work

In the matter of employment even the thirty-niners varied widely. H. E. Day enlisted in 1939. He had just turned 21 and was earning 'full money' (£3 6s 0d a week) as an industrial designer. J. E. Black enlisted in 1939. Sacked from a wool-broking firm when he reached 21 years, and being two years out of work, he joined up because he was 'in one word – unemployed'. F. P. Melrose enlisted in 1939. Married with three children, he was a well-qualified toolmaker with a radio corporation, earning over £6 a week. He had difficulty with the manpower officers until he told them at a recruiting depot that he was an unemployed labourer – and at the radio cor-poration later 'it nearly caused World War III'. F. F. Parkin-son humped his bluey from the time he left school to enlistment in 1939, aged 18, because he was sick of being on the road and in and out of gaol. All four men were thirty-niners, but was there any pattern in their backgrounds?

O. J. Jenkin, 23, had struggled from 1933 to become first a primary schoolteacher and then, in 1940, to gain a secondary school appointment, from which he was earning about £6 a week. He enlisted in that year. 'Storeman' was sacked at 20 years of age in 1940 and enlisted after being unemployed for a month: 'The army was a job.' G. N. Bissett, a single 24-year-old station overseer and member of the Pastoralists Association, went to Victoria from Western Australia to escape his 'reserved occupation' classification and to enlist in 1942. W. H. Blestowe, single and 29 years old, earning £10 per week as a night-shift worker in a woollen mill, left that protected occupation in 1942 to join up. G. C. Burr was a 19-year-old farm labourer when he went into a field regiment early in 1940. For him, whose working fortnight had pre-viously won him under £2 in cash, the army's £3 10s 0d was 'pretty good' and it had been a prime attraction; but he was unusual, he thought – 'most chaps came down a peg on join-ing'.

After listing his own wide range of jobs – from digging potatoes to digging for gold – Maurice Melvaine grumbled that the questionnaire he was tackling so long afterwards did not give sufficient scope for 'answers geared to the un-certainty of the 1930s'. His father was also unable to find secure employment in those days, having to take whatever work opened up at an electricity supply company, a granite quarry, on shire relief, as bridge carpenter, on shearing shed plants and as fruit-packer, goldminer and lorry-driver. Other men Melvaine knew 'went rabbiting for a living, did inter-mittent work like fencing, or risked their lives getting cedar logs out of gorges'. Melvaine joined the army in 1940. So did the migrant 'Jock'. Losing his job with General Motors Holden at 21, he was unemployed for a time before grasping one of those straws that authority, not entirely uncaring, offered to some in his plight. Under a Government Youth

Training Scheme he learnt sheet-metal work, which secured him a position in a factory that was soon fulfilling war contracts for bomb boxes and ammunition cases. 'When one contract expired we were stood down until more work came in. It was during one of those breaks that I joined the army.'

So the individuals differ, those few and the thousands of others who were in and out of work, yet broad generalisations are still possible. In 1939 unemployment in Australia was quite high. Among males it was about 10 per cent according to trade union figures, although the national register* showed 15 per cent, and only in 1941 was there a dramatic fall to 3.7 per cent, followed by 1.6 per cent in 1942. Therefore the jobless who joined the army in 1939–40 almost certainly made up *at least* 10 per cent of the total intake.

Most of the respondents (58 per cent) were in the army by the end of 1940, before unemployment fell so significantly, and the rate of unemployment among them was 5.2 per cent of the 1939 enlistments and 3.4 per cent of the 1940 enlistments. For the respondents as a whole, between 2 and 3 per cent were out of work on enlistment – one-quarter for up to seven weeks, one-quarter for up to six months, and one-half for even longer. There were also cases in which the real position was unclear. Another 2 to 3 per cent were students not then earning an income: Ken Knox was still at school, but feeling a bit guilty and sure he could do a reasonable job – 'I went to school one Monday, left at lunch-time, and was in the AIF that night'. One lucky man in a thousand had no need to work: aged 26 and single, 'Irishman' had the backing of a father who was of the professional class; he had left Eire to visit the World's Fair in New York and later casually decided to visit New Zealand – and on that leg of his comfortable journeyings was caught up in the war. Yet overall something

* The *National Registration Act* 1939 required all males of from 18 to 64 years to complete a form showing their occupation, income, unemployment etc.

From these young men on the production staff at Horwood Bagshaw's machinery works (Adelaide), in 1939, came recruits for army, navy and air force

like 94 per cent of the respondents were 'working' at enlistment. 'Tom' joined the 2/17th Battalion in 1940:

In my unit we had wealthy graziers, farmers, most trades, stockmen, a stud master, solicitors – down to uneducated young blokes like me. I think this is important: I only remember one man who was unemployed. I was the only man in my platoon who got more money in the army than in civvy street. I resent the remarks often made about the AIF having many unemployed in its ranks.

Let his point be well taken. Nevertheless, without wishing to offend 'Tom' or anyone else, it must be insisted that there were in the army more of the unemployed than 'Tom' came across. (Former soldier Charles McCausland, indeed, thought that many men lied about the good jobs they had given up when, in fact, they had been unemployed.) Even allowing for the difference between the first in and the last, the unemployed who went into the army in World War II were considerably under-represented among respondents. It is a pity, but probably not surprising, and certainly not fatal for a sympathetic understanding of the economic difficulties of the time.

Under-employment emerged clearly among the respondents. Almost 13 per cent (and nearly 15 per cent of the

Depending on the Salvation Army in the depressed Melbourne of the 1930s. When Australia looked to some of these men for service in the 1940s, the Salvos were still found to be good for a cuppa in the most unlikely places

thirty-niners) said that the prospect of steady pay and three meals a day made the army attractive to them, and a few men were in the regular army when war broke out because of lack of other work in the 1930s. Many men were like Melvaine and 'Jock' in reporting breaks between seasonal or contract work, or had been unemployed at some time, and about 2 per cent of the whole group's surviving and unretired fathers were out of a job. Such things were reported often enough to show that life could still be hard around 1939.

Nevertheless the happier and larger aspect should not be lost to sight. Day, Melrose, Jenkin, Bissett, Blestowe and a great many others were also part of the scene – secure in their jobs and earning good money. Most respondents simply ignored a suggestion in the questionnaire that 'employment' could have affected their decision to go into the army – it was just not relevant; and nearly 6 per cent (about 4 per cent of the thirty-niners) emphatically rejected the idea. The fact is that in 1939 from 85 to 90 per cent of the Australian male work-force was in work of some kind, and by 1941 the proportion was even higher. It is a warning against such parrot talk as 'Oh, the 6th Division – it was *all the unemployed*'. If there were some solid grains of truth in the remark, there was always much more chaff in it. Respondents to the questionnaire, although including too few of the unemployed, still stand as a healthy reminder that even in 1939 most of the Australian army was made up of men who did not have to enlist to get a living.

The art of survival

The wartime army was not exactly generous to all who had to live on its pay, and there were unfortunate anomalies. Volun-teer Militia privates continued to receive the 8s a day set in 1938 to attract recruits, but conscripted privates were paid 5s a day. The daily pay of single AIF privates was also 5s while they were in Australia, with 2s deferred pay added after embarkation, and married AIF privates got an additional allowance of 3s a day for their wives and 1s for each child. Although a private could allocate from his 5s another 4s a day to his wife and children it still left perhaps the worst anomaly. For the married private it meant that, in Gavin Long's words (*To Benghazi*, p. 66), 'the most his wife and, say, one child, could receive was £2 16s a week. The average basic wage was £3 19s and only a fraction of those who enlisted had been used to living on this minimum sum'. With their keep thrown in and a few fringe benefits, the financial rewards offered by the army were reasonable for lieutenants (15s), single sergeants (10s) and even single privates (especially if they had been receiving a dole of, say, 8s 6d per *week*). Ultimately postwar aid helped many too, but subsistence during the war could be difficult for the wives and children of private soldiers, and thin for those men who made the maximum allotment to their families from their pay.

That basic wage in the six capital cities, averaging £3 19s 0d a week in 1939, had risen to £4 7s 0d in 1941. Some 15 per cent of the respondents claimed to have been earning much more – from £6 to over £10 – when they enlisted, and probably 40 to 50 per cent of the entire group were getting *at least* the minimum adult wage. It did not put the respondents as a whole into the class of big earners: at the halfway mark in the group the weekly earnings were about £3, and it is likely that from 50 to 60 per cent were getting *less* than the basic wage. It would not have mattered if the same percentage of men had been under 21 years of age, and so not entitled to an adult wage, but only 43 per cent were still juniors. The information provided by respondents was not sufficiently complete or free from oddities, and the changing circumstances over time and all Australia were too complex, for precision to be possible; but it might not be too far from the mark to suggest that one in ten of the respondents enlisted when he was legally an adult but was not getting the income laid down by law as the minimum. Thus the shadowed underside of economic life appears again.

The range is illustrated by J. D. Thompson, who enlisted in 1940 as a 28-year-old businessman with a weekly income of around £10; and WX354, who joined up in 1939 and, aged 25, was 'doing well' on less than £3 as a door-to-door salesman of Watkins products. C. J. Butwell joined the AIF in 1941 when he was 24; he had been forced to leave the city in search of work as a lad, but had achieved a full adult wage from the age of 17 years, working at a saw bench in a country timber mill. On the other hand T. J. Toohey, enlisting in 1939 at 23, had worked on his parents' property and then gone droving and lorry-driving, but was getting only about £3 a week – barely making the basic wage, if that. When J. C. Thomson enlisted in 1939, aged 23, he had been hawking fruit and vegetables and making under £2 a week; but E.J. joined up in 1940, aged

No bulk handling between the wars; just lumping bags for 'a few bob'.
'Is it any wonder', asked a respondent, 'that I have a flattened disc in my
spine, when I was loading bags of wheat on my own at 14?'

36, after bringing in £8 10s 0d as a travelling salesman. E. H. J. Searle, aged 24, was earning about £9 when he enlisted in 1942, and had difficulty in getting release from his job as a welding works foreman. He was one of the many who (unless they won promotion) earned much less in the army than in civilian life: strange were the priorities allotted to industrial workers and private soldiers.

On the principle of 'anything for a quid', young men had changed between manual and clerical work according to what was available in the 1930s, but in broad terms respondents divided into 52 per cent blue-collar (including farm) workers, and 42 per cent white-collar workers (including professional and managerial, and rising nearer to 45 per cent if students are counted in). Almost 3 per cent were dubbed 'self-employed' to distinguish farmers from farmhands, and contractors from wage slaves. The 'self-employed' segment could have been enlarged by taking some of the professionals out of the white-collar category and some of the rabbiters out of the blue-collar lot, but not many of this essentially youthful group were employers, and the most interesting division seemed to be between those who got their hands calloused and dirty, and those who went to work in office clothes.

A.H.M.'s doctor made yet another distinction in 1942. With his father in the prewar permanent army because of a shortage of other work, A.H.M. left school to become a messenger boy and a junior salesman in a music shop. Then he worked for one year as a furnaceman in an iron foundry, turning 18 while he was there. His doctor said to him, 'This work is too heavy for you. It is ruining your health. You should join the army.'

6 • BELONGING

'Aub' had a good secondary education shortened by the death of his father – largely due to the effects of the depression. It turned Aub into a rural worker for several years, but it did not turn him to the political left. He simply 'did not like the uncouth, tough, belligerent types of the Labor Party', and although he belonged to the Australian Workers Union, it was only because it was 'compulsory for a shearing shed worker'. There were other respondents who were similarly reluctant unionists, as well as those who believed whole-heartedly in unionism, and those who managed to buck the union system altogether. The tough L. A. Hintz, 17 when he went into the army after being in and out of many factory and rural jobs, used to *say* he was 'Labor', but only because his 'old man' was. Young Hintz would join no union: 'I was boss of me.'

Trade unions and politics

When the respondents went into the army, about 30 per cent of them had been members of a trade union. Of that group, 52 per cent favoured Labor, and 1 per cent the Communist Party, but the United Australia and Country Parties were preferred by 25 and 8 per cent respectively, while 12 per cent had no real party preference (and 3 per cent gave no answer). Ignorance and indifference often meant that young men failed to reconcile their political leanings with their status as

unionists. WX3623 *thought* that he had found the logical solution: as a *worker* he was a unionist, a member of the AWU; but
as a worker on a *cattle station*, he favoured the Country Party. It
made sense to him, although he had not had 'much time to
think of politics'.

The inconsistent position of R. J. Anson was a little more
surprising. He was an 'avid reader of the *Worker* and the poems
and philosophy included', and yet he remained loyal to the
Country Party. But then this AWU member and head stockman 'knew nothing about politics in Canberra the "Bush
Capital", except that [the Country Party's] Earle Page and
Charles Hawker seemed to be interesting men'. E. J. Long,
having been an improver butcher, a drover, and the manager
of his father's 1000-head cattle property, had been in the
AWU and the Australian Meat Industry Employees Union –
'both compulsory', he said. Before he enlisted he had just
qualified to vote, but he could not really make up his mind
between the Country and Labor Parties – a large part of the
truth being that he was not much interested.

There were plenty of others who were straight down the
line, and some who knew very well what unionism and politics could be about. D. K. Parker, one of a family with five
boys in the services, had been raised in a trade union atmosphere. His father held office in a union, and an uncle had led a
meat strike. Parker belonged to the WA Amalgamated Society
of Railway Employees, and was ALP all the way. Most people
would think that Parker represented those respondents who
had got their act together, and there were enough like him to
produce a tendency for union membership to go with support
for parties of the left. Whereas 53 per cent of the unionists
favoured the ALP or the Communists, only 35 per cent of all
respondents preferred those parties; so the trend was there,
even if it was not overwhelming. Non-Labor was favoured – at
least vaguely – by 47 per cent of the whole group, 15 per cent
had no political preferences at that time, and the rest gave no
answer. Thus neither Labor supporters nor trade unionists
came close to forming even a small majority among the re-

spondents. They are points of importance in understanding the composition of the group, and they possibly reduce its representativeness of all recruits, although it should be remembered that many unionists and Labor sympathisers were kept out of the army by their reserved occupations.

Of the respondents who did belong to a union at enlistment, 13 per cent were in the Australian Workers Union – and that was the highest score of any union. The AWU mainly consisted of rural workers but it was not restricted to them. AWU members among respondents included NX98521, who had a job at a wire works; 'Bluey', who was a fuser at a stove factory; and F. C. Crellin, who had worked as a fibrous plasterer and maintenance mechanic as well as in cork manufacture, had been a member of the Miscellaneous Workers Union as well as the AWU, and saw himself as a townsman who favoured the Country Party.

Running second among the respondent unionists was the Bank Officers Association, with 10 per cent, but these men were often uncertain whether they belonged to a union or a professional association – in other words, whether the body's main purpose was to improve pay and working conditions, or to promote common interests of a broader kind in a less militant way. When some unions were lumped together, Public Service with Postal, Shop Assistants with Storemen and Packers, and various transport unions, each grouping provided between 7 and 9 per cent. Ranging from just under 5 to about 6 per cent were unions connected with food, printing, building, teaching and (together) clerical and insurance work. Because of war production – not necessarily lack of patriotism – other unions had still lower representation. Workers in metal, clothing and textiles, various engineering, vehicle and other manufacturing each supplied from about 4 per cent down to 2 per cent, while miners, electrical tradesmen, boilermakers and wharf labourers had only a token presence.

Other men besides bank officers had difficulty in deciding if they were in a union or a professional association. Members of the Australian Journalists Association (noticeable in number) had similar trouble classifying themselves, and there were various others – musicians, surveyors, some men in teacher associations ... What journalists and bank employees *now* belong to are certainly unions, and perhaps it is right to see them as such even then. If tellers and reporters are called unionists, the proportion of the respondents who belonged to 'professional' or 'employer' associations was small – not much more than 5 to 6 per cent. Accountants led, followed in descending order by pastoralists, medical and related professions, engineers, surveyors and architects. But the *range* of interests represented was wonderful: the Royal Society (a geologist), Advertising, Commercial Travellers, Retail Traders, Professional Photographers, English Teachers, Garage and Service Station Proprietors, Librarians, Metallurgists, Master Hairdressers ... It was that handy mix appearing again; in the army almost anything could be done by someone, somewhere – if only he could be found at the right time and place.

Social class

Respondents were asked to say which social class they thought they belonged to at the time of enlistment. No answer was given by 6 per cent, and 1 per cent believed they were upper-class – a claim usually given some support by their privileged backgrounds. QX16129 was a university graduate, an articled law clerk and the son of a very comfortably placed Darling Downs dairy farmer who never used the word 'unionists' but only the term 'damned agitators'; the father went berserk when he learned that his son – then, not later – was voting Labor. F. V. Rudduck, born in the United States and coming to live in Australia when he was 4, had a father who was manager of an international company and a mother who had been an opera singer in New York and London. The father of VX13985 was in a managerial position, and his mother was a doctor; he had been born in England, came to Australia at the age of 10 years, and was a part-time university student at enlistment. Philip Russell's father was a Western District grazier, and his school had been Geelong Grammar. Such were the men who had reason for putting themselves in an upper-class bracket.

Middle-class was chosen by 26 per cent, working-class by 38 per cent, and a large 28 per cent maintained that they were not class-conscious. Nor should that last claim be too quickly dismissed. Some people rarely see class distinction in its starkest forms; some can move easily and unselfconsciously between classes; and class divisions can be confused by factors like extended family connections, local community identification and codes of football, or cut across by such other divisions as country versus city, and Catholic against Protestant. Certain things will inevitably be noticed from time to time, but often they will not be analysed sufficiently to make a young man fully class-conscious. Even when pressed, he might have great difficulty in fitting himself into any class, the lines are so blurred and the definitions so changeable.

F.S.J.I. had long been convinced of one thing: he was called to become an Anglican clergyman (and he achieved this, after war service). About other things he was pretty muddled. He told an army recruiting sergeant that he was torn between a sense of duty and a pacifist conscience – and was treated with complete sympathy and posted to a medical unit. He was inclined towards the United Australia Party, as his father had been before being 'savaged' by the depression and converted to Labor. That father had been a self-employed salesman, unemployed, manager of a vacuum-cleaner hiring service, and a self-employed gardener. The mother had been forced to work extremely hard to help keep the household. The son was a state school boy with part of a secondary education behind him and, on enlistment, was trying to complete his Leaving Certificate at night while employed as a salesman. He knew he was *not* upper-class, but was he working-class or middle-class? He did not know; anyway, he 'was not very class-conscious' at 20 years of age.

A Victorian Catholic, W. P. O'Shannessy was illegitimate

and had been dragged up in an orphanage and by two sets of
foster parents, 'both bastards'. He was 18 in 1941 and had
known unemployment, although he was then a hotel boots
and kitchenhand. He had reached 8th Grade at school, belonged to no union, favoured no political party – and, he said,
was not class-conscious. J. H. Briggs was called up at 20 in
1940 after growing up in Sydney, the son of a fitter with the
railways, and becoming a journeyman carpenter and a member of the appropriate union. His Baptist faith meant much to
him, but he claimed not to have been conscious of class –
although he favoured Labor. L. V. Letwin was Jewish and a
Victorian. His father was a clothing cutter and pattern-maker,
and he himself – with a fair education behind him – belonged
to the Australian Metal Workers Union; but, at 19 in 1941,
Letwin had no political preference and was not class-conscious. Ted Tremaine, from Queensland, was a 24-year-old
married pharmacist in 1941. He was a rare attender at the
Church of England; he voted for the Country Party; his
deceased father had been a stock and station agent and his
mother a 'professional' woman before her marriage. But
Tremaine put himself down as not class-conscious. The strapping Ken Knox (6 ft 5 in and 15 st 7 lb at 18) left Melbourne
Grammar for the AIF; he had a father who was a company
director – and knighted – and a mother who was 'almost a
full-time honorary charity worker'; but he described himself
as being not class-conscious. Even some who classified themselves as upper-class, such as Philip Russell, added 'but not
very class-conscious'.

No definitions of class were offered as a guide to the respondents, but only the choice between 'upper', 'middle',
'working' and 'not class-conscious'; they answered according
to their own perceptions. Sometimes the perception appeared
to be that to talk of class at all was too wicked or communistic
to be proper. 'It seems like you people are very class-conscious', wrote C.E.S., 'probably socialists or fellow travellers. I
don't think normal people will, voluntarily, find your book
readable.' His shop steward father back in England was never

able to understand C.E.S., nor he his father. A self-made man, C.E.S. had done, and was yet to do, all sorts of work and to prosper in the end; but he stubbornly refused to acknowledge any consciousness of class. Nevertheless people are affected by family background, status, income and opportunity or lack of it, and it seems worthwhile to apply some crude tests to the answers that respondents gave to questions about class, especially those who were 'working-class' or 'not class-conscious'.

Those who saw themselves as working-class usually had a low level of education: 80 per cent no higher than 'some secondary', compared with 59 per cent of the 'not class-conscious'. The working-class were also much more likely than those who were not class-conscious to be blue-collar workers, domestics or unemployed: 74 per cent, compared with 46 per cent. It was clearly easier for the more privileged to ignore class; yet it was not entirely simple, since there were the poorly educated blue-collar workers – like W. P. O'Shannessy – who claimed not to think in class terms. Also, if 66 per cent of the working-class had no skills, a larger 72 per cent of the 'not class-conscious' had none – reflecting those who were, and were not, learning trades, and showing that advantages did not all run one way. The proportion of the working-class in trade unions (38 per cent) was higher than the average for the whole group (30 per cent), and 58 per cent of those who described themselves as working-class favoured the Labor Party or the Communists, compared with 35 per cent of the respondents generally. Young and politically ignorant many of these men were, and often more ready to accept the status quo as something given than to analyse and challenge it; yet others had at least begun to perceive their identities and where their interests might lie.

City and country

When asked about one other dividing line – town or country – a solid third of the group did not answer. Why that happened remains a puzzle, but it might be reasonable to think that some found it too hard to say whether they belonged to city or country because their backgrounds had been so mixed. If so, they would properly have joined those 19 per cent who did say that they had moved between city and country, or lived on the boundaries of both, and therefore were neither the one nor the other. Some 20 per cent reckoned they were countrymen, and 27 per cent saw themselves as townsmen. Judged by where they were living when they joined up, they were an urban group: only 13 per cent were on farms or similar places, and 85 per cent were in a town of some kind. Yet that criterion is never good enough. A countryman born and bred may move to a city, and often does, without losing all of his country characteristics. And, if 15 per cent lived in a small country town, and 39 per cent in the outer city, they were often not in a very urban environment – especially in 1939.

Two points are probably valid. First, this group (and probably the whole Australian army) was *not* essentially 'made in the bush'. Too few men could say that they were just countrymen for so much to be claimed for rural influence. Nevertheless there is a second point. Those with stated 'country' or 'mixed' backgrounds together made up 39 per cent, and half of the entire group might have been properly included in those categories if the 34 per cent who gave no answer had given one. It is likely that a significant degree of country experience – living, working, playing or drifting – lay in the background of a very sizeable proportion of young male Australians at that time. It is not impossible that only a minority were townsmen pure and simple. If so, country experience could have been an important factor in the making of the army, even while other factors were equally – or more – formative.

NX22467, single at the age of 25, was where he had always been – on a dairy farm. He had completed primary school, was nominally 'Prespeterian', and he 'just voted', without particular interest, for the Country Party. He was so much a countryman that when he joined the army in 1940, in the 2/1st Pioneer Battalion, he was grateful to it for showing him

Fishing and shooting along the Yule River in Western Australia's northern sheep country

that 'the world didn't end at our boundary fence'. In contrast, 'Snow' was solidly of the town: he attended the Alfred Crescent and Falconer Street state schools in North Fitzroy, became a telegram messenger and then an apprentice with the Easyphit Slipper company, and was mainly interested in roller-skating and crystal sets (wireless). 'Snow' was also a Pioneer, and after service in the Middle East and captivity in Japanese hands decided that men from the country did best – and then immediately blurred any such division by remarking that business and professional men, and those with trade experience, 'also coped quite well'. So there might not have been much between town and country as far as effectiveness in the army went. 'Snow' chose another distinction: those who had come from, or close to, the criminal element and could not settle down to discipline were the least effective soldiers.

Blurring town and country in himself was 'Tom', who lived in hard rural circumstances   shooting, trapping and selling rabbits at 7 years of age, and at one stage helping an uncle who broke horses – before moving to Sydney and a state school that was poor in every way except the quality of the teachers. Thereafter, while working as a wrapper of catalogues and parcels, and pining to be an artist, he tried 'to get out of the city as often as possible – so far removed from the bush I came from'. The cause of the poverty was his father's vicious alcoholism (the father enlisted on 4 September 1939), and 'Tom' himself became an alcoholic after service in the Middle East and the Pacific, followed by the trauma of appalling housing conditions in Sydney after the war, and the struggle to survive as he trained as a commercial artist. After fifteen years of hell he was saved by the serenity of his wife and the efforts of psychiatrists and Alcoholics Anonymous – to whom he was pointed by the persistent care of one of his old officers, who also persuaded 'Tom' that it was a good idea to become a respondent. That officer, in answering his own questionnaire, was one of those who left blank the question on whether he was from town or country. He could hardly be blamed. Born in Scotland, he had been in the permanent forces for nine years at the outbreak of war; he was also a qualified plumber and had been living in a country town when he joined the army in 1931. He probably should have said that his background was 'mixed'.

Politics and patriotism

Despite some instinctive class-consciousness and leanings to right or left, politics was actually of little interest to most of the respondents. Under 3 per cent were members of any political party, and nearly half of the group were too young to vote anyway. Almost 60 per cent had nothing to say about Australian politics, unless it was that they had simply been ignorant. Not many (15 per cent) were positive, some (10 per cent) were ambivalent, and a larger number (17 per cent) were critical. The group was only marginally better informed about the world politics that was catching up with them. Over half (53 per cent) again said nothing or admitted to sheer ignorance. For some (24 per cent) the world just seemed to be in a mess, while others (17 per cent) nominated some specific enemy – Hitler, fascists, Japan . . . A clearly defined left-wing understanding emerged among just over 1 per cent, but only another 4 per cent gave very positive answers about the *politics* of things worth fighting for. The politics of war – at home or abroad – was quite beyond most of the group when they enlisted.

L.H.F., a 19-year-old Sydney storeman, was Labor-oriented but too young to vote, never gave domestic politics much thought, and found world affairs way over his head. F.C.J., a farm boy and garage hand who was conscripted at 20, had no interest in politics or party: 'Before I was called up, a girl asked me my opinion of conscription. I had none. The only paper we got was the *Weekly Times*. I remember my father and a visitor saying there was going to be a war. That worried me.' 'The Gink' never did 'really find out what the war was all about'. Although 'a lot of foolish people have had their say, the Japanese attack on Pearl Harbor never made sense'. Having been shop boy, rural worker and Sydney fitter until conscripted at 20 in 1943, he remarked that, without a vote, he and his mates did not think for themselves about politics but 'if asked, would follow the parental line' – in his case, United Australia Party. 'In the army we just did our best and for some years were happy enough to describe ourselves as patriots.' R.F.B., at 19, had done all sorts of work from post office to farm and building site, and he was 'Country Party'. Yet

while aware of the names and parties of the prime minister and premier, most country people of my age would have had little knowledge of politics in Australia and overseas. We seldom listened to news bulletins; newspapers were at least 24 hours old when received, and – if my parents were typical – politics were seldom if ever discussed with the family.

The Western Australian railway worker D. K. Parker, a dunce at school, had an unusual family background of Christian Science combined with union militancy and romantic tales told by a grandmother who had been a goldfields pioneer: 'she filled me with stories of the mateship of the fields; of "hearts of gold" prostitutes (can you imagine?); of kangaroo courts meting out rough justice to "baddies"; of strong loyalty always between the battlers.' Even so, the teenage Parker

'thought very little about Australian politics, except that all
parties were crook – Labor better than others. World politics
was above my head, except that Germans were bad, Japs bad,
Poms pretty good, French laughable'.

Some at least had strong preferences. In 1932 A. I. Allan had
joined the New Guard – the right-wing 'private army' organised to prevent a communist take-over. He was a cost clerk
inclined towards the Country Party, and was only 16 at the
time. Still, he grew to be 6 ft 6 in, so was probably man-sized
even then. For the 17-year-old Sydney clerk Gordon Geering
the United Australia Party was the only one, and the ALP was
'a bunch of dangerous Irish twits'. He had no thoughts on
world politics, apart from the empire being 'the most wonderful organisation that ever existed'. Yet he was 'a republican at
heart' and, with six or seven other recruits, refused to take the
oath of allegiance to the king. SX22812, a compositor and
unionist who was just at an age to vote when conscripted in
1939, thought 'the ALP always right, the UAP always wrong'.
Also, as 'an avid reader of *Life* magazine', he had 'formed the
opinion that Herr A. Hitler was not a Nice Person'. The certainty of L. W. Wood, a 24-year-old timber-faller, rural
worker and Labor voter, was that 'there was a job to do' and
that there should be 'no room for dissension' between parties.
T.J.A., a university student not concentrating on his studies
because 'the French were being beaten', was more interested in
those international affairs than any politics at home –
although he thought the UAP were 'more my sort of people',
and that the baneful Catholic influence 'was supposed to be
strong in the ALP'. He had read a lot about Germany, and was
against Franco in the Spanish civil war, but did not like communism any more than fascism: Soviet Russia 'seemed pretty
awful'. Anyway, 'the Führer somehow had to be stopped'.

On the other hand, R. G. Parry, a young worker in a
clothing warehouse, admired the efficiency of Nazi Germany
and thought Australia must be backward; he really had 'no
political feelings at the time', and from the volunteer Militia –
to which a love of horses had drawn him – he transferred to

the AIF in 1940 for the sake of adventure, mateship and the Anzac tradition. R. H. Ferguson was a UAP voter (even thinking of joining the party) and an Australian who had been educated in England; before returning home in 1938 to start up his own business, he had several times visited Germany and was 'convinced they wanted war'. SX9054, a bank clerk and 23 years old, had been introduced early to politics by his father – a returning officer – and his own study of economics had confirmed his ALP sympathies. He was profoundly disturbed by the conservatives' actions against J.T. Lang in New South Wales and J. H. Scullin in federal politics, and by the lopsided representation in his own South Australian parliament. Equally disturbing to him were the threats to democracy posed by the rise of dictatorships overseas, and everywhere 'the spectre of poverty amidst plenty'.

Jim Guy, coming from an English mining background and in Australia a worker at whatever he could get, 'often voted informal as the only avenue of protest in an Australian political system that did not meet the needs of the masses, in a world that was repressive, unfeeling and dangerous'. Australian-born, with a background as a fitter and turner, professional boxer and footballer, 'Little Sav' went further and joined the Communist Party while in the army (he served with the artillery in the Pacific). Before enlisting – he had trouble there because he came from a reserved occupation – he had started to get interested in politics, and gradually moved to the left. His father's business had been smashed in the depression, and 'the inhumanity of man to man' strongly affected 'Little Sav'. He resented the ruling class, and enlisted for adventure, escape and mateship's sake – with 'patriotism a poor last. I owed Australia nothing'.

The carpenter J. H. Briggs would have been shocked at such a thought. He was 'proud to be an Australian, proud to have a father and uncle who had been Anzacs, and proud of King and Empire. I wanted to serve my country very much'. That did not stop him from thinking after the depression that the political system should be 'more helpful to people', and from hoping for a Labor government; but he did not want Nazism or communism to take over the world. 'Jab', an apprentice survey draftsman, was 'thankful that Australia had been chosen as "home" by migrant ancestors' – although he was too poor to belong to a cricket team – and he saw 'the British Empire as a democracy under threat'. R. A. Eeg, a 24-year-old with part of a university degree, was 'a little cynical about politics', but Australia was his homeland and he would 'go to great lengths to protect it and the empire'. Trainee teacher Gordon Gibson 'thought Australia the lucky country, the land of the free, with a comparatively classless society that offered opportunities for the young'. He was an Australian first, but still had a strong sentimental attachment to the British Empire , his grandparents on both sides having come from Britain. The bank clerk G. S. McLeod put it this way:

Politically naive, I dimly sensed the need to put the Nazis down, and I'd read the school's Honour Roll. I was always so proud to see the red patches on Mercator's Projection, and I was a sucker for newsreels showing the Royal Navy's battleships butting their way through heavy seas while some band blew its guts out playing 'Land of Hope and Glory'. Oh, yes, I was a believer. But Australia was unquestionably the greatest place on earth. Where else would one find the diversified talents of Bradman, Kingsford Smith, Jack Crawford and Gladys Moncrieff?

C.R.B., 25 and a grocer, thought it good to belong to the empire, and believed that Australia was God's country. He wryly added, 'I had not travelled then', but at the end of the war he still thought of Australia as 'a desirable place to get back to'.

Most respondents had been taught to love their country and the British Empire, and happily did so, spreading their love fairly equally between the two. Of those who answered the appropriate questions (and something like one-quarter did not), 81 per cent called Australia the 'best' country or at least were loyal to it, and 80 per cent were 'proud' of the empire or

Empire Day, 20th (for 24th) May.

EDUCATION DEPARTMENT
VICTORIA · AUSTRALIA
SCHOOL PAPER
GRADES III AND IV

No. 407.] *Registered at the General Post Office, Melbourne, for transmission by post as a newspaper.*   MELBOURNE.   Price 1d.   [MAY 2, 1932.

THE HOUSE OF EMPIRE

THE EMPIRE THAT GIRDLES THE WORLD

The World Book.]

The British Empire and its Seat of Government.

The Empire is made up of many countries, states, and settlements scattered round the world and owning King George as their sovereign.   The upper picture shows the Houses of Parliament at Westminster, London.

'I was always so proud to see the red patches'

at any rate felt a duty to it. The 19-year-old butter-factory storeman N. K. D. McGrath wrote that every child knew (and he still knew in 1983) the words:

> It's only a piece of bunting,
> It's only an old coloured rag,
> But thousands have died for its honour
> And shed their last blood for the flag.

SX9054, worried about the paradox of Australia's exporting the necessities of life while families lived from hand to mouth in dugouts on the banks of Adelaide's River Torrens, nevertheless thought – 'probably due to schooling' – that the empire was 'an enormous brotherhood for good'. At his school the flag was saluted every morning, with the pupils repeating:

'I love my country, *the British Empire*. I honour her king, King George V. I salute her flag, *the Union Jack*. I promise cheerfully to obey her laws. [And added by some teachers] May God defend the right.'

No wonder I was imbued with a spirit of empire. I was familiar with and proud of the exploits of English, Scottish and Irish soldiers and statesmen and their kings and queens. I just wasn't too keen on George III and the American fiasco.

Not quite so deeply affected was NX65735:

Balgowlah Primary (close to Sydney but very rural). No Anzac ceremony that I remember. But on Empire Day the school marched through the headmaster's room (where classes 5 and 6 were taught), which had two entrances. On the way through, each child was given a meat pie and a bag of boiled lollies.

Family moved to Bankstown, still semi-rural although a large school of 1000 pupils. Anzac Day: teachers who were returned soldiers paraded in uniforms with gasmasks, tin hats, rifles . . . a performance that impressed a boy. Empire Day: school marched down to local picture theatre for speeches. I preferred the meat pies, but was glad of the half-holiday. All this may have had a subconscious effect on me when joining the army, but I doubt it. Other influences were probably at work, e.g. my reading.

Only 13 per cent of the respondents were notably critical of Australia (and then they were mostly thinking of the 'politics' of the land, not other aspects of life in it), and 14 per cent were completely sour on the empire. J. N. Barter, a youthful farmer, was unhappy with New South Wales's J. T. Lang, and Labor, and lack of development; but 'if the British Empire fell apart, the whole world would do the same'. Catholic furnace-hand Stan Brahatis, at 21, was 'not in favour of the empire', thought 'Lang was right', and had a poor opinion of R. G. Menzies; Brahatis went to war simply because Australia was threatened. 'Aide-de-camp', a 29-year-old banker and prewar Militia officer, thought that Labor governments in the states could do no permanent damage, but a federal Labor government 'would do lasting harm to freedom, and their views on defence and foreign affairs were a danger to the future of Australia'. He went on to be mentioned in despatches; he endured years as a Japanese POW; his wife had twins he did not see until they were 4 years old; and – a royalist to the end – he was once aide-de-camp to the queen. R.L.D., a travelling salesman, believed that Australia should assert itself more in the world, although the empire was the great bulwark of strength and decency.

J.B., sacked from the furniture trade when he was due for full adult wages, and then months out of work, thought everything everywhere – Australia and empire – was 'rigged to exploit the ordinary people', and resentfully remained in the Militia from 1940 to the end of the war, 'because I was called up to serve my country when my country couldn't give me a job for ten months'. He found some mates in the army, but did not like it, especially the training and discipline; yet in the finish he thought Australia 'the best country in the world', and postwar rehabilitation gave him 'trade training and a better-paid job'. R. F. Emonson, the young railway worker who could only remember 'being hungry all the time as a child', was 'cynical' about Australia – since he 'never saw an underfed politician or member of the church'; and he was 'bitter' about the empire – 'always involving us in wars and treating us like children'.

A few young men notably lacked any sense of being Australian. VX12454, a storeman who joined the permanent army just before the war, thought he was really a Victorian rather than an Australian, although he was a 'loyal royalist' about the empire. For NX72561, a 19-year-old butcher, Australia was 'just the little town I lived in – in tough times', and the empire was no more than 'the countries coloured red on the map of the world'. He enlisted solely for the adventure, and he discovered a mateship that would only die when he did. The sport-obsessed clerk NX3700 'lived in a self-centred small world and gave little thought to either Australia or the empire' – yet somehow felt it his duty to enlist on the very first day of recruiting, and did so. After service in all major Australian theatres, he finally took part in the Victory March in London in 1946. By then he thought Australia 'great' and hoped the empire would 'continue for all time'. An insurance clerk, L.H., had been well taught at school to believe in the empire, but he was too busy enjoying himself to realise 'what a fortunate thing it was to be an Australian'.

A married man, and an assistant manager in the retail trade, V.P.J. was ambivalent about Australia. It was perhaps close to the top in sport, but few Australians knew about the gifted writers and artists it was producing, most of its books came from overseas, and – again apart from sport – the available entertainment was limited. He had no doubts about the empire: it was invincible. Dennis Bird, born in England, had migrated twice to Queensland – for the years 1926–29 and again in 1939 – as part of his roving and adventurous life. He found the place 'a little disappointing. I had been a keen applauder of the arbitration system and it was a pity to see it manipulated by both the establishment and the unions. Still, it was a good country and recovering well from the depression'.

WX11470 was born in England (never knowing his father, who was killed in World War I) but at the age of 13 came to Australia, where he 'lived and worked in the northern wheat-belt, on a friend's farm'. More unusually, he had 'ample time for reading, wrote some verse and became addicted, through the wireless, to serious music'. He was 'never a jingoist imperialist', thinking that the empire could be better and could be worse (he enlisted to fight Nazism and, much later, was expelled from the Returned Services League because he was for several years a member of the Communist Party). Australia had immediately won the heart of this English boy: 'I fell in love with the country as soon as I set foot in it, and would never wish to live permanently in any other.'

Some such sentiment was felt by most respondents. Few of them went to war because they understood the politics of it. A great many went, at least partly, because they identified themselves as Australians and members of the British Empire. They felt a sense of loyalty and duty, a feeling that often cut clean across class and all other divisions. Then, ironically, a split in the community was widened: the gap between returned soldiers and the stay-at-homes. But within the comradeship of arms many men found a degree of belonging they had never known before.

Having started life with a handicap, F. F. Fenn was freed by being thus bound:

I, with Aboriginal blood and illegitimate, have a bond among men which can only come about through the experience we had during the war. I meet with all types of ex-servicemen, and in no other way in my lifetime could I have been able to face [them], shake hands [with them], and have respect for [them] and they respect for me, unless . . . through the experience I mentioned. I can count Brigadier Generals, Colonels, right down the line to fellow privates as equals, and I am so proud that no way have I ever regretted joining the army.

JOINING UP

On guard, Geelong AIF camp, 1940

7 • THE THING TO DO

It was not just 'Country and Empire' that got men for the army. Compulsory call-up into the Militia brought in about 22 per cent of the respondents, and they rarely appealed against it. Only about 5 per cent were involved in an appeal, and literally half the time it was instituted by their employers against the wishes of the conscript.

> *I* didn't appeal. I was manpowered out by my boss, an electrical manufacturer, who was friendly with the local area officer [NX49243].
> My employer appealed (protected industry) and I was rejected. So I re-registered, named a fictitious employer, and that time was accepted [R. E. O'Farrell].
> As my employment was in the pastoral industry, my employer appealed each time, and the appeal was always granted. Finally a call-up arrived while the boss was in hospital. It was my opportunity to leave and to be too far involved for an appeal to work [N. F. W. Banks].

Employers were possibly correct in thinking that some employees would be of more use to the country in their civilian occupations than in the army. Employers had vital roles to play, and they had problems; yet they also seem to have often been harsh and selfish. Respondent J. W. Howard was one of the many apprentices sacked as soon as they were entitled to full wages, after doing a tradesman's work for a couple of years at apprentice rates (in Howard's case the offending

129

firm was a brass foundry in Launceston). Removing to Melbourne, he was in a protected industry when war broke out and was refused permission to enlist by the managing director. When that man died in 1941, his successor not only allowed Howard to join up but also made up the difference between what he had been earning and his army pay – an amount that continued to be sent to Howard's wife even after he became a sergeant.* So a different side of employer behaviour emerges.

Sometimes more than one factor operated to keep a man out of the army for a while. 'My employer appealed because of the loss of all his station hands, and because my parents were against me joining up. I had a brother in the RAAF and one in the AIF, both in the Middle East, and another one elsewhere in the AIF', said N200699.

Appeals for at least deferment had a reasonable chance of success; they worked in the case of nearly 60 per cent of the applicants among respondents. On their own account they sought deferment on such grounds as illness (theirs or their family's), the imminent birth of a baby to a wife, or to complete an apprenticeship or university examinations. It was very unusual to object entirely to going into the services, but it happened.

I was deferred for approximately nineteen months, as I was classified medically unfit. (I was nicknamed 'Tubby'.) It was later changed to B2, which was acceptable to the Militia. I did what I had to do, with bad grace. Otherwise, in the terminology of the time, go to gaol and stay there until twelve months after hostilities ceased. I was not interested in politics. I don't know what I thought of the Empire then. I'd left school after primary, and was a fur cutter, 18 years old.

---

* Other employers noted as making up the difference between civilian and army pay included Woolworths (B. J. Porter), Sydney Water Board (P. D. McPherson), Sydney Gas Company (NX10773), Commonwealth Bank (VX56661), NSW Public Service (J.C.H.) and Dalgety (QX6945).

A.A.F. Mob. 31.

AUSTRALIAN MILITARY FORCES.

NOTICE TO RECRUITS

Area 57A
Drill Hall
Raglan St
Preston N 18 ____ (Place)

_10/4/41._ ____(Date)

Surname ____ _DEAN._

Other names in full ____ _Albert Murray_

You will report to ____ Area 57A
Drill Hall
Raglan St ____ (Name or appointment)

at ____ Preston N 18 ____
(Place)

on ____ _3ʳᵈ May 1941 — time notified later._
(Date and time)

prepared to proceed to a Camp of Continuous Training at ____
for a period of three months.

On entering camp you will receive a free issue of the following articles, in addition to uniform:—

Two singlets.   Two pairs socks.
Two pairs underpants.   Two towels.

The following articles will not be provided by the Defence Department, and if you are in possession of them you should bring them with you:—

Hair brush.   Piece of soap.
Comb.   Shaving soap.
Tooth brush.   Tooth paste.
Shaving brush.   Pair of braces or belt.
Razor.   Cardigan, jersey, or sweater.
Razor strop (if required).   One pair sand shoes or light shoes.
Small padlock and key (for kit bag when issued).

When uniform is issued to you your plain clothes will be despatched to the address desired by you free of charge.

REMARKS.

_____

_____

_____

_____

_____

____ (Signature and Rank)
Captain
Area Officer ____ (Appointment)
57A Area

Conscription notice for a married man without children, nearly 26 years old, and an urban labourer and part-time radio mechanic

My interests were movies, reading, ball games in the park (not team games), bike riding and young ladies [A. W. D. Hall].

For all these ex-soldiers, of course, any exemption turned out to be only temporary, and mostly they wanted it that way. As R. H. Carlson said, 'I was exempted after three months training in 1940, due to having to support my mother and two sisters, but I rejoined my unit when it was finally mobilised for active service against the Japanese'.

Volunteer militiamen

For another 19 per cent the Militia was the gateway to the army, although they were not conscripted. They were mainly men either already in the Militia at the outbreak of war, or too young to be accepted by the AIF for the time being. Others found that the Militia was the only service that would take them at the time, or at their level of fitness. All such men were volunteers, and there were a few others whose reasons for choosing the Militia may shed some light on men's thinking about joining up. Some went into it because, for family reasons, they preferred not to go overseas. Some were prepared to defend Australia as such, but would not fight in an 'imperialist' cause. Occasionally Militia service was a compromise between pacifist principles and doing nothing for Australia. The odd one or two were frankly too scared to join the AIF. A few were aliens and therefore ineligible for the overseas force. Only a tiny number of men gave such reasons, but they supplied part of the web of motives.

W. T. Dedman joined the permanent forces in 1938; when war broke out he was in Darwin, where he was obliged to remain for years, a disgruntled 'militiaman'. By the time J. D. Thompson overcame a medical problem that had kept him out of the AIF, that force was temporarily taking no more recruits, so he joined the Militia and only got into the AIF after months of effort. C.P.C. was rejected on medical grounds

THE THING TO DO   133

by both the RAN (1940) and the AIF (1943) but finally got
into the Militia.

Son of a returned soldier from World War I, C.H.F. could
not get his parents' consent to his joining the AIF at 18 in 1941,
so he went into the Militia while waiting to turn 19. A. T.
Macfarlane joined the Militia in 1939 because he was an only
son and this step was 'a softening-up process for Mum'; in
1940 he crossed over to the AIF. 'Rusty' came from Irish stock
that was anti-England, and as an only child after his mother's
five unsuccessful pregnancies was regarded as 'something
special', but he beat parental pressure at 19 in 1941 by the
Militia route to the AIF. Anyway, after Japan came into the
war, his father completely changed his tune on it – but his
mother's hair 'turned from ginger to grey almost over-
night'.

Ronald G. Moss transferred to the AIF in 1941, when he
was 21, but in the previous year had gone into the Militia and a
base job (army records) because of his mother's attitude. Who
could blame Mrs Moss for standing in her son's way? Grandfather Moss, a Boer War veteran, lowered his age to join the
First AIF and was killed at Gallipoli. His son (Ron's father)
served there too, and was later so badly wounded in France
that he was totally and permanently disabled until his death in
1937. Ron and his twin brother Keith benefited greatly from
help by Legacy, and Ron from the interest of an employer,
who was a returned man from World War I. But the suffer-
ings of war had not finished for the Mosses. Ron's health was
affected by service in Borneo, and Keith – who also joined the
AIF in 1941 – went to Malaya and died as a POW two weeks
before the war's end.

R.A.C. had unusually good parents, both of them battlers
and generous to all in need, poorly educated yet avid readers,
well informed and ready to discuss community and world
affairs with their children, whom they educated 'well past the
compulsory primary schooling of the day'. R.A.C. grew up
antagonistic to British imperialism and could not conscien-
tiously join an imperial force, but he came increasingly to hate

'I irreverently call this "the last supper" ', wrote D. L. Whittington
(centre). 'With the girls and the tea and cakes in 1939 are Colin
Balfort (air-crew, Europe, Middle East and south-west Pacific), myself
(2/10th Battalion, United Kingdom, Middle East and New Guinea)
and, on my left, Alan Watson (2/3rd Machine-gun Battalion, Middle
East, Java and death on the Burma Railway).'

Nazism and Japanese imperialism, so he voluntarily enlisted
in a Militia battalion. E. M. Waddington was a Christian
pacifist who volunteered for a Militia medical unit as a compromise; and a young salesman admitted that he was too
scared to go all the way with the AIF, but went into the Militia
because he felt he should do something. John Gardener, born
in Vienna of a Jewish family and coming to Australia in 1938,
was at first classed as an enemy alien and then as stateless; as
such he was ineligible for the AIF (though he was able to
transfer late in 1944) but was accepted in the Militia as a
volunteer in 1942, as were his father, foster brother and
brother-in-law.

There were other sorts of volunteers in the Militia. T.C.
was conscripted in 1940 and immediately rejected for poor
eyesight. He indignantly *asked* to be sworn in, and a surprised
officer told him to return the next day. He was examined by
another doctor, who did not test his eyes, and T.C. was in.

'Was I a volunteer?' he asked forty-five years later. As for A.A.T., he was only 17 when his older brother was called up. The brother was not at all keen, so A.A.T. 'packed a cut lunch' and replaced him.

But still the questions remain. Why all the acceptance of the call-up by the men involved? Why so few appeals? Why all the volunteering, with about 60 per cent of respondents going straight into the overseas-bound AIF, and another 36 per cent later transferring to it from the home-defence Militia? It was *not* usually because men were short of work, and it *was* often because of identity with Australia and the British Empire. If there was a single factor motivating these men, it was a sense of duty – sometimes vague, perhaps just a matter of 'the right thing to do'. L. W. Piper put it this way: 'I think "duty", the unquestionable thing to do, a sort of compulsion which I am still unable to define. I had no illusions about high adventure; I'd known too many World War I men.' At any rate, 72 per cent of *all* respondents chose 'duty' as part of the explanation for their readiness to go to war, thus putting it above all other single elements. (As percentages of the same total, and as specifically mentioned motives for enlistment, the next highest were Australian nationalism at 58, and empire loyalty at 56.) Mick Sheehan maintained that most men enlisted for adventure and only in later life thought it the right thing to say that they enlisted because it was their duty to serve. Yet there were too many respondents like Piper – with some gut feeling about the proper thing to do – for the role of duty to be so sceptically diminished. It had a high place, whether solemnly declared at the time or not.

'I just felt I should'

V. F. Barclay enlisted in 1939, aged 20. He was a Victorian, a Methodist, favoured the Country Party and, although work was scarce, had always managed to get something – clearing land, cutting wood, rabbit-trapping. His sense of duty was

reduced to simple logic: Australia was at war, I was an Australian, therefore . . . Aged 22, B.E.O'M. (Queensland-born,
enlisting in New South Wales in 1940; Catholic, no political
preference) had a fair education but had found work a matter
of what was available rather than what might be desired;
nevertheless he was enjoying his job as a window dresser, and
for him enlistment was 'very much' a case of duty since he
was young and fit – a duty backed up by Australian nationalism, empire loyalty and the Anzac tradition in descending
order. F. V. Rudduck (Victoria, but born USA; salesman;
Anglican; well-educated, upper-class and United Australia
Party) was 19 in 1939. He had been trained in the Militia
before the war and no one was going to stop him from doing
his duty. W. M. Johns (New South Wales; Presbyterian;
Country Party) was farming with his only brother, who was
married, so it was up to the single man – 31 in early 1940 – to
enlist. SX180 (born England, arrived South Australia 1925;
Anglican; United Australia Party; milk pick-up driver, aged
28) also saw enlistment as the duty of the single in 1939; he
had empire loyalty rather than Australian nationalism to
inspire him. NX134297 volunteered for the Militia in 1941,
aged 20, and transferred to the AIF in 1942. It was a case of
'duty – a little bit; I just felt I should' for this Labor sympathiser, nominal Anglican and factory worker. His employment had 'quite a bit' of influence because, although his was a
protected job, it was not a very good one. And there was a mate
to go in with him, and he did belong to the British Empire
Boys Brigade. WX1872 (20 in 1940; Salvation Army; no political preference; post office worker) in retrospect thought
that a deep-seated sense of duty would have moved him,
although at the time he hardly realised it.

For one reason and another

About 27 per cent of the respondents simply ignored the suggestion that duty might have been a factor in their enlistment,

or remarked that it was not an important motive for them. Only 0.4 per cent were expansively negative, and even then the rejection of duty was not always complete. F. P. Sherry (Victoria; Catholic; junior railway porter; unionist but not politically minded) was 18 in 1940. He said he had no sense of duty because he was in a reserved occupation and there were plenty of older men who had not joined up. He was influenced by having brothers in the army, the chance to go overseas, pride in Australia and the Anzac tradition, and a bit of loyalty to ' the greatest empire in the world'. Yet there was also public opinion, and that seemed to be suggesting that he should 'do his bit'.

Complete rejection of duty as a motive came from men like 'NSW Butcher' (Methodist; unionist; United Australia Party): conscripted in 1939 at 21, he saw service in the Pacific, remained in the Militia throughout, and was there simply because he had to be – 'If I'd had a sense of duty, I'd have been in the AIF'. A.J.B. *was* in the AIF, with a three-figure VX number as a 1939 enlistment, but he was another angry young man who 'owed Australia nothing' and 'even in 1939 was a republican'. Labor-voting, a non-unionist and a totally indifferent Anglican (with deep respect for the Salvation Army's relief work in the depression), A.J.B. was in the prewar Militia not because of king and country, but solely because it was 'absolute bliss for a city kid' to ride a horse as an artillery signaller, and because the six-day annual camp was the nearest thing to a holiday he had. That training, plus the opportunity of a lifetime to travel, made him join the AIF at 23 and leave the only decent job to come his way (head storeman and despatch clerk) after years of being kicked around from job to job (including sustenance work) since leaving school, fatherless, at 13 years of age. SX15148, who preferred horses to humans all his life, for whom politics did not exist, and into whom enough Anglicanism had been instilled as a child to last the rest of his life, reckoned that Australia owed him some adult wages – which he got from 1939 until 1941 as a station hand – before he enlisted. He joined up, aged 21, because of the pres-

On Anzac Sunday 1960 D. L. Whittington, with sons Peter and Stephen, admire the Victoria Cross won by Roy Inwood at Polygon Wood, near Ypres in Belgium, in 1917. Inwood was an original Anzac, and the Anzac tradition influenced many young men in World War II

sure of public opinion and fear of invasion ('this place was and is wide open to canoes'). But it was not a sense of duty, he claimed, as he had no part in starting the war.

There was seldom a single motive for enlistment. Many motives were perceived, some more often than others. Over half of the men thought that the Anzac tradition influenced their decision. As a highly placed PMG engineer, N. J. McCay went into the army to implement its postal service in World War II; but on the matter of previous military experience he was able to say, 'I landed at Anzac Cove, 25 April 1915'. M. J. McKenna had 'something to live up to', with six uncles killed in the Gallipoli campaign. So had G. L. Throssell, whose Uncle Hugo had there won Western Australia's first Victoria Cross. F. N. T. Brewer's father had been in the New Zealand part of Anzac. SX3995 could still recall the impact of the brass 'A' worn on the shoulders of genuine Anzacs returning to Australia from about 1918. C. J. Selby was so ashamed that his father had *not* been an Anzac that he served from 1939 in the Militia, then the AIF and, finally, the RAAF. R. J. S. Johnson rejected Anzac as a motive because the campaign had been a blunder.

But no awareness of war's terrible price deterred 'Smiler'; having 'just been kicked in the arse by a brutal manager in the Myer furniture department for not flicking the feather duster correctly', he went off in his lunch hour and joined the Militia in 1940. He was 14 years old. He thought that Australian nationalism was not much apparent then (it was 'more so from December 1941'), but he had 'lived in a world of jingoism' centred on empire loyalty, and he was proud of his brother in AIF uniform, and one-eyed enough to believe that 'the Anzacs saved the empire in World War I and would do so again'. His schoolbooks (but not the Irish nuns who taught him) had supplied some of this identity and loyalty, and his mother used to sing 'Roses are blooming in Picardy' and other Great War songs while she stirred the copper. Yet 'Smiler' had no delusions about what war – and peace – could do to men:

Elsternwick was full of broken men on crutches, in wheelchairs, with gas-green faces and noses eaten off by gas. There was even one case known as 'The Man who Walks Backwards', probably shell shock. He would get off a tram at Kooyong Road to go to the Repat. late at night, with a white face, spats and a cane, and proceed to walk backwards like Charlie Chaplin. There were the poor ex-diggers who constantly knocked at our door in 1933 and 1934 trying to sell Mum clothes props, home-made medicine (cough mixture made out of honey and vinegar), home-made Mickey Mouse toys, rabbits at 6d a pair (nothing was over sixpence), books of poems they had written, little booklets on their experiences . . . They talked to Mum, and I listened. I felt an affinity with them, despite a father who was anti-war and had not been to World War I. Directly opposite lived a rich young man (a bank clerk) who would strut off to drill one night a week in full Light Horse uniform – emu feathers in slouch hat, bandolier, breeches, leggings and spurs. He looked like the Duke of Gloucester. And there would be Mum singing her war songs . . . Yet they couldn't understand me when I ran away to enlist.

'Smiler' was discharged from the Militia on his determined father's insistence: he had gone through thousands of photographs to trace his son. But 'Smiler' was just as persistent and managed later, still under age, to get into the AIF and serve in

A dashing militiaman between the wars

THE THING TO DO   141

the Middle East before being discharged again for lying about
his age. Six months after that he joined the RAAF.

An important element, recognised by 55 per cent of respondents, was some personal desire to prove themselves or go on
the great adventure. D. E. Thompson, under 18 in 1939, had
never left South Australia and the idea of adventuring abroad
appealed to some extent but, more than that, he wanted to
show that he could do as his father had done in the previous
war. He found that heavy casualties soon wore adventure thin,
and long service in the major theatres settled his wanderlust
for a time. A. J. Guy's father, gassed in World War I, died soon
after the son enlisted in 1940; but Guy, a 19-year-old hairdresser, believed that 'Australians don't back off' and at the
end of his war service felt that he had proved to himself that
he was a man. P. G. Webb, who wore glasses, hated sport and
was a day-dreamer, enlisted in response to an older brother's
jibes. E. J. King wanted to show that he had not been in the
prewar Militia just as a chocolate soldier. At 26, N. E. Davies
wished to escape being a mother's boy and do better than his
father, who had not served in World War I. NX72561
thought over all the possible motives suggested in the questionnaire and replied, 'Truthfully, it was just adventure'.
There were others who saw deeper from the start: at no time
had K. M. Sillcock any desire to be shot at, but he gritted his
teeth to serve in the Middle East – and then to transfer to the
RAAF and a Lancaster squadron in the United Kingdom.
QX4728, who was in both the Middle East and the Pacific in
armoured units, pointed out that 'us cowards will go to any
lengths to prove we're not'.

Mateship

R.H., a regular and a regimental sergeant major, preferred to
call it comradeship. G. C. Ayrton, a wool-buyer and a crusty
type, denied that there was ever such a thing as mateship,
except between man and woman, and homosexuals. Ayrton

can sort it out with the 46 per cent of respondents who claimed 'mateship' as a big factor in their enlistment. The Adelaide clerk A.D.C. wrote of seven friends joining up together after the fall of France in 1940. At the same stage of the war, the Melbourne factory worker G. R. C. Lancaster and four friends, all under 18, dared each other and walked in from Brunswick to enlist. L.M.K., an Adelaide compositor, also joined in the second half of 1940 with four friends, all of whom were killed in the Middle East – and the most difficult week in L.M.K.'s life was the one in which he returned to visit the parents of his friends, each of them obviously wondering why it could not have been *their* boy who came home.

Eager *for* mates were men like W. K. Favell, who had never met many people in the backblocks of New South Wales; C. V. Barkla, a Queensland orphan; and R. Hoey, an only child and always appreciative of company in sports teams and cadets (he married during the war too). VX1959, educated at Melbourne Grammar, rather dreaded having to mix with 'a rough element', but he ended up a sergeant, serving with a petrol company in the Middle East (no easy berth, with Stuka dive bombers about) and an air maintenance company in the Pacific; what he found he liked most in the army was the 'comradeship'. He was representative of the many men who, not drawn to the army by mateship, certainly found it there. The Queensland teacher and pious Methodist M.N.K. 'never had a real mate' until he escaped from his education department by being called up in 1943, and thereby 'extended his circle of friends' in a most welcome way. L.D., a Victorian printer with a pacifist family background, was simply called up; but once in the army he was surprised by the 'quantity and quality' of its mateship. Colin McKinnon, conscripted at 18, having just left high school at North Sydney in 1943, went in as a loner – and longing for a girl – but found that his greatest moment came in May 1945, just before the 31st/51st Battalion went into action in North Bougainville for the third and last time. A group of men invited him to share their tent, making him suddenly realise that he was accepted and wanted.

Call the bond what you will, it was there and strong. It took men in together, or they found it together; it carried them along, and it often developed into something they still wondered at as elderly men. At times, previous identities and even any sense of the overall purpose of the war might be lost in the stress of a moment, the strain of months; a man and his mates became all. C.R.B. reflected that a soldier could be

a straw in the wind, pushed here and there, with the only constant need being survival. And only those near you were important, your own and their strengths and weaknesses soon apparent. It was not possible under other circumstances. Things like respect, tolerance, compassion, fear, were learnt and are still basic to the relationships that continue. Those who have not experienced such conditions might not understand, and some might even denigrate what we developed: mateship.

Family and the wider community

Many respondents (over 40 per cent) mentioned 'family' as a positive influence on their enlistment. Sometimes it was 'to keep Australia safe for family and Aussies', as in the case of J. F. O'Neill (19 in 1942, a Catholic and Labor sympathiser), who also offered other reasons: escape from the hard work and boredom of a cattle station; meeting people and seeing places; the glamour of the uniform; and some sense of duty. E. K. Edwards (23 in 1940, a Presbyterian and UAP voter) was very family-conscious when he left his office to enlist because he had 'three older brothers, but they were married, and surely one of us should go'. The clerk K. V. Ireland (17 in 1943, a Methodist and ALP) falsified his age to join up to protect his mother and four sisters. P. E. Pechey (19 in 1941; Church of England; Country Party; sheep station hand) did not think that family was a prime cause of his volunteering, yet still believed his parents would have been 'dismayed and chagrined' if he had waited to be conscripted. As one of his

Original Anzac No. 159,
Private J. L. Cheal, about 1917;
and an Anzac's son, NX81159,
Private F. C. Cheal, in 1942,
aged 17

A recruiting poster of World
War II

motives, W. M. Johns had a desire to get even for his father's being killed in action in France in 1918. For some men escape from home was the spur: NX116025 had a dominating mother, and K.B. a father who was a 'bad drunk'. Among those who faced opposition from parents were SX25946, whose father was a returned soldier from World War I and had hated war ever afterwards, and QX60566, a butter-factory worker, who had two older brothers in the forces and was 'the only support at home'. Both of these young men welcomed conscription.

Respondents were surprisingly unwilling to grant that public opinion had determined their enlistment – only one man in five gave it any role. Certainly there were some highly independent men among this lot, and there was manpower control, with its reserved occupations, to provide young male civilians with some cover, but it still seems likely that many of these men were much more influenced by public opinion and propaganda than they realised. Quite apart from the white feathers at VX42047's boarding house in 1940, and 'the posters of big brave Aussies' recalled by VX45445, there were the newsreels that moved D. K. Parker, at 15, to wish he were old enough to enlist:

They just used to make our hearts soar. We kids were being left behind. The battleships ploughing through the seas, the glorious armies marching prior to embarkation . . . In Perth the planes overhead, the blackouts, the mournful wail of sirens when we had a couple of practice raids, an older brother getting his wings and a commission (he crashed and died later; I read of it in a newspaper I picked up on the floor of a lavatory in Queensland) . . . Rallies in front of the GPO, the Warsaw Concerto played by a dark-haired violinist, the crowds, the emotion . . . Would the time *never* come when we could join up? In the end my mother was able to place three stars in her window to show that she had three serving sons.

There was R.M., a stock and station agent, who found it intolerable to be selling farms because sons had enlisted, and

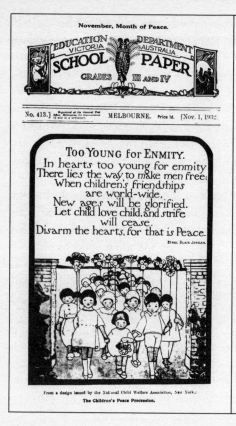

November, Month of Peace.

EDUCATION DEPARTMENT
VICTORIA AUSTRALIA
SCHOOL PAPER
GRADES III AND IV

No. 413.] MELBOURNE. Price 1d. [Nov. 1, 1932.

TOO YOUNG for ENMITY.
In hearts too young for enmity
There lies the way to make men free;
When children's friendships
are world-wide,
New ages will be glorified.
Let child love child, and strife
will cease.
Disarm the hearts, for that is Peace.

ETHEL BLAIR JORDAN.

From a design issued by the National Child Welfare Association, New York.
The Children's Peace Procession.

School literature between the wars gave prominence to both world peace and Anzac Day. Was there necessarily anything contradictory in that?

felt the emptiness of the Mosman rowing club. G.T. remembered commercials on the wireless, and embarrassed silences at parties. SX10941 heard a woman remark to another, 'Notice how all the better boys have joined up?' SX9054 knew the pressure in a small town, and SX25946 the 'silent blackmail' of a boss who had won the Military Cross in World War I: he had the distinct feeling that the future in that firm would be none too bright for the young man who did not volunteer. K.F.G. at least 'imagined that people thought less of you unless you were in uniform'. Only the very strongminded like A.R.M., who joined up in 1940, aged 26, for his own reasons, and who thought the recruiting propaganda 'crude and naive'; or the isolated like 'Bertie', still under age in 1941, and working on a farm – only such men could be comparatively little moved by public opinion. Nevertheless, *something* got through to all respondents, if only the conscription broadly favoured by 'public opinion'.

Not very many respondents (15 per cent) thought that their school background pushed them towards the army; but they were usually thinking in terms of the old school tie, rather than of what they so often mentioned in other contexts: the duty inculcated at school, the observance of Anzac and Empire Days, and the atlases liberally daubed with red. Something must have taught them duty, and to love Australia and the empire as often as they did. If any evidence is required beyond that already given in Chapter 6, take the case of G. L. Zierk, who joined the AIF in 1940 at the age of 15. To be sure, he had a brother and brother-in-law going in at the same time, and he had not had enough employment since leaving primary school a year before; but at that school he had been 'taught duty to empire, taught duty to country, taught the Anzac tradition (teacher an ex-Anzac). It was important to recognise the empire as part of our daily lives, and every Monday morning there was the ceremony of raising the flag'. Very few respondents had known a schooling quite like C. J. Weir's: 'I was educated in Western Australia by the Christian Brothers. Under the guise of beating the good Lord into me, they only succeeded in beating Christ out of me; and, with my school background, I would have been more likely to join the IRA than the AIF.'

A politically conscious minority

As readers of the previous chapter might expect, few men professed to having had any clear 'political' reason for wanting to serve – not if politics is narrowly confined to parties and parliaments, as was the tendency among respondents. But some men had very clear and highly developed political motives. The few like John Gardener, the Jewish refugee from Vienna, 'saw the necessity to win the war'. So did the 19-year-old son of a primary school headmaster, A.D.M. (bank clerk and Country Party):

I was concerned about the spread of totalitarian movements – nazism and fascism, socialism and communism. The coming struggle appeared to be between left and right extremists, with no room for anything else, and I could see some danger in these movements in Australia and thought we should preserve our basic system. That's why I joined the volunteer Militia in 1938 and the AIF in 1939. At that time I thought the empire would go on, and be a great force for reasonable government generally.

T. W. Mitchell (later Victoria's Country Party Attorney-General) at 29 was running the family cattle station, but had been educated at the universities of Cambridge and Harvard, and had qualified for the Bar in London. He had travelled in Germany, Italy, Japan and Russia (his train was shot up by bandits in Manchukuo), and he strongly feared an invasion of Australia when he joined the AIF in 1940. He wanted neither foreign rule of the country nor a left-wing regime in it, and he deplored the notion often drummed into school pupils in the 1920s and early 1930s that the League of Nations had ended war and dispensed with the need to be prepared for one. That is a point to be laid alongside the other evidence of Empire and Anzac Day celebration, but Mitchell, who was the son-in-law of General Harry Chauvel, did not for one moment believe so naively in the League.

At the opposite extreme, bush worker and prospector Harley Taylor was a unionist (AWU), a member of a 'professional association (Swagman's Union!)' and a communist. World politics was bedlam; Australia was a land dominated by squatters, with a very poor political system; and the empire was 'an out-of-date left-over'. From the way Australia had treated Gallipoli veterans like his father, there could be 'no way' in which Australian nationalism and its Anzac tradition would move Taylor to serve. He joined the AIF in 1941, aged 21, mainly for the political reasons that 'the Russian army was falling back, Japan seemed dangerous, and it appeared that a new dark age was beginning'. Dennis Bird was different again. A 28-year-old Englishman, he had been a wanderer over the face of the earth, a sportsman, a cane-grower and a British Regular, among other things. He had seen the fascist Mosley's 'antics' in Britain, and 'a string of pacifists – MacDonald, Baldwin, Chamberlain' leave England ill prepared; it was another aspect of that disarmament mood complained of by T. W. Mitchell. The United Kingdom, Bird thought, was not even reading the signs – rising independence in many of the dominions – that the empire's days were numbered. With the League of Nations a 'dead loss', he was predicting war before it broke out, and was so convinced that Hitler had to be stopped that he enlisted in 1939. Thus the political angles that took respondents into the army varied widely, even when they had a view they could have spelt out in some detail. And for most of them it was more a matter of being Australians than any explicitly informed and developed political understanding.

Was religion a motive?

The ramifications of religion were not well followed through either, even among this group of whom one-third claimed to have been serious churchgoers. Only 8 per cent offered some religious motivation *for* enlistment, and a mere 2 per cent said that, if anything, their religion was a reason *against* going to war. The matter is vastly wider than the question of a 'just war' versus the 'peacemakers', since it comes down to whether or not Christianity – or any other faith – involves the whole of life. However, most respondents did not seem to see it that way, but blandly separated their religious beliefs from their patriotism, duty, mateship, adventure or whatever else combined to get them into the army. It seems that religion was an individual's optional extra rather than the very fabric of life;

it simply had nothing to do with most of the real world – enlisting for a war, for instance.

'Bertie', 18 and a farmhand in 1941, believed that the church was 'a necessary part of society' and went 'fairly often' to Methodist services – but 'why should religion have any influence on joining up?' I.N.R., though married with two children in 1940 and aged 34, enlisted as a longstanding militiaman and for the excitement of being a real soldier at last. He went quite often to an Anglican church, and was 'very tolerant' of what a person believed or did not believe – but religion had 'not the slightest' bearing on his joining the AIF. Aged 18 in 1939, a grocery deliverer and – under family pressure – a Presbyterian, N.C.B. went into the army to escape from home and 'modern slavery' at work, to develop himself and do something worthwhile, including his duty along the lines of the Anzacs. But religion as a motive? 'None at all. If you had faith, trying to relate war to religion would put you in the funny farm.'

Yet there were the others. R.J.W. was 24 in 1940, a farm manager and a Methodist for whom religion was 'a guide to reasonable behaviour' – and that included enlistment 'to defend what I believed in'. VX105004 was a Baptist clerk for whom his faith was the most important thing in life, but that did not make him a pacifist: he believed in the protection of family as a Christian duty. For QX12612, a Catholic labourer, his war service had similar religious point: he saw himself as resisting an aggressor, and it was the aggression that was unchristian, not the resistance. NX28601, telephone mechanic and good Methodist, joined the AIF in 1940 because his country and Britain seemed to be defending freedoms, and his religious training 'gave a sense of responsibility and a con-scientiousness about duty done in a voluntary spirit'.

C. S. Pearlman enlisted in 1939 as an Australian-born Jew; there was nothing in *his* religion to conflict with going to the aid of Jews in Hitler's Germany. VX112974, a farm worker in 1941, wanted badly to join the AIF but could not get his Methodist parents' permission, so at first he went into the

Militia; among his various motives for wanting to do his bit
was information that the Nazis were persecuting *church* people
too. Broadest of all, cutting across the boundaries of the religions, was the reaction of F. J. Bennell, a student at a Baptist
theological college in 1940: 'The anti-Jewish atrocities by the
Nazis horrified and really angered me.' There could hardly be
a more Christian anger than to spring to the defence of anti-
Christians, although Bennell preferred to be a non-combatant
and chose a field ambulance unit to serve in. Anglican office
manager SX4430 had one religious motive, among other and
stronger ones: he thought he would ultimately be 'assisting
world peace'. So relating religion to war might be seen as the
pathway to madness, or as part of the travail and paradox of
the coming of the kingdom of God. Even when they thought
about it, which was not so often, respondents disagreed on
which it was.

But R.H.S. knew something of the personal travail that
could be involved. He was in a reserved occupation when he
finally made his break for the army in 1942, a married man
and father, and a committed member of the Churches of
Christ. He thought that the 'influence of the church was
against serving', but he 'felt the time had come when every
able-bodied man should serve his country (not the empire) and
Christian principles should be put aside'. It was his private
judgement that war and Christian ethics could only be separated, and never reconciled. Similarly, his assessment of his
church's position was a personal one. Where any particular
church stood was always a matter on which respondents differed according to their individual perceptions. Two of the
Catholics among them illustrate the point. N. R. Ford was a
bank officer in 1939 and an army major by 1945; he had strong
motives for enlisting – family service in the army, excitement
instead of work for a 20-year-old, and a sense of duty to a
threatened country and empire – but, although he was deeply
committed to the Catholic Church, he 'always had the feeling
that it held itself remote from the war and did not encourage
enlistment'. Yet another 20-year-old, K. L. G. Smith, a shop

assistant and ex-seminarian, had never forgotten a wartime headline in the *Catholic Weekly*: 'Resistance to tyrants is obedience to God.'

Other influences on enlistment

Conscription was not usually seen as a tyranny to be resisted. Despite the compulsory call-up that caught over one-fifth of the respondents, the latent threat of legal action did not worry many of them. Mostly they were ready enough to go, and saw call-up as simple or welcome notification rather than the big stick, although there were exceptions. V52797 was 25 in 1941 and had been doing 'farm work, council work, any damn work you could get a few shillings out of'. When he was called up, it was 'gaol if you refused, so what option did I have? I did not believe in war, call-up or gaol. We were badgered every so often to turn AIF. So I remained firm and the army could get F——'. He was wounded in 'the bloody Sanananda massacre', and no man 'who had to put up with the stinky bloody jungles ever came back 100 per cent'. 'Kyogi' was 25 in 1942, working with his mother in a delicatessen. 'I let the army join me, rather than vice versa. I saw no reason to wear a "rainbow" on my shoulder on active service, but there was no point in being gaoled.' A.V.B., a clerk with pacifist parents, was called up in 1941 with his thoughts in confusion: he was very pro-Australia, did not like to be called a coward, and wanted to avoid the public shame of being taken to court . . . It was the legal sanctions as much as anything that took him into the army. But the farm worker VX5416 enlisted in the AIF in 1939, aged only 19. The big factors for him were the Anzac story learnt at school, and mateship. Legal action? Well, yes . . . There *was* some talk of that: he owed ten quid for a bike.

It is sometimes thought that the entry of Japan into the war, in December 1941, had to happen before Australians were convinced that it was *their* war at last. There may be elements

of truth in the idea, yet it was the fall of France – in June 1940
– that was the real turning point in enlistments for the AIF
and the building up of the Militia. It was reflected in the
enlistment of respondents: 57 per cent of them were in the
army by the end of 1940, and the largest annual intake (38 per
cent) occurred in 1940, followed by 24 per cent in 1941. The
war with Japan broke out on 7–8 December 1941, and a proportion of the respondents doubtless enlisted almost immediately afterwards, but at least 70 per cent were in the army
before Japan was in the war. C. E. Lemaire personified the real
trend. He offered himself in June 1940, but he was not called
up until November because 'all the camps were full after
Dunkirk'.

The fear of Australia itself being invaded was, in fact, no
motive at all for most respondents when they joined up,
although it was probably an indication of their generally poor
grasp of international affairs that they could think of Europe
and Great Britain falling without Australia ultimately suffering the same fate. But perhaps they had in mind *immediate*
invasion, and some were off to help *prevent* England from
going under anyway. For only 34 per cent of the respondents,
mainly those joining up after Pearl Harbor, was the spectre of
invasion real.

T.A.D. was a steelworker from New South Wales who enlisted so early that he was a three-figure man, and too early for
the invasion of Australia to have any meaning for him. John
Routley, a Tasmanian pharmacist's assistant who volunteered
in 1940, explained that he did not think of an invasion because
Japan had not then entered the war. Yet some of the early
recruits were well aware of the possibilities: a Shell employee
aged 20, 'Artilleryman', was afraid of eventual invasion by
Germany; the young farm manager R.J.W. was 'very much'
concerned about invasion, 'remembering German control in
New Guinea once'; the 23-year-old store manager H.E.C.G.
was 'not so much afraid of an invasion in that early period, but
saw the universal danger of world domination by the Third
Reich'; and the station worker QX11548, who went into the

army via the Militia at 21, always thought that 'if the war in
Europe was lost, we would fall too'. All four men joined up in
1940, and their judgements were sound.

From the start Japan was in the minds of a few men. 'Brisbane Accountant' enlisted in 1939, but even then was uneasy
about Japan's ambitions. Pearl Harbor itself drew VX67833
into the AIF. He had previously been rejected by the RAAF
and RAN for colour blindness – although his reserved occupation was as an illustrator for aircraft production. But in
December 1941 he had had enough; he did not want unleashed
in Australia the same ruthlessness shown by the Japanese in
China and Manchuria. L. H. Ballagh and B. B. Bennett were
two of the 18-year-olds conscripted early in 1942; as they saw
it, 'the war was getting close' and 'for the first few months
Australia's invasion was always a possibility'. E. J. Fuller was a
teenage member of the 9th Division, still in the Middle East at
the time, where he chafed at the thought of Australia's being
directly threatened while he and his mates were left out of the
fight. E.J.D. left his work on a sheep station in 1942 partly
because there was then 'a threat to Australian womanhood',
while L. R. McDougal had left his bank as early as 1940 with
some fear of invasion and a desire to 'protect the Australian
women folk from rape, etc.'. Sometimes there and sometimes
not, the invasion fear peaked around 1942. By the time C. M.
Porter got into the army he did not think at all of Australia
being occupied: 'that fear had passed by September 1943.'

So, for most men, what took them into the army was a sense
of duty, their Australian nationalism, which easily combined
with empire loyalty, the impetus of the Anzac tradition
(including its mateship), and the eagerness of young men to
prove themselves and have a share of excitement. Clichés?
Hardly so, when they took men to war. One way or another,
their families often came into the picture, but only for a time
after the very end of 1941 did a substantial proportion of the
young men go into the army thinking they might be preventing an actual invasion of Australia. Other motives also
found a place but, consciously at any rate, as minor ones for

the group as a whole. Probably such a summary of motives is reasonable. And yet . . . NX68718 volunteered for the Militia in 1940 and transferred to the AIF in 1941. He was only 16 and 17 years old then. Over forty years later he studied the questions and suggestions on why he might have joined up . . . Some proving of self, mateship, Anzac, empire loyalty – all 'possibly'. But 'to this day I honestly do not know. Perhaps the potential of the army way of life appealed; they were "uniform" days. Yet I believe in retrospect that 17-year-old potential soldiers really do not know what they are about'. Much the same might be said of many considerably older potential soldiers. Many others, though, knew very well what they were doing, and still went off to see it through.

Why the army?

Why was it the army for these men, rather than another service? A majority of respondents (57 per cent) declared that it was a deliberate choice on their part, even if it was no more than E. L. Bromfield's 'She's rough, but she's honest'. But – apart from 4 per cent who gave no answer – a large 28 per cent reckoned that they had no say in it: the army was forced on them, mostly by conscription but sometimes by their inability to meet what the navy and air force set as minimum standards of education and fitness. The final 11 per cent said yes, they had a choice, and no, they didn't: in theory they could have gone into another service, but in practice it was much easier to get into the army.

There were, in fact, many negative reasons for enlisting in the army. Some 10 per cent mentioned a preference for the RAN, and 19 per cent (including some of the would-be seamen) would have been in the RAAF if that service had accepted them or called them up quickly enough after acceptance. For another 10 per cent the other services had no appeal – 'I didn't like heights and I got sick in a boat', wrote C.E.S. – or there was no conveniently located recruiting depot for

Some soldiers would have preferred the navy, and some were in the army because they feared the sea. Either way, many of them saw plenty of the sea's menace – as in their escape from Crete

anything but the army. TX2548 went into the army in 1940 because of a 'delay in navy recruiting'. C. E. Lemaire, a clerk and part-time university student, opted for the AIF in 1940 because of the long wait on the aircrew reserve. He was only 17 at the time, but the young executive J.O.M. was 23 when he volunteered for the RAAF at the outbreak of war. He became so impatient at not being called up that he went into the AIF in 1940 – and the army gained a recruit who was a captain at war's end. L. M. Campbell, 16 and a cadet reporter in 1940, chose the army simply because both the navy and the air force required birth certificates. F. G. V. D'Aran, a 22-year-old bank clerk in 1941, had been accepted for the RAN but was still awaiting call-up several months later. Meeting some mates who were doing one of the compulsory Militia training periods, he and they got a little drunk and all proceeded to a recruiting office and joined the AIF. (The keeping of service records must have been a nightmare for those concerned.) A Sydney factory worker and partly trained motor mechanic, aged 22 in 1939, T. C. Birch claimed to have 'joined' all three services in the one day, and the army got in first with the actual call-up; he thought joining *something* was the right thing to do. Paddy Alford was 20 in 1941. He had worked at various jobs, although he was then a farm labourer, and he thought about all three services; but he knew he 'lacked the schooling' for the air force and was too afraid of water to be a seaman. Anyway, it was the army that his mates seemed to be joining.

Negativeness took varying forms and emerged to varying degrees. A 19-year-old labourer in 1941, J. G. Henderson had actually gone into the navy at 16, put in six months at Flinders Naval Depot and been sent to join the *Sydney* during a war scare in 1938. He and his class never returned to the depot, and Henderson never rejoined his ship after Christmas leave. Old hands in the service had discouraged him from staying in it. When war broke out he rang to inquire about re-entry, but the navy was definitely not interested in him – very fortunately for a deserter. J. R. Moran was a farm worker facing the common problems of an inclination to seasickness and too poor an education for the air force. He had other problems too. He was restless at 24, early in 1940, but he had not been game to leave a job while so many swagmen were still calling for a feed. It was the army that gave him the chance to get away – 'with food thrown in'. His decision was 'definitely *not* for patriotic reasons'.

M. J. Radel was not unlike Moran, and he should be heard at length because of the prominence of the negative factors in his story, and the way in which negativeness extends even to what most respondents were so positive about. Radel was a Queensland farm worker, educated only to primary level, and 21 in 1940.

Being a country bumpkin, I didn't know anything about the services, and all they seemed to want was the army, so I just followed the mob. There hadn't been any future in my life and to join up was a change, and perhaps a means of seeing outside my own district – not because I thought of being patriotic; like lots more, I had nothing. Whether I was killed or not didn't particularly worry me, but I only hoped I didn't come back a cripple. I was in the 2/25th Infantry Battalion right through (Darwin, Middle East, New Guinea twice, Borneo), and what made me sour was the fact I wasn't thought worthy of two stripes, but I was refused a transfer to other units 'because you are too good a soldier and we can't afford to lose you'. What bull! To this day I can't bring myself to join the 2/25th Battalion Association.

Radel did not get much rehabilitation assistance, but finished up managing a research farm, with a wife who helped him by thrift and hard work.

There were plenty of positive reasons for choosing the army, and many men gave them. The conscripted had no choice, and some respondents gave no answer, and together these men accounted for one-quarter of the whole group. But, of the rest, some 25 per cent had already chosen the army, being members of the permanent or (more often) citizen forces when war broke out. Another 15 per cent had either had some army training at one time or calculated, in a very positive way, that their civilian occupations best fitted them for the army. Actual service in World War I had been done by a mere fourteen respondents, not only because comparatively few original Diggers served again, but also because most would not have lived into the 1980s to answer the questionnaire. Family service in World War I, or some wider military tradition in the family, prompted 11 per cent to carry it on; and about 4 per cent chose the army because it was the service in which members of their families were already placed in World War II. But where their family members were serving often seemed to be of less account than where their mates were headed: 9 per cent went into the army because of friends joining it. Even so, the influence of family could be strong and poignant.

L.M.W. was 20 in 1942 and in a protected industry – the De Havilland Aircraft Company. But his brother was a POW, and L.M.W. got his wife to take over his job so that he could fill his brother's place in the army. (The brother survived four torrid years in Germany.) QX13349, a 24-year-old AWU battler from Queensland, reckoned that his path was laid out for him, with a father, stepfather and five uncles all having served in the First AIF. F. C. Cheal, 17 in 1941, also followed in the steps of a father and uncles in the First AIF, and of a brother serving in Malaya with the Second. Tramway worker VX24499 had the service of three brothers with the First AIF to combine with his own eight years of Militia service in keeping him loyal to the army. V. C. Wilson went to war 'to keep a block of land 60 ft × 100 ft, and for the Australian way of life', and he chose the army because of 'family tradition' – his father was a professional soldier, first with the British army and then with the Australian.

Their personal backgrounds were alone sufficient to point some men towards the army. D.C. was 27 and had been educated at a Catholic primary school; after 'four years as a butcher on a cutting cart in the depression' and then 'six years learning the building trade', he thought his life best fitted him for the army. F. J. Baxter was on a sheep station in 1940 – his main relaxation drinking beer; but he had been born in the United Kingdom in 1898, and had been with the British army from 1915 to 1919, which had involved him in the Third Afghan War. Hitler was 'annoying' this trained soldier, so he went off again – as an artillery sergeant. He had no time for army 'bull dung', but then he was a sheep man in civilian life. NX7619 had done compulsory training from 1922 to 1929 (when it was suspended), and had actually broken a record set by the British army for mounting a Vickers machine-gun; so he thought the army was for him. He rejoined the volunteer Militia in June 1939, with the idea of gaining a commission before war began, but it did not work: he had to wait until 1942, and see out North Africa and Greece, before that happened. G. W. Spence, born in New South Wales, had been a sergeant with the Shanghai police in 1932–33, and had fought the Japanese as a member of the Chinese army in 1933–35. Back in Australia, and acutely conscious of a threat from Japan, he was a member of the Militia in 1939 with 'no wish to join either of the other services'. And why should he have had such a wish? He was well trained for the force he promptly joined – the AIF.

There was many another interesting individual, yet respondents could not show much of a military tradition in the sense of families continuing a commitment to the army and a proud regiment. Australian association with the service had tended to be casual and occasional, an aberration rather than normal. Most surviving members of the First AIF would have been saddened by any idea that the next generation would again need to do what they had done, and few members of Australia's World War II army would have been long expecting that their turn was to come. When it happened, though, they knew they had a fine example to follow, for they had been taught about that. However, Australia still had little of a military tradition in the sense of 'universal' training. Citizen military training had been so spasmodic and selective that almost 60 per cent of the respondents had done none whatever. It was hardly a satisfactory background for what lay ahead of these young Australians; but here again they had the inspiration of the First AIF, whose preparation for war had not really been any better.

8 • GETTING THEIR MEASURE

The younger a soldier was in 1945, the greater his chance of still being around to answer a questionnaire forty years on. Yet even allowing that there were the older soldiers, the fact is that men in wartime armies have tended to be very young in years. Writers such as Paul Fussell – who concentrates on homosexual trench-poets of World War I in his book *The Great War and Modern Memory* – develop psychoanalytical arguments about male love associated with war and partly revealed by it, and they become very clever about the homosexual overtones of calling soldiers 'boys' and 'lads'. Whatever may be said for such theories, it does no harm to remember that most of these soldiers *were* boys in years, and that it was entirely normal to think of them as such.

There was one sight I've never seen the like of, before or after [wrote QX7328]. When we went on leave for the first time after returning from the Middle East, there was a mother on the Stanthorpe (Qld) railway station welcoming home her four sons. As they engulfed her, she uttered only two words: 'My boys.'

The heterosexual J.W.B. asserted:

The 39th Militia Battalion was the mother of us all, and it gave 1500 half-trained, 18½-year-old, beardless youths pride in the battalion. Now on Kokoda Day, when the names are read out of those killed in action, I know them all and *still* see them as they were. They will never become old or embittered. Just laughing kids forever.

161

Three AIF 'boys' who joined from Western Australia in May 1941 – 'Crid' (left), Fred Smith (sitting) and Cyril Doyle – and served with the 2/2nd Independent Company. Nine months after this picture was taken, Smith was killed in action in Timor. Doyle was killed later

Of the respondents, nearly 6 per cent joined up when aged between 14 and 17 years, and 26 per cent when 18 or 19. Over half the group (53 per cent) were between 18 and 22 on joining, and the most common ages of entry were 18, 19 and 20 years, in descending order. At the opposite end of the scale were a couple of 46-year-olds, but 90 per cent of the whole group were under 30 when they went in.

On the whole, the earlier a man joined the AIF, the lower was his number. And some very low numbers turned up: VX6 (Captain I. G. Webster), WX8 (Major I. J. Bessell-Browne), NX20 (Lieutenant C. E. Raymond), DX33 (Lance-Bombardier G. E. Wignall, of Darwin), SX80 (Gunner F. H. Thompson), WX96 (Private A. M. Sweetapple) . . . Most men with low numbers were proud of them, and one with only four figures in it ensured status. Bob Holt, whose own number was NX7984, wrote about an original member of the 2/3rd Battalion in his book *From Ingleburn to Aitape* (p. 154):

It had been raining heavily . . . and the slit trenches around the camp were half full of water. The beer had been flowing freely when the popular Clarrie Bourke fell and got stuck in one of the foxholes . . . He called for assistance. 'Will some four-figure man come and help me out of this hole?' No one took any notice, so after a while Clarrie

'Dingo' Burgess, 2/2nd Field Regiment, and his cobber from the 2/7th at Bardia, 1940. If the little mate had been enveloped in Burgess's greatcoat, he might still be trying to find his way out of the army

tried his luck again. 'Will some five-figure man come and help me out of this hole?' Everyone was going about his own business and did not notice Clarrie, so in desperation he called for a third time. 'Will any bastard at all come over and give me a hand to get out of this bloody hole?'

Most respondents finished the war with AIF numbers, but only 4 per cent could boast of a number *below* four figures, and 17 per cent of one *with* four figures. Most had to make do with five- or six-figure numbers, the highest of which were over 300 000 and, as L. J. Blake recalled, dubbed 'jeep numbers' by the haughty four-figure men, because every American jeep had a long number too.

'The long and the short and the tall'

One of the more possible ways to describe the 'typical Digger' might be by physical measurement. Among this group the height at enlistment, by one measure of average (the mode), was 5 ft 8 in and, by another measure (the median), 5 ft 9 in.

Between enlistment and discharge from the army, the median was unchanged, but the mode rose to 5 ft 10 in. What this means is that many young soldiers were growing boys who increased their height by a couple of inches during their service, but the 'average' height throughout was 5 ft 9 in. About 13 per cent remained 5 ft 6 in or under, and about 19 per cent were 6 ft or over.

Pity the hard-pressed quartermaster, having to fit out this foursome:

Ken Knox	6 ft 5 in	15 st 7 lb
SX24816	5 ft 4 in	8 st 0 lb
TX6010	6 ft 1 in	19 st 12 lb
David Milne	5 ft 2 in	8 st 5 lb

Come to think of it, quartermasters were not famous for caring very much anyway – although that might be a libel on a fine body of men.

Overall, the average weight (however calculated) was in the 11 st range both at enlistment and on discharge. There was a slight increase in the group weighing under 10 st and down to 7 st, due to sickness in the islands and wasting in Japanese prisoner-of-war camps, but there was a greater increase in the number weighing 13 st or more – so some men certainly developed physically. But your typical Australian soldier? He is elusive to the last, alas. If he was one of the respondents he was 5 ft 9 in tall, and weighed just over 11 st – but the only known 'official' record made him 5 ft 7.6 in and 10 st 7 lb.

Left at home

Marriage had not claimed many of the respondents at enlistment. There were 14 per cent married, 0.4 per cent divorced, 0.2 per cent widowers and 3 per cent engaged. Not quite 10 per cent of the whole group had become fathers, and half of those men had only one child, usually a very young one; only 1 per cent of the respondents had an eldest child aged 10 or more years. Yet that still meant grief as husbands and fathers departed.

Early in 1940 Roy Gould went to war while his wife was expecting their fourth child, and a fifth was born when Gould was in New Guinea. Mrs Gould shared her husband's sense of duty and no harm was done to the marriage or the family in the long run; but Gould hated their separation – it was the worst thing about his service in the Middle East and the Pacific – and he felt much for his wife, who 'was made to suffer more sacrifice' than he did as a soldier. The wife of NX37108 bravely seemed 'always prepared for the inevitable' when their partings came after a wartime marriage, yet 'it became a great burden to return to the service' and, when a leave was granted elsewhere in Australia, 'the desire to "shoot through" and return home' was ever present. Another New South Welshman, NX28127, became engaged on his return from the Middle East, and married while on leave from New Guinea. His first child was six months old before he saw her, and twelve months of age when he was discharged: 'Each parting was more upsetting.'

J.W.B. was still single when he watched the goodbyes of a married couple at Roma Street station, Brisbane, late in 1943:

A party of 9th Division men – nothing to do with us – was boarding a troop train, in the charge of a cracking fine sergeant wearing the Eighth Army ribbon and straight out of the *Soldier's Manual* – neat, clean, equipment just right. He was letting four men at a time go over to the pub, and four more when each lot returned. His wife was there, and a son of around 14 – with one of those dreadful hats schoolboys used to wear then – and a daughter of about 9. The last men returned. The sergeant called the roll, got his men comfortably settled, kissed his family, and the train pulled out. His wife waved until the last carriage disappeared, then started to shake – great spasms along the length of her body. She collapsed into the dust of the platform, rather like a shot elephant, slowly, in sections. The boy was patting her awkwardly, embarrassed, and the little girl began to cry

. . . I *do* hope that sergeant survived the fighting. That dreadful scene was typical of incidents all over Australia, night and day, all through the war. When in my dribbling dotage I am asked to tell a war story, I'll tell that one. The agony and misery were not all at the sharp end.

The army family

The breaks made, and the soldiers no longer at home, where did they find their 'home' in the army? Or, in military terms, which 'arm' took them in? For the sake of tidiness, some anticipation of things to come is made in the following table, which shows the last arm in which respondents served, as well as the one they joined after their initial training battalion. (During their service, 32 per cent were to stay with their original unit, 32 per cent were to make one change, 19 per cent two changes, and about 17 per cent three or more.)

Percentage of respondents in various arms

Arm	Initial	Final
Head Quarters, Intelligence	1	6
Armoured	6	3
Artillery (incl. Ack-ack etc.)	18	13
Engineers, Pioneers, Workshop	9	12
Signals	7	6
Infantry (incl. Commando etc.)	42	35
Supply, Transport	9	11
Medical, Dental	5	6
Provost and Other	2	7
	99	99

The trends in the table are roughly in line with what Jane Ross (in *The Myth of the Digger*, p. 135) has pointed out about the Australian army over the course of the war: changes in the proportions serving in different arms, with the emphasis away from fighting and towards support troops. Here the armoured, artillery and infantry went notably down in number, while headquarters, engineers/workshop, supply and transport and 'other' went up significantly. Yet that is to go beyond these men's joining the army, and far into their years of service.

Before following them there, look at what came in the mail from the postman himself. The make-up of the 2/19th Infantry Battalion, 8th Division, was vividly described by Peter Wellington, of Bathurst (NSW). Partly based on estimates, his account was very much more than merely impressionistic because Wellington knew his battalion unusually well.

As 'Battalion Postman' I became acquainted with all the members of the unit. The postman has a Nominal Roll – a detailed and accurate record of all members, maintained to show the movement of outgoing men (to hospital, training schools, other units and so on) and those joining the unit. As a morale booster the mail service was vital; the battalion post office was the direct link between home and the soldier. The postman made a thousand friends, and knew their civilian backgrounds – whence they came, and what they left behind. Indirectly, he was linked with all their families, and was privileged to be told of wives and sweethearts, children and parents. He was shown the most valued photographs in hundreds of wallets. Whenever and wherever he met the troops the greetings were much the same: 'Where's my parcel? Did you get my letter off?' I say all this to support my claim that I have the knowledge to write down all sorts of details about the battalion. I do have a retentive memory, and also have had access to the 2/19th journal, published in Malaya up to the end of 1941, and the battalion history.

FORMATION OF 2/19TH BATTALION

From full-time Militia (15 July 1940)

Officers	37 (World War I service: 4)	
Warrant officers	6 (2)	
Sergeants	36 (1)	
Corporals	44	
Privates	<u>350</u> (2)	473

From part-time Militia (15 July 1940)	150	
New recruits from country holding centres (29 July)	329	
Final intake from base recruit reception depot (20 August 1940)	<u>48</u>	1000

The battalion was known as the 'Riverina Mob' because (approximately) 650 men came from south-west New South Wales. There were 200 from western NSW, from Penrith to Broken Hill, 150 from Sydney, and very few others.

RELIGION

We were not a religious battalion, nor were we irreligious. It was important to some, but not to others. Roman Catholics – 100. Protestants – 900.

POLITICS

Although the topic of politics was almost never seriously discussed, there's no doubt that the parties favoured were Country and United Australia – 70 per cent – with Labor making up the rest.

STRUCTURE OF BATTALION

Battalion Head Quarters

Commanding officer, supporting officers for administration and orderly-room staff – adjutant, medical officer, padre, pay clerk, postman, quartermaster, medical orderlies, band personnel (who in battle became stretcher bearers). Approx. 60.

HQ Specialist Company

Officer in command, and supporting officers. Platoons of signals, anti-aircraft, mortar, machine-gun carriers, pioneers (engineers and other tradesmen) and transport. Approx. 420.

Rifle Companies (Infantry)

A, B, C and D Coys, each of 130 all ranks. Approx. 520

So, within the battalion itself, to establish 520 infantrymen on the ground prepared for battle, there were 480 specialists to support them. Because of the grim battle formation at places like Muar (Malaya), all members could more or less become frontline soldiers.

WHERE LIVING AT ENLISTMENT

Victoria (VX number)	1 (The padre)
New Guinea (NGX number)	7
New South Wales (NX number)	
City and suburbs	160

Large towns	250	
Small towns	450	
Farms, etc.	<u>140</u>	Approx. 1000

AGES (estimated)

16–18 years: 50. 19–20 years: 150. 21–30 years: 550. 31–40 years: 200. Over 40: 50.

HEIGHT (estimated)

5 ft to 5 ft 4 in: 200. 5 ft 5 in to 5 ft 8 in: 400. 5 ft 9 in to 6 ft: 300. Over 6 ft: 100.

OCCUPATIONS

Engineers 2. Doctors 2. Dentist 1. Minister of religion 1. Lawyers 4. Accountants 2. Farmers/graziers 10. Orchardists 8. Shearers 8. General rural workers 714. Rural carriers 4. Store/dept managers 2. Bank clerks 12. Railway clerks 4. Railway workers 5. Engine driver 1. Schoolteachers 4. Radio announcers 2. Newspaper cartoonist 1. Journalists 2. Golf-club secretary 1. Postal worker 1. Shop assistants 20. Labourers 130. Carpenters 5. Bricklayers 2. Blacksmith 1. House painter 1. Bakers 2. Hairdressers 3. Band leader 1. Salvation Army musicians 12. Hotel managers 2. Hotel workers 6. Plantation over-seers 2. Motor mechanics 4. Apprentices 3. Students 2. Jockeys 3. Prize fighters 8. Speedway cycle rider 1.

MARITAL STATUS

Single 700. Married 300 (of which at least 30 occurred after joining in July 1940, up to final leave in January 1941).

FAMILY MEMBERS IN BATTALION

There were two father and son pairs; both of the fathers were killed, but both of the sons survived. There were three brothers from one family, all of whom returned. There were twenty-one pairs of brothers. In six cases both were killed, and in four cases one was killed. (Many other members had a brother – and one had a father – in other units.)

DEATHS

Of the 1000 men, 282 were killed in action, and 131 died as POWs. Of the remaining 587, about 400 had died by mid-1982, often as a result of war-caused disabilities.

So Peter Wellington also leads us far past joining up, on to war service and its results – which in the end are the sort of thing most worth measuring.

Sporting soldiers

What of the service of leading Australian sportsmen? Did they measure up to the test of war? NX4320, just back from the Middle East, used up part of one of his precious fourteen days of leave in August 1942 to sit enthralled while Newtown beat St George 55 to 2, but he went on to say, 'No one was impressed by "sporting heroes" parading their reserved occupation status'. Other respondents also suggested sometimes that many top sportsmen did less than their bit for the war effort, and doubtless there was justification for their resentment in certain cases. On the other hand there were leading sportsmen who might justly be angered by sweeping remarks of that kind. SX9054 described his workmate SX6977 as 'a good friend, citizen and officer'. He could have added that SX6977 was one of South Australia's most promising cricketers and all-round sportsmen. Twice wounded, winner of a Military Cross, and rising to the rank of captain in the army, SX6977 commented in his own questionnaire on ways in which he was harmed by his war service: 'It deprived me (from the age of 23) of six years of civilian life in which I would have finished a university degree, furthered my career and developed my sporting abilities to their peak.' In fact he had a distinguished career after the war, but nothing could restore to a sportsman six years lost in his twenties.

To help explain his pride in the 24th Brigade, part of the 9th Division, Paddy Alford sent in a copy of *Red Platypus*, a book compiled in the field and published in September 1945 to celebrate the brigade's achievements. Included in it is a chapter by Corporal E. Mathews on 'The Field of Sport', in which he listed dozens of prominent sportsmen who served in the three battalions that made up the brigade – the 2/28th, 2/32nd and 2/43rd. Only a sample of the names can be given,

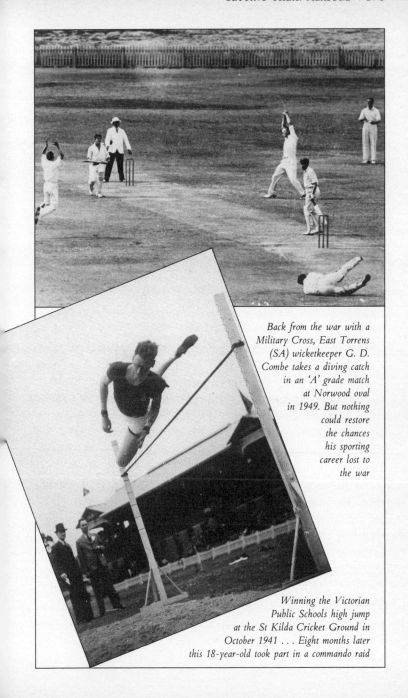

Back from the war with a
Military Cross, East Torrens
(SA) wicketkeeper G. D.
Combe takes a diving catch
in an 'A' grade match
at Norwood oval
in 1949. But nothing
could restore
the chances
his sporting
career lost to
the war

Winning the Victorian
Public Schools high jump
at the St Kilda Cricket Ground in
October 1941 . . . Eight months later
this 18-year-old took part in a commando raid

and it is not much more than a catalogue; but it is a record of sportsmen's sacrifices of what was very dear to them. Men from the southern states being predominant, Australian Rules footballers were notable among them. Bob Quinn, wounded in New Guinea, had captained South Australia. J. Mackay had played 202 games for South and North Adelaide. Don Waite, killed at Tobruk, was a West Torrens player. F. Hardy played in Sturt's 1938–40 premier teams. F. Cotton, killed near Lae, was a prominent country footballer. Leo Opray had played for Carlton and Victoria (and also won the Jeparit Gift). Cliff Tyson, originating in West Perth, was in the Port Melbourne team, as was J. Irvine. A top Kalgoorlie footballer, T. Nettleton, was killed near Lae. Four others who died in New Guinea were H. Burton (Perth), Hugh Guthrie (Claremont), J. Woodhouse (West Perth) and L. Oliver (East Perth). 'Stew' Daily and L. Stack (the latter captured on Ruin Ridge, in Egypt) had played for Subiaco. L. Bowen won the Sandover Medal for West Perth in 1942.

Among the cricketers was B. O'Shaughnessy (wounded on the Huon Peninsula, New Guinea), who had played for Western Australia against an Australian team and bowled Bradman. W. McCulloch represented Tasmania. M. Agars and H. Webber were South Australian country champions, and C. Plant played for Sturt. G. D. Combe (decorated and twice wounded) kept wickets for East Torrens, and A. Edmonds was also in that team. J. Gorman played for Toowoomba district against G. O. Allen's England test team in 1936–37 (and was in the Queensland soccer eleven). G. Hutton might have represented South Australia, given his chance, but was killed in New Guinea. Morgan Herbert was a brilliant country cricketer from Western Australia.

Athletes from Perth included O. Chapman, of Christian Brothers College, and F. Rush, of Wesley. Winner of a Nathalia Gift and second in an Echuca Gift was A. E. James. In 1938 A. A. McInnes had won the Mildura Gift. J. J. Thornton had won the Warrnambool Gift, and Ron Smith and

K. Wyatt were promising South Australian athletes. Bill Norris represented Queensland in Rugby. T. D. Hollywood and F. Fields were good Union footballers from New South Wales – and Fields was a hard-court tennis champion. Ted Levy was beach sprint champion of the Bondi surf club, and for three years held New South Wales and Australian breast-stroke titles. W. Weir had won Victorian medley and 400 metre championships; he was wounded at El Alamein, and underwent twelve operations, but lived to swim again. H. Nankivell (wounded at Katika, New Guinea, in 1943 while winning the Distinguished Conduct Medal) had won Western Australian and national swimming titles. J. Sharp was Victorian featherweight boxing champion in 1933, and J. Cooper the heavyweight champion as early as 1920. W. W. Crellin, who commanded the 2/43rd Battalion at first, had represented Victoria and captained Queensland in hockey. Johnny McPhail played soccer for Western Australia. G. Budd was one of that state's great cyclists, and 'Laddie' Hiron had broken one of Budd's records. L. Reynolds was a leading lawn tennis player from the West, and F. Thompson (POW at El Alamein) a top South Australian golfer. F.Turner played baseball for South Australia, and R. Black (POW at Ruin Ridge) represented the West. J. Leonard, one of the West's foremost axemen, was killed in an attack on the way to Lae.

Fifty sportsmen, a mere selection from those mentioned by Corporal Mathews – who was sure he must have missed some . . . So many leading sportsmen, and from only a single brigade in one of the three services . . . They and their peers elsewhere deserve to be remembered. They are the counterbalances. In the middle were top sportsmen in genuine reserved occupations, and even members of the AIF like L.R.N. who, as an outstanding sportsman, was removed from four overseas drafts so that he would be available to play football for 'Sydney Showground' and the AIF. (He complained bitterly each time but later realised his luck: each draft was for the 8th Division, so he was saved from 'four years as a

POW with the Japs *at the best'*.) On the other side, of course, there were the wanglers – those supremely fit young men who, when Australia was fighting for survival, still chose to play games.

<u>SERVING</u>

Born in Wales but brought up on an Eyre Peninsula (SA) farm, Private David Jones reports back with his Bren gun after a week of battle with the Japanese in New Guinea

9 • TAKING IT AS IT CAME

'How did I react to army life? With astonishment at first', replied W. H. Martell, who went into the AIF at 18 years of age, straight from a private school, and was an acting warrant officer five years later. Another 18-year-old who won parental consent to his joining the AIF was VX140919, and he 'took to the army like a duck to water'. He came out of a business position, and he enjoyed both training and action, including a commando-type raid on Lieutenant-General Nakai's HQ in New Guinea, and a successful attack on a position held by the Emperor's Own Tiger Marines. 'How did I react?' responded a third 18-year-old volunteer, who was a Militia signalman for a few months before transferring to the navy. 'I hated it. What did I like? Nothing. I suppose companionship was the best aspect. What did I dislike? Everything. Crude toilets, crude kitchens, flies on food . . .'

There were many initial – and later – reactions to the army, but 93 per cent of the respondents fell into one of two large categories: those who thoroughly enjoyed the life and some-times spoke of pride in their role (43 per cent), and those who adapted readily enough, perhaps with some initial difficulty or continuing reservations, yet with little hassle (50 per cent). These men were often not very expansive: 'loved it', 'loved every minute of it', 'revelled in it'; or 'took it as it came', 'accepted it philosophically', 'reacted fairly well', 'didn't mind the life', 'adjusted okay after a while'. Such brief and repeated comments are not very quotable, but *nearly all* of the respondents made one or other of them. A few other men gave

vague or complicated answers, or no answer at all, but under
4 per cent clearly said that they disliked the life intensely and
from start to finish. Men will talk about what they coped with
very adequately, or liked very much, or – in some cases –
desperately loathed. Some could not talk about what they
hated, and there were probably many men who found their
army life simply boring and so would not answer a questionnaire that promised to be equally boring. At any rate, the
respondents fell overwhelmingly into categories ranging
from the positive side of neutral up to tremendous enthusiasm
– and there were plenty of the last.

   Nevertheless, army life is one thing when it is regular food
and pay; a group building up into a skilled team; a proud uniform; travel and the occasional leave pass. It is quite another
matter when the army means being badgered by martinets and
frustrated by red tape; bored by inactivity or activity without
point; smashed up – this wonderful team – by enemy action,
or humiliated in captivity. And army life is different again
when – however good it has been, and whatever it has
achieved – it simply goes on for too long. Even those who said
they mostly enjoyed the life often had to say that it had its
limits, one way or another. The respondents rang many
changes on the theme of how they reacted, and when.

   Training camp could come as a shock. NX87457, a bank
clerk, outwardly a conformist Presbyterian but privately sceptical, was 'initially aghast at the crude, insensitive, amoral
world I had let myself in for'. He survived well enough in that
world to end up as a sergeant. J. R. Moran had a different
background. He was a large young farm labourer who joined
an Independent Company in 1940, but he too had his eyes
opened to a new world:

I was terrified at first impressions. The new recruits were billeted at
Caulfield racecourse, upstairs in the grandstand. Some had
wristwatches and other valuables, and these were being stolen by
professional thieves. One evening a soldier, half asleep, saw one of
these thieves going through the kitbags. He called out and a number

*Training at
Puckapunyal (Vic.),
1940*

of soldiers caught the thief and threw him over the balcony, killing him. I had been visiting my aunt at Hawksburn and, on returning, couldn't find my sleeping position. A laconic Aussie voice very drily said, 'I wouldn't wander about too much, mate. They threw a bloke over the side tonight.' In that instant I found my palliasse. The shock that *one could be killed in Australia, by Australians, opened up a frightening new dimension to me.*

Nor was that only Moran's story; it was independently supported by J. W. Howard, another respondent.

Most men got into the way of things quickly. John Cassidy, aged 34, had been a carpenter, unemployed, and a farm worker:

I liked army life after I'd done the early squad drill and been allotted to a unit, where I was at home among friends. The first few weeks were not so easy . . . The loud-mouthed Sergeant Major, 'You broke your mother's heart, but you won't break mine.' You could not afford to answer back. There were petty pinpricks to adjust to, but the army was fair, if you knew the rules.

D.S.A., a bank officer, was 'not happy initially. Too many men about who were more practical than me'. Yet he eventually became a sergeant in a Supply Depot Platoon. R. A. Burke had once entered the Order of Friars Minor and studied in Belgium, but at the outbreak of war was a chief inspector of drugs and poisons for the Queensland Department of Health, a married man of 28 years, with a child: 'I accepted army life after a while. I was a mature man, and could cope with change.' Much more hesitantly did the timid G. W. Bray reveal his talents. He had been sacked from his job as a steam presser when he turned 21, and there had followed six years out of work:

Before the war I would have been called a Mum's boy. I had to look after my invalid mother and sister who was too young to manage my mother. I couldn't get a job, so I cooked and sewed and whatever else needed to be done. When I joined up, the things I could do were regarded as sissy, and I wondered how I would be accepted by the other fellows. I *was* accepted; no one seemed really interested in what anyone had done before. It wasn't until after Japan had attacked Malaya, and we were retreating, and our uniforms were being torn and someone was needed to cook, that I admitted to being able to do them. It was appreciated and from there, through our POW days, I cooked and sewed when I had the opportunity; even on the boat coming back home I was taking clothing in to fit some of our skinny bodies. Sorry I've rambled on a bit.

Those who were never really happy with army life could still become effective soldiers, and their attitude to the army did not stem from one sort of background. P. E. Buddee was a Western Australian schoolteacher who was to be wounded at Tobruk, and finally became a lieutenant in the Army Education Service: 'I accepted the army. I liked nothing and disliked everything. I just took army life as a necessary evil; but I had volunteered, and had to make the most of it.' Young H. W. J. Austin, a conscripted Queensland meat-worker (whose father was also serving in the army), was not much different from Buddee in his reactions: 'I didn't love it (I liked leave most), but I was a soldier, so that was it.' 'Victorian Insurance Clerk', who finished the war as a captain, said, 'I put up with it, and tried to get my troops to do likewise'.

Left: *Army linesmen at Madang, New Guinea, 1943*

Below: *It was some explosion that tore apart this tank – and the men in it – during a North African campaign*

Bottom: *Members of the 2/4th Field Regiment in the Syrian campaign*

Among some of the more positive there remained lingering objections, or an occasional breakdown occurred. A youth from a poor, politically conservative, staunchly Methodist family, who had just secured his best job – as a wood machinist – left it to become a four-figure man, NX7971, and he mostly got on well enough, if not entirely: 'I accepted routine and discipline, except when inconvenient – e.g. I used an army vehicle to go to see my brother, had a dispute with English provosts, and lost my sergeant's stripes.' VX73795 was 34, married with two children, and working a small, leased farm when he enlisted. Although he was a staff sergeant on discharge, he remained 'cynical of regimental nonsense, and disliked the waste of material', but he was 'proud of the malarial control achieved' by his specialist unit in Papua New Guinea.

The points beyond which enjoyment of army life could not last were clearly indicated by some men:

> No real worries. General frustration when war seemed never ending [NX4320].
> I enjoyed the first three or four years – the pride in my regiment [2/12th Field Regiment], the friendship and the achievement, but I became a little restless after that [VX22492].
> Having already had some Militia training, I reacted well. I liked it to begin with, but before my years were up I hated not being able to quit – even though I'd enlisted without parental permission, had been subsequently discharged, and then re-enlisted [VX89033].
> I reacted most favourably – like a fish to water. I'd done some Militia camps, and I used to read Field Service Regulations and Manuals of Infantry Training in the train going to work. Yet it faded. I left with relief after five years, with a hearty dislike of regimentation; and I'd started to lose my fascination for guns about the same time as they started to go off at me ['A Sydney Clerk'].
> It was good – as long as the opposition were not shooting ['Hook' Anderson].

I liked it. Not so keen on the action [SX2386].
I found the first three years pleasant enough, if one could say
that in wartime, but when the battalion [2/10th] changed – after
heavy casualties – it was not the same [D. E. Thompson, a three-
figure man].
Enjoyed it – until action, and the Japanese POW days [P. J.
Cook: his tall, strapping frame was reduced from 14 st 7 lb to
9 st].

Even the duck-to-water type, VX140919, who enjoyed action,
had finally to admit to fears that the Japanese near his isolated
post might not have heard the news that the war was over.
    Yet still the acceptance or enjoyment came through
overwhelmingly. It was okay, or it was much better than that.
It was good for trivial-seeming reasons, or deeper ones. It was
good in the end, or at the start, or at some stage, or in some
ways. And again, these reactions did not come from men with
only one sort of background, but startlingly different sorts.
K. L. G. Smith, a 20-year-old shop assistant and a devout
Catholic, did not like the vulgar and obscene language; but, he
said, 'I cooperated fairly willingly in everything, and was
proud of my uniform'. SX2963 was a truckdriver, English-
born but resident in Australia since 1928. He found army life
'great; the roughing it, the outdoor feeling'. He was to lose a
leg in Syria. VX133648 had known hard times and had a
chequered career in the course of his twenty-four years, and
he said, 'After working alternate night and day shifts in the
malting industry for two years, I enjoyed the regular hours
and meals'. C. K. Hart was a farmhand who had switched to
work in a dairy factory, and for him going into the army was
little different from the farm to factory move – just a matter
of adjustment. L. W. Piper, a shop assistant, had 'liked the
Scouts, and the army was grown-up Boy Scouts'. G. L. Zierk
had gained only his Merit Certificate at school, and found
only part-time work delivering groceries after it. He joined up
in 1940, aged 15, and found army life 'Good. Improved my
standard of education and showed me mateship'. NX112503,

aged 22, had done any rural work that 'returned a coin' and helped support his parents, four sisters and three brothers. He was matter-of-fact: 'I simply took the army in my stride like any other job.' And R. C. Beilby reacted 'very well. Hobo-ing had taught me, at 21, the essentials of surviving amidst a large crowd of men'. A young farm worker, D. G. Bourne, had an angle all of his own: 'I enjoyed most of it, as I'd expected it to be worse.'

But those who had roughed it were not the only types who could slide smoothly into army life – or perhaps there are other definitions of roughing it. J. D. Blanton was a young shop assistant who 'adjusted easily, having been in boarding school'. R. H. Timperley, 18 years old at the time, spelt it out more fully: 'Fitting in was no problem at all in any way. Nine years boarding school gives ideal training for the army: you'll eat anything, join in or stay out of activities, defy authorities, stick to your mates, and generally have fun – at the teenage stage, anyway.' But having roughed it – whether in camps of workers or the unemployed, or at boarding school – was not the only good preparation for the army. The confidence of H. Wittenberg, a Jew, had been undermined by both unemployment and poor jobs, but he was beginning to make good with an assurance company when he enlisted at the age of 25. And he went in with a particular attitude of mind: 'I did as I was told, and tried to be a model soldier. I appreciated the discipline and the friendship.' Nor did NX99513, also aged 25 but a confident schoolteacher, have any trouble with army life; he was like Wittenberg in that, and for one of the same reasons: 'I was amenable to discipline, as I had expected it from children. I realised that discipline in my new situation was important for survival.' For WX28144, a 24-year-old drapery assistant, 'discipline was no problem' because he had been 'a member of a well-knit family' of ten children. NX129884 went originally into the Militia, due to family objection to overseas service for him – although, before he was through, he was in the lonely, dangerous work of coast-watching as a member of the Australian New Guinea Administrative Unit. He said:

'The regulatory atmosphere prevailing in an established army unit appeared as an extension of the benevolent, authoritarian family society in which I grew up. I hadn't then been exposed to anything else.'

'Discipline' and 'roughing it' are not necessarily poles apart. When the self-described hobo, R. C. Beilby, spoke of knowing how to survive among rough men, one part of the knowhow would have been self-control. When 'Victorian Insurance Clerk' found that all he could do with the army was to 'put up with it', yet still became a captain, it could only have been through great self-discipline. External army discipline may often have been petty, crude and overbearing, but as discipline – at its best – makes an army, it must run through army life, around it and over it. It is bearable when a man has his mates to help him, and it begins to work as men realise that they can rely on each other to play their allotted parts. Discipline can be a high form of mateship, and mateship a steady teamwork under the roughest of circumstances. Something of the kind made many men appreciate army life.

It was 'mateship', in fact, that the respondents particularly liked about the army. It was the first choice of 59 per cent of them, and 62 per cent included it somewhere among several valued aspects. Everything else came *far* below it, but favourable mention was made of 'discipline and teamwork', 'doing something worthwhile', 'travel or adventure' and 'improved physical fitness'. Among the aspects singled out by a few men – perhaps 2 or 3 per cent – were 'regular food and pay', 'escape from home restraints' and 'active service'. It is a point worth noting that hardly any – under 2 per cent – of these Australian soldiers really liked fighting and being under fire; and if the old soldier wryly remarks, 'Who would?', one reply is that legend sometimes has it that the Australian is eager for action. According to the respondents, however, it was not so, or not for long. On the contrary, for most of them, action rather spoilt army life – somewhat as the regular colonel is alleged to have complained: 'I'll be glad when this damned war is over, and we can get back to *real* soldiering.'

Orlright. Who is goin' to bloody fix the bloody puncture? I bloody fixed the last bloody one. Actually, the accompanying description was: 'Members of HQ RAA, 9th Aust. Div., relax in August 1942.' A pity!

Any hole is better than none, especially if a bomb has dug it for you

October–November 1942, and part of the battle of El Alamein has just rolled through this spot – viewed through battered mesh

What did the favoured 'mateship' mean? Almost anything could be implied by the many short answers: 'The mates I made', 'Companionship', 'Comradeship', 'Being with my mates', 'The people I met'. Many sorts of meanings were indeed intended. For 'Chooky', a drycleaner who served only in Australia, the best things were 'mateship and no worries', and it was not unusual for men to say that they were sheltered from 'responsibility' by the army – which was partly because of all those mates, as well as just being a 'number' shuffled here and there. S.F., a 19-year-old apprentice in the shoe trade, who had earlier been treated like dirt by sheep farmers used to employing state wards, welcomed 'mateship and being accepted as a man'. A. C. Flannery was an assistant projectionist, and something of a loner at 19. The army gave him two previously unexpected privileges: 'Travel and mateship – which despite some trendy contemporary thinking is not an indication of latent homosexuality.' He enlisted in 1940 and married in 1943. For QX9616, a young taxi-driver and bandsman, who had hoped to get into the RAAF but seemed to have been forgotten by them, the army meant 'comradeship and a sense of belonging'. VX7051 had a 'casual' primary schooling, and experience as a rabbiter, share-farmer and foreman of a road gang before enlisting at 32 years of age; what he gained most from the army was 'association with intelegent and educated people'. For a Baptist clerk, VX105004, the expanded and appreciated companionship was 'with Christians who knew what they stood for, from various denominations'.

The apprentice printer R. C. W. Foster said that the things he liked most about the army were 'Training. Friends. Discipline. Different'. How much can the 'friends' be separated from the rest? Probably very little. Army mates tended to be much more than just friends. A 20-year-old tyre-retreader on enlistment, 'Bars' reckoned he was

5 ft 5 in when joining, and two weeks later 10 ft tall and all heart. It's very hard to put the finger on exactly what it was all about. The instant friendship was truly amazing. Men whom you had never

known were immediately your best friend. Maybe it was just because we were on the same team, but I think it was something more than that.

C.A.B. called it 'comradeship in camp, on leave and in battle' – and he was captured on Crete, as a member of the Army Service Corps, and lost a leg while a POW as the result of Allied bombing. NX52013, a master butcher who served in the Middle East and the Pacific, described mateship as 'the utter reliability each man inwardly knew he could expect from the other. The bond was stronger than brotherly love, and never failed to surface in times of crisis'. A 20-year-old labourer with an engineering firm, VX11842, saw it later as 'the satisfaction of a silent bond, personifying that we had volunteered for the infantry, we were the "front line", and the vein of mutual respect for each other, from officers to privates, was ever present'.

Some of that was occasionally denied, of course, particularly when respondents had 'rank' in mind. Doug Baker, a Queensland foundry hand, for whom the best thing about the army was getting his discharge, said that 'esprit de corps was a myth; the "Jack system" was the order of the day', but even he found that it no longer applied during POW days in Italy – and he *was* thinking specifically of relationships between men, NCOs and officers. It was also strongly affirmed that mateship permeated all ranks, especially in a fighting unit compared with a less active one. G. M. Fry, a lieutenant for most of the war but finally a captain, said that what he valued most in retrospect was 'the privilege of knowing so many fine men'. He claimed that the men in the ranks of the 2/5th Battalion never gave any indication that they considered themselves inferior to officers. He followed the Australian trend of relying on discipline based as much as possible on consensus – 'We will' rather than 'You will'. Nor could he recall an order ever being queried in action, which he saw in both major theatres of war.

Nevertheless, a difference in rank complicated relationships that were already hard enough to describe. Even on the level of the same rank NX31016 was eloquent, yet still defeated by mateship's fullest meaning:

Over-riding all other considerations in army life was mateship. We all had our particular mates; mine was a West Australian one year younger than me whose birthday fell on the same day. I do not believe I have ever loved a woman more deeply than my mate. None of these were homosexual relationships – we would have been disgusted at the thought, if at that age we had even known what homosexuality was. In all the millions of words I have read on every subject under the sun, I have never read an explanation of the meaning and depth of that love, because 'love' is not the right word either. Your mate was your tender companion, the rough-house drunken bum you went on a spree with, the bloke you could depend on in life or approaching death, who would never let you down, would always forgive, whose moods and desires slotted like a mechanism with your own. In those lonely places, far from home and Mum and sister and wife and sweetheart, your mate was the alter ego of each of them. Someone should write a thesis on this – based on a questionnaire such as I am struggling through now.

When asked for their dislikes, 13 per cent of the respondents ignored the question or said 'None'. M. B. Orken, who rose to the rank of lieutenant, disliked 'nothing really. I was amenable to discipline, and was given responsibility and opportunity to use whatever talents I possessed'. Some of this group did add a qualification (F. A. Patterson 'didn't dislike much – maybe extremely adverse conditions, e.g. in New Guinea'), but it is to be remembered that respondents on the whole did *not* react unfavourably to the army.

However, some 36 per cent singled out and covered between them a wide range of special grudges – and about 1 per cent had a broad range on their own, including 'Everything'.

Sometimes utter loneliness; also short-arm parades [SX13875:

he meant inspection of the penis by the MO as a check for VD].

As a non-smoker, having to pick up butts dropped by others [F. A. Peebles].

Train journeys of up to five days. Being canteen officer on the *Queen Mary* [R. S. Walsh].

Exhumations, as an officer in a war graves unit [G. McQueen].

Climbing mountains and cleaning latrines [VX124868].

Army Education Sections [G. C. Ayrton: he did the question-naire, but also despised historians].

Being a POW [W. P. Barber].

Females giving out white feathers when I was not in uniform [M. J. Holten: he joined at 16 in 1942. R. H. Attridge too, at the age of 17 in 1943, was given a white feather by a 'rotten female', and hated women ever after; but he also hated everything about the AIF the feather forced him to join].

The b—— cook [VX2995].

Breakfasts, usually doubtful, and sometimes only a soldier's breakfast – a cigarette and a piss. (Being a non-smoker I was down by 50 per cent.) Lying down for a rest in a jungle swamp; could anyone say, 'I'm going to enjoy this'? [L. J. Peterson].

Dust and dirt of the desert [F. C. Barnet].

Attack from the air [NX8078].

500-plane air raids in Greece [R. S. Stacy].

Stuka bombers, without Allied fighters to combat them [Frank Lyons].

Loss of mates in action [C. F. Young].

Deaths of others [NX41216].

Low pay [J. F. Joseph: he had left a box company, at 18, to join up].

Lousy pay [C. V. Barkla: he had been shovelling gravel on main roads at 17, when he went into the Militia for – among other things – economic security].

Heavy drinking among some colleagues [NX147039].

Strong drink [VX60529].

An army marches on its stomach, although the food seldom pleases. Early breakfast in the Sinai Desert; and a mess line-up, Cape York Peninsula, Queensland

Drinking; gambling; the few cowardly officers – most were good [C. L. Barnard].

Men who were a nuisance and thereby got everyone's leave docked [TX4537].

Away from home and buggered around [A. L. Rudder].

The list could go on and on. About 2 per cent complained of the crudity of their companions. Home was badly missed by 6 per cent, and the lack of privacy troubled 6 per cent.

One large group (34 per cent) was made up of men disgruntled by monotonous routine, boredom, hopeless military types, waste, and the frustration of not being committed to action. It did not take much action to cool most men's ardour, but the ideal came somewhere between a mouth dry with fear and one constantly yawning. As T.B. put it, he disliked both '*excessive* danger and periods of boredom'. Most men knew fear; it was what quickly blunted their keenness for battle. Yet for the majority it came and went like being out of breath. Only 5 per cent of the respondents admitted (at any rate) that fear during action reached such a level that it preyed on their minds as the great horror. The difference can be illustrated by two cases. F. C. Barnet, who chose the dust and dirt of the desert as his great dislike, was a regular soldier who ended up a major. Army life was 'okay' for him, and he was pleased to be 'doing something against Hitler'; it was almost as an after-thought that he added, 'I was scared in the Middle East'. On the other hand, VX44380 was one who hated the death of mates *and his own 'fear under fire'*. Captured in Crete, he was held for three weeks, then escaped to rejoin his unit in Palestine and later serve in the Pacific – all of which demanded pluck. Even so, he could neither forget nor *like* his fear.

Any control of fear showed its own courage. The salesman Ernest Badham was blown up by a shell at Tobruk:

Personally I feel I was not a particularly good soldier as, after my shell-burst episode, I became terrified of all shellfire. Although I tried hard not to show my feelings to others, and continued to carry out the duties of an infantryman, I felt I could break at any time and therefore become cowardly. This did not occur, but I could not hide this fact from myself, and at times felt ashamed when others appeared to be so adjusted and, to me, rather heroic . . . I think it would have helped me greatly if my parents and brothers had asked me more about my experiences when I was again settled in at home . . . and therefore alleviated the tensions and horrors I was keeping within myself . . . I will *never* forget the tension of combat, the fear so great that I used to repeatedly urinate, and sometimes worse, *unknowingly* in the heat of battle.

Poor, brave Badham. He endured the Middle East, went to
Java where he was taken prisoner in March 1942, and survived
three and a half years of that.

Fear of being in action, and a hatred of seeing mates killed
and wounded, combined to make L. M. Ferguson develop his
own kind of courage. He was a regimental police sergeant
('The Sheriff') with the 2/14th Battalion in Borneo when
three officers were killed, and two wounded. Ferguson took
charge. Under fire, he crawled to casualties, dragged in a
wounded artillery officer, crossed a damaged bridge to repair
artillery signal lines, took a stretcher party up a fire-swept
road and then guided a water ration party along it. For two
days he led every stretcher and water party to the forward
companies, spent a whole night tending the wounded, and
returned next morning with a burial party. He was awarded
the Military Medal because – as the citation concludes – his
'courage and coolness inspired the confidence in forward
companies that casualties would be returned and supplies kept
up whatever the circumstances'. And there we have it all:
discipline, mateship, compassion and courage – while hating
every minute of it. After the war Ferguson bought his own
grocery business. The deliveries would have been reliable.

Another military policeman belonged to a tiny minority of
respondents (0.5 per cent) who gave as their great dislike the
thought of *taking* life. QX62468 ended up as a 21-year-old
sergeant involved in the trial and execution of Japanese in
Rabaul for 'war crimes':

I was brought up in a Christian home where life was sacred . . . It was
my lot to organise the transport of condemned prisoners to the execution site, and conduct those to be hung or shot up the steps of the
gallows or strap them into firing squad positions. After discharge I
did not quite know what was wrong with me . . . It was several years
before it was accepted that I had an anxiety state due to my experiences at Rabaul . . .

His religious faith, and his wife's, and contact with the widow of one man he befriended (though still having to escort him to execution), helped QX62468 to ride out the stress. H. J. Barnicoat felt for his enemies even during battle – and not because he had been a churchgoer. There was little chance of that for a young fellow who had been on a Queensland cattle station from the age of 13. In the army at 32 and sent to New Guinea, he was 'always on patrol or put out on a mountain to count the movement of men of the enemy, in and going. It was a nerve raking job and really cruel to see the enemy get blown up. You don't really know till you see it'.

'A Sydney Clerk' commented: 'If you mean to include action, then danger of death is the thing. If you mean army life in general, then boredom, inaction, loneliness for want of female companionship . . .' He brings us back to the 34 per cent who complained of monotony, muddle and frustration of one kind or another. B. G. Newton detested 'the absolute boredom of camp life; there was never any enterprise shown with regard to training, you just did the same things'. P. T. Ward and J. W. Jacob objected to 'wasting time; not getting on with winning the war', and Garvin White to 'the waiting, always waiting'. R.S.S. took a dim view of being 'up at 2 a.m. to pack, then waiting two days for transport; coming out of hard action to find that some bright officer has decided on drill to keep the men occupied; and raw troops being sent to the front while men with two years of training sat around in Australia'. VX64780 was frustrated by being kept in Australia for years as a member of an armoured division, and D. E. Pike was still resentful of having been in the permanent army and a member of probably the first contingent to leave the mainland, yet going only to Port Moresby and being kept there in 1939–40, denied the right to become part of the AIF and refused accreditation as being on active service. NX774 bemoaned the early lack of equipment and supplies, even in North Africa; and the ex-lieutenant VX6513 was bitter about 'my men being sent to Greece for nothing'. D. M. Thompson found it hard to take 'the lack of incentive in the final year of the war', while VX109124 (a former office junior) thought that the army in general tended to 'completely lack mental stimulation', and K. M. Sillcock – a dairy supervisor – found himself inclined to become 'mentally lazy'. (On the other hand, R. A. Burke 'was in a survey team and had plenty of stimulation in the mathematical field'.) E. F. Ticehurst felt that one of the worst things about the army was the way it was so completely 'cut off from all other society'.

Officers and other ranks

One block of complaint centred squarely on officers and NCOs, but it has to be treated cautiously. The complainants were only about 15 per cent of the whole, and they did not necessarily make it a blanket criticism. Many were like C. L. Barnard, who disdained the *few* cowardly officers, and R.S.S., who complained only of different food and conditions for officers in camp and on troopships. Another point is that only 34 per cent of the respondents remained privates (although 5 per cent gave no answer), while 42 per cent were non-commissioned officers (from corporal to warrant officer) and 26 per cent were commissioned. So the bias was towards those who won promotion, but it is also to be noted that almost all the NCOs, and nearly half the officers, had risen from the ranks – so the worm's eye view should not have been altogether lost, and sometimes NCOs felt they were still regarded as worms.

Sergeant James Moore, a tradesman, spoke of 'being insulted by officer bastards not worth spitting on'. He added that the 2/10th Battalion would have been better commanded by the NCOs than its officers – with some exceptions (those, let us hope, that Moore will meet at reunions). Lance-corporal P. H. J. Hayman, a toolmaker, did not have much confidence in officers generally, although some were well liked, and those who had got commissions through pulling strings were usually the first to panic. Bitterly anti-officer was Driver W. C. Jones, a farmer's son, who appreciated discipline but resented incompetent officers stifling initiative, throwing their weight around, and neglecting their men in Japanese POW camps. He made no exceptions. Private W. A. Sarkies, a clerk and a POW at about 18, joined in the 'universal suspicion' that officers were usually 'aloof snobs' and 'impractical, white-collar types'; he *knew* that 'some were absolute horrors'. The mature and talented R. A. Burke resented 'the assumption [it was a regulation] that, if you were 30 years old or more, you were not suitable for a commission [as lieutenant]', and he deplored 'the arrogance of a lot of young officers':

I twice witnessed cowardly actions by troop commanders (captains), both of whom were subsequently returned to Australia, and I was threatened with arrest after objecting to the stories told by an officer of his participation in a pack-rape in London during the blitz. My skin was saved by another officer – a Duntroon graduate and a professional soldier (I always found these types excellent characters).

NX22435 hated the regimentation imposed, and L. H. Thomas added that the objectionable regimentation was not the same thing as discipline. F. H. Wood, who went in as a captain and ended the war as a major with an MBE, commented on 'the pettiness of surprising people' – and he certainly was not talking about the men in the ranks.

WX33713, a sergeant, found officers usually good, but not all of them. *Some* officers and their 'suck-holers' were his pet hate, while the Greta camp – when he knew it – was a disgusting and degrading 'chocolate city' run by a 'boy bastard' captain and far too many NCOs and RSMs, all of whom were deep in graft at the expense of those unfortunate enough to spend time there. J.V.R. finished up as a WO II himself, and believed that many officers and NCOs did a good job, with the situation improving over the years, but he detested

NCOs and officers who were misfits; bullies at first and walked out on us in action. One captain handed a patrol over to me in New Guinea because he didn't know what to do, but afterwards he accepted the credit. He was later sent back to Australia. Battle soon weeded out the undesirables, and they were replaced by proven men from the ranks.

Indeed most of the resentment was directed at a limited target. J. F. Tannock, who became a lieutenant, thought the relations good between officers and men in general; what he disliked was 'having to take orders from inexperienced reinforcement officers'. VX73305 had the same trouble with a few 'over'-experienced officers, too clever for anyone's good. NX3251 did not like 'being pushed around' – he had been a head stockman – but he 'deeply respected *good* NCOs and officers'. He had to say that it was a 'mixed' affair, some good, some bad, but he was due for promotion himself – above 'Gunner' – when he was captured on Crete, and that ended that.

Even clearer patterns emerged as respondents moved on to questions specifically about relations between various ranks. The majority of men expressed opinions, and most who did so maintained that 'good' described relations between NCOs and men (67 per cent), NCOs and officers (60 per cent), and officers and men – the last only just forming a majority (51 per cent). Hundreds of respondents therefore agreed with the 'excellent' relations between 'all ranks' spoken of by VX87208, who began with the Victorian Scottish Regiment (5th Battalion) and ended up a corporal in the Army Service Corps, with service in Australia and Borneo. VX145712, a trooper, joined up at 18 in 1943 and served in the south-west Pacific. He had a special reason for his claim:

In commando units the calibre of officers and NCOs was outstanding, and the mutual respect high. They ran great risks, showed great courage, and were generally fine officers. And where would we all be without the Troop Sergeant? They were wonderful people.

P. J. Gilchrist, after service with about eight units, ended as a lieutenant in the Army Service Corps unit he had joined as a private upon enlistment. He found relations good throughout;

it was up to the officer or NCO to command respect – and Gilchrist's implication was that it was normally achieved. D. G. Armstrong, a Company Quartermaster's Store staff sergeant with the 2/14th Battalion in the Middle East and New Guinea, maintained that after action, the transfer of the unsuitable and promotion from the ranks, the relations were very good. 'Hook' Anderson, a corporal with the 2/31st Battalion (Middle East, New Guinea), chose the 'good' category because 'after the blooding of the unit, most officers and NCOs came from the ranks'. For R. J. Berry, who went from lance-bombardier to WO II in a light anti-aircraft regiment, relations within the unit were fine because most officers and NCOs had come from the same prewar permanent army regiment and understood each other, and the NCOs – in closer contact with the men – could be relied on to iron out any problems. The ex-clerk W. H. Harding, a private who began in the 3rd Militia Battalion, thought the officers and men in the unit got on well because nearly all of them came from the Goulburn (NSW) area, had known each other beforehand, and understood each other as they trained. Some of the NCOs, he recalled, 'were terribly keen and did a lot of bouncing', but that ceased after embarkation for New Guinea.

Much depended on the personal qualities of the officer. Serving with the 2/22nd Battalion, C. E. Edwards was a former salesman who steadily rose in rank until he was commissioned in the last year of the war. He once saw a platoon of battle-hardened infantrymen lose their officer, a big man with much experience, and get as a replacement an officer of small stature and no experience of action at all, but the new man 'took only a few weeks to completely gain his platoon's confidence and respect'. VX191618, rising from private to staff sergeant, attributed good relations in his unit to the commanding officer, a decorated soldier from World War I, who instilled into his officers the notion that they were *responsible* for the men under their direct command; it was a spirit that endured into the postwar unit association of the 2/2nd Pioneers. W. A. Flowers served as a private with a field ambulance unit and was not entirely happy with all the NCOs – 'some walked into trouble' – but had good relations with his officers, who were doctors and very tolerant of the raw young men under them. And there are two things to note in particular about Flowers: one is that he spoke well of his officers although he and they became prisoners of the Japanese, whereas some POWs were bitter about their officers; but the second point is that Flowers's officers were medical men, and among POWs the doctors usually won high praise.

Yet, whatever the differences of opinion, the main points to be emphasised are that a majority of all respondents – if a small one – generally spoke well of their officers, and that a much more convincing majority spoke well of the NCOs. Respondents who, in describing relations between ranks, could not settle on 'good', usually did not choose the category 'poor'. Instead they applied the word 'mixed' – NCOs and men (29 per cent), NCOs and officers (33 per cent) and officers and men (38 per cent). Again the NCOs did better than the officers.

'Jack', a gunner, came close to saying that the relations were good all round, but could not get past the fact that there were 'some disagreements' because NCOs were usually first-rate and could 'see the soldier's point of view', but some officers were poor – mainly those who had 'no military experience and had obtained commissions through influence'. Another gunner, Ron Beeck, found the NCOs good – 'one of us' – but had mixed reactions to officers: 'Peacetime officers were not as good as those from the ranks.' F. G. V. D'Aran, a former bank clerk private with the 2/1st Battalion (Middle East, Ceylon, New Guinea), said that all relations were 'mainly good in action', but 'otherwise men despised the officers' petty pomposity (with notable exceptions) and accepted NCOs with a fair degree of tolerance as necessary evils'.

A. R. Johnson was more positive. A bank officer, whose ten years with the Citizen Military Forces made him a sergeant straight off in 1939, he rose to captain in 1943 with the 2/6th Battalion (Middle East; New Guinea). Johnson reckoned that in a good unit there were only odd cases of bother between officers and men, although sufficient overall to make him decide on 'mixed' relations in his reply. As for the NCOs – again in a good unit – 'they were only men who had been promoted; they were all members of a team who depended on each other'.

NX14409 was in Tobruk and New Guinea as a private with the 2/17th Battalion, and chose the good side of 'mixed': 'There were the usual tiffs, seeing how most of us were together for six years. Some NCOs and officers played on their rank, but in action their attitude changed and they were one of the boys.' W. H. Caffrey saw service in the Pacific and towards the end was a lieutenant with the 2/12th Battalion. He thought that a lot depended on the calibre of the individual, the capacity of an officer or NCO to win the confidence of his men, but even a substandard officer was likely to be 'suffered' by his NCOs, who were usually too well disciplined to do anything else.

But different possible reactions were sometimes hinted at or asserted. The militiaman Q104668, an ex-orchardist, fought in New Guinea whither his unit was sent with rifles dating from 1916, and very short of ammunition. Nevertheless 'each soldier still had five rounds of personal ammunition and, *therefore*, even those officers who were inclined to be overbearing generally *behaved*'. Q104668 actually claimed that his 61st Battalion was very well disciplined, and remarked that relations with officers were only sometimes a little mixed, yet his veiled threat was perhaps not just a joke. C. J. Selby – a Sydney carpenter – served in a small, tight unit that had 'good' relations, and the message *from the ranks* was, 'We'll all pull together'.

Army life was a good one as long as a fine line was kept between discipline and bullshit. We drew that line after a few weeks in Palestine, when our OC was *told* that he had to treat us as *men*, or the first bullet fired by us in anger would be up his arse. He was fantastic after that . . .

Selby also knew officers who *gave* the right message:

I remember being only a few yards behind the firing pits at Sana-nanda, December '42, when there was a rustle in the bushes behind me, and Major-General George Vasey stood there – red epaulets, swagger stick, the lot. There stood a brave man. 'How's it going, boys?' With leaders like that we *had* to win the war. How leaders can order men to their death I don't know; thank God I was never in the position of having to do it, although I realise that someone had to do it.

C. E. Edwards, as an acting platoon sergeant, had to order men to what might be their deaths – and as a direct result nearly met his own. They went into the Syrian campaign with a platoon member who had been 'a bloody nuisance since he had joined up'. Anti-everything, he kept saying what he would do when they got into action, and how little stripes would protect NCOs then. In a critical phase of an attack, climbing towards a hilltop swept by enemy fire, Edwards was in the rear when this person came back with the claim that he had a message to deliver. Since the trouble-maker could repeat no message, Edwards shoved his Tommy gun into the man's midriff and made him turn for the top again. In the final phase of the attack, as Edwards was going down the far side of the hill and towards the next ridge, he was wounded by a shot from behind – and was ever afterwards convinced that it was no accident but was fired by the renegade member of the platoon.

That was a case of the bad soldier. Other soldiers scoffed at suggestions that better men would ever call part of the tune by threatening to turn their weapons on those above them, and probably such menacing was at least unusual. Relations between ranks were more likely to be changed by the need to *depend* on each other in tight spots, than by *fear* of one another. Even so, the fact that every member of a unit was armed must from time to time have affected relations and modified behaviour – whether it was that of a soldier thinking of running away, or that of an officer inclined to treat men like dirt.

Comparatively few respondents summed up as 'poor' the relations between different ranks. The categories of 'only fair' and 'poor' together yielded under 5 per cent for NCOs and men, 7 per cent for NCOs and officers, and 11 per cent for officers and men. Yet the few have every right to be heard.

QX5170 served with the engineers. To explain his belief that relations with officers were 'only fair', he gave an instance that he claimed was true and thought to be typical. During the El Alamein battle one of his officers retired – allegedly with burst eardrums – and the unit saw him again only when the battle was over. Nevertheless, according to QX5170, that officer collected a Military Cross for what the unit had done, while the sergeant who took over command won nothing. Sidney Buckley, a private who had been a railway tradesman's assistant, also took a cool view of relations between officers and men. In his 2/4th Battalion 'the original officers were okay, but reinforcement officers thought they were "upper class". Their coming prevented the promotion of NCOs to officer rank and – when there were promotions in the field – poor officers could choose men they liked instead of those with ability'.

Buckley's was a generalised grouch, and C. E. Edwards has already been quoted on a reinforcement officer who filled his position very well. The coming of any reinforcements – officers or men – into a close-knit unit was a difficult change to cope with for everyone concerned. R. J. Berry finished up as a WO II in his light anti-aircraft regiment, coming up through the ranks, and he put the other side of the matter. Private soldiers joining the unit as reinforcements could cause trouble occasionally by resenting discipline – although, he added, that did not last long. Similarly J.J.C. witnessed and took pride in the way a battalion could pull everyone into line. He had been a battler. As far as he knew, his father had been killed in World War I, and he himself left school to become a messenger, labourer, sheet-metal worker . . . He was sacked at 21 years of age, as was so common then, but had found work

again before enlistment. He then served in both major
theatres, at times with one or two stripes up, but mainly in the
ranks with a pioneer battalion, a field company of engineers
and finally with the 2/3rd Battalion. 'I picked well', he wrote
of the latter. 'They were very colour proud, having fought all
four of the King's enemies (Italians, Germans, Vichy French
and Japanese) and losing a lot of men in the process. They had
splendid officers and NCOs, and any men who joined them
were smartly showed how to do it the Battalion's way.'

Still, some men were never easily reconciled. Jim Guy had
migrated to Australia from the north of England a few years
before the war, and had been a miscellaneous worker at spasmodic jobs in that time. Conscripted in 1940, liking the uniform but hating the army, unimpressed by the men in the
'Malitia' and determining to be a real soldier if he *had* to be in
the army, Guy transferred to the AIF and saw service in the
Middle East and the Pacific, all the time carrying his indi-
viduality with him. He summed it up this way:

The typical digger is an UNMITIGATED ASS with remarkable
abilities to capitalise on mistakes. Officers' relations with others
were poor. I hated the stupidity of the officers, the training, the
protocol. Give two pips to a schoolteacher or bank clerk and he
thinks he is Jesus Christ above a carpenter. Officers were not mature
enough for their jobs, and were not well enough tested and trained.
Between NCOs and men relations were only fair; promotion was
given to the more amendable soldier, rather than the more efficient
fighter. I was promoted to corporal at the end of the war, rank post
dated (I believe classified unamendable to discipline). After a con-
frontation with a battalion commander on the boat over to the
Middle East, a whole company was charged (all charges dropped in
the end). I was the first to be fronted.

Some who were among the 10th Reinforcements to the 2/5th
Battalion, or in the 2/23rd Battalion, would remember Jim
Guy. The rest of us may well believe that he might be the first
fronted.

SX24816 was a welder who had been to the Churches of Christ Sunday school as a child, but had decided that religion was a waste of time and a 'rackett', and developed 'a lot of time for the Communist Party'. He was conscripted in 1940 and sent to the Northern Territory. He 'realy didn't have time to work things out', he was despatched so fast, but he transferred to the AIF in the hope of going overseas. He served in Australia only, however, with medical units and Z Force – a mixed-service force for special operations. He became a corporal, yet he did not think that the transport drivers in northern Australia had ever got – from the RSL or anyone else – the recognition they deserved for their arduous work; at first no roads, just dust, flies, bad water, poor food, skin diseases . . . But it was the officer system in the army that most troubled him, and its heartlessness. Never mind his writing style or spelling; catch something of his passion:

I realy think the army was a sought of a class society, officers mess, NCO mess, all the cigerettes they wanted, spirits, beer. Rank and file few cigerettes, beer rations no spirits, women in their mess not in mens, ext. You are here to do and die and I mean do whether it be right or wrong, yes sir no sir, stand up straight now stand there for a couple of hours, get the picture. Medical officers mostly students in early part of the war, they could do most anythink and not have to answer for it. One instant – I will cut that out, no you won't, yes I will, died of cancer 6 months later. Quite a lot more but I have said enough. A little bit more. Call up 18 year old, never been away from home, I should say Mothers boy fretted to death (I can see him now). Poison letter to a mate of mine, shot himself. Officers a class above you, aloft, realy not a good fellow to privates. Supreme outlook. NCOs above corporal not good contact because of segregation.

Despite the harshness of SX24816's war environment, it was not the one that often brought all ranks together – the environment of battle. And it was from another and even harsher non-battle environment, the Japanese prisoner-of-war camps, that some men emerged with an ineradicable contempt for their officers. VX35898 declared his officers useless, with very few exceptions. They kept away from the men on working parties, but were very much around in the compound where the Japanese were few:

We used to say that when the war was over the officers would have to have an operation to get the bed from their backs. They did not have to work, but they had better rations. The junior officers who came up from the ranks used to say they were not *allowed* to work, but they built up resentment among the men.

In fairness – although the whole situation was grossly unfair – the officers were right. Strictly, though there were plenty of exceptions in practice, they were *not* permitted as officers to work. They were, however, made responsible for maintaining order in compounds, which was difficult work of another kind, and could be extremely stressful. WX2836 saw his medical officer, Colonel Edward Dunlop, continually going to the guardhouse to protest against sick men being made to do heavy work. Being very tall, 'the Colonel was forced to stand in a 2 ft deep hole outside the Guard House so that a fanatical 4 ft 6 in Japanese could slap the Colonel's face repeatedly to demonstrate his power'.

Nevertheless, NX65735 would argue that such a comment missed the point – and not only because it was illustrated by reference to 'Weary' Dunlop, that distinguished doctor whose unremitting work for prisoners belied his nickname, and for whom probably no soldier who met him felt anything but admiration and gratitude. No, NX65735 would say, keep to the real point. Relations between the usual run of officers and men in his POW days were poor because, while there was no promotion or increased pay for anyone else, his captain became a major, retained a batman so that he could be kept in the station of life to which he had become accustomed, and was notorious for putting men on charges. The officers' better rations did not prevent an Army Service Corps captain pilfering from the stores. Nor was that captain punished when

his stealing was detected and a group of men petitioned for
something to be done about it; on the contrary, their own
officers forced them to withdraw the petition or be charged
with mutiny. NX65735 saw officers supplied with a covered
waterproof dugout while their men slept in a morass, un-
protected; and the best he could say was that, when his
stretcher was coveted by an officer, and a WO was told to get
it, the WO refused to do so.

Even in the financial settlements with former prisoners of
the Japanese, F. W. Jackson and others believed that officers
were given a bonus denied to other ranks. Yet that idea seems
to have arisen from 8th Division officers *not* being docked the
3s per day normally levied for extras in the officers' mess. The
real 'beef', wrote the president of the NSW Ex-Prisoners of
War Association, should come from other *officers* – those from
German and Italian camps who, on a technicality, *did* lose that
money. Nevertheless R.W.B., a driver captured by the Japanese, thought that the social differences were so marked
between officers and men – the officers expecting a 'master
and servant' relationship – that the NCOs were much to be
preferred. In particular he developed contempt for chaplains,
who held a minimum rank of captain. Although he went into
the army a devout Presbyterian, he was discharged from it
believing that religion was 'just part of the establishment'. The
chaplains, he considered, had 'put rank first, church second,
soldiers last'.

Not all the prisoners of the Japanese had the same poor
view of Australian officers. Ernest Badham retained respect
for them throughout his POW experience, no doubt helped
by the fact that his commanding officer was Colonel Dunlop
– who, as a respondent himself, was simply 'irritated' by the
questions on relationships between ranks. 'A good officer or
NCO', he said, 'gets on well with all subordinates, and most
AIF officers and NCOs were fair to good.' How possible is it
that Wal Gotch (though never a POW) summed up a great
deal about short-term and long-term attitudes, strong complaints and general acceptance? A veteran of World War I,

Gotch was a commissioned officer (lieutenant and captain) with electrical and mechanical engineering units in Australia and – despite his age – in the Pacific. He wrote: 'The young 18-year-olds thought I was a bastard, but later in civil life they thought I was okay, and they made me president of their unit association.' What Gotch might have been implying was that soldiers all along did appreciate the distinction between 'a bastard' and 'a *fair* bastard'.

'Crimes'

One test of men's reactions to army life is the kind and number of 'crimes' they were charged with. About 26 per cent of the respondents were put on a charge, nearly 9 per cent more than once. Most offences were comparatively trivial, and many men who were repeated culprits still took it very lightly. R. W. Bentley, a sapper, casually went 'absent without leave a few times'. QX3506, a gunner and POW in Germany, said that his were 'all AWL offences, can't recall the number'. R.E.G. ended up a lieutenant, but had been four times AWL. WX345, a private mentioned in despatches and captured on Crete, was 'AWL every time near a town to see', but he had no complaints about his officers and NCOs: 'All treated me as I deserved.' The 39th Battalion's J.W.B. had 'the usual – AWL; failing to attend parade; looting when Burns Philp was bombed at Port Moresby – two bottles of whisky, taken off me by Sam Templeton [the colourful, almost elderly Captain S. V. Templeton, killed in action in 1942, and whose name was perpetuated in Templeton's Crossing on the Kokoda Trail]'. W. A. Catton served in the Middle East, Greece, Crete, Ceylon and New Guinea, and was once an acting corporal. He was also up on a number of charges: 'AWL several times in Australia. Once for failing to obey a lawful command, fined £1. I settled to army discipline reasonably well, but I always spoke out at things I believed to be unfair.' E. W. Chambers was a private who refused promotion; his view was that NCOs were respected, but lost real respect when commissioned. He was wounded in Syria, wounded in New Guinea, and mentioned in despatches on the Kokoda Trail. He also had 'three counts of AWL. Various other misdemeanours – I can't possibly remember – all in Sydney after contracting illnesses and being wounded'. VX73305, a tough little apprentice fitter and turner, was pulled out of the AIF by his family with the backing of manpower officers, but he got back into the 127th Australian Electrical and Mechanical Brigade Workshop, served 654 days in New Guinea, and was a corporal in 1943; yet his record showed: 'AWL. Insubordination. Attempted to fight an officer and NCO.' VX85728, an ex-storeman and several times a corporal, was AWL more than once, and also lost his two stripes for abusing an officer ('too many dickheads among them; NCOs and men appreciated each other').

So there was some ill feeling, but not too much, and the crimes were not serious in most cases. The prevailing crime was, in fact, being absent without leave: 73 per cent of the respondents charged had committed that offence. Rather than being a worrying absence, it was often more a matter of being back late, or going off on a bit of a wander, or – as in the case of Arthur Mothersole – being charged with twenty-one days AWL from a base workshop, due to taking himself into action at El Alamein.

Yet being AWL *could* be very serious. WX12841 sent in a newspaper clipping that discussed his own case, somewhat graver than usual, but contrasted it with another that was much worse. With a good record overseas, WX12841 was granted leave on his return to Australia and much of it he spent in bed, both because he decided to get married and also because he had a bad bout of malaria. The upshot was that he overstayed his leave by twenty days, and fiddled his pass before rejoining his unit, when a court martial severely reprimanded him. The other case involved a young Western Australian militiaman who had become so browned off with the army that he decided to desert, although he was charged only

Escorting surrendered Japanese was one role of the military police, in this case a provost of the 9th Division (indicated by a platypus over a boomerang)

with being AWL. He had been AWL for sixteen weeks, and had attempted to escape from custody, before he came before the court; his sentence was nine months in detention.

There were similar features in the case of respondent NX1854. He was in camp at Tamworth (NSW) when a telegram arrived, telling him of his foster mother's death, but a two-day delay in delivery (for which he blamed the army) meant that the funeral was over by the time he reached Sydney. The whole affair so upset him that he could not settle, and – dodging some MPs – he went AWL for twenty-three weeks, living with his wife at the address he had given the army, and working in a box factory. Then he gave himself up and was sentenced to sixteen weeks in detention, mostly served in Victoria at the old Bendigo and Geelong gaols. With no smokes whatever, and 'barbarously' reduced food, he suffered a nervous breakdown, after which the authorities allowed him to work each morning in a regimental aid post. Upon release, he soldiered on and was quite soon a corporal, but continued to think that too little leniency was shown for his voluntary return. Yet in the light of the penalty imposed on the Western Australian militiaman – nine months for sixteen weeks – NX1854's four months for twenty-three weeks probably *was* lenient.

Where men were serving when they committed their crimes was not always clear, but it seems that in about 65 per cent of the cases it was Australia, and perhaps 20 per cent of the time it was the Middle East and Europe. The south-west Pacific was not much of a place for crimes, if only because it was not so tempting to go AWL there, although even New Guinea produced its small crop. Naturally there were many offences everywhere that went undetected ('Never caught' was a common enough remark), and detected misdemeanours that were not followed up. J.P.L.R., a farmer's son and a private with service behind him in the Middle East, was placed on no charges at all, yet he added, 'Quite a bit of AWL when opportunity offered, but got away with it. Just missed a court martial in New Guinea'.

After applying to the Engineers for a transfer back to the 2/28th Battalion, I contracted a poisoned hand and was evacuated to Port Moresby. After hospital, I was sent to a transit camp, where I was told I would be for six weeks. One of the staff was a sergeant who had been with us in Tobruk in '41, and he told me not to jump camp, as it was a mandatory court martial charge. Next morning I walked out of the camp at 5 a.m., down to the airfield, asked a Yank for a lift in his 'Biscuit' Bomber. Got back to the Engineers and pushed for a transfer and movement order to Finschhafen, where the old battalion then was. Returned joyfully to it and my beloved Vickers guns, then went straight to the CO, told him what I'd done and asked him to fix things if the MPs came after me. Apparently they did ask for my close arrest and return to Moresby for court martial, but he told them what they could do. The CO was one of the old lot from 1940–41, and took great care of the old ones like myself, for there were so few of us left by then who had started four years before.

It was in New Guinea that NX1854 was charged with – of all offences – speeding. He drove a jeep along a jungle track, taking a couple of mates to the beach for a swim, and was booked by the MPs. Before his commanding officer next day he claimed that his foot had developed a cramp, so he could not lift it from the accelerator for a time. He was reprimanded. Then the CO chuckled, NX1854 chuckled, his escorts chuckled . . . Yet a moment's thought about soldiers

who were often still boys, all kinds of drivers in a whole range
of states, tearing along all sorts of tracks in a variety of army
vehicles – and the absolute necessity of trying to regulate
speed becomes soberingly apparent. The military police?
They had a job to do, as many respondents remarked.

There were not only persistent offenders among the respondents, but also some who were charged with very serious
crimes. We have called one 'Storeman'; that is what he was
until sacked at 20 in 1940, and what he became again after the
war. He had left school at 13 'to earn the price of a loaf of
bread'. His father had been an Anzac, and 'Storeman' himself
joined the volunteer Militia at 16. Brought up a Catholic, he
remained 'a good Christian', but he became a heavy drinker
and a keen gambler. In Chapter 12 he is quoted on the divisional MPs being okay, but base provosts being mercenary,
and he always tried to assess people fairly. He could name one
chaplain in particular who should have got the Victoria Cross,
and the Salvation Army welfare officers were always appreciated. The Germans had 'good fighting qualities', but the
Italians 'did not want to fight'. As for officers, 'some thought
their shit didn't stink, but could name a few good ones'. Most
NCOs who were in battle with him were 'just like good mates,
but 10 per cent thought they were going to be colonels'.
'Storeman' was in the Tobruk siege, and served also in the
Pacific. He enjoyed visiting foreign places 'and learning their
language'. His attitudes seem good, and there was nothing
wrong with his physique: he was nearly 6 ft tall and filled out
in the army to weigh 12 st 6 lb. He was proud to be in the AIF,
yet his career as a soldier went sour. Why?

Crimes too numerous to mention. I had more red lines than blue in
my paybook. Being ex-Militia, I used to drill the boys at Warwick
Farm until one Saturday night a mate and I decided to go AWL. That
was the end of any promotion for me. The provosts raided the
Leagues Club in Sydney, and we ended up back at Warwick Farm
under escort. We were the first to be charged in the Regiment, and
were the black sheep from then on. It was all right to take over a gun

at Tel el Eisa, when the bombardier got half his back full of shrapnel, but I was soon relieved of that command. Needless to say, I ended up with some larrikins as mates and was never out of trouble. If you ever get hold of a paybook of mine, I would like to have a look, if that is possible. There is some interesting reading. Even one line has FGCM. Yes, a Field General Court Martial, where they shoot spies.

The paybooks may be lost forever, but the proceedings of an FGCM in 1942 survive, at which 'Storeman' was charged with desertion: absenting himself while his unit was in an area of operations against the enemy, with intent to avoid such service. He was found *not* guilty of desertion, but guilty of being AWL, and was sentenced to field punishment for seventy days, with loss of all ordinary pay for that time. His anti-tank regiment had been on mobile reserve, the understanding being that at any time they might be given fifteen minutes notice to move into action – notice that might not come for days, and might never come. One afternoon 'Storeman' was found to be missing, and he did not reappear until the middle of the following morning. Everyone believed that he would turn up, and witnesses said as much at his court martial. A major spoke for him, saying that he had known the accused for a long time and had found him satisfactory in action, but in periods of inactivity he was inclined to be easily led by company that was bad for him – he was not led by his own viciousness. 'Storeman' had already had eight summary awards made against him for being AWL, conduct to the prejudice of good order, drunkenness, failing to appear at the place of parade, breaking out of camp and being beyond limits *in* camp. His real trouble was that he was too fond of drinking, and had begun to feel that he was a marked man in the army.

His own explanation to the court was simple enough, and was believed. Finishing a Mine School in the morning, and knowing that many men would be driven to the coast for a swim in the afternoon, he and some friends (the bad company?) had decided to skip the swim and look for some beer instead. Finding some at a South African canteen, they became very drunk – it was their first beer session for three months – and he remembered nothing beyond waking up next morning and starting back to camp. No, not guilty of desertion, but certainly guilty of being AWL – and of drunkenness, and of conduct prejudicial to good order, and of potentially handi-capping his gun crew. A pity, for he had real possibilities even then, at the age of 23.

Other respondents had personal problems similar to those of 'Storeman', and it would be important to describe them if they were typical; but here, in the context of a group of men who mostly liked army life, or survived it with a minimum of bother, it would be misleading to instance case after case of deep trouble. Yet it might be appropriate to listen to several of the respondents who spoke of *whole units* taking protest action. The men who recounted the incidents thought them to be important happenings, of a kind that are usually hushed up. They described the events from their own points of view, and there could be very different descriptions of those events.

R. H. Byrnes, a gunner turned signaller, with part of an economics degree already behind him, had been in the army for three and a half years by September 1945. He was among 1300 men sent – without much real purpose – from Borneo to Rabaul, where about 900 of the men refused to disembark. The ship was going on to Australia, and they thought it was time they went with it. Food and water were promptly cut off, and Major-General K. W. Eather promised that if the men disembarked no charges would be laid, and they could put their case for repatriation to the Minister for the Army, F. M. Forde, who was in the area. The troops replied that they would wait until he came to them, but Eather said, 'No, by then you'll be so hungry you'd eat him.' During the afternoon the soldiers gave up in twos and threes, and were all off the ship before Eather's deadline. At the meeting with Forde,

the army tried to prevent the Borneo men from speaking, and we got no sense from Forde – who didn't have much, anyway. The papers and ABC reported that the incident involved only a few young

Lae, 1945: no home leave in nearly two years for Keith Battye (left) and Jack Hollway

troops with short service – a fraudulent misrepresentation typical of army public relations. Most of the Borneo men stayed in New Guinea until June 1946, when Mr Chifley directed that they should all be home by September – i.e. before the elections.

VX131996, a railway worker and eventually a WO II, recalled a 'mutiny' won by the troops. It happened late in 1940 or early in 1941 at the training camp at Darley (Bacchus Marsh, Vic.) and he had never seen it reported anywhere. The trouble was that the men believed they were being granted only half the periodical leave enjoyed by other camps, and members of the 2/6th Training Battalion requested the extra leave, warning that they would march out in a body if it were refused. With particular care and smartness the whole battalion paraded under the command of their company sergeant majors, and refused to disperse until the commanding officer agreed to meet with them. It took several days, with all leave cancelled, telephones cut off, one company CO threatening that the machine gun battalion would be used against them, much coming and going from company areas to regimental parade ground, and much conferring between battalion commanders and brigade HQ, before the denouement: 'A special parade was called, and the news was given out that the leave had been granted. "But do not think", said the colonel, "that it is because of your actions over the past few days." Whatever would have given anyone that idea?'

William Pye did well in the army, rising to captain and staying on in Borneo for a time, on loan to the military governor; but the cooks and catering officer did not do well for 9 Battery of the 2/3rd Anti-tank Regiment after its return from the Middle East to the Atherton Tableland in Queensland. The men and NCOs finally rejected the food and refused parades, and were all charged with mutiny, fined or demoted. Soon afterwards the battery was broken up and the men allotted to other units: 'it was a great shame, really, because it had been a happy regiment and the loss of this battery destroyed the regiment's continuity after several years and all the battles of the Middle East.'

Demotions such as those mentioned by Captain Pye were meted out as punishment to under 5 per cent of the respondents – overwhelmingly from NCO rank, perhaps giving some point to another of Pye's remarks: 'Of course nothing happened to the officer who was most to blame for the cause of the mutiny; and in later civilian life he got a good post.' Most demotions were not punishments but were voluntarily accepted by respondents (nearly 8 per cent) as a means of transfer to another arm or unit. Indeed it would be quite misleading to round off reactions to army life on a note of mutiny, charges and punishment. Delinquencies had to be paid for, when detected, and sometimes good men – individually or en masse – jacked up with good reason. But these were *not* the experiences and reactions of most of the respondents or their mates. On the contrary, acceptance of discipline was characteristic, along with a good deal of pride and appreciation.

NX3403 would not have claimed anything out of the ordinary for himself. He once had a leg broken in a bomb blast in Greece, and suffered from malaria in New Guinea, but he was never charged with a crime, nor decorated, nor demoted – indeed he was never promoted from gunner during his 1939–45 AIF service with the 2/1st Field Regiment. He had some training with the Militia from 1938, and he was single when he joined the AIF, although he married during the war. Before and after the war he was a shop assistant in a men's wear store. The most unusual things about him were that he was older than average, aged 34 at enlistment, and that the effect of the depression on him had been to make him politically minded. He reflected in a balanced yet positive way on his six years of army life.

The unit in which I served consisted of approximately one thousand men, with such variation of type and character as one would find in a similar number of men in civilian life. We had our entrepreneur who ran the two-up game or, in camp in Australia, was the SP bookie. We had the con-men, the fellows anxious for promotion, the no-hopers and many more. The great difference in army life was that they were all linked in a bond of loyalty not usually present in civilian life. There was a remarkable tolerance, as in a family where all protect the one delinquent. However, this spirit of brotherhood developed only after time and shared experiences. At first there were many clashes in all ranks between men who were still raw civilians and permanent army instructors who knew more about their weapons than about managing men. But relations improved as we got to know each other and learnt the necessity of the discipline imposed, and as unsuitable officers and men were transferred to other units. The 'esprit de corps' took a leap forward when all were tested in action; a unit pride was born, producing not so much a different man as one living by a different code. I can recall my feelings, on returning from a dangerous mission, just to be again in the company of my comrades; never had I felt such a love for my fellow man, with all his faults. I do not wish to imply that we lived in a utopia. We had our arguments and fights, and had to get over them because we could not escape to another place. Men came from all walks of life and, as we had to rely a great deal on conversation, views and experiences were exchanged and all our horizons were broadened. I have listened with great interest to young men from affluent backgrounds talking with those who had been poverty stricken – and marvelled at the latter's ability to define the truth. I feel that I emerged from a great experience a much enlightened and improved human being.

10 • 'IN PLACES I DID NOT LIKE TO BE'

Queensland stockman H. J. Barnicoat supplied the phrase. 'Will you kindly send to me a questionnaire,' he wrote, 'as I have been in a lot of situations in the army . . . and have been in places I did not like to be.' War service took many respondents to places they did not like, under circumstances they liked even less.

A. J. Kilner was a four-figure gunner from New South Wales who was captured in Greece but escaped and fought alongside of Tito's partisans in Yugoslavia for a month before being retaken by the Germans. G. R. Dwight, born in England and captured in North Africa, escaped in 1944 and joined the Russians – whom he disliked as 'modern vandals, cruel and destructive'. So Australian soldiers sometimes turned up in unusual spots among unexpected company. The respondents, however, mostly served in the more predictable areas: 10 per cent never left Australia; 43 per cent were in what is often loosely called the Middle East (including North Africa, Greece and Crete); and most of them returned to swell to 80 per cent those who served in South-east Asia and the south-west Pacific.

Many would have agreed with the respondent who said that the Middle East campaigns could be better coped with than those in the tropical jungles.

Events, places, faces, actions which took place in the Middle East remain in clear focus. It was a chivalrous war, if there is such a thing. However, it is with extreme difficulty that I remember New Guinea,

Stuka dive bombers were about when this photograph was taken in 1941. Regimental Sergeant Major 'Dingo' Burgess does his best for a Cretan family that had attached itself to the 2/2nd Field Regiment. The family could not be taken aboard the rescue ship, the Perth, *but it was given all the food and money the men had*

no doubt brought about by detesting my long stay there under vile conditions . . . with the constant thought of being cooked and eaten by the Japs (as a number of our fellows were) if killed or wounded.

There was complaint about the futile gesture of sending troops into Greece and Crete. VX5416 was game to the last. Looking back on his life in a thankful spirit, he filled out his questionnaire while suffering from cancer; but he had reached Crete after being sunk at sea in the evacuation of Greece, and later was a POW for four and a half years. 'We done the rearguard to get some New Zealanders off. Good men. Along with them we became the second Anzacs – proudly, despite the odds.' But the odds included being 'scapegoats . . . poorly

equipped . . . used up by the British'. J. G. Thom was 'amazed
on landing in Greece to find British troops being shifted out
of the country', and he later wondered about Churchill as a
leader, since lives seem to have meant so little to him. The
NSW gunner Kilner – very bitter, very anti-British in spite of
English parents – denounced the

stupid commitment to Greece, where the Anzacs were formed again
to be sacrificed for Churchill's ego. The Greeks were doing quite
well against the Italians until the Germans were forced to come in by
Churchill's action ... There's nothing worse than being outnumbered on the ground, in a strange country whose troops have given
up, without air cover and subjected daily to attacks from the air.

Even more frustration and anger were expressed over troops
being left unused in Australia, or misused in the 'unnecessary'
island campaigns in the last year or two of the war.

> From 1943 my unit was stationed for long periods in Australia
> and New Guinea with no action, just waiting for our masters to
> decide to commit us again. New Guinea was stupefyingly
> dreary. I often ponder on this, and on how demoralising it
> became. All credit to those commanding officers who devised
> educational, recreational and sporting programmes to hold
> men's interest. The attention that Australian field commanders
> paid to the welfare of their men has not been properly recog-
> nised; it was far superior to the British and American armies
> [T. J. Barker; private, 2/4th Battalion, 1939; lieutenant, 2/1st
> Machine Gun Battalion, 1945; served with British army in
> Burma, 1945–46].
> The last twelve months of operations in New Guinea, Borneo
> and Bougainville were completely useless. The casualties were
> 'throw-away expenditure' for postwar political expediency
> [S.V., corporal, 2/1st Pioneer Battalion].
> In the early part of the war I thought my death was very pos-
> sible, particularly in Greece and Crete ... However, in the
> Aitape-Wewak campaign I found the death of anyone I knew

Top: *Last machine-gun post in Greece . . .*

Above: *As if eating dinner in the paddock, three Australians have a meal in Greece before evacuation – and someone snaps them*

Left: *German leaflet dropped on besieged Tobruk in 1941. 'I remember when these came down', wrote SX9054. 'I thought it was lavatory paper blowing in the wind – and so it was really.'*

pretty sad, since we all realised it wasn't really necessary to dig the Japs out of there. 'Bluey' Burridge was a young soldier of 18 (I was a veteran of 24 years). He died in that needless campaign, but would be alive today – with many others – had the division been used to better advantage [D. B. Cade, private, 2/4th Battalion].

Even at the time I saw the Aitape-Wewak campaign as a political push to keep the troops in the public eye as seeming to be doing something. The Americans considered us mad to push down the coast to Wewak; they had established a perimeter around Aitape and were starving the Japanese out. The Japs outside the perimeter were receiving no supplies and, although still capable of fighting strongly, were in a bad way. I saw two cases of cannibalism by the Japanese in the area, one involving the body of a Jap, and Australian bodies in the other case. But, like the Syrian campaign (swept under the carpet because of the involvement of French troops as the enemy?), the Wewak campaign gets little publicity – although it's a glaring example of the stupidity of war [WX7927, sergeant, 2/3rd Battalion]. The labour market was kept tight so that no strike could fail. To disguise the fact that the army was doing very little, servicewomen were recruited for jobs that could easily be handled by soldiers doing nothing. By 1944 the Americans were ready and did not want the Australian army; they found it a political nuisance and kept it out of Dutch New Guinea and the Philippines. Wewak and Bougainville were quite unnecessary. The Borneo campaign was to cut off Japan's oil – but US submarines had already done that [R. H. Byrnes, signaller, 55th/53rd Battalion].

On Morotai, on the way to Tarakan, an American conscript driving our landing-craft said, 'Bluey, keep your head down on Tarakan because we have a big bomb to drop on Japan'. He did not say 'atom bomb', but if he knew so much, why were we being sent in? We could have waited a couple of months. 'Diver' Derrick, VC, was killed on Tarakan, and a lot of other Australians – some shot each other in the night by mistake. For the Shell Oil Company and the Dutch the Australian government let those Diggers die. Tommy Cook, of Gunbower, who fought with me right through the Middle East and New Guinea, got blown out of a tree by the Japs, rolled down the hill to my feet and died in my arms. That is the picture I see every night when I try to sleep. To think he had only to live another week . . . [H.M.W., private, 2/23rd Battalion].

Awards

Each of the major theatres of war threw up its due proportion of medals for bravery, and honours for outstanding service of perhaps another kind: the Middle East and Europe produced one award to two gained in South-east Asia and the south-west Pacific. Decorations for valour such as the Military Medal, the Military Cross and – in one case – the Victoria Cross were made to just over 4 per cent of the respondents. The fact that about 12 per cent of these medal-winners were private soldiers, 41 per cent non-commissioned officers and 48 per cent commissioned officers shows who were favoured in the matter of medals. Another 5 per cent of the respondents were either mentioned in despatches (literally mentioned by name and probably recommended for an award that was not granted) or had their achievements recognised by the Efficiency Decoration or one of the grades of the Order of the British Empire – and only in the case of mentions in despatches were private soldiers really in the race. That is not to imply that the decorations awarded were not usually merited by those who wore them; it is to be expected that those who gave a lead should stand out for an award, and the leaders should be the NCOs and officers. The real implication is that many more medals were deserved than were ever granted – even to officers and NCOs, let alone privates. Decorated men often say, indeed, that they are only the holders of what was won by their units.

J. W. H. Atkinson, MC, once a lieutenant with the 2/23rd Battalion, wrote of fear to the marrow of the bones and the chattering of teeth before and after hand-to-hand fighting, despite his two commendations for 'gallantry in action' and 'disregard of danger'. Then he continued: 'I saw plenty the same, but they still went on. The ordinary soldier was absolutely tops, and all did their best. If some did better than others it was because they were born with a higher limit. I don't believe in decoration for that reason, although I wear one for all my men. I was proud of them.'

The difficulties of making awards and the oddities of the system were well noted. R. G. Penny, a sergeant with the 2/2nd Machine Gun Battalion, said that the company sergeants were asked to nominate possible names for the Military Medal after El Alamein, but they decided to put none forward because almost all would have qualified. QX13154 was promoted from private to staff sergeant in one jump at the beginning of the Owen Stanley campaign (he replaced a man taken away with a self-inflicted wound). Convinced that the 'entire Kokoda Trail campaign was an example of military mismanagement', with too much attempt to push the Japanese back instead of wearing them down, he was equally certain that 'every man who went over the Kokoda Trail deserved a medal'. He saw enough to believe that 'medals didn't mean very much in the way they were awarded'. W. W. McKay, a bombardier with the 2/2nd Field Regiment, understood that he was recommended for a Military Medal in Crete, but he thought that it did not go through because the army was not keen on distributing awards after a defeat. Alexander Fraser, a captain with a commando unit and made a POW in Rabaul, was still sore about no decoration being allocated to anyone in his unit. A commando lieutenant, Mick Sheehan, remarked that a citation was made out for him once, but his commanding officer quashed it because he disapproved of officers being decorated; some other units, however, 'went flat-out after awards, since they reflected favourably on the CO'.

TX1539, gunner and specialist signaller with the 2/8th Field Regiment, certainly saw action. He never forgot the noise and sight of the Alamein barrage opening up at 9.40 p.m.

A section of the opening barrage at El Alamein, 23 October 1942, 'taken from the Pimples at 2145 hours on time exposure of 15 mins'. It was 'difficult to get breath', and 'it seemed that the air was on the move'

on 23 October 1942: 'Nearly a thousand guns firing at once and for long periods, with aerial bombing combined, made it difficult to get breath. It seemed that the air was on the move; it would gradually take a loose blanket from the body of anyone lying prone.' But he thought awards were a contentious matter: there were the COs who would pass no recommendations on; the COs themselves who got DSOs for what their units had done; the observation post officer badly wounded beyond the wire, brought back by his driver, and awarded the MC while the driver got nothing ... On the other hand, R. G. Reeves – with the distinguished number WX52 – recalled a platoon commander getting the Military Cross because the members of his platoon recommended it as a body.

A. N. Dick, as an infantryman in New Guinea, was put up for a medal he never got. This dairy hand and textile worker, a very simple man, was moved to write verse about the ambush of his forward section ('A' Coy, 2/4th Battalion) and the death of its Bren-gunner.

If I earned a good conduct medal
for some trivial thing,
pin it on some soldier
who has been shot dead.
The reward should go to him.

There was a young Victorian,
Richard Addison by name,
who had twice the courage
of some types of men
who were seeking medals and fame.

The qualities their medals did not have
Richard stored within his heart so bold,
but the medals some heroics had
were stained by Richard's blood.

Yet not all who died were heroes, and many who won medals were brave – or at any rate were fully committed to the task at hand, and no more could be asked of them. They are not to be belittled.

The one winner of the Victoria Cross among the respondents was Lieutenant-Colonel C. G. W. Anderson. Born in Cape Town, he won the Military Cross in the jungles of East Africa during World War I, and was well equipped to command the 2/19th Battalion in Malaya. He was made a POW, but not before his force of Australians and Indians in the Battle of Muar had destroyed ten Japanese tanks (Anderson's men had none) and four guns (in an attack Anderson led personally), and caused hundreds of casualties among elite Japanese troops, thus saving another Allied force from probable annihilation. In four days of continuous fighting Anderson disregarded his own safety, set a magnificent example to his men, and refused to leave the many who were wounded in the persistent Japanese attacks by land and from the air (of which the enemy had almost complete command). So runs his cita-

*'What a hell of a place for mankind to settle a difference.' Remnants of
'B' Company, 2/17th Battalion, at Thompson's Post after El Alamein.
Nearby, three posthumous VCs had been won in 1942 by men of the
2/48th Battalion – Privates A. S. Gurney and P. E. Gratwick,
of Western Australia, and the English-born Sergeant W. H. Kibby,
of South Australia*

tion; all Anderson wrote was '1939–45 war, VC'. But he did
describe his unit: 'My battalion was a splendid cross-section of
Australians, with well chosen officers; a unit of high morale
and exceptionally well trained. About 20 per cent were ex-
Militia, and the battalion being in the 8th Division – the third
raised in the war – they were generally men who had to make
a special sacrifice to join up.'

No questionnaire could be answered by one man from
Berri (SA) whose father had served in the 48th Battalion, First
AIF, and himself served in the 2/48th. T. C. Derrick, VC, was
dead. But Jack Ralla was with 'Diver' Derrick in North
Africa and 'saw him attack enemy positions aboard a Bren-
gun carrier, upon which he stood firing the Bren while enemy
bullets just rained on the carrier, and a Very light stowed in it
caught alight and lit up the place like day. Derrick carried on
up and down and around until the Germans were wiped out'.
That action won Derrick the Distinguished Conduct Medal;
the Victoria Cross had to wait until New Guinea in 1943.

There his company was ordered to outflank a strong Japanese position on a precipitous cliff-face and attack Sattelberg. After some vain attempts the company was ordered to withdraw, but Sergeant Derrick asked for one last chance. Permission granted, Derrick went ahead alone at about last light and destroyed an enemy post with grenades. As an Australian section moved in, he went on and repeated the process for a second section. In all, he personally destroyed ten posts, so enabling the company to seize ground from which the battalion moved out next day to take Sattelberg. Then, with Derrick promoted to lieutenant, came Tarakan in 1945. WX2672, as forward observation officer for the 2/7th Field Regiment, was nearby when Derrick was hit in the stomach and thigh but carried on for some hours. He died in hospital next day. Being with him was the most inspiring experience WX2672 had in the army: 'He was a born soldier (a warrior, really), left nothing to chance in training and was the ideal fighting soldier. The effect of his loss on the men was most poignant.' Derrick had served for five years, and he died in a campaign that many soldiers believed was unnecessary.

Yet sometimes it is the survivors who are most to be pitied. QX5634, a corporal with the 2/15th Battalion, was the Digger of legend: a lean 6 feet, a station hand from New South Wales. In North Africa in 1942 he ran ahead and personally disposed of three enemy posts a couple of hundred yards apart, using the bayonet, his boot, grenades, and a Tommy gun he picked up (first firing it and then swinging it, empty, as a club). His section thus got ahead, but QX5634 had killed fourteen men before his comrades caught up. He was awarded the Distinguished Conduct Medal and made a sergeant; and he survived the war. Yet

I would not go to another war after the way I've been treated since. I was twice wounded, and I'll never close my left hand again. I've had stomach operations, and all private doctors say I should be on an 80 per cent pension, but the Repatriation Board won't go above the

An Australian shadow falls fleetingly on a German corpse. For survivors, the mental shadows of such horror were often permanent

20 per cent I came out with. I'm 67 and I still think my stomach and nerves are due to war service. It's hard to forget putting the bayonet in one side of several men, and out the other, and bashing a fellow's brains out with a Tommy gun, which I had to do to stay alive and save the company from the machine-guns.

All sorts of respondents won medals, and for different reasons – the odd one well after World War II. 'Chas', a pearl diver and houseboy from Thursday Island, joined up in 1939 'to protect father, mother, brothers, sisters and country' and stayed in the army until 1961, meanwhile winning the Military Medal in Korea as a corporal. R. G. Scott, a young South Australian farmer commanding a troop of the 2/4th Armoured Regiment, was awarded the Military Cross in Bougainville for twice going ahead of his tanks on foot, and directing their movements and fire, so that enemy posts were destroyed and the infantry could advance. G. C. Bingham was a theological student who considered himself something of a pacifist, but he won the Military Medal as a sergeant in Malaya for leading a bayonet charge that freed 22nd Brigade headquarters from enemy pressure. (Not that it worked in the end; Bingham spent over three years as a POW.)

J. H. Burns was 19 and an apprentice baker in a small town on the River Murray. He lived not far from 'Diver' Derrick, in fact, and was also like him in that his father had served in

an original First AIF battalion, the 27th; the son went into the
2/27th. Burns senior, a captain, had been decorated in World
War I, and his son was awarded the Military Medal as a corporal in New Guinea, essentially in recognition of young
Burns's ability to keep up morale. Mention was made in his
citation of his courage at Gona where, until wounded, he
maintained wireless communication throughout an action;
but most of his citation was devoted to an earlier time in the
Owen Stanleys when he was one of a party cut off and forced
to take a difficult track, carrying several wounded men. For
ten days Burns worked untiringly, encouraging comrades to
keep going and keep carrying the wounded. Once comparatively safe from enemy patrols, the wounded were left in the
care of Burns and one other man while the rest of the party –
desperately short of food – went on. Through another ten days
Burns cheered the wounded, found food for them, kept them
comfortable in heat and flies, wet and cold. He gave them
talks on the Bible and any topics he could think up. Two men
died, and Burns scraped out graves for them with bayonet and
tin hat, before Papuan carriers arrived to take charge of the
remaining men. So gentle care, determined cheerfulness, and
talks on the Bible helped win a Military Medal for a baker's
boy grown quickly into a man.

NX4320 came from an inner-city area of Sydney, the son of
a tram driver. After a series of urban jobs as a junior, ending up
as a metal grinder in a pipe-fittings works, he was sacked at 21
and remained unemployed for six months or more. It is
instructive that the *Official History* describes him as a metal
grinder, not as unemployed, and that he was two of the things
that some respondents said characterised the worst soldier –
not only unemployed but also inner-city urban. He enlisted in
1939, partly to relieve his parents of the need to support him,
but basically because he felt that the Germans had to be
opposed. He took part in the first Australian action in North
Africa – the attack on the Italian fortress of Bardia – and there
won the Military Medal. His description of this baptism of
fire is not notable for flashy heroics, but for wide-eyed

wonder at what was going on, and the steadiness of those around him.

After dark on 2 January 1941 the 2/3rd Battalion moved out to an assembly area where, after a hot meal, we bedded down. At about 2 a.m. we were roused and served another hot meal, fortified with a tot of rum. Suddenly the orders came to prepare to move. Quietly the men assembled in their platoons, mostly seeking their closest friends. To barely audible commands the battalion began to move out along a route here and there defined by petrol tins perforated to allow a minimal light to filter through from hurricane lamps. The march seemed interminable. Abruptly the opening rounds of our artillery barrage burst upon our ears and I, for one, left the ground by two feet. Our shocked comments were drowned by the crashing of guns and whistling of shells passing over us. Out of the darkness came the order to halt. While the leaders sought the start line marked by service flannelette ('4 × 2' we called it), my straining eyes caught what seemed to be silent columns of blackness rising, hanging suspended and then falling. I considered the matter and then decided that they were Italian shell bursts exploding unheard under the din of our own guns. Instantly I distanced myself the regulation five yards from anyone else.

Lying down at the start line we noticed the abatement of our own barrage and the audibility of the enemy guns probing for us. In a while we could detect the methodical lifting of their range, and could almost anticipate the gunnery officer's commands ... Then for some brief moments their shells, with indescribable fury, were stamping the ground amongst us – odd silences being punctuated with startled comment, 'Jeez, that was close'. Then the range lifted and it was our turn to breathe freely.

We advanced when it was fairly light, and the widely spaced battalion made an impressive sight as it moved towards the Italian wire. With the movement, the enemy shelling increased. As a shell came my way a kind of automatic release in my knees had me flat on the ground with the OC's voice roaring, 'On your feet and keep moving.' A section on my left was suddenly obscured by a great gust of smoke and dust, and I despaired of anyone escaping, but they came marching steadily out, ranks unbroken. A blue light bobbed and floated across the battlefield, arousing wondering comment, 'Blimey, what's that?' Why should a tracer bullet drift so gently as to give the impression that one could reach out and catch it? And was it dangerous?

As we came in sight of the outer defences, we were a bit ahead of schedule, and the adjutant came dashing up in a carrier and told us to hold fast where we were. We went to ground. Almost immediately a projectile of unknown identity but of damaging size passed diagonally across the gap between me and my neighbour, uncomfortably close to my head and his feet. It was pursued by the now universal question, 'Blimey, what was that?'

The advance resumed, the OC called to me to go ahead and indicate the opening in the wire. In a very small voice I said, 'Who, me?' I was loath to leave the 'safety' of my comrades to mark an opening I could already see two or three hundred yards away, and even then secured by our sister battalions. He said, 'Yes. Those people you can see are prisoners' – as a small comfort to my fears. I increased my pace and headed for the opening, becoming more apprehensive about what was going on ahead. Hovering around the break in the wire was our friend the RAF Lysander observation aircraft, pursued by a pattern of shellbursts from the Italian ack-ack. I did not relish the thought of *that* curtain hanging over my head, then falling. Arriving at my marker's position, I was further discomforted by the sight of a rifle stuck in the ground by its bayonet, a helmet hanging on its butt. Beside it lay the body of one of the boys from the leading units, the first Australian killed in action I had seen. I kept moving about, rather superstitiously, but had the satisfaction of seeing a sliver of shell slice into the ground near me. That curtain *was* falling.

The company all up, and the line of advance settled, we set off towards our objective – still out of sight. We joined some men from a leading battalion sheltering behind a wall but, after too brief a stay, over the wall we went among an increasing hail of bullets. I have a vivid recollection of a burst of three bullets kicking up the dust from a spot where my foot landed an instant later. With the sun in our eyes, and thick dust and smoke rising, we began the approach to the final assault.

We moved into a small gully, up to the crest and there, across another gully and at the top of a slope, stood an immense sangar [a stone breastwork]. Without any instruction, it seemed to me, my platoon went to ground and opened fire. I emptied my magazine of ten rounds before I realised that I had not adjusted range and the bullets were striking low. Then the men rose and began to advance the 250 yards. I watched their deliberate calmness almost as a detached observer, and glowed with pride at belonging to such a company in our first battle.

From that point I have little recollection of what was going on to either side of me. The whole of my concentration was on getting there, and to the firing I was deaf. I saw Italians throwing handfuls of their 'tomato bombs' and, as our men came to grips with them, throwing up their hands in surrender. One of our boys, hit in the leg, hopped across our line of advance and sat on a rock. I asked if he was all right, and he answered, 'Go in and bayonet the bastards.' I said, 'Aw, you don't want to be too rough.' The sangar loomed up ahead and suddenly I found myself on top of it, and there were five Italians and a medium machine-gun in the position. I made some threatening gestures with my bayonet and, when they put up their hands, I jumped down and ran on into the inner ring of the sangar. The Italians were beginning to stream out in surrender now. One character gave me a moment of perturbation when he dashed out of his gun pit with a Breda light-automatic on his hip. I bailed him up and made signs for him to dump the gun. To my amazement he put it down . . .

NX4320 continued his story: the fort taken; separation from his section; attaching himself to another platoon sent out beyond the sangar to consolidate the position; lying behind a small rock to fire on a tank and having the rock shattered by an answering shot; thinking he was dying, wondering what his family would feel, and then lying doggo in case another shot did get him; fearing the tanks might run over him; a wounded runner moaning for water as he died; and after a long time the coast becoming clear. The Italian tanks were destroyed by artillery, at very short range, as they attacked battalion headquarters. Next day a soldier returned NX4320's identity discs, which were where he had lain. And when NX4320 went to look at his lucky stone, he found that the shell had pulverised it into bits ranging from gravel to 2 inch pieces, the fragments distributed in a perfect arrowhead where they had sprayed past his steel helmet and shoulders.

He said, 'Bullshit. What for?' when told that he was being put up for a decoration. Two signallers said that the OC and 2IC had discussed the day's activities and thought that everyone's performance had been worthy of a medal, but decided that NX4320 should be one of those recommended. An official account says: NX4320, 'very young and excited, ran as fast as he could, jumped on the wall and stood thrusting with his bayonet at an Italian machine-gun team. Another Australian close behind kicked the heads below with his heavy boots'.

Who was that other Australian? Who was the other man who stayed with the medal-winner J. H. Burns in New Guinea? Who marked the path for the Bardia advance with hurricane lamps in petrol tins? Who went far out to lay the flannelette for the start line? Who kept making those hot meals possible? How many of these men gained due recognition? As respondents kept saying, many more medals were earned than were ever awarded.

Health

Men's health was affected, though not always adversely. As far as their general health went, there were no complaints from 46 per cent of the respondents, including 12 per cent who thought that it had improved. But one-quarter of the men claimed that their health had deteriorated from general causes. Another 2 per cent specifically blamed the Middle East for poor health, and 14 per cent the tropics. Life in German POW camps ruined the health of 2 per cent, and 7 per cent attributed bad health to Japanese POW experiences. Half of the respondents therefore reckoned that war service had adverse effects on their general health. Most men had some kind of physical illness during their service, and 11 per cent recognised and admitted to serious psychological troubles – 'bad nerves' or worse. (Reading between the lines suggests a higher percentage.) The war in the Pacific produced a high proportion of the illnesses, both because of the proportion of men who served there and also because of the particularly difficult conditions.

If N.J.S., a shop assistant, felt a lot healthier in the army, the farmer WX12381 suffered badly during twelve months of isolation in Timor, as boots fell to pieces and supplies and medicines were almost nil. Another farmer, VX15269, seemed to harden physically as the war went on, yet the long-term effects on his health were bad. The young labourer NX170955 simply kept on growing up, his health good before and after service in the islands and Japan; but the young clerk R. S. Walsh, although discharged A1, had aged prematurely and was grey-haired at 26. The health of lorry-driver U. J. Yates improved because the army gave him prolonged treatment for his asthma. On the other hand, telephone mechanic NX28601 wondered why he was losing weight in the Pacific; he had in fact contracted tuberculosis, but had neither diagnosis nor treatment until after his discharge from the army. His comment was that 'war service carries more than ordinary risks for both participants *and bystanders* – it is not to be recommended'.

NX28964 emerged from the army impotent. Sergeant Clyde Cook became 'unable to love' after the death of his best friend, who was carrying out Cook's order. He could form no more close relationships and did not even know the names of two men who were killed after being under his command for a week. His frozen emotions, which could not be admitted, and his unresolved hatred of the Japanese affected all his human relations – including his 1954 marriage – for thirty

Port Moresby accommodation in 1943. A bit rough? It was luxurious compared with living farther up

years before he was helped to bring his 'personal war' to an end, and he knew that many others were still emotionally crippled, consciously or not.

Salesman VX38771 lost weight badly in New Guinea, where his isolation brought on serious depression. The clerk D. A. Welch – wounded and ill at Tobruk – dropped from 12 st 8 lb to 4 st 7 lb. 'Bega Dairyman' was thirty-seven times in hospital with malaria, dengue fever and nervous disorders. TX667 became deaf from gunfire and suffered a complete nervous breakdown. J. Arthurson was a veteran of the Middle East and Singapore (not a POW) who was toughened up in the army, but he wrote that many he served with were dead: 'Some of them died surprisingly soon after the war . . . In quite a few cases they couldn't adjust . . . so they drank themselves to death.'

Long lists of illnesses cropped up, sometimes complicated by injuries. M. J. Brincat's included haemorrhoids, bronchitis, dermatitis, dysentery, extreme nervous tension and damage to the right eardrum by gun blast. TX1450 had dysentery, dengue and sandfly fevers, malaria, back and neck troubles – and eight weeks in hospital having his face rebuilt after being bashed in Cairns by 1st Australian Corps provosts for being without a leave pass. (At the time he was a sergeant, a regular soldier and a Middle East veteran.)

But it was among the former POWs, particularly those in Japanese hands, that some of the worst cases appeared. B. H.

Holland's ills included septic sores, blast ear and whiplash from a shell, dysentery, vitamin deficiency, circumcision due to fungus on foreskin, malaria, scabies, beri beri, being in a coma for a week (cause unknown), cystitis, palpable liver (cause unknown; no treatment) . . . At 55 years of age he was classed as totally and permanently incapacitated. A.D. returned from Japan feeling sold out, bitter, and incapable of facing people – even his own family, for a day or two; a deep anxiety neurosis overlaid various physical illnesses.

J. G. Mellor suffered over a dozen serious illnesses, including cholera, while he was a prisoner on the Burma–Siam railroad. In 1947 he had made an affidavit for the War Crimes Commission that described also the severe and numerous bashings he and others endured at the hands of their guards. One man, weak from diarrhoea, was refused permission to break from work. Because he then got excrement on his shovel handle he was knocked unconscious, thrown on a fire, laid across a light railway track to be run over by a skip filled with rocks and, even after other prisoners intervened and pulled him from fire and track, still had half the load tipped on him. He died a few days later.

'Sydney Joiner' had malaria eighteen times, scurvy, dysentery, beri beri – 'every disease except cholera'. When the war ended (for other people; it never really ended for him) he was 'no longer of this world, literally about to die and more or less mental'. Coming in the nick of time out of the coalmines in Japan, he saw Nagasaki after the bomb and, forty years on, the horror of its total devastation still shocked him even more than the unspeakable barbarisms he had already seen and suffered.

Wounds and injuries

If, for the respondents, the worst place for illness was the Pacific theatre, wounds were more likely in the Middle East and the Mediterranean area. Nearly as many wounds were received there as in the Pacific, although only about half as many respondents served in the Middle East. With 47 per cent of their wounds received on the other side of the world, the respondents only slightly distorted the trend in the official figures: of all army wounds and injuries in action, 40 per cent were suffered in 'the war against Germany'. (Death was much more likely for Australians in the Pacific than in the European war, but that was because of the appalling death rate in Japanese prison camps; more Australian soldiers [7777] died in them than died as the direct result of battle in the region [7284].) Nearly one-quarter of the respondents were wounded, mostly once but sometimes twice or more times. Half of the wounds were serious, at least at the time, and 10 per cent of all respondents claimed permanent effects from their wounds.

NX139702 was not wounded in war, but claimed he had sustained a strained hand while answering the questionnaire. QX6945, a sergeant who served in the Middle East and Pacific, also escaped a wound, and he even questioned the whole aura around a war wound:

Why is it that a wound is proof of the fighting man? I sympathise with the wounded, but what about the poor bugger who has to see a whole campaign through because he happens not to be hit? The worst coward I knew was wounded, although it's a mystery how shrapnel could travel faster than he could. There are also comparisons like that of chaps wounded in the islands who were evacuated only after days or weeks, and those wounded in Europe after D-day who might be in an English hospital in an hour.

He had a point: there are wounds and wounds; some are happy shortcuts from service. Paddy Alford received flesh wounds in the leg at El Alamein; they were not serious, he said, just a soldier's dream. Later, though, he slogged on through the New Guinea campaign, so he knew also the strain and stress of day after day with no escape.

Men like S. W. Creed offered the strongest answer to QX6945's query. See Creed in Tobruk. 'Junkers 88' dive

For some Germans the last battle was over. Were they less fortunate than men who went on to other battles, and those who emerged crippled in body and spirit?

bombers come over in mass attack with a scream to produce terror in a moment and nightmares for life. There is the urge to run but no power to do so. Machine-gun bullets spatter the dust. A bomb . . . Its roar becomes silence . . . Then heat, stabbing pain, shoulders wrenching in sockets, tin hat stretching to the full length of the chin-strap before whacking back; blood, standing up, blackness . . . Later he finds insult added to injury: shrapnel tearing into his haversack has destroyed every roll of film. Later still he is invalided back to Australia and discharged. Later yet, disillusionment sets in as all the sacrifices in war seem to be frittered away by leaders still prepared to send the pride of youth to shed blood and die. 'And nothing will ever give back my former strength.' Old campaigners, though unwounded, can be reduced in health, suffer from nerves and know great disappointment; but others have wounds as well.

H.M.G. was unwounded, but had plastic surgery to his face after a truck overturned near Gona. He suggested that the questionnaire should have asked not only about wounds and illnesses, but also about the injuries suffered. He too had a point, since army figures show more cases of injuries and wounds out of battle (over 33 000) than wounds and injuries *in* battle (over 22 000). Still, there was the possibility of NX139702's strained hand to be considered and respondents often described injuries without prompting anyway.

'Tiger' Lyons was never sure whether he was wounded or injured at Finschhafen. He seemed to see something black across his nose before he fell, but others said later that he had simply fallen back and hit his head on a shovel. The injury was slight, so he did not argue. What was more troublesome was having been so 'bomb happy' after Greece and Crete that he no longer trusted his nerves; back in Egypt he was actually charged with being AWL (and got twenty-eight days field punishment), but he had been in the camp all the time, dodging drafts going up to the line at El Alamein. H. C. Halligan hit his head when he fell with a full pack as Japanese bombers passed harmlessly overhead. He was unconscious for a time, but was generally considered to have suffered only a bit of a scratch. It was years before a hairline fracture and brain damage were discovered, as he became epileptic. It was an accident with a grenade at Bathurst training camp that made K. M. Pitts partially deaf. T. A. Lawler's back was crushed while he was serving with a forestry company in Scotland, leaving him 'crook ever since'. Jumping from a train in Italy in an attempted escape while a POW left R. A. E. Conway with a badly dislocated right arm and a broken shoulder blade. During an air raid in New Guinea, part of a pile-driver fell on VX105607 (was it an accident or a wound?). It put him in hospital, where he several times became completely paralysed – and lived with the dread of the disability becoming permanent. Yes, there were plenty of injuries apart from wounds, and plenty that were a bit of both.

QX6794, an army driver, survived a moment in September 1943 that resulted in the virtual wiping out of 'D' Company of the 2/33rd Battalion, about fifty of its men being killed and sixty-two others maimed. Encumbered with all the ammunition they could carry, the men sat in trucks just off the end of a runway near Port Moresby, waiting to be flown into the

Markham Valley. An American Liberator bomber failed to become airborne and crashed 20 yards from the trucks. Bombs exploded, flaming high-octane fuel sprayed the vehicles, men became blazing torches and their own bullets, grenades and mortar bombs went off – rescuers also becoming victims of the fire and explosions. Another respondent, NX52013, was close by and heard, even amid the other din, 'the dreadful screams . . .'

Men charging around with clothes on fire would suddenly disappear as the grenades and mortar bombs they were carrying went off. Others, rolling on the ground, would give a quick jerk as their bandoliers exploded. We did our pitiful best, all the time with one eye on an unexploded 500 lb bomb, while horribly burnt men pleaded to be shot; and, as a medical man said to me not long ago, it would have been better so, rather than letting some of them die after weeks of excruciating pain.

A total of at least fifty-nine men died because of that crash; two US airmen walked out of the tail of the aircraft, but died of shock the next day. Such strict censorship was imposed on the incident that for over thirty years NX52013 wondered if it had all been a nightmare, until his psychiatrist hunted up verification of it. Repeatedly over the years the scene had returned to haunt his dreams. At first the recurring picture was blurred and grey, still and silent; but later it took on full colour, movement, sound and smell. 'I must stop here for a while,' he wrote, 'the thoughts racing through my head are unbearable, and I will cry if I keep going. After forty years, what a legacy.'

NX52013 himself was never 'wounded'. Who were the wounded? Who the unwounded? Who are the more to be pitied, the young dead or the young survivors carrying horror on into long lives?

There was a particularly bitter irony about some of the wounds men received after going out of action and into prisoner-of-war camps. It was while C.A.B. was a POW in Ger-

The surrender of the Japanese was important enough to one ex-serviceman to make him treasure this photographic record. But what had the war cost him? He brought the prints with him when admitted to Larundel Psychiatric Hospital

many that he was bombed by Allied planes, and lost a leg. But it was not so much on that grim twist of fate as on his liberation that he wished to dwell. Released by British troops, he was given white bread; and to one who had been four years a prisoner, it tasted like cake. Soon he was on a DC3 aircraft and seeing his first English girl of the war – a WAAF with lipstick, powder, short dress and beautiful legs. Her captain was from Adelaide, so she fetched him to talk to this Australian sergeant. 'It was the best day of the war.' In England he was 'on show' because what was left of his leg was covered with butcher's paper, the Germans having run out of bandages by that time.

F. A. Hillier was wounded by Chinese bandits. Taken as a prisoner of the Japanese to Hainan Island, off the Chinese coast, he saw many local inhabitants cheerfully executed by the Japanese. The day came for Chinese revenge, and they did not care if whites shared the punishment. Hillier was going out for road-building in a truck loaded to capacity with twenty-three POWs, armed guards, tools and supplies when it was ambushed by bandits whose arms included a machine-gun. About a dozen of the Australians and a couple of the guards made a break for the jungle, and some of them survived. The guards who stayed with the truck put up a stiff fight, but the bandits (one of them in a complete Japanese uniform) killed almost every man left. They jumped into the truck and ripped off Hillier's boots and belt – he was feigning death – and bayoneted him three times in the back in an attempt to make sure that he was dead . . . They did not succeed, and Hillier was rescued by a Japanese patrol.

In Bougainville, after a brush with the Japanese, QX35534 began carrying back the seriously wounded Q28077 – Private Sydney Stacey. He lost contact with some of the patrol but struggled on until the wounded man said he wanted to be carried no farther – but would someone visit his mother? QX35534 left him with two others (one of whom won the Military Medal for his part in the operation, and the other promotion to corporal), and set out for help. He wandered in a circle and into the Japanese perimeter, where he had to lie low. He was aware of the enemy by signs (bootmarks), sounds (wild-dog calls) and smell (excrement) that were of more use than the rifle he carried; but the Japanese were also aware that he was somewhere about. A barrage was sent over and he was hit in the eye, but he began to move after applying a makeshift bandage made from his beret. A low-flying Douglas aircraft that had apparently just dropped supplies gave him direction, and he judged the paths by the colour of the signal wires along them: yellow meant Japanese, brown Australian. So he made his way and got into the 9th Battalion perimeter only a split second away from being shot as a Japanese infiltrator. A few days later he was flown out, but the sight in the wounded eye was lost forever. Long before that, somewhere up the track and watched by a couple of helpless mates, Private Stacey had died worrying about his mother.

It was not unusual for hurt young men to think of their mothers. The highly cynical yet deeply sensitive 'Lawyer' described some of the action at El Alamein and spoke of wounded men – not in the brilliant action so often pictured, but in the confusion – calling in 'lonely little-boy-lost voices for aid, and I swear that more than one cried out "Mumma". Oh, mothers of these frightened little boys who so badly needed you then, how glad I am that you do not know about this thing . . .' And NX65735 spoke – by hearsay – of a lieutenant, 22 years old, who led a platoon attack on some advancing Japanese one night in Malaya, and halted them. The Australian platoon then returned to its position, but the lieutenant was held up by a fence, lost his bearings, and shouted for direction. No one answered. NX65735 maintains that it was the platoon sergeant's responsibility to reply, and rank cowardice for none within hearing to have done so. NX65735 may have been right, and certainly he seems to have been well informed, for he continued: 'The lieutenant was hit by a machine-gun burst, and died crying out for his mother.'

Some other wounds have been known to draw different

sorts of responses. R.F.B., an acting corporal, sport-mad and in
the company football team, was wounded at El Alamein. On
'Alamein night' he laid the tape for 'C' Company, and then
moved to his position as flankman for the battalion (2/17th).
They moved forward, R.F.B. with the Bren gun, and the next
thing he knew he was trying to get to his feet, falling, trying
again . . . Some time later two stretcher-bearers passed with a
wounded Italian, his stomach exposed. They dumped him in
favour of R.F.B., who spent months in hospital with a head
wound before being discharged medically unfit. He was
thankful to still have a head, but regretful at losing a tin hat
with a hole in it large enough to pass a Jaffa orange through;
he had tried to keep that as a good talking point. Later he was
told that when he was brought into the Regimental Aid Post
someone remarked that it looked like goodbye to R.F.B. A
mate then grumbled, 'So it looks like I'll have to take the
bloody Bren.' Another retorted, 'F—— the Bren. What about
our footy team?' Thinking on this, R.F.B. was touched by
their affection.

Prisoners of war

E. B. Shepley was wounded only in one way: 'in my pride
when taken prisoner by the Japanese.' Frank Chard, captured
by the Germans, regretted that the army had given men no
training to help them if they became prisoners: 'The Australian press had poured scorn on the Italians, and we were not
sure what they would say about us.' Another prisoner of the
Germans, G. R. Dwight, felt much the same: 'Being taken
prisoner was a great indignity. We had thought of being
wounded or even killed, but never of being captured, so we
were materially and psychologically unprepared, and had a
sense of letting the side down. It was years after the war before
some of us would willingly admit to having been POWs.'
   In one form or another the psychological problem of being
captives often affected men badly. QX7535, taken by Ger-

If Australians were left mentally unprepared for capture, it is hardly likely that the Germans were any more ready for it; but a lot of them were taken near El Alamein in 1942

mans and guarded for a time by cruel, trigger-happy Libyans, commented that 'the shock of surrender had a mind-numbing effect, and for some men it brought on quite severe bouts of retching and physical illness'. VX11480, wounded in Greece and taken prisoner while in hospital, thought his army career 'not very impressive: thirteen months training, nine days action, four years POW'.

The tragedy for one 21-year-old lieutenant (he and his in-separable companion were collectively labelled Bib and Bub) was that he became a POW in Malaya soon after his only engagement with the enemy, in which he felt that he had failed as a signals officer. The Japanese cut the signal wire to the forward company, and Bib blamed his inexperience for not better protecting the wire. Then he worried about his judgement in sending out to repair the wire the two men who had originally laid it; one of them was wounded in the attempt. He had sent a sergeant with them; should he have gone himself? Had he done wrong or right? Was he afraid or, as he hoped, just confused? Given the chance, Bib could have learnt from any mistakes he made, but he was denied that chance. Into the POW bag he promptly went, a secret agony in his heart because he believed that he had let everyone down – and for forty years he had been ridden with unconfessed guilt. Without it, he and those close to him 'would have led happier lives'. Bib might find comfort in the remark of J. G. Henderson, who served in the Middle East, Ceylon and New

Guinea, that 'many service personnel believe that they didn't do their best', and that he himself had to learn to live with a complex over finding out that he was 'no hero'.

As a lieutenant with the 2/30th Battalion, G. S. McLeod was captured by the Japanese in Singapore and always resented the army's failure to prepare Australians psychologically for coping with the Japanese – who, they had gathered, were totally inadequate little yellow men. The truth was a shock: the British defeat in Malaya was inevitable. What is more, instruction about the Japanese 'reverence for authority, concept of honour and casual contempt of death' would have helped prisoners 'understand the indignities soon to be heaped on them'. It said much for Australian adaptability, he thought, that prisoners managed to adjust as well as they did to captors who were philosophically so far removed from themselves.

The hurt pride of some prisoners was healed by attempted or successful escapes. It was the news of the Japanese bombing of Darwin filtering through to a German prison camp that prompted A. G. Baxter to embark on the first of his two escapes. He did not finally reach freedom (although he was planning a third attempt, with forged papers, when the war ended), but F. N. T. Brewer did make it. Brewer met his brother after several months in German hands, and they escaped together from Salonika and got back to Egypt, where Brewer (already a Military Medallist) joined a special British force formed to penetrate POW camps, contact underground movements, set up safe houses for escapees, establish routes into Greece and Yugoslavia for special personnel and equipment, and undertake 'special tasks as allotted from time to time (no clearance to elucidate these)'. He made three such trips before returning to normal duties in the Pacific.

VX19853 was not technically a prisoner at all, but was one of the many Australians who hid for months in the mountains of Crete, sometimes housed and fed by local people, sometimes living in caves and eating snails, until they received information about escaping. There were eighty-four men in the successful escape party, so it was well organised as well as

Respondent H.C.S. at last receiving proper treatment – even with (propaganda?) flowers – after developing tuberculosis as a prisoner of war and going down to 6 st 7 lb in weight; the Czechoslovakian farmhouse in which H.C.S. was hidden when he escaped; and a photograph, taken from a window in the house, of Allied POWs – at that stage apparently well clad – being marched past on their way from Poland to Austria

lucky. VX19853 then went on to the Pacific, rejoining his 2/7th Battalion. He served in this battalion for six years – less his six months in Crete. That had been no holiday, but with his wife and son he gladly visited those brave and friendly Cretans later. H.C.S., taken prisoner at Tobruk and sent into Poland, eventually escaped and spent the last months of the European war with Czechoslovakian partisans. But he was even then a sick man. Like the prisoner VX11480, who starved and slaved in factories and forests in 30 degrees of frost, H.C.S. developed tuberculosis; his illness began while he was still in the Polish coalmines.

VX26672 was taken by the Japanese on Ambon, but after six weeks joined a party of seven men who broke out and, helped by 'very brave Ambonese friends', hopped from island to island in small craft on a successful journey of about a thousand miles to Darwin.

My wife and I went to Ambon some thirty-five years later, to be met by some of the old Ambonese friends. We visited the war graves, and I walked past the plaques that spelt out the names of comrades . . . Even the bones of three hundred massacred men, whose intermingled remains in a mass grave could not properly be identified, each had a plaque: 'An Australian soldier known only to God.' I left with tears in my eyes. I shall not return.

That escape was organised by another respondent, Lieutenant W. T. L. Jinkins, of the 2/21st Battalion. He was awarded an MBE for the escape and the intelligence the party was able to supply. Alec Chew, who was of Chinese descent, was in the little group and several times had gone 'under the wire' at night with Jinkins as outside contacts and arrangements were made. Chew also answered a questionnaire, and his great regret was that his mate Ken Lawson felt too weak with malaria to join the escape. Chew still worried over whether he should have tried harder to persuade Lawson to come. He did not insist because he did not think the odds were in their

Italian soldiers not too depressed by being prisoners of war to perform some gymnastics for the camera

favour, but the odds were the other way and 'Smokey' Lawson died in captivity.

An escapee in Europe was E.K., a Catholic bush worker and the only child of a former bank clerk killed in action in France during the year E.K. was born (1918). He served with the 2/23rd Battalion in North Africa until captured in 1941.

The last thing I expected was to be a POW. We went into attack with a full company, about one hundred men, but three officers, several NCOs and twenty or so men were killed, another thirty wounded and taken prisoner, while ten just vanished. Only about twenty of us got back to our lines. We probably advanced too far in the attack, and we had to kill a lot of the enemy, but I understand we sent back over sixty prisoners. In position again, we were cut off, surrounded and pinned down by German automatic fire for two days. Then they sent in their tanks – and we had no option but to surrender.

The death all around E.K. obviously troubled him – 'we *had* to kill a lot . . . but . . . we sent back prisoners'.

Mad with battle, men do sometimes go on killing beyond what is necessary. Outraged by atrocities committed or believed to have been committed on comrades, some men will perpetrate their own cruelties in return. In deadly danger, with declining numbers on their side and loose arms lying around, men sometimes have to kill prisoners they can neither guard nor trust not to turn the tables. 'When the battle was over,' wrote 'Lawyer' of his part in El Alamein in 1942, 'the Bren-gunner said that a group of about six Germans put up their hands to surrender, but he didn't trust them not to play tricks like throwing grenades, so he mowed them down to be on the safe side.' W. G. Smith, with the 2/8th Battalion, said that before Tobruk in January 1941 his company commander's orders were to take no prisoners. Smith's platoon commander, Mick Dwyer, told them that it was a divisional order but none of them was to obey it. Nevertheless Smith knew of times when Italians under the white flag were shot or bayoneted.

R. H. Ferguson served in New Guinea with the 2/9th Battalion and then with the Australian New Guinea Administrative Unit. When his mates saw for the first time the result of some Japanese atrocities – two militiamen who had been tied to a tree and bayoneted – they swore they would kill rather than capture Japanese. Yet the men were in fact upset when a cook – 'practically a non-combatant' – grabbed up a rifle and shot dead a Japanese pilot brought in uninjured after crashing. Ferguson believed that the Militia's 5th Division held an inquiry after some members on Goodenough Island shot several Japanese survivors of the battle of the Bismarck Sea in 1943. S.T.B. too was saddened by the sight of captured and sick Japanese troops being ill treated by Australians. Savagery was not all on one side.

Sometimes blame was wrongly attributed. J. G. Henderson and his company found the body of Private M——, one of their mates, with the flesh cut from his thighs, and they thought that it had been done by the Japanese. On the same day or the next, they caught two men from Rabaul, whom the Japanese had brought over as carriers and who, throughout much questioning, insisted on declaring that they had cut off the flesh themselves because they were hungry.

Death and cruelty followed E.K. into Europe after his capture in Africa. Prisoners died. German soldiers were shot for desertion. He escaped from the Polish coalmines (expecting to

Top: *An official German photograph of Allied prisoners at a convalescent camp in Berlin. There (and in some other German camps at times) the conditions were good enough to make it almost 'a holiday camp' – even down to costumes for dramatic performances. Mostly the men in German hands were less fortunate, though not usually so badly off as those in Japanese camps*

Above: *Anton, a Czechoslovakian partisan leader; and Stefan, a 15-year-old member of the group H.C.S. joined after escaping from a POW camp in 1945*

be shot if recaptured), reached the Russian lines late in 1944, contacted a British ship in Odessa and was taken to Egypt and then home. It took him years to adjust mentally and he had persistent health problems. 'It was no picnic', he wrote. 'I think that any returned man who says he would like to go again did not see much the first time.' Then this ex-Europe prisoner generously added, 'But we were not as bad off as the POWs with the Japs'. One of those prisoners, 'Aide-de-camp', wrote that 'no one who was not on the Burma railway for eighteen months or more, and spent a total of almost four years under the savages who controlled the Japanese camps, has any right to comment . . .'

Some respondents had that right. About 4 per cent of the entire Australian army in World War II became POWs, but 12 per cent of the respondents were former prisoners, and 7 per cent had been in Japanese hands for several years. More than might have been expected, they were prepared to talk about it.

I.C.W. was Lieutenant-General Gordon Bennett's driver in 1940–41, and considered it to have been a privilege to serve and be made the friend of so courageous and inspiring a man, who was unjustly blamed instead of acclaimed for his escape from Singapore. I.C.W. – personnel officer with Griffiths Sweets before enlistment – went through four and a half years as a POW, including a time on the Burma railway.

The refusal by the Japs – brutal, sadistic, inhuman bastards – to allow Red Cross medical supplies to be distributed was a major factor in the death toll, particularly in Thailand. I once lay on bamboo slats opposite another hospital patient who had such shocking ulcers on his leg that the only way to save his life was to amputate at the knee. Next day all the sutures broke away completely, exposing the stump, which became infested with maggots. A week later he died. When we were moved south on the completion of the railway I discovered four small ulcers on my knee. I had the great good fortune to meet a mate who, when I told him of my ulcer worry, amazed me by producing one M & B [May and Baker sulphonamide] tablet, which I crushed and packed into the four small holes in my knee, before wrapping a palm leaf around it. Within a few days the ulcers had healed. Just one M & B was all that was necessary. If supplies had been made available up the line, many lives would have been saved.

One other thing saved I.C.W.'s life: thoughts of his family at home. 'As I lay on the ground at night I could conjure up an image of my mother, talk to her and feel I had a link that no Jap was going to break. I would hang on.'

J. G. Mellor's sworn evidence, supported by W. S. Ross and originally supplied for war crimes trials, described 'H' Force, formed from POWs on Japanese orders to help build the infamous railway.

The party comprised about six hundred Australian POWs who were told by the Japanese commandant that they were leaving Singapore because of the poor conditions there, and would receive better food and medical supplies in a new country. The men were selected on their physical appearance; though poor after many months of starvation, malnutrition and partly healed war wounds, they were the best of a bad lot. They were crowded into enclosed, steel goods-trucks for their long tropical journey. Their particular camp was Hell Fire Cutting, and their job was to hack and blast through the rock. Those provided with tents were no better off than those without, for the canvas was rotten. The Japanese quartermaster known as Puss in Boots diverted most of the food supplies to the Japanese staff quarters, but always carefully produced for senior officers' inspection papers showing that the food issued for prisoners had been consumed by them. Very few prisoners possessed footwear of any kind, and their cut and blistered feet made movement difficult on the stones. Those unable to walk were half-carried, half-dragged along by the fitter men, a terrible strain being imposed on both. No medical treatment was available, and The Silent Basher told the prisoners that sickness was a crime to be severely punished. Only those who collapsed and could not be kicked onto their feet – those with cholera, perhaps – were not forced to work. The continual beatings with

Lance-sergeant L. C. E. Cheal and friend 'somewhere in Malaya' in July 1941. Cheal was not so plump when he emerged from a Japanese POW camp

picks, shovels, bamboo poles, fists, boots, fuse wire and rocks were part of the general treatment meted out by guards over the whole of the Burma–Thailand railway. And to speak of the illnesses – dysentery, beri beri, malaria, pellagra, dermatitis, etc. – which prevailed would again be to repeat the story of all POW camps in the area.

At Hell Fire Cutting, when the three-minute fuses were lit for blasting, the prisoners had to hand in all tools, run to pick up two large rocks, stagger back across the area to be blasted, clamber up a steep slope and place the rocks on a path under construction. If the stones were not suitable, the prisoner was beaten and sent back to get another two. Only by some miracle were prisoners not killed in that repeated process – and these were men for whom every movement was an effort.

How badly Japanese and Korean guards and soldiers could treat living creatures, human or animal, had never passed from the mind of SX10941, a trainee teacher when he enlisted in 1941 for a war that was mostly spent in places like 'the Death Railway' and 'the Bridge on the River Kwai'.

In every victorious group there would be some whose behaviour left much to be desired, and no doubt there are nasty things in British and Australian history to live down. I haven't seen those things, but I have seen the Japanese. As POWs – soldiers who had surrendered – we were the lowest things possible, and were treated accordingly; but there seemed to be more to their behaviour than that. I have seen the Burmese police sergeant at Victoria Point hung by his hands while a fire was lit under his feet to make him talk. Each night he was dropped into the coals before being dragged to a kennel before a repetition on the morrow. He lived for three days. He screamed for two. I have seen Japanese cooks keep a hungry dog near the kitchen, feeding it just sufficient to keep it alive; the point of it all being to amuse themselves by tipping boiling water over it. I have seen Japanese soldiers bayonet a dog just to see how long it would take to die.

SX10941 hoped that education might be the answer to the Japanese problem.

'Medical Officer' would not complete a questionnaire, but he sent in a record he had written up in Thailand during 1943. In it he described a POW camp at Kanchanaburi.

Open ditch latrines . . . The camp could be smelt some distance off. So many men were sick that it was difficult to get working parties. In the monsoon the camp was a quagmire, yet some patients had not washed for a month. They had all been working on the railway . . . The camp was newly occupied and strenuous efforts were being made to improve it against Jap resistance and indifference. The term Jap includes Koreans. Death rate, 6–9 daily. Morale, remarkably good. The general ward had about 140 patients. Many of the men had only sacks for bedding to cover the hard irregular bamboos . . . Take one case of beri beri. Solely through lack of drugs his entire body became horribly swollen until the skin in both feet and one leg burst. The wounds became gangrenous before the last breath left his water-logged lungs. His spirit never failed. He had nursed men through a cholera epidemic.

Can you see this hospital? Before we left, all the available space for latrines (and there was a whole dysentery ward) had been used. The Japs would not shift camp, and they made us bale out a latrine all day to keep it in use . . . There were two lots of Japs. The first bunch was well-disciplined and reasonable. Also their sergeant dispenser used to send drugs to the camp. The second party were badly disciplined, diseased, physical wrecks and mentally deficient.

Naturally prison guards varied. W. A. Flowers recalled 'our only victory over the Japanese – when we played them basketball at Changi, under a Jap umpire too'. Brewery worker Tom Fardy often commented on the guards in a painstaking record he kept while working in factories in Japan. He even reported that late in 1943 the Japanese ordered them to keep diaries, which would be censored. The stamps of the censor appear on various pages of two small volumes, but if the intention was to use diaries as evidence of good treatment, the censor did not know what he was doing. (Perhaps he was like the guard spoken of by NX65735. The man understood English but not the vernacular, and so complained to a working party, 'You think I know fuck nothing. I know fuck all.')

No one died today, which is almost a record . . . [In ten days at the start of the diary Fardy had listed by name nine of the dead: Don Fraser, Wally Lewis, Bill Ashford, Dinny Connor, Tommy Power, Bob Farley, Doug Bowden, Ralph Cordorey, Eric Bell. But the death rate was not consistently so high. A list in another of Fardy's diaries gives fifty-nine Australians – including Lieutenant-Colonel A. E. Robertson – who died in that camp in about eleven months.]

Sgt Oaki [suddenly] wishes to be our friend . . .

Two apples on issue. I swapped one for a fish head at tea time.

Herb Lamb put in a report about the way the light duty men were made to work. Sgt Oaki found out and we thought he was going to do Boof and Commy. He had all the dog wallopers [guards] lined up ready . . .

Good fish head for tea tonight, though a bit high.

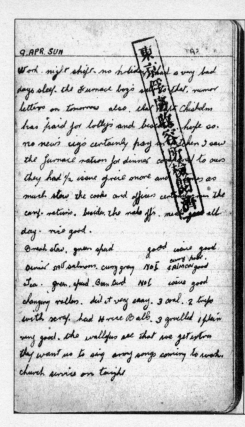

A page from Tom Fardy's POW diary (with Japanese censor's stamp) shows some of the tensions between prisoners. The Japanese guards (wallopers) appear this time in a good light

Boot inspection by Suzuki. Any man whose boots did not pass had to lick them. Nearly all in our squad had to do so.

In an earlier, uncensored diary Fardy gave a remarkable rundown on some of the guards.

Rabbit Ears (wears furs over ears during snow). Very dangerous. Has done most of the boys over. *Robin Hood* (wears green clothes). Very good. Will give you a fair go, but do not try to put anything over on him. Ex-soldier. *Happy*. The best we have. Has not been known to give anyone a slap yet. Has been good when we were out of smokes. Ex-soldier, Singapore. *Commercial Traveller* (always carries bag). Got to be careful with him. Will do you over if he thinks you are bludging, but has given boys a little weed to tide them over. *Churchill* (like his name's sake). Sticky beak about what and how we eat. Not bad. Has done several boys over. Got to watch him. *Monkey Face* (is like one). Very dangerous. Gave one man a hell of a bashing – over 112 slaps on the face – through a misunderstanding. Was sorry afterwards. Has done quite a lot over. *Osner*. Very dangerous. Has done over quite a few of the sergeants. *Homer*. Very good to boys. Always carries a bottle of iodine. Very concerned about sick. Does not like to see the boys dying so fast. Has cleaned up kitchen.

L. E. Le Souëf (an army medical service lieutenant-colonel, captured in Crete) thought that, broadly speaking, the guards from different nationalities tended to behave differently. He gathered that the Japanese were inclined to treat POWs much as they did their own troops – both were expendable. The Italians, he thought, were often frightened of the Australians and consequently became very difficult at times. It may have been some such twitchiness that produced bad blood between an Italian commandant and the Australian prisoners E. L. Milgate was with. Perhaps there was strain between the commandant and his garrison too, because the atmosphere was very tense all round at the time that two guards brought a photograph of the commandant to some prisoners decorating a concert programme. They asked if anyone could do something with it, although Milgate was never sure whether they meant an insulting cartoon or a flattering portrait. He decided on the latter and – being an amateur artist – worked on it with materials provided by the padre. He chose well. The commandant accidentally saw the finished study and was so delighted that he relaxed, threw a party and provided the prisoners with a case of wine. Immediately the strained and dangerous atmosphere evaporated. Milgate brought the photograph home, and after the war received a gift of books from the commandant – while the ex-POW was living in a garage because of the housing shortage, and losing rehabilitation possibilities because of chronic pain in a frost-bitten foot.

Le Souëf concluded his discussion of national characteris-

From this photograph of the commandant of an Italian POW camp, Australian prisoner E. L. Milgate painted a portrait that so pleased the commandant that the whole tone of the camp changed for the better

tics by saying that the Germans simply regarded themselves as the master race and others as their servants or slaves – and they treated the inhabitants of each occupied country differently, the Russians getting the worst. 'Lofty' (captured off Greece and eventually freed by Russians, who treated him well) was appalled by the Russian compounds he saw as a POW:

inmates starving to death or dying of typhus; the Germans afraid to enter the compounds because of disease and cannibalism among the occupants; attempts to keep them back with stockwhips when urns of cabbage and potato soup were placed inside the gates, yet still the urns rushed and overturned so that prisoners went on hands and knees to lick soup from the ground.

Yet 'Lofty' found that the German soldiers who captured him abided by the Geneva Convention, although the SS troopers were a different matter.

Another prisoner from Crete, N. W. Pritchard, contrasted the elite paratroopers (soon to die on the Russian front) with the deteriorating types who progressively took charge of

them, prison guards being the very worst. Though he became
so hungry that he once took a crumb from an ant to eat, his
group did sometimes get Red Cross parcels – but there was no
Geneva Convention to protect the Russians; the Germans
treated them like animals, and vice versa.

NX3251 became very friendly with some Russian prisoners, who were getting neither better nor worse treatment than
he – a rather tough nut – was getting himself. He also had
differing experiences with guards. He saw courageous Greek
civilians bashed or shot as they tried to pass food to marching
POWs. He lost his groundsheet to Germans who (helped by
two Australian WOs – later courtmartialled) were stripping
all they could from prisoners. He was in a camp where even
dysentery patients were often shot at, and some killed, as they
tried to get to the lavatories at night; and he was once among
those held in damp cattle-stalls, in bitter cold and with little
food, so that tuberculosis began to develop among the men,
while each week the SS troopers searched and wrecked the
place. NX3251 was in that camp because he would insist on
escaping; but once, after an appalling train trip that had sent
some prisoners 'peculiar', they had arrived at a camp where
they not only got Red Cross food, but were also put on double
rations for a couple of days by the German officer in charge.
Then NX3251 joined a work party in the Munich railway
yards, and that had all sorts of advantages – even better than
double rations. They once persuaded a guard that one of their
number, who had got onto some champagne, was suffering
from malaria, and they were allowed to wheel him back to
camp in a barrow.

G. R. Thompson was lucky to survive both the first and the
final stages of his European imprisonment, which began with
captors of a very mixed sort.

The German paratroopers treated us well, but they handed us on to
third-grade men. On the way to camp, five soldiers robbed us of
anything of value, like watches. I had a gold ring sawed off my finger
with a knife that cut so deep into the flesh that I have a scar to this

day. They seemed to be working themselves up to shoot us, but a paratroop sergeant appeared and seemed likely to shoot one of them for a few minutes. Then he escorted us to camp and wished us luck . . .

Towards the end of the war I went on the death march from south-west Poland to Hanover. We were four and a half months on the road, with probably millions of refugees fleeing from the Russian army. We walked a thousand miles, and thousands must have died. When released by Americans I weighed just over 6 st.

Such marches were often strafed by Allied planes – seeing columns of moving figures in German territory . . . NX3251's last march was attacked, and Australian POWs were killed. R. W. E. Werry, however, was able to add that 'once the Allies had established who we were, we had constant fighter protection until the Americans met us'.

As a prisoner in Japan, C. W. Marsh was gunned by Hellcats from American aircraft carriers for a few days after the first atomic bomb was dropped – the bomb that saved his life and the lives of many thousands of Americans who would otherwise have had to invade a still strongly defended Japan; the bomb that resulted in his handling at Hiroshima railway station many severely burnt women and children . . . He refused to bear grudges or condemn either side, and had visited Japan three times since the war. 'Some of my POW mates, who spent their three and a half years in other parts of the Far East, still can't understand, but they only saw the guards – the lowest type of their race.'

The behaviour of prisoners towards each other was without doubt remarkably good on the whole, but it too varied. According to Corporal Werry, 'In four years captivity I only saw *one* fist fight between our men. There was an unbreakable bond'. Gunner J.S.D., a prisoner of the Japanese, wrote that 'the humour created in the situation made endurable the seemingly unendurable, and in the midst of tragedy and fear there was the inspiration of daily acts of courage, generosity where selfishness might have been expected, and compassion in many whose physical demeanour belied the inner sensitivity'. But Sergeant Fardy's diary notes some of the other side, although it does not always make plain who gave the resulting punishment.

There was four tins of Bully [beef] stolen from Captain Chisholm's room. When we came home we had to stand at attention till the man confessed. We had no tea. S—— was thought to be guilty, but was let go. I—— was next on the list. After standing up all night he confessed. He was slapped by every man on parade a week later. B—— pinched cigarettes off a chap, they were found in the leg of his pants. He got sent to the guardhouse . . .
A lot of Bully was stolen from the chaps by their mates. F—— was caught eating Lewis's tin in the lavatory. He was reported. A lot went off while we were at work . . .
R—— admitted to Red Cross thefts, tried to commit suicide and was put in the guardhouse. They made him stand out in snow in underpants only. He was brought back in a very bad way . . . [A week later he died of pneumonia.]
Had pkt cigs stolen from me this morning.
Fight between P—— and T——.
Boot inspection tonight. X—— pinched mine and dubbined them. Left me in a hole, but I found them by accident. Don't know how he got on.

As 'Aide-de-camp' asserted, outsiders can hardly condemn anyone. Fardy weighed under 60 lb at that time (having enlisted at 140 lb), and all those men were in a similar state. Temptation must have been overwhelming to men half crazed with hunger and weakness, fear and despair, illness and the craving for comfort. The wonder is that more did not break.

In a European camp, G. R. Thompson witnessed both solidarity and depravity among prisoners. A German spy was unmasked among them and the ten NCOs in the compound – Thompson was one, as a corporal – drew lots to decide which of them would kill him. That duty done, the German was buried so cunningly that, although all camp inmates were stood out on farmland in the snow for two days and three nights while the camp was virtually demolished, the SS never found a trace and none of the ten men gave way. It was self-defence, and it was group loyalty.

But the camp's Glasgow Compound was evil, made up of about 150 Scottish criminals and thugs, handy with a razor. (At Camp VIIIB, NX3251 also encountered a razor gang of British toughs, possibly the same group, although he thought that it was dominated by a Londoner.) The Glasgow Compound lived in comparative luxury, part of the gang working in the cookhouse and being hand in glove with the Germans in such rackets as pilfering cigarettes and chocolate from Red Cross parcels. Two fresh-faced English lads were put into the compound, where they were homosexually pack-raped and made to serve the leaders. Telling the whole story to the Anzac Compound when they were detailed to bring food to it, the lads were kept there and the Glasgow Compound was watched. It happened that the guards were much reduced due to Germany's need for soldiers, and more lenient because they could see the writing on the wall for the Fatherland, so it became possible to move at night from compound to compound. The crunch came when an Australian was slashed on the face by one of the Glaswegians. Sergeant Alan Snedden (a district cricketer from Western Australia, and brother of Sir Billy) led an attacking party that night, with two results: within four days the Glasgow Compound was moved from the camp, and everyone received a 50 per cent increase in their rations.

Thompson partly explained the rapes this way: 'as the Scots were well fed they had sexual desires; no one in most compounds spoke or thought about sex, only food.' QX7535 said the same thing: 'In European POW camps there was of course no sex, and when food got so short no one even thought about it.' From experience in the Japanese area, SX10941 also commented that for years the prisoners thought of food above all; without more food it was impossible to enjoy anything much. Nevertheless some respondents spoke of homosexuality among prisoners of war. 'Artillery Captain' won the MC in Greece before captivity ('forward observation officer and proved useful'), and after four years came home to an 8-year-old daughter ('who did not like having another boss'). As prisoners in Germany, he said, 'we had cases of homosexuals really falling in love. In the interests of general happiness we re-arranged some room occupants and eventually got all homos in one block'. Of Changi camp in Singapore, W. A. Flowers remarked, 'Homosexuals were about, and what's more did a trade – only to be expected, I suppose'. Ernest Badham, captured in Java before being sent to the Burma railway, claimed that 'homosexuality was evident in many cases in POW areas', even adding that 'doctors said the rice diet had much to do with it'. Angry and scornful denials of more than one thing in those assertions are to be expected, but they were made and would be as seriously defended.

At least when conditions were comparatively good, and POWs had some freedom from barbed wire, starvation and pain, heterosexual activity occurred. While 'Lofty' was a POW he 'had sex with a Polish girl, and a friend had it with a German girl, on a number of occasions'. WX1042 was more expansive.

For prisoners of war, Ray and I were well off after a while. We were daily marched from our camp to the *Ashphaltwerke* to prepare bitumen mix for road repair. The mix was transported to the road works in two tank-like trailers pulled by a tractor. Hans, a German worker, drove the tractor, and Ray and I rode on the trailers to apply the brakes as necessary. It could be a cold job, but we'd just been supplied with clothes and food parcels by the Red Cross.

Ray somehow found out where the brothel was situated. I don't know how. Maybe he had an instinct. After weeks of negotiation, Hans agreed to have a mechanical failure outside the establishment. We paid him the fifty cigarettes he demanded, and on one of our return journeys he organised a breakdown simply by closing off the gas bottles. While he grabbed a spanner, Ray and I ran in. Half a dozen men of the *Afrika Korps* stood there, talking to some girls. For some reason we hadn't expected that. Two of the biggest strolled over.

'You're not German?'

'No.'

'Not Dutch?'

'No.'

'So. What are you?'

'Australians.'

'Have you been in Tobruk?'

'Yeah. We've been in Tobruk.'

He stuck his finger in his mouth and drew a wet outline on the table. It was Tobruk harbour. Dropping an extra large blob of spit outside the perimeter, he said:

'We were here. Where were you?'

'We were outside too. We took Tobruk. From the Italians.'

'Oh! The Italians!'

His eyes rolled upwards. His hands were raised as if to implore Heaven's forgiveness that the Fatherland should have associated itself with such an ally. There followed a discussion, in broken German, on the failings of Italy in general and of its soldiers in particular. Suddenly one of them broke off in the middle of a sentence.

'Do you men want a woman?'

'Er, yes.'

'Blonde or brunette?'

Ray doubled up with laughter. 'What is it?' woofed the *Afrika Korps*. 'Jeez,' said Ray, 'we haven't been near a woman for over two years. Any colour will do.' A roar of laughter, and one of the Germans turned with two fingers up and a bellow for two women.

I won't recall much else, except a woman's uncontrollable laughter as she lay on a bed waiting for action while one Australian hero peeled off army boots and socks, blue worker's overalls, battle-dress, pullover, grey flannel shirt (oversize), long woollen underpants . . .

Ray and I met at the top of the stairs, worried about Hans lying under the tractor in a snowstorm.

'How much did you give her?'

'A two-ounce packet of tea. And I got five marks change.'
'So did I. God bless the Red Cross.'

Neither sex nor Japanese guards caused as much trouble to WX6691 at Changi as British military police and a British colonel did. WX6691 claimed that he only once saw Japanese in his part of the camp because they had largely delegated the control of prisoners to the British and Australian officers. So it came about that he was charged by Red Caps with being outside the wire they 'policed to the letter', and was subsequently sentenced by the English colonel to ninety days solitary confinement. His own colonel and several other officers, including a chaplain, interceded for him and managed to have the sentence reduced to forty-two days. So WX6691 thought there were good and bad officers.

His story raises again a matter mentioned in the last chapter: the attitudes to officers developed by POWs in Japanese hands. From the 137 respondents who had been long-term POWs in Germany, and the 271 who had been in Japanese custody, it emerged that the latter were *less* likely to say that relations between officers and men were good – 51 per cent (Japan) to 59 per cent (Germany) – and *more* inclined to describe them as poor – 4.1 per cent (Japan) to 1.5 per cent (Germany). The trend is clear without bothering about two other categories, mixed and only fair. Part of the reason might be that in Europe officers and even most NCOs were held in separate camps from the men. 'We had no commissioned officers or warrant officers in our stalag,' wrote G. R. Thompson, 'and a minimum of NCOs. They opted to go to their own camps.' But in places like Changi, as WX6691 illustrated, the Allied officers rather than the Japanese gave the direct orders, and they were in the camp to do it. NX65735, a prisoner on Blakang Mati (Singapore), complained bitterly – almost obsessively – of 'the wide gap between officers and men' and the officers' readiness to pamper themselves and punish other ranks. Tom Fardy, in his diaries, recorded mixed reactions as the weeks passed.

Bill Latham was exceptionally handy to us. He stood up for us . . .
and got us in out of the bad weather as much as possible. The only
mistake he made was to have his favourites, encouraging the Nips to
reward some as 'No. 1 diligent workers'. I was never very diligent
and never will be.

The officers are certainly doing their bit to keep the camp running
smoothly.

The officers ought to be ashamed to look the men in the face. The
rations they get is a damned disgrace. Tonight they had their stew
bowls overflowing as usual, but we have the same bowl half
full.

Signalman J. M. Eddy, who worked on the Burma railway,
firmly insisted on relations between all ranks having been
good. QX17835, a lieutenant who became a POW in Malaya
('through no fault of the AIF or myself') and who also worked
on the railway, maintained that relations between all ranks
were not only good but also *had* to be good – 'survival
depended on it'. J. G. Mellor gave an instance: it was Lieutenant Mansfield who hurried to the scene when 'Hunchback'
tried to kill a prisoner already knocked unconscious, and
Mansfield kept intervening even though twice viciously
beaten himself. Driver and despatch rider M.R.L. was not
going to complain about officers, especially those who were
doctors and chaplains. Some of his quick notes were: 'To Siam
on the Burma Railway of Death. 180 miles forced march. The
courage of all involved. Doctors with nothing to help them
performing amazing operations. Padres with their love of
God trying to give to all, no matter what religion. They were
men.' He knew he was very lucky to 'get home to good old
Aussie and a Sargent's meat pie', carrying with him a record of
the 'grand effort' made by the cooks for Christmas Day 1943,
and an order of service for the Festival of Nine Carols conducted by Padre Duckworth, an Englishman and ex-cox for

Cambridge University – 'a wonderful experience enjoyed by all under those shocking conditions'.

So some of them came home. G. R. Thompson, returning from Europe, was very nervous and drank heavily for five years, along with many mates. They thought they were forgotten while the ex-Japanese prisoners 'got the goodies'. L. E. Le Souëf returned to be met by men from his old unit ('much appreciated') and to begin again as a consultant surgeon. He remembered it being said that POWs from Europe were more difficult to rehabilitate because they were fitter than those from the Far East: 'As an observation only, and not a criticism, it was said that men from the Japanese camps were so down physically and mentally that they accepted what was done for them with greater gratitude.' It might have been so, or perhaps much depended on the individual and on the time he needed to find his feet. 'Lofty' returned from Europe to drink heavily and 'over-indulge in all things' for a while, but finally married his prewar girlfriend (then a widow with two children) and developed a close-knit family and a successful career. Tom Fardy got no assistance; he just went back to Toohey's after release from Japan, but found it 'a bit hard' to settle. R. W. E. Werry came back from Europe to drift rather aimlessly until he and his wife, dissatisfied with their lives, became practising Christians. Others, having survived captivity in either theatre, never really survived postwar Australia, never really became free.

In his wartime logbook, while a prisoner in Europe, Captain R. A. E. Conway wrote out his thoughts in an attempt to prepare himself and others for a POW's return. This is the gist of his meditation:

We are not returning to the same Australia. How many and how drastic the changes, we do not know, but we will be sceptical about them. You will find us cynical in many respects. You must be prepared to find us rude. Being enclosed in an all-male camp leads to frankness and swearing. You will find us moody, easily elated and easily depressed. We will lack small talk. We will want to sit for hours and read old papers and magazines. We will not eat as much, due to the shrinkage of our stomachs. We will want delicacies, and as little out of tins as possible. We will want to go to parties, but won't be able to stand them for long. We might be shy of the opposite sex and awkward through trying to remember our manners. We will have the habit of giving our opinion on any subject under the sun. Used to routine life, we will get annoyed if this is put out. Little things may anger us very much – we ask you to forgive this. One very good thing is that few of us will ever take things for granted in future, and we will appreciate what our families and friends do for us. We will be like convalescents. But do not try to fuss over us and, if we do not want to do a thing, do not press us.

A prisoner of the Japanese might have written much the same.

One need of most POWs, whether in Europe or the Pacific, was so simple that it might never occur to non-POWs, and the prisoners themselves might not have fully realised it. But N. W. Pritchard found it out even before he got back to Australia. 'I was flown to England and, stepping from the plane, was hit by something I had not known in four years of living in stench: fresh air.'

11 • SOLDIERS GOOD AND BAD

What background produced the most effective soldier? It is a thorny question that needs careful handling. About 13 per cent of the respondents recognised the difficulties by either dodging the question altogether or replying that they did not know. A few men shrewdly pointed to some of the thorns: any answer depended on what was meant by 'effective' and 'soldier', what sort of service was required of him, and at what level.

V.P.J., a corporal with advanced ordnance (supply) depots, preferred ex-storemen. 'Artillery Colonel' wanted men with enough education to handle technical equipment, as well as the ability to cope with stress. N. K. D. McGrath, a signals NCO, said that ex-clerks seemed naturally fitted for communications work, while schoolteachers and scholarly types often made good instructors or filled higher command positions well. 'There was so wide a diversity of roles in the army', he continued, 'that it was possible to fit almost anybody into a slot.' N185992 carried the argument to an even pricklier conclusion.

A chap at a recent reunion was saying, 'A lot of fellows reckon they were in the army in World War II, but most were never really soldiers. They were doing a work function, in uniform and even on the other side of the world, but they were never soldiers.' The man who said that had been highly respected by his mates, a twice-wounded Bren-gunner. And he was right. The number of people required to maintain one man in the firing line is astronomical. I imagine it was worse for the US army, but the Jap travelled light and would have had considerable advantages over us.

The points have to be taken, although it would be dangerous to make much of them at *some* reunions.

Most respondents took 'effective soldier' to mean a useful frontline serviceman of not very exalted rank, an infantryman or someone closely associated with the infantry, in a battle or other very testing situation. In that case the background of the effective soldier was sometimes seen as rural: 18 per cent selected the countryman only, compared with 4 per cent who chose the townsman with equal exclusiveness. 'Most men were from the country in the few AIF infantry units I knew. I have no doubt about the most effective soldiers being countrymen, and the least effective coming from the poorer urban areas of Sydney and Melbourne', wrote QX16129, an infantry training officer from a mixed rural and urban background, who had to admit that he hardly heard a shot fired in anger throughout the war. NX65735, also from a mixed background, but a private in Malaya and then a prisoner of the Japanese, was one of the few who chose townsmen as the best: 'Country soldiers were too passive and took too much from their officers. The best came from the city – and the closer to the slums the better.' If those two respondents were to meet, they might have a bitter argument, and would need to define their terms.

Yet, to this point, the vote favoured the countryman. And a further 10 per cent of the respondents specifically nominated men from the country for inclusion among the best, along with certain types from the town. So, with a total of 28 per cent giving the countryman a special and favourable mention, he scored very well. It is not hard to see why that should have been so – quite apart from a slight tendency for countrymen to vote for themselves.* Respondents spelt out some of the

---

* Nevertheless, although countrymen were a little more ready than townsmen to nominate the rural man as the best soldier, most men from the

advantages of a rural background; yet, having done that, they often wandered on to write of non-rural men who were just as effective.

In the end, indeed, the vote did *not* go to the countryman. He was widely recognised as being good, but the final weight of opinion among respondents favoured a variety of backgrounds – wider than rural Australia, as wide as Australia itself. Listen to some of the respondents musing.

> The most effective soldier is one who does his job well according to the needs of the time, be it as an individual or part of a team. Irrespective of his origin, or whether he be an enlisted or conscripted man, the all-purpose most effective soldier must be a very special man. Personally I leant towards the countryman of around 23 years of age and upwards. He had many natural advantages in New Guinea – an understanding with nature, a quick eye, good hearing, an acute sense of smell. He was alert to the movement of birds and animals, and was quick to learn the ways and habits of local people. Most, with practice, could move through jungle and tall grass with quiet ease. They were not afraid of their weapons – often, from early training, liking particular weapons – and they were confident in using them. They had a good sense of direction. And yet the most effective forward scout I knew was a man who picked himself for the role and came from suburban Sydney. This remarkable 19-year-old militiaman positioned us right time and time again. And, strangest of all, he would not – could not – fire a shot to defend himself even when, as happened once or twice, his very life seemed to depend on it. God saw him back to Australia [N180258].
>
> Obviously a bush worker used to hard physical conditions, handy with a rifle and tools, used to being in the open in all weathers, and able to walk long distances over rough terrain is going to have advantages – certainly in the initial stages – over

country (about two-thirds of them) did *not* single out their own type for special mention.

Regimental aid post at the foot of Mt Prothero, New Guinea. It was terrain that tested men from all backgrounds

the bank clerk living at home, with his mother making his bed, washing his clothes and getting his meals . . . But it would be reasonable to assert that any man who in civilian life had been an orderly citizen, proficient and conscientious in his work, would make the grade in the AIF. What was basically needed were the elements of education (the three Rs), enough sense to comprehend training, the ability to work in a group and get along together, a stable temperament and a readiness to accept discipline [N. K. D. McGrath].

If you mean by 'best' a fighting soldier, anyone brought up in the bush . . . Yet, thinking about it, that's not correct, because we had a hell of a lot of city fellows who were splendid soldiers. Our 2/48th Battalion had a mixture of country and city blokes. The country chaps were all very fit and strong, and had already learnt to live off the land, and so on. They didn't really need much instruction or training to become good soldiers, but they might be a bit slow up top. Most of the city blokes were not so fit, but they were a lot smarter. The shrewdest and toughest were the fellows who had been brought up as juveniles in the city dead ends and then gone to the bush in search of work. They usually ran the swy schools . . . [D. H. Adams].

The thorniness of the problem was repeatedly shown by the same type of man being chosen by different respondents to illustrate both the good soldier and the bad one. The form of the question itself – which was 'What peacetime background do you feel produced the most effective soldier?' – was sharply criticised sometimes. VX3511 wrote, 'It depends on what you mean by "soldier", which is not the same thing exactly as "fighting man". The best fighting soldiers were from the bush or the slums, but – oddly – bank clerks and teachers were almost always good'. B. A. Brown took a swipe at the question and at the countrymen: 'Your meaning is obscure. However, city types were by far the best soldiers; they had a "group" background and worked as a team. Generally, country boys were least effective, tending to be loners and suspicious of city slickers.' Brown commented as a townsman (a potter) and from four years experience in Australia and the Pacific, in five different units as a militiaman and member of the AIF.

The postal worker Peter Wellington was of a very different opinion. He considered the question to be 'loaded' – liable to blow up into an argument – and he included among the best the active sportsman and the man 'from a well-brought-up family, of reasonable education', but he put high on his list 'a rural background'. R. A. Aitken might want to debate some points with Wellington. As a commando sergeant, Aitken found that a bush background 'was not necessarily what mattered, despite popular views', and that 'nationally known sportsmen did not have a good record' in his original unit. Intelligence combined with 'ability to obey stupid orders' proved more important, and the best men were often bank clerks, civil servants and tradesmen.

Ernest Badham was another who found the question 'very difficult'. Perhaps country boys were 'more adaptable', but 'in some cases shop assistants were as good as any'. W. C. MacAdam certainly wanted to include countrymen among the most effective, but insisted that blue-collar workers generally should also be listed. VX26672, who rose during the war from private to major, was one more respondent to move far beyond the men from the country in debating who was best.

As an infantryman with the limited experience of one brigade and, in particular, one battalion with attached troops, I believe the most effective infantry soldier (front line) was perhaps the unsophisticated farmer boy – possibly because in a volunteer infantry battalion there is always a preponderance of ex-farmer boys. It is the country boy's personal tragedy that he has all the basic qualities for an infantryman. He was more easily disciplined, perhaps more self-reliant, and had a stabilising effect on other members of his platoon. With 'farmer boy' I include small-town boys generally – brought up to hunting and shooting.

Very effective infantrymen also came from the big cities, usually from middle-class to lower middle-class stable families, boys of limited educational qualifications. Officer ranks, initially filled by ex-militia (peacetime) men, were often very dedicated; they were mostly private-school boys nurtured in traditions of duty to their country and empire. There were also exceptions – excellent officers coming from less privileged backgrounds, especially as the duration of the war extended.

What defined a countryman anyway? VX26672 wanted 'country town' included in 'country', which was perfectly reasonable but demonstrated the problem of definition. He himself grew up on a farm, yet by the time he enlisted at the age of 27, with some higher education and a £6-a-week position, he saw himself as a townsman. QX16129 enlisted at 23 as a university graduate and articled law clerk in the city, but still thought of himself as a countryman because his father was a farmer. Was either of them quite what he claimed, really the one thing or the other? What was WX5094? His father had been the sanitary man for a town council, as well as a wreck from World War I, and WX5094 had been very poor, a street urchin, a trouble-maker at school and a seller of newspapers and boronia to help out at home. He had worked in shops and factories – and been unemployed – in town, and he had been a farm labourer and a member of the Australian Workers Union. The backgrounds of all three men, however different, were similar in their mix of urban and rural experiences. With 19 per cent of the respondents actually saying that they came from too mixed a background to be labelled either town or country only, and with question marks hanging over many of the rest, it becomes very difficult to categorise a lot of men anyway.

NX3251, a true countryman turned artilleryman, wrote of the infantry that although 'a good, practical countryman was hard to beat in action, the 2/1st Infantry Battalion was mostly made up of city men and was an outstanding unit, so it's difficult to make any judgement between backgrounds'. There were many 'city' battalions, very different from those like Peter Wellington's predominantly rural 2/19th – 'The Riverina Mob'.

Take the 17th Brigade and its three battalions as an example. Two respondents disagreed somewhat on their composition. In his published memoir *Not as a Duty Only*, 'Jo' Gullett described the 2/6th Battalion as mainly country, but respondent J.W.B. thought it 'a rather snob unit with a lot of men who had been earning £5 a week or more in the city and suburbs'. To Gullett the 2/7th was mostly suburban, but J.W.B. would have called it *outer*-suburban, made up in the main of men from semi-rural places like Dandenong in 1939. The 2/5th was from industrial Melbourne according to Gullett, but J.W.B. argued that although this Scottish regiment's headquarters might have been in working-class Richmond, most of its original members were from middle-class suburbs. Another complication arises there – the possible changes in a battalion's composition over the course of the war; but, whoever had the rights of it about the original members, J.W.B. and Gullett agreed on two things: neither man chose the countryman – the one not at all, and the other not exclusively – as the best soldier, and those 17th Brigade infantrymen were *not* overwhelmingly from the country. Of the Australian infantry generally, whatever was true of some battalions, it is highly improbable that most were rural in origin.

Because of this need to run to and fro among the possibilities, it is no wonder that A.R.M. became quite caustic

about the whole issue – a false one in his estimation, and that
of many others. A.R.M. was a Sydneysider, definitely a
townsman. He was also a sportsman, a mechanic (actually
managing a garage and towing service) and aged 26 when he
enlisted to serve in various units in Australia and the islands
and rise steadily from private to lieutenant. For him the question on the background of good soldiers was 'impossible,
almost inane (sorry). "Effective" soldiers came from all walks
of life and from every social level: farm labourers, schoolteachers, bus drivers, shearers, clerks, squatters, shop assistants, solicitors, carpenters – the list is endless and one can't
generalise'. William Gairey, a WO II with an artillery survey
regiment, agreed wholeheartedly with A.R.M. and gave the
question up: 'There were too many possible reasons for effectiveness to be named.' R. W. McAdam left a grocer's shop to
join the Army Service Corps – the right man in the right place,
and therefore effective? At any rate he gained a commission,
and he thought that 'men from all backgrounds proved themselves'.

In fact a round quarter of the respondents – little below the
28 per cent who mentioned the countrymen, alone or with
others – would have *none* of this particular background business. 'There is no answer. The person who one thought would
be a good soldier in action sometimes failed, and the one
expected to be useless could be the most effective', wrote J. G.
Henderson, a townsman who had five years as a private with
two units – the 2/1st Battalion and a workshop platoon – in
the Middle East and the Pacific. A.J.B. was basically a
townsman but had done a lot of country work in the course of
trying to earn a living. He was a thirty-niner with service in
both major theatres, and progressively sergeant, WO II and
lieutenant with the 2/2nd Field Regiment. He said:

The majority of enlistees became good soldiers, and the 5 per cent or
so of no-hopers came from all walks of life. A good peacetime
background does not necessarily produce good soldiers, nor does a
poor peacetime environment always spawn the bad soldier. Among

good soldiers (including officers) I can recall an ex-racecourse urger, a barman, an ex-SP bookmaker and people from the ranks of the unemployed. Bad soldiers I remember include two utterly useless scions of well-known Victorian families, a prize fighter who was a coward, and a bank officer who was the greatest bludger of all time.

Reg Hastings said that the effective soldier was 'just the ordinary man in the street' – and the least effective was 'the boaster'.

The city boy and Military Medallist NX4320 concluded that a broadly *Australian* background was the only important thing. There were

a few no-hoper types – alcoholics who had to be discarded, and some street-corner lairs who found the going too tough and took their own steps to escape (self-inflicted wounds). But in my experience neither class nor racial origin had any bearing on it as a general rule. In the 2/3rd Battalion we had [Australians who, by parentage, were] Maltese, Italians, Greeks, Aborigines, Lebanese, Irish, English, Scots, a Pole and a Chinese. They were all rated effective.

C. W. Waters was very much a countryman and he held strong views, including an arrogant AIF condemnation of all militiamen. On the question of where the good men in the AIF came from, however, he was uncharacteristically baffled.

Impossible to say. There was a little schoolteacher, thick-rimmed glasses, a pansy-looking little fellow. I often used to wonder what the hell's this? And he shot three legionnaires just like I'd shoot rabbits, and never took the grin off his face. Cool as a cucumber. As hard to pick who'll be a good man under fire as it is to pick a bloody winner on a racecourse.

The largest group of all among the respondents (30 per cent) moved away from 'town and country' in a different sense.

Gunners 'Chick' Rendell and 'Kiwi' James in the Middle East in 1941. James, a New Zealander, was learning wine-making in Australia when war broke out, and Rendell was very young when he enlisted from his native South Australia. Both men survived the war

They simply chose one or more background influences that could affect urban and rural men equally. What produced the best soldier was the experience of battling for a living (9 per cent), growing up in a stable family (5 per cent), having had army training (5 per cent), involvement in sport or outdoor activities (3 per cent), a belief in what was being fought for (2 per cent) or certain other factors, singly or in combination (6 per cent). Their choices were perfectly reasonable – even when contradictory. Together they supplied necessary modifications while adding to the ingredients of an effective fighting force.

> I'd want to pick the man who had known a hard life during the depression or in rural work, someone who had already learnt to take hard knocks. But I don't know. I was in the permanent army at the outbreak, a corporal with the tank section and used to acting on command without thought, and transferring to the AIF was an eye opener. I was thrown among men of all kinds – graziers, industrialists, lawyers, taxi-drivers, even male nurses, and one of the male nurses ended up being colonel of the regiment. To try to make all these men into a fighting unit was a

big task but, with all this talent, they became some of the best
fighting men the world has seen [John Moody, WO II, 6th Divisional Cavalry Regiment].

Any civilian rich or poor, lawful or unlawful, outgoing or
sheltered, believer or unbeliever, timid or aggressive, educated
or not, can be *trained* to be an efficient fighting soldier, doing
what he has been taught to do instinctively in the hour of
action – given of course the right kind of leadership that builds
esprit de corps [C. F. Hartmann, lieutenant, permanent military
forces, AIF service (anti-aircraft) in Middle East and New
Guinea].

The best had soldier relatives, came from a good family and a
good home-town environment, had been disciplined at home
and school and, above all, were aware of the threat to the nation
[R. J. Hall, lieutenant, 2/28th Battalion].

The gentle type, those from a humble background or who felt
humble, and those with no previous army experience. The least
effective were those who enlisted 'to kill some bastard' – and
there were plenty of them [QX12612, gunner, 2/1st Tank-
attack Regiment].

He could come from any walk of life, but he had to be a
volunteer [E. M. Lawlor, trooper, 2/4th Armoured Regiment,
who spent frustrating years in Australia with 'no equipment
and going nowhere' until his unit at last saw action in the
Wewak area in 1944].

Voluntary Militia service, done with pride, and school and
family discipline [TX537, lieutenant, 2/1st Anti-tank Regiment and 11th Australian Army Small Ships Company].

I've absolutely no idea where the most effective soldier came
from. I had them in barristers, garbos and circus hands. But
remember that our volunteer army in war all started with the
blokes who were in the Militia before the war [VX69, major,
2/2nd Field Regiment and 2nd Mountain Battery].

The best came from among the self-employed. They were able
to cope with an emergency [D. H. Grant, lieutenant, 2/3rd Field
Workshop and 73rd Light Aid Detachment].

The question of background is too complex to generalise about.

Overall, however, middle to upper classes had more to fight for [C. S. Harle, lieutenant with engineers and infantry].

The most effective was the person who hadn't planned his future. The way the army was run would make it fail as a business venture [SX454, farmer's son, POW, gunner, 2/3rd Field Regiment].

The best was someone with a middle-class background whose upbringing and education had given him the ability to weigh his responsibilities in a rational manner. The worst was someone who had known so many hardships and had battled so much against the odds that he thought everybody under him should have to do the same [A. H. Massina, sergeant, who served with too many units to list].

Education and good employment ['Mil', an Aboriginal lance-corporal, 2/12th Battalion].

The single man in his late teens or early twenties, placed in the right unit and with an interest in sport. Education not necessarily important [D. B. Bailey, sergeant, last unit the 41st Australian Landing Craft, and member of the Australian Victory Contingent, London, 1946].

The soldier with the best potential was young (initially 19 to 22 years) and educated to fourth or fifth form at secondary school, with good passes in English, Maths and probably Science – but especially with an adaptable, inquiring mind. However, the 'professor' type, who knew too much for his own good, was a sheer handicap; and the uneducated and illiterate were taught and protected by their mates [J. M. Bowman, corporal, 2/1st Battalion].

The best thing a man could bring into the army was basic honesty [J. M. Macansh, gunner, 2/12th Australian Field Regiment].

What the good Australian soldier most needed was pride in being Australian [W.F.H., sergeant, 1st Armoured Regiment].

To be effective a man had to have a cause to fight for, a background of knowing right from wrong and not thought of self first, last and always ['Little Sav', sapper, 2/1st Field Company; communist and RSL member].

The most effective soldier was the most dedicated, conscientious, truest believer in what he was fighting for. Apart from that, background had little to do with it [NX48848, corporal, 2/19th Battalion].

That final opinion came from one who enlisted as a young dairy farmer. He had gone only to primary school, and his spelling of 'conscientious' and 'believer' had to be corrected, but his considered opinion was as good as any. Probably no one should be dogmatic about what it was in men's backgrounds that made them – in their various ways – good soldiers. Such a conclusion comes, not from dodging the issue, but from considering the evidence.

The least effective soldier

'*Were* there ineffective Australian soldiers?' asked R. F. D. Owen, once a private with the 13th Australian General Hospital and a POW in Japanese hands. 'They were soon culled out', he added. Respondents were less willing to hazard an opinion on what backgrounds produced the weaker men than to point to the sources of effectiveness. On ineffectiveness 24 per cent gave no answer or did not know, compared with 13 per cent unable or unwilling to explain what produced good men. One man in a hundred said that none was ineffective, but that was to be loyal beyond belief. A wiser 1 per cent settled for saying that most were okay, particularly if they were given good leadership and placed in the right units.

The largest single group (16 per cent) insisted that, as with the effective soldiers, ineffective men could come from any background at all that had somehow failed to develop in them the necessary qualities. M.G.R., who served in the Middle

East and the Pacific, ending up as a lance-corporal with the
2/33rd Battalion, pointed out that 'any mind can crack under
tension, no matter how strong, healthy, confident and well
adapted its possessor might seem'.

Almost as many respondents (15 per cent) found the ineffective coming from the no-hoper element – the bludgers
(according to C.G.), the drifters (P. L. Bladen), the shiftless
unemployed (TX15991), the least educated (DX100), 'the
drunks – AWL just before embarkation' (QX13154), those
who 'could not cope with civilian life' (G.W.B.), 'a bum in
peace and a bum in war' (J. Puddephat), cowardly street
'toughs' (W. N. D. Bow) and 'the criminal who wouldn't
work as a civilian or fight as a soldier' (N. Zenos). If the no-
hopers could in a sense be called 'hard', there were the very
opposite – the 'soft' nominated by 12 per cent of the respondents as being poor soldiers. These were the boys who had
been 'Mama's pet and Daddy's darling' (C.E.S.) or, as A. H.
Drummond put it: 'Those from affluent homes, particularly
an only child. Suddenly thrown into the vortex of real life, it
took them so long just to come to terms with it that they were
left with little time to really learn teamwork and how to
fight.'

Too soft and too hard often came together as 'city' types.
Some 10 per cent of the respondents pointed to the city as the
producer of the worst soldiers (contrasted with only 0.2 per
cent who chose the country). Sometimes it was the slums that
were to blame, but quite as often it was the soft life of an
office. Edwin Badger felt it of himself. He had been a mis-
sionary to Japan and was in the army as an interpreter. Having
said that the best soldiers were 'manual workers with initiative', he added that the least effective were 'chair-borne office
workers (my own type) who go to war knowing that they will
never be quick or ruthless enough to shoot anybody'.

Hard and soft backgrounds could also combine to produce
other qualities that some 8 per cent picked as the mark of the
worst troops: selfishness and conceit. And many elements
came together in a 9 per cent category of miscellaneous causes

of ineffectiveness. They included the snob-school product, the university student, the religious man, the male mannequin, the homosexual, the man with a low mentality, the very ordinary types who were also too young or too old, the person made timid by family friction and those with substandard health, education, work and standards of behaviour. Clearly, too much and too little could equally be blamed, and what some men damned as fatal for success in the army was nearly always selected by others as one source of the best soldier.

As the worst soldier, about 5 per cent of the respondents nominated either the permanent army man or the militiaman – if not both. The regular and the *prewar* militiaman were rarely criticised, but when they were it was for being parade-ground soldiers and camp martinets who could not manage men, or were unwilling to go to the real thing, or were no good at it when they did go. More often the dislike was of the wartime conscript, and even then it was frequently toned down in such ways as '*some* conscripts' (TX6030), '*some* of the *city* conscripts' (P. E. Pechey), or 'those drafted *against their wishes*' (R. F. Morgan). According to A. W. Nash too the worst men were those who carried into the army 'a resentment at being called up', but he believed that the grudge 'disappeared almost entirely after about a year's service'.

J. A. Alexander was one of those science undergraduates whom some men would immediately have dubbed hopeless and others would have welcomed as full of potential. He was not conscripted, but volunteered from the Sydney University Regiment for the 53rd Militia Battalion and joined it as a corporal. Originally destined for Darwin, the 53rd was diverted to Port Moresby in late December 1941. Made up mainly of conscripts, it was committed to battle against the Japanese without real training – an 'iniquitous' lack, sufficient in itself to explain the 53rd's poor initial performance in action. Yet there may have been more to it in the case of some of those conscripts.

Many in the platoon I joined were labourers from the Sydney dock area who hated being called up, and I couldn't understand their attitude. They weren't given any information on why they were in New Guinea, and weren't trained – but they didn't *want* to be trained. Most in my section were drinkers and brawlers, bullshit artists and, some of them, bullies. They and I were probably oil and water, and one or two of them I even feared. They would have been difficult to train even if they had been willing and proper training had been available. Still, the battalion as a whole was made up of ordinary young Australians, and they deserved better. Get them on side, get them motivated, and I guess they would have made adequate if not good soldiers. I left them after an ankle injury in May 1942 and never saw them again.

In August 1942 the 53rd met the Japanese and, not surprisingly, were judged to have been hopeless. But A. W. Nash's assessment (resentment finally disappearing) and Alexander's hope (get them motivated) seem to have applied to many in that battalion. With some of the weak men culled, and the remainder reorganised as the 55th/53rd Battalion, the unit finally won high praise from such people as respondent I.N.R., who served with the 2/1st Battalion but knew the 55th/53rd well: 'There was none better in New Guinea than the 39th and 3rd Battalions and, later, the 36th and 55th/53rd.' *Some* conscripts, some *city* conscripts, some drafted *against their wishes*, were no doubt among the least effective. But so were some from many categories, and all soldiers needed time and experience to become really good.

The AIF and the Militia

Considerable tension developed between participants in Australia's 'two army' system – the AIF volunteers for service anywhere in the world, and the stay-at-home Militia with its many conscripts. A lot of AIF men despised what they saw as the militiamen's lack of wholeheartedness, avoidance of the

Four members of the 2/10th Battalion in a Lebanese fig-orchard. Norm Lloyd (wearing hat) survived the Middle East, to die on the other side of the world

heaviest burden of the war and, sometimes, their promotion over men already seasoned in overseas campaigns. Some in the Militia resented AIF conceit and narrow-minded misjudgement of the situation – and complained of incompetent AIF types placed as officers over more able militiamen. Respondents who were in the AIF throughout the war, and particularly the Middle East veterans, were least likely to say that relations between the two armies were good. Their vote was 13 per cent for good relations, 43 per cent for mixed or improved later, and 44 per cent for always uneasy or poor. Those who began in the wartime Militia (as conscripts or volunteers) but later transferred to the AIF were a little happier about relations: good, 19 per cent; mixed or improved, 46 per cent; uneasy or poor, 36 per cent.

The resentments sometimes led to unpleasantness and brawling between AIF and Militia, but they were often apparently left unspoken or voiced only in AIF camps, for those respondents who were militiamen all through the war (only a small 4.4 per cent of the total) were the most ready to describe AIF–Militia relations as good – a category chosen by 36 per cent of them, with 40 per cent going for mixed, and only 24 per cent selecting uneasy and poor. Nevertheless, the unhappy fact remains that (with one-tenth not answering) over one-third of all respondents (36 per cent) described the relations as pretty bad, even more (39 per cent) did not think that relations were very wonderful, and a mere 15 per cent opted for an unqualified 'good'.

Follow a few individuals as they lead this way and that in their arguments about the Militia. The AIF member A.R.M. said that it was only the prewar 'carpet knights' who were called 'chocos' – those peacetime militiamen who had been so scornful of others and so boastful about what they would do to save Australia, and then at the crunch 'followed the [World War I] example of the Hon. R. G. Menzies by deciding that they should not be put at risk in a vulgar war'. *They* were the 'chocos', and the term was never applied to the 18-year-old conscripts who, 'when properly led, acquitted themselves splendidly'. But C.H.F. corrected A.R.M.: 'When I was in the Militia, even at 18, I was considered a "choco" and had a couple of good blues over it.'

VX100383 was originally a volunteer militiaman but transferred to the AIF when his father relented and consented to his changing over; by that time he had seen much more action than his elder AIF brother had. He tried to get the record straight in another way.

The first volunteers for the AIF left a large number of former peacetime men in the Militia – those under 20 or over 34, and many married men. The first 'call ups' required to do three months training with the Militia were not called militiamen but 'Universal Trainees'. They and the Militia together were the Commonwealth [Citizen?] Military Forces, and this CMF plus the AIF made up the Australian Military Forces.

Strictly, VX100383 might have been right, but most respondents knew whom *they* called the Militia, as well as who was called a 'choco' – and both terms were widely applied to the non-AIF part of the army.

A Middle East and Pacific veteran who despised, not the militiamen, but those in authority who maintained the system, was the artilleryman WX8388: 'This situation should

never of occurred. The Militia done a mighty job.' C. S.
Wright was a married man aged 31 when he joined the AIF in
1941 to avoid 'the degradation of being called up'. He served
in the Dutch East Indies and really had no contact with the
Militia, which was 'a non-existent army' for him, but in the
1940s he came across a piece of 'hate', and kept it for forty
years.

The Answer to the Unwrapped Chocolate Soldier
by One of the AIF

We have read your letter, and we think it rather balmy,
Written by a choco in the Aussie Conscript Army ...
They were forced into the army, they were forced across the
foam
To the island of New Guinea, a home away from home ...
Before those Nips got started in this bloody rotten war
The AIF were fighting on a lousy foreign shore ...
Our boys were up against it there, their backs against the wall,
They called for reinforcements and to Aussie went the call.
The chocos didn't heed it. 'We cannot go', they cried,
While their cobbers went to battle, went and bled and died ...
Keep writing, chocolate soldier, sit down and sigh and write,
And leave this bloody battle to the fellows who will fight ...
But your callous heart should hurt you, Jack, Bill, Tom and
Geoff,
As you never were the type of man to join the AIF.

QX17835, a volunteer militiaman (in a special security job)
from 1939 until transferring to the AIF in 1940 and ending up
a POW in Malaya, recalled 'before going overseas quite a lot
of strife in Brisbane between AIF and Militia, which seemed
to be provoked by the AIF'. Another prisoner of the Japanese,
TX3809, thought that too few men allowed 'the possibility of
a legitimate reason for others remaining in the Militia'.
NX7619 was in the 2/1st Battalion as a private one month
after war was declared and was a captain before the end of it.

He saw service on both sides of the globe, but he was contemptuous of the 'stupid propaganda' that caused the AIF–Militia problem: 'My eldest brother was unfit for the AIF and joined the CMF to do a clerical job (he was an accountant). Only after two years was he allowed to transfer to the AIF, classified B2.' NX58425 was in a volunteer Militia unit that managed to transfer to the AIF in July 1940 (its members wanting a more active role), but he said that 'most AIF men did not understand the restrictions placed on Militia transfers to the AIF'. J.V.A., ex-Militia and ex-AIF, said that relations 'varied from place to place. More generally it was the Middle East Mutual Adoration Society against the rest'. K. R. Battye, originally in the Militia because his father (a badly incapacitated Anzac) would not consent to the 19-year-old joining the Second AIF, was in a mixed unit in New Guinea where relations were 'extra good', but he noticed a difference on return to Melbourne, where 'a couple of smarties in Menzies Hotel started giving the Militia the treatment. Probably neither of them had left Melbourne, but by the time the argument finished they wished they'd left the day before'.

J. M. Bowman became a member of the AIF in 1942 at the age of 17, and he saw service in the islands. 'Some Militia battalions were very good,' he remarked, 'some very poor. Some good men would not transfer to the AIF because they were proud of their battalion.' R. A. Browne was a case in point. His father had won the Military Medal in World War I, had been at Gallipoli, and had got his son into the 45th Battalion as a cadet when the boy was only 11 years old. Although Browne served a number of years with that peacetime Militia battalion, he did not enlist when war broke out (for reasons not made clear) but was conscripted at the age of 20 in·1941, when he found himself in what became the infamous 53rd (later 55th/53rd) Battalion. Browne was far from agreeing that its notoriety was deserved. On the contrary he wrote:

The mention of my battalion could start a brawl with any AIF mob, but the Militia and the AIF were played off against each other, and to me 'choco' was an honourable name, not the slur implied. To change to AIF would have lowered the honour of the name, and I didn't like the methods and attitudes of officers and men in trying to influence us to transfer – join the AIF or lose your stripes. I stayed as I was.

One such transfer was eventually made by 'Charlie', but only because there seemed to be no point in passing up opportunities for promotion – men of lesser ability often being promoted simply because they were AIF. 'Sniper' also transferred when he could, but before that the slur had done him no harm: 'AIF reckoned conscripts were chocolate soldiers – melted in the heat – so a lot of us at 18 had things to prove.'
    L. W. Wood was in country work when he volunteered for the AIF in 1940, only to be

knocked back as essential service. Had the idea then that, if you don't want me, I'll go in my own time. Found I could volunteer for the 49th Battalion (Queensland Militia) in August 1941, and did so. It was better than being called up. The whole 'choco' business was upsetting and unnecessary – being thought of as having done something terrible. I transferred to AIF in 1942 because Japan was in the war and the Militia could not cross the Papuan border, and I served away from the Militia in Morotai, Labuan and Borneo. Relations between AIF and Militia are supposed to have got better the longer the Japanese war went on.

There is no doubt that, in many cases, those relations did improve. 'I find this rather an unfair question', grumbled R. G. Scott, MC. 'Until I worked with the Militia I regarded them as poor, but my ideas changed as they showed courage and proved as good as any others. Much depended on their training and their officers.' L. R. Martorana was rejected by the AIF in 1939 but taken into the Militia for full-time service. Nearly three years later he was a sergeant with the 39th Battalion when

Papuans of the type who served so well as carriers, bearers, labourers, guides, armed constables and infantrymen

on the Kumusi River, news reached us that the Japanese had landed. On 6 July 1942 we fired our first shots at the Nips but, outnumbered ten to one, could only hold them for a few days. We were almost surrounded but our guide, a native soldier and Military Medal winner named Sinopa, led us out of the trap. Anyway, after the Kokoda campaign we were tops. I was later a member of the AIF, but my period with the 39th Militia Battalion was the proudest time of my service.

It was not only the militiamen who had to put up with derogatory remarks and worse. Sometimes the boot was on the other foot. VX16738, having had some prewar training with the 6th Battalion (Royal Melbourne Regiment), joined the AIF in the early months of the war and bitterly recalled how the 6th Division was 'sneered at as being merely "Cook's tourists" by many of the public and many of the Militia, including old "friends" in the 6th Battalion'. It was one other attitude that needed changing and was hard to forgive.

But perspectives continually changed. One Middle East veteran said that 'the certain degree of contempt we had for the Militia disappeared after we saw them in action at Milne Bay'. D. C. Hampstead was at Singapore when it fell (although he escaped), and he was then fully aware of how much the Militia was needed to protect Australia. 'It depended on the time and the comparisons', wrote J. H. Fawkes, as he revealed another prejudice: 'Before the Yanks arrived, the Militia seemed poor. After the Yanks came, the Militia was good.' S. J. Bruton served with the 7th Division through the Middle East campaign and then, back in Australia, had a hand blown off while training a Militia unit in guerilla warfare at Canungra (Qld). So he was discharged from the army in 1942. At that time, he said, 'We were glad the Militia were here to defend our country, and they were glad that we of the AIF had come home to help'.

Bruton made much sense, yet the respondents overwhelmingly remembered the strain in the relations between the 'two armies'. Some AIF men will take to their graves an ineradicable contempt for all things Militia, and one such man appeared in C. W. Waters, a veteran of Syria and New Guinea with the 21st Anti-tank Regiment.

Back from the Middle East, the 7th Division piddled off to do battle with the Nip, and we were met at Moresby by the Militia running off the Owen Stanleys like a mob of sheep with a dog after them. I actually talked to several who had mud maps to island-hop back to the mainland. The 7th Division halted the Nip, and the remnants of the Militia were hanging around and our brigadier sent in his report: 'I have six hundred men and some Militia.' At the end of a week he lined the Militia up and said, 'You're only eating good men's tucker, get down and unload bloody boats at the wharf at Moresby', where they deliberately dropped crates into the sea, so they'd be sent back to Australia in disgrace. This is true. What was handed out to Australia in the way of information I wouldn't know, but our opinion of the Militia – well, it couldn't be anything but contemptuous, could it?

I'll give you an example of the choco types. We had 10 tons of cement coming and nowhere to put it. I said, 'We'll shoot into Moresby and get a few sheets of iron.' And we got one load. The next time the bloody chocos had the military police on us, so I went down to the town major – a choco again – and I told him the story. We had to cement a gun in, and it rained every bloody five minutes . . . 'Every sheet of iron is being put to the maximum use for the war effort in Moresby,' the major said. And I found it hard to take. They even had iron screens around their dunnakins, that's how plentiful it was, but he finished up threatening me with arrest if I didn't pull my head in. While he was talking I saw through a window a beautiful gabled roof on 4 × 2 posts. I thought, bloody hell, there's our shed. So I went out duly abashed, jumped into the truck and said, 'Drive around behind and back in. Keep the engine running.' A couple of hits with an axe on each of the 4 × 2s, and the roof sat on the truck. Tailor-made shed. But that's the Militia. Bastards wouldn't give us a sheet of iron to cover cement for a gun emplacement.

Waters will have his believers, but the Queenslander R.A.C. would not be one of them. An unrepentant militiaman, he would not join the AIF on principle. He was a great lover of peace, well aware of the 'extravagant lying' by Britain and her allies during World War I in the 'atrocities propaganda', but he also believed that some wars might be shown to be just and necessary, in which case service should not be left to volunteers but should compulsorily involve all citizens.

Educated ignoramuses have recently suggested that my generation had an attitude to war derived from the dark ages. It wasn't so. No one wished for war. No one wanted to waste their lives, and the more thoughtful dreaded the very idea of war. There was no blind rush to enlist except by a small percentage of the population, and even then it wasn't usually for blood-thirsty patriotism. Some sooner, some of us later, saw that we were engaged in a war of survival and decided to take part in it. Any informed person must admit that our war, particularly with Japan, was one for survival. Japanese treatment of Koreans, Chinese, other Asiatics and POWs can leave no doubt that, had Japan won, Australia as we knew it would have disappeared forever. The evidence against the Nazi regime mounted too. I couldn't act a part I didn't believe in, and join the AIF, but I could join a 'universal service' Militia battalion, which I did in 1941. So we rather hurriedly learnt 'fire-fighting', and did rather well as 'firemen', but that didn't mean we were 'fire bugs'. As a matter of fact, I was one of the best shots in my battalion, yet I haven't shot anyone since the war – not even radio and TV commentators, nor yet (and they are far more tempting a target) any sociologists. After my service began, I volunteered for this and that. One job would have involved serving alone in forward areas, but doubtless the 'powers-that-were' didn't believe a mere militiaman could handle it. Then a mate and I responded to a call to join another brigade, and so we ended up in the 61st Battalion, forming part of the reception committee for the Japanese at Milne Bay.

R.A.C. was not so foolish as to claim that no one was panicky. His first morning in action came after a night in which others had been doing plenty of shooting. His company had spent it quietly, simply lying dispersed in ambush positions. Then came the dawn, and with it the sight of enemy ships and barges close to shore when they were supposed to be still a good way off. It left him with a sense of unreality, a feeling of helplessness he would always recall. Sardonic humour came to his aid, for at least one man seemed in a worse state.

A little later we were visited by our company sergeant major, a fine figure of a soldier when on parade. In a flustered half-stammer he told my mate and me that a large landing had taken place, fighting had occurred, A—— and B—— and C—— were dead, the Japs' green uniforms made it impossible to see them coming, and we were to shoot on sight. Hardly the Duke of Wellington heartening his troops. I was amused then, and have enjoyed the memory since. I was scared too, but the green uniforms were no surprise and I never had thought that a .303 was for shooting mosquitoes.

The important part played by militiamen in the repelling of that attempted invasion at Milne Bay has long since been written into the history books – and into the memories of some AIF men. R.A.C. continued to serve with combined forces of AIF and Militia, and in mixed units where 'nobody cared which their mate was'.

N185992 acquired that Militia number, one he was to keep throughout his service, when he was suddenly conscripted in

January 1942, aged 18. (He had wanted to join the navy or the air force, but his parents would not sign the papers.) Five months later he was in New Guinea.

I first met the AIF veterans of the Middle East in the foothills of the Owen Stanleys. The 25th Brigade, 7th Division, were taken by truck from the wharf to a point just below the famous climb with the hair-pin bends and sheer drops. There they changed to smaller trucks. The situation was very serious, and I remember I drove a small truck (it only held eight men) for 22 hours non-stop till these men were taken as far as motor vehicles could go. They would dye their khaki uniforms green that night and be in action, taking casualties, the next afternoon. They were brash and patronising to me, but very confident and acted very professionally. They were particularly aware of the youthfulness of the Militia battalions. They came straight from desert warfare. They had the wrong uniforms, equipment and training – and were clobbered as a result. The Militia battalions already there proved to be most informative to us and, as they mastered jungle warfare, became more than a match for the enemy, but in the beginning neither the Militia nor the AIF had the correct training. (In Australia they had taught us all the ruses and tricks learnt in World War I trench warfare.) I spent a few nights with some wounded AIF men from Milne Bay, and they spoke of the Militia doing an excellent job. The AIF and Militia relationship was a strange one, different in different circumstances. Competitiveness between them was encouraged, but the AIF was given the spectacular jobs and were far ahead of the Militia units in the matter of decorations and promotions. Our own CO in the 36th Battalion had come from the 2/27th and was none too pleased to be lumbered with a Militia unit, and we took some AIF reinforcements who didn't like their posting at first, but after a time there was strong mutual respect.

Another member of that battalion, K.C.H., thought that the commanding officer in question, Lieutenant-Colonel O. C. Isaachsen, had 'a change of heart after the 36th had won him the Distinguished Service Order'.

Thus the supporters of the Waters view of the Militia would not win hands down, and probably not win at all, in the debate over the merits of the AIF and Militia, even though so few respondents could say that relations between the two forces were good. Let VX100383 speak again.

There is no simple answer. Most soldiers, AIF or CMF, who reached the point of no turning back, kill or be killed, also reached the point where, without perhaps being aware of it, they ceased to point the finger at others – and were quick to say to anyone, 'Stay out of it, if you can'. There were all too few who *served* in the King's uniform. There were probably more who only *wore* it, and this was the group that stirred up trouble against the 'chocos' – who, on their part, never failed to give the AIF their due. Having been one for a while, I admire the CMF man, maybe lacking parental consent, or being married, who accepted defence of his country without chasing fights overseas. Sticking by that decision was just as hard as being a glamour boy. When dead, AIF and Militia looked quite alike.

The qualities of the Digger

The AIF private who lost his hand in an accident at Canungra, S. J. Bruton, recalled a time in the Middle East.

Our company was guarding a road, and an enemy armoured car was approaching when I found the anti-tank rifle. Resting it on a rock, I kept firing it, and it bounced up in the air every time and hurled me yards away. I can still see Lieut 'Butch' Bissett looking down on me from a higher rock and barracking as though at a beaut footy match. 'C'mon, Stan. Give it to 'em. That's the stuff. Let 'em have it.' The same Butch, at the head of his platoon, met me on the roadside at Canungra just as I'd blown my right hand off. 'Gawd, Stan. Wotvyer done?' He and many others were killed on the Kokoda Trail within three weeks, and I was wishing I was there with them.

When asked what quality most characterised the Digger, the

biggest group of respondents said he could be relied on to be with you when you needed him. The dependable mate was the typical Digger for about a third of the respondents. When 'determination' is combined with 'reliability', almost one-half of the respondents said of the Australian soldier something along the lines of 'a dependable comrade, determined to see things through'. Very few chose to apply the term 'disciplined', presumably because the word conjured up to many the images of parade grounds and military automatons, but of course discipline belongs to the inner core of reliability and capacity to stick. 'Not the usual distorted view of "big wild Australians", please', wrote A.J. McDonald, from the angle of the 2/13th Battalion. 'They were sensible, reliable, no-nonsense soldiers, quick to learn.' Adaptability and initiative were in fact the qualities applied to the Australian soldier by one-quarter of the respondents, while some 14 per cent spoke of his 'cheerfulness' – of a wry and peculiar kind, perhaps. So the Digger was neither a larrikin nor a glittering hero. He was just determined to see the job through and not let his unit down, and as he did the job he showed a lot of quick thinking and found some humour in unlikely places.

Some denied that any qualities were sufficiently common to enable a 'typical Digger' to emerge; real soldiers were 'just ordinary Australian men' (G.R.), and 'each individual was what he was – although he could be changed' (VX117890). In World War II, according to E. C. Fancote and others, even the word 'Digger' was little used, and he sourly added that 'anyway, not too many had the esprit de corps the term "Digger image" implies'. Many respondents would indignantly reject the last part of Fancote's claim, and it did seem that respondents' reports on their comrades often reflected as much about themselves as about the 'typical' soldier.

NX3251 and E.R.W. were both original members of the 6th Division, but NX3251 chose to comment on the blues and brawls, strikes, drunkenness and general wildness he took part in, whereas E.R.W. wrote of the many older, steady, married men in the division. He thought they got in after the gov-

Sketches done in North Africa in 1942 – probably by a member of the 2/12th Field Regiment – might support the idea that there was not a 'typical' Digger

ernment found that the division could not be filled by young men from the Militia, and he was very conscious of the 'heart wrenching' it caused – particularly when some of those men went with him into captivity as POWs. So two individuals produced contrasting impressions of the men in the 6th Division, although their brief summings up of 'the Digger' were not so different: 'carefree and hardy' (E.R.W.), and 'a bit wild on leave, but solid and practical, able to take over in an emergency' (NX3251).

Some respondents were critical of the Australian soldier. He had, in the judgement of D. V. Goland (a lieutenant-colonel by 1945) 'an erroneous impression of his natural fighting abilities'. J. R. Linscott, a captain in both the prewar Militia and the AIF, complained that his own 'workaholic' approach was appreciated neither by his CO, who could not get over what he imagined he had done in World War I, nor by the troops, who seemed to think they were going to a Sunday school picnic (instead of Malaya and the POW camps) and took the line, 'We'll enjoy ourselves while we can, and when the time comes we'll be there'. That was from an officer with the 2/20th Battalion, but a corporal with the 2/16th in the Middle East, A. T. Fogarty, was also bitter about a common lack of responsibility and a spirit of 'take it as it comes'.

Whatever justice may lie in the – few – critics' denunciations, the same tendency could be assessed differently, and often was. The sceptical Jim Guy said that the Australian soldier could 'capitalise on mistakes'. W. J. Warriner saw him as 'an individual who was never completely dominated by the military system but still achieved the desired goal'. Ernst Heckenberg (born in New South Wales) admitted that the Australian could be 'hard to get going', but he was really there 'when the whips were cracking'. The artilleryman Allan J. Guy pointed the accusing finger above and away from the ordinary soldier in this matter of careless lack of preparation.

My father's unit marched through Melbourne to the troopship in fatigues because uniforms weren't available in World War I. We had uniforms, but a lot of our equipment was of World War I vintage. When we came out of action in the desert we handed over our guns to the relieving regiment. The 6th Division had to use Italian equipment to keep up their advance. In Syria we took over the 7th Division's guns. Not till Alamein [October 1942] did we seem to have our own regulation equipment. It's a good thing that Australians can take matters into their own hands when officialdom blunders.

B. O. Ellison (born in the United Kingdom and emigrating to Australia at 19) thought that the Australian was marked by his initiative – very different from 'the regimented Pom'. M. J. McKenna, an infantry sergeant, also chose initiative as the characteristic – at least of some person in every group: 'No matter if all NCOs and officers were killed, someone would take over.' And it was not to win a medal: 'There is no man to my knowledge who has cold-bloodedly contemplated going for a decoration.'

To NX4235 the Digger was 'man enough to admit being scared, and man enough to fight'. L. H. Sloane thought Australians would 'attempt the impossible, and give miracles a

A 1930s Smith's Weekly *cartoon by Frank Dunne. High ranking officer: 'Things pretty quiet today, eh?' Unregimental Digger: 'Yair, what with the birds singin', 'n' you blokes strollin' 'round, a man'd hardly know there wuz a —— war on.' Some respondents rejected that legend of the Australian soldier, although Vane Lindesay (from whose book* The Inked-In Image *the cartoon is reproduced) believed, from experience, that there was substance behind the myth*

horrible fright'. 'Sydney Joiner' wanted to characterise the Australian soldier by 'his humour even unto death'. The bushman TX4537 believed that the Australian strength lay in 'an ability to treat the army as just another job', although E. F. Ticehurst added something else: 'The soldier was an ordinary guy who had the ability to do a job that was contrary to all his beliefs.'

Ordinary plus . . . That about sums it up. 'The Australian soldier was *not* the *Smith's Weekly* type', said G.S.S., who was with the 2/3rd Battalion in the Middle East and the Pacific, and a sergeant in 1945. 'He was moderately intelligent, with a stable and independent personality, but disciplined.' Jack

Ralla thought of 'guts – readiness to have a go'. Speaking of himself, and thus opening a window on many Australian soldiers, he reflected on 'mixing very well with members of the unit. I took my role seriously, worked when necessary and played when it was playtime. There was nothing enjoyable about being in combat, but there is a great sense of achievement in knowing I was an Australian soldier who played a part ... I feel proud of our servicemen and servicewomen'.

And why not? WX7309 spoke with something of that 'confident modesty' that W. S. Howden said was very common in the army. The Western Australian commented:

What image people have of the Digger is their own affair. I have mine, which others probably don't agree with. In my eyes he was one who during trying times, whether in training, on leave or in actual operations, could be turned to for advice and help, and always gave it. The Digger was not the beer drinker and flashy type depicted on TV and in books. He was the one who never let you down.

Some men indeed probably don't agree with his opinion, but most respondents would have gone a long way with it.

Other services, other armies

'The Digger who actually experienced service under fire', wrote L.R.N., 'was the *second best* soldier in the world. I still say the German was best in the Middle East. What made the Aussie terrific was his fear of showing fear. He was a pure egotist, and so afraid of showing fear to his mates that onward he went regardless, and washed his underpants when things quietened down. Thank God our underpants were also khaki.' D. C. Randall said, 'The Japanese were very good soldiers indeed. What else can I say? In Malaya they had us looking like a pack of girl guides in an earthquake'.

Respondents, on the whole, were very ready to give credit

where it was due, and not anxious to claim it all for themselves. There were the few like S.D.F., who dismissed airmen as 'blue orchids' and damned the seamen for 'leaving soldiers on Crete', and rather more like QX10428, who admitted that he found it hard to 'relate' to men whose service was not a frontline, face-to-face combatant role. Yet only 2 per cent were utterly negative about the air force and navy, while 66 per cent were completely positive. VX16221 recalled

the cool courage of the pilot of the spotter plane from No. 4 Army Co-operation Squadron who drew the fire on Shaggy Ridge so that we could locate the enemy positions, and the pilot of a biscuit bomber, dropping boxes of mortar bombs by parachute on the Kokoda Trail. When one box became caught on his tail, he dropped to tree-top level and wiped the box off by bashing it on the trees. The air force and navy were one hundred per cent.

VX43611, as a sergeant in the pay corps, had to take a suitcase of new money into Tobruk, and was ferried into and out of that dangerous harbour on HMAS *Vendetta*, a little old destroyer that made the trip regularly, and whose officers and crew showed a skill, courage and good cheer that impressed all who benefited.

Interpreting the question a little differently, the infantryman Julian Waters said that he wanted to praise the medical corps; they did much for him – saved his life, in fact – and his opinion of them 'went up 200 per cent during the Owen Stanley show'. J. Arthurson's comment was that he had 'great respect and liking for air force and navy, and *loved* the Australian Women's Army Service, the Women's Auxiliary Australian Air Force, the Women's Royal Australian Naval Service . . .'

Many respondents ventured no opinion of British troops because they had nothing to do with them, but of those who made a judgement 64 per cent were favourable, 29 per cent mixed, and only 8 per cent quite disparaging. TX4997 thought the British soldiers' discipline was good, and 'they were okay when well led, but lacked initiative'. C. E. Pickrang said that British troops 'never questioned an order, but might have died of thirst alongside of a creek without a mug'. K. A. Withers found the British army good in the Middle East, but poor in the Singapore region. Neville Haughton wrote that 'the British were our teachers in the Middle East, and we gave them grateful admiration for that and their sense of humour. But after Australians began to defeat the Japanese many British officers wisely came to New Guinea to learn from us'.

Other distinctions were sometimes made: the *regulars* were good (said A.T.V.B.); or the regulars like the Royal Horse Artillery were 'the best in the world, but raw Britishers probably the worst' (R. J. Weston); or the RHA and the Northumberland Fusiliers were 'fantastic', yet had a different attitude: 'They said, "Look what the bastards put us in for", while we said, "What bloody mugs we were to put ourselves in for this." Their letters from home weren't as happy as ours' (O.W.). But unstinting praise of the British army came from Middle East men like J. E. R. Clarke, who said that it was 'certainly as good as the AIF', and NX22467, for whom the British soldier was simply 'the best in the world'.

Yet other dominion troops received a lower percentage of negative votes than the British did – 4 per cent of those giving an opinion, compared with 8 per cent. (A lot of respondents – 44 per cent – said nothing, having not served with men from elsewhere in the empire.) Perhaps the Gurkhas were regarded with most awe. D. G. Armstrong offered a list in order of merit: 'Gurkhas best, Maoris next, New Zealanders as good as Australians, Canadians average.' The New Zealanders were usually well thought of – 'better than us' ('Marconi'), 'as good as us' (C. Cook), 'great – but mean sods when drunk on leave' (J.J.C.), 'very good – and on leave they were on our side in a brawl' (QX1020). Nevertheless NX3700 was disappointed in Greece, where he claimed that on two occasions he found New Zealanders unwilling to stand and fight. He also thought the South Africans 'arrogant' – and, while they had their

'For me? Twenty drachmas?' In March 1941 a little Greek girl can hardly believe it

champions, they were sometimes neither admired nor liked by respondents who judged them as 'never above the ordinary' (J. M. Callinan), or were offended by their attitude to their black troops (NX28127 and 'Patche'). Australians were popular with other soldiers, W.S. felt, and therefore it was easy for them to return the goodwill – which suggests that meetings on leave and in transit depots could become as important in respondents' minds as actual assessment of troops' effectiveness at the front; but at least it was an opinion, and not without its value. About the only other empire troops mentioned were Malayans, 'deplorable' according to C. J. Butwell, and Indians, who were 'very good' in the judgement of T. H. West, but for whom – the Gurkhas excepted – men like J.S.D. had 'little respect'.

Reflecting what they knew, only one-fifth of the respondents commented on the Greeks as soldiers, but their views were overwhelmingly favourable. They lacked arms but not guts, said R.L.P. – left alone and given a break, they would have taken Italy. L.A.M. would have granted them all Australian citizenship, and recalled the courage of the Greek women in trying to give food to POWs. J. R. Ferguson was deeply impressed by the Cretans – 'a different type of Greek'. D. B. Cade thought the Greeks in general superior to the Australians in that they did not give up; yet W. E. Butt felt that the Greeks, although good against the Italians, had given up too quickly in the face of German might. Indeed, E. J.

A captured photograph of Italian soldiers on parade in Libya

A print taken from a German parachutist who surrendered on Crete, showing his comrades embarking for their attack on the island in 1941

Riordan considered them to have been good soldiers but penetrated by a fifth column, and R. E. Ryan also suspected that there were many Nazi sympathisers among these otherwise fine troops. Their opinions were merely those of individuals, to be taken for what they might be worth, but the Greeks came out well.

The Italians did not. Of those respondents who answered the question on Mussolini's troops, over 70 per cent were negative, 10 per cent mixed, and only 2 per cent entirely positive. Some praised the artillery (M.G.B. and NX59154). R. F. Row 'witnessed an act of extreme personal bravery by an Italian during an attack on Tobruk'. A few men thought the Italians usually underrated as potential soldiers – they were just poorly led and did not know what they were supposed to be fighting for (S.A.R.B.), or were 'demonstratively anti-Mussolini' (K. A. Lodewycks). But T. J. Barker thought the Italians as soldiers were so hopeless that he was sorry for them. R. H. Lovett wondered how he could admire them after 'capturing' eighty-nine single-handed. 'Clancy' despised them and resented Australia's permitting Italian immigration. L. R. Sutherland pitied the Italians but would not trust them – and neither would '2/14th Sergeant': 'They were poor fighters, but sneaky and would shoot you in the back, given the chance.' Yet the prevalent attitudes among respondents were summed up by two of them. K. M. Rouvray (also known as 'Nude Nut' and 'Desert Head') said, 'The Italians just didn't want war'; and Lester Royle remarked, 'Italian troops? They made excellent opera singers'.

The French, sometimes pitted against the Australians and sometimes on their side, were occasionally mentioned by respondents. J. W. Backhouse considered the Free French to have been 'hopeless' allies, but J. M. Callinan certainly found the Vichy French admirable enemies. He wrote:

Cornered, with the British driving from the east and the Australians from the south, with poor equipment and no hope of reinforcement, the French in Syria fought for [Vichy] France with the courage of despair. At Merdjayoun the Foreign Legion and the 2/2nd Pioneers fought each other to a standstill . . . At Barada Gorge the French inflicted on us our first and only defeat . . .

The Poles were described as formidable, even savage. They were eager to fight, said S.C.B. – with their homeland overrun they had nothing else to live for. J.J.C. noted their hatred of the Germans, and R. J. Weston developed the point:

The Polish troops who relieved us at Tobruk were the most ferocious and callous soldiers (equal to Gurkhas) we had ever met. They literally butchered any Germans they came across. Their listening patrols always turned into battle zones. Their favourite trick was to tie up a German's hands, put a hand grenade with the pin out in his pocket and tell him to run. They would laugh all next day.

There was a respondent with an Italian name whose best friend was an Australian of German ancestry, so that their army mates described them as the Rome–Berlin Axis. The Italo-Australian became a WO II in the 2/17th Battalion, so Italian blood was not necessarily fatal for a soldier, and he remarked, 'We Australians did not hate the Germans as the Polish troops at Tobruk did. The Germans were good soldiers who fought as fairly as you could expect'. And so said 80 per cent of the respondents who gave an opinion on German troops. 'They could be out-fought, but they were tough, disciplined and superbly led by Rommel' (NX12384). 'Good soldiers, and fair. When taken prisoner, they would help our wounded back to our lines' (QX15226). (Two prisoners of the Japanese, 'A Victorian Plumber' and 'Queensland Theatre Manager', reported on the kindness shown them by German sailors in Singapore, feeding the prisoners against the wishes of the Japanese, whom the Germans hated.)

A few respondents disliked the Germans as 'arrogant'. W. F. Tolhurst would make 'no comment on Germans (or Italians) except that they were our enemies', and NX17811 considered them good soldiers, but real Huns and never to be trusted. Others distinguished two kinds: those 'as good as Brits and AIF, and the rest – the brutal SS units' (J. E. R. Clarke); the 'good troops, with a surprising sense of humour, and the arrogant, ruthless SS "political" soldiers' (M.R.C.); and, from a POW, 'the frontline men okay; those behind the lines not' (S. A. Phillips). But, without a doubt, most Australian soldiers who encountered Germans at the front had a deep respect for them, and not much hatred.

For the Japanese soldier there was a different mix of attitudes: a kind of respect was often there, but so was a revolted detestation. Statistically, the respondents were coded as 24 per cent speaking positively about the Japanese, 29 per cent negatively, and 22 per cent expressing a mixed opinion. (The remaining quarter did not answer.) Expectations played their part in men's assessment of the Japanese. Meeting them early in the Pacific, K. A. Withers commented that 'they were better than we were told', but Alan Coe came with the 9th Division comparatively late against the Japanese and thought that they had been falsely built up as super-soldiers just to cover the early Allied lack of preparedness. Perhaps their best units had already gone, but those Coe found had serious weaknesses; they would camouflage their positions well but give them away by being noisy, and when forced back would become badly disorganised because their training had not allowed for defeat. For other respondents the Japanese were 'very good in the jungle, and it took us a long while to get their measure' (K. J. Irwin); 'so strictly devoted to duty that we could learn from them' (Ray Reece); 'ready to die; when we overran their positions, their personal papers had been laid on the edge of their weapon pits' (L. M. Opie); 'prepared to fight to the death, giving and expecting no quarter' (C. J. Selby); 'courageous and adaptable, good to have on our side next time' (D.R.S.).

The Japanese could inspire fear. VX1959 was so scared of them in the 1940s that he hated them still in the 1980s. L.M.D. was one of the many who applied to the Japanese the word 'fanatical' – ambiguous in its meaning: dedicated, or mad, or

September 1945. Lieutenant-General Hatazo Adachi surrenders in New Guinea. He is met by Lieutenant-Colonel P. K. Parbury, of the 2/7th Battalion – and by the visible hatred of another Australian officer

both. He noted *their* terror of being taken prisoner, and their 'strange [give-away] habit of blowing bugles and whistles before attacking'. 'The Japanese were not an honourable foe,' wrote D. J. Doran, 'I saw some of their atrocities.' To the ex-POW R. G. Goodman they were 'yellow barbaric animals', but an Australian who took charge of some Japanese *as* prisoners, V. T. Wright, found them spic and span, humble family men, often speaking English and wishing to visit Australia some day. R. H. Nowland, another former prisoner, would not have been entirely surprised by either comment: 'The Japanese were cruel and arrogant to those beneath them and subservient to those above. They could stand pain, although they didn't like being bombed any more than others did. They were brave and would obey orders, but seemed dull witted.'

Japanese private soldiers were 'useless without leadership' (T.W.K.); 'willing, but mostly no good without leaders – and filthy in personal habits' (A. G. Baker). In general they were 'fanatical, and filthy in fighting, hygiene and morals', thought SX4430, who nevertheless had 'respect for their marines – big men'. Alan Dower also thought the 'marines excellent, but the peasant types were just dogged without the same perception and initiative'. VX93755 knew the Japanese were 'good; but we were trained to take advantage of their weaknesses. Thank goodness their equipment was not good [in

Bougainville and Rabaul]'. After the war he was part of a
firing squad that executed Japanese convicted at the War
Crimes Trials in Rabaul: 'I have had no regrets. It was a simple
extension of the killing during the war.'

R.G.P. hated the Japanese arrogance and cruelty, but was
bitterly impressed by their 'ability to do so well on very little'.
Underlining the point of how much the Japanese war
machine was running down in the remotest areas, J.V. commented that 'many Japanese troops, having been in action
since the "Rape of Nanking" in 1937, were completely
exhausted by the end of the Solomons campaign in 1945'.
W. S. Howden, who commanded the 2/48th Battalion, concluded that 'at the regimental level the Japanese were not very
intelligent or enterprising, but their inbred fanaticism rendered them always dangerous, and their reluctance to
acknowledge defeat was always a handicap in dealing with
them'. J. A. Henderson knew what defeat meant to one Japanese.

In 1942 I was sent out to bring in a prisoner – a Zero pilot shot down
near Milne Bay. He looked small and helpless, and I was worried that
I might slip on the several miles of muddy track and accidentally
shoot him, or that he might make a run for it – and I had no desire to
shoot this slight, weary figure so different from the marines who had
landed on 26 August. I handed him in at the signals office with great
relief. When I searched for him in Japan in 1983, I learnt that he was
dead, but his brother and sister gave me pictures of him as a proud
fighter pilot. He had hanged himself, in the shame of being a prisoner, at Cowra Camp in 1944. I later found his headstone there, and
was sad with the memory of the small, defeated man and those who
mourned him.

Animals and people, terrifying and capable of being beaten,
able to do much with little yet finally exhausted, excellent
jungle troops but restricted to routine procedures, not honourable and very honourable, brutally arrogant and humbly subservient, filthy and spic and span, excellent marines and

dull-witted peasants. Ready to die, unwilling to admit defeat. Fanatical. That was the Japanese soldier, good and bad.

Respondents' opinions of the Americans were about as mixed as their judgements of the Japanese, and almost as strong. A positive decision was made by 35 per cent, a negative one by 24 per cent, and a mixed comment by 41 per cent. It was sometimes fighting ability, and sometimes social relations, that loomed large in the memory. It might have been either personal qualities or equipment that left the impression. It could have been the saving of Australia or Yankee talk about it that remained in the mind. There were many things, and widely diverging views.

'Without them we would now all be Japanese subjects, if alive', said E. C. Risden. 'They were at the right place at the right time, had all the gear and equipment, and would hop in and get a job done.' VX43388 had only five words: 'Thank God for the Yanks.' E. G. Wild, although not impressed by some negroes and base troops, thought the US air force, navy and marines 'the tops – and they saved Australia'. For a young Australian of the time, as R. G. Helyar was, the trouble lay in Americans on leave making their role as saviours of Australia offensively plain – and, what was more, he was probably jealous of their equipment and pay. Still, in the islands he got on well with them.

It did not matter to VX68246 where the Americans were: 'They did some magnificent things in both combat and leave situations.' NX15584 found them 'terrific blokes who would share anything they had with us'. The cavalry commando K.R.J. initially had no respect for Americans, but changed his mind about them after patrolling with the 9th US Texas Cavalry: 'they were no different from us.' (What never changed was his hatred for the Japanese, who 'booby-trapped our dead', and *were* 'different from us'.) The only contact '2/12th Gunner' had with Americans was with their landing-craft personnel, and they impressed him.

The kindness of Americans struck QX3506 when they released him from a German POW camp, but E. K. Edwards

*Buna Beachhead, 1942.
Whatever natural charm it
possessed has been pitted
by bombs and shells into
'Bloody Buna'*

(German POW) and A. W. Webster (Japanese POW) considered that Americans were poor survivors as prisoners – the
withdrawal of comforts affected them particularly badly. B. J.
Freney much appreciated American cigarettes and candy, and
the value of their plentiful gear and fire-power, but thought
them poor soldiers. They were good soldiers, Charles Armstrong decided, but he feared their fire-power because they
were so trigger-happy. Still, it was fire-power and numbers,
according to L.C.N., that made the Americans win; they were
a very mixed lot of men, although their marines were 'real
soldiers'. Indeed the marines 'were the very best', wrote
VX14618.

The Americans were good and bad, like the British. They had too
high an opinion of themselves, and I was sometimes disgusted by the
attitude of some Australian girls to the Americans' higher spending
capacity; but on reflection I can understand and realise that perhaps
we had caused a somewhat similar reaction in the Middle East.

J. R. Davies hated Americans, being 'probably jealous of their
uniforms, food, icecream, sex appeal'; and T.W. muttered,
'Rotten lot. One stole my girl'.

At Buna, W. L. McGee found the Americans 'poor'. The
2/10th Battalion 'crossed swampland the Japs declared im-
passable and attacked the airstrip next morning while the
Americans were 600 metres off, unable to move'. Yet F. J.

Rolleston, of the 2/9th, fought at Buna alongside of the American 32nd Division and said that 'they lacked training, but they did their best'. W. N. D. Bow blamed American failures on their being 'badly led', and NX12179 – who commanded the 2/3rd Anti-tank Regiment – was critical of the fact that Americans 'never saw their officers except when going into action. The Top Sergeant (RSM) ran the unit'.

C. V. Barkla preferred American equipment to American troops, and generous individuals to collective skites, while J. D. Donohue preferred Americans in New Guinea to those he met in Sydney and Brisbane – and so the wheel of the evidence almost turns one complete revolution . . . Let it go full circle with the comments of two more respondents. Andrew Muir was also a proud member of a sometimes despised group of men – he was a militiaman in the 36th Battalion – and he said of the sometimes despised Americans, 'I had quite a lot of contact with them. The negroes were gentlemen, and some American units were very good, even if others were not so good'. But it was NX10773 who produced a version of a very old one-liner: 'The Americans were over-paid, over-fed, over-equipped and over-dressed; thank God, though, they were over here.'

There is a babel of voices, some fresh, others heard before. The British were best . . . The Germans were best . . . The New Zealanders . . .

'The *Japanese* weren't invincible, anyway,' says R. C. Tompson, 'I've seen them run in the face of bayonet charges. They were no better or worse than other troops.'

'Nationality had nothing to do with it,' breaks in VX34007, 'though some people like to think so. The better the *discipline*, the better the troops.'

In some units there were all sorts of racial and national types, all rated effective . . . Still, they all had an *Australian* background . . . A *country* background was best . . . The best came from *all sorts* of backgrounds, as hard to predict . . .

'Background?' interjects NX17811. 'It was *training*, like we did in Syria before Alamein, and jungle training at Canungra, and amphibious training at Cairns . . .'

'I served in the regular army in various places after World War II,' remarks J.W., 'and I've been most impressed by the highly trained Alpine troops . . .'

Italians?

When experienced *AIF* troops were put into a place with the wrong equipment and wrong training they got clobbered . . . It was equipment that made the Americans, and their numbers . . . Some Americans were tops . . . Look, the best was the volunteer . . . Fair go, there was none better than some Militia battalions . . . It depended on leadership . . . The best was the man who believed in what he was doing . . . It depends on what you mean by a soldier, and what he had to do . . .

'And it depends on where he was,' adds C.R.T. 'In *open country* the British were among the best . . .'

On and on, round and round, the argument goes among Australian men who served. Most of them would agree on three things: they met some worthy foes, although not all were honourable; they had some worthy allies, although some were better than others; and they were proud of their Australian comrades, even if individuals sometimes privately doubted their own worth.

12 • FRANKLY AND PERSONALLY

Russel Ward once wrote that the Australian reputedly 'hates officiousness and authority, especially when these qualities are embodied in military officers and policemen'. His own assessment too was that 'dislike and distrust of policemen . . . has sunk deeply into the national consciousness' (*The Australian Legend*, 1966 edn, pp. 2, 160).

As a respondent Professor Ward still favoured that stereotype of the Australian. He himself finished the war as a WO II with a psychology testing section, and he believed that relations between different ranks were seldom better than 'only fair', while those between officers and men were downright 'poor'. Furthermore, the military police were 'all bastards', an opinion formed 'especially after living in their barracks with them for two month-long periods'.

Yet there is more to be said, and many other respondents helped to say it. A mere 3 per cent of them labelled as 'poor' the relations between officers and men (in a group of which one-third remained privates, and another third rose no higher than corporal or sergeant). On the military police, or provosts, only 16 per cent of respondents agreed with Ward in totally despising them, while 17 per cent went to the opposite extreme of singing their praises. That left most respondents with a more moderate or ambivalent attitude to MPs, and often they made clear distinctions.

There were 17 per cent who said that their own divisional MPs – or other frontline provosts – were first-rate, but that the MPs in and around base areas – especially the British 'Red

Caps' – were less good, and sometimes overbearing or sadistic. Since Ward's service was mostly done in Sydney, his judgement was doubtless coloured by his being in one of those rear areas where MPs – and military officers – were often at their worst, their harshest and most officious. There can hardly be any argument about normal Australians disliking officiousness – and viciousness of one kind or another; but as troops moved from base areas, officiousness necessarily declined anyway. Pettiness, red tape and abrasive distinctions of rank diminished; there was less alcohol; many poor types did not get so far, or were pulled into line at last, or got rid of; and, as danger and clear purpose increased, everyone – officers, other ranks and MPs – drew closer.

Differences in rank and role remained, but attitudes changed. It was a kind of 'frontier' situation, and it had some of the marks of new societies: status having to be matched by performance, the practical having to be preferred to protocol, and some shackles being lost in the process. It came comparatively easily to Australians. To quote Ward as historian again, and this time to fully agree with him, the settlement of Australia did not so much change the institutions among the white settlers as it did people's attitude to life, 'and so . . . the way . . . these institutions . . . work in practice' (*The Australian Legend*, p. 240). One of them has been the Australian army. Despite its basic model, hierarchical structure, phases of bastardry and continuous discipline, no Australian army has been entirely British. Even action scarcely blunted the sharp edge of petty rank in the British army.

As an infantry private from Echuca, A. C. Smith had some British troops alongside of him at El Alamein. 'What amazed me', he said, 'was the way the British sergeant gave the commands to his men – really yelled at them – different altogether from the way our sergeants spoke to us.' Ivor White was 'very, very impressed with the Tommies, but distressed at the way the one-stripers and one-pippers stood over them'. Something very deep, and from a long way back, was being carried on there. Australians, in whom it was neither so deep nor complete, could more readily let some of it go. They toned it down progressively the farther behind they left Puckapunyal training camp, Sydney railway station and Brisbane and Beirut bars. Behaviour was modified on all sides; they saw the job in front of them; and men got on better with NCOs, officers and MPs.

C. F. Hartmann thought an 'intense dislike of base and leave-centre MPs' was widespread, but knew no one who had anything but 'great respect for divisional and unit (Australian or British) MPs, who often remained behind directing traffic in retreat long after it was safe to do so'. Apart from the checking of leave passes, K.C.H. had no contact with line-of-communication provosts (MPs in rear areas), but still believed that the divisional MPs were a different breed: 'A 7th Division provost carried my Bren gun and helped me through [at least seven miles of] swamp from Soputa to Gona.' 'Storeman', a soldier who was often in trouble in both base and forward areas, considered that 'divisional provosts were okay, but base provosts were mercenary – never seen action and never gave any leeway'.

Other distinctions were made. Various respondents – Ivor White, E.K., J.W.B., K.R.P. and R.F.E., among others – warned against confusing *any* military policemen with 'the lowest of the low', the warders in military prisons. R.F.E. was never in one but had talked to men who were, and he was still wondering if the government ever knew of the brutal treatment handed out in them. After 'a bit of AWL', Ivor White was an inmate. He had nothing against MPs – they did good work in Greece and helped his unit even in a base area like Cairns; but he was 'appalled at the way the "screws", all staff sergeants, treated the detainees at Geelong Detention Barracks'. Although only once punched and kicked himself, he watched the fist and boot frequently used on others, and various humiliations inflicted on particularly the duller inmates.

Another group of respondents broadly approved of the MPs yet had to say that the provosts sometimes emerged in a bad light: NX41216 had two brushes with them, and was treated fairly in Warwick but unfairly in Cairns. When these men are added to the 17 per cent who distinguished between base and divisional MPs, the combined total is 25 per cent who refused to put all provosts in the one basket, either all good or all bad. One more large group (26 per cent) simply said that MPs were 'necessary', leaving it impossible to know if they liked, disliked or were neutral about those who performed a duty that had to be done. The necessity of the job was well illustrated by three respondents.

One said that he thought many MPs tried to be fair and tolerant, 'but when the boys started to break up a bar, they *had* to move in'. NX4320, already wearing his Military Medal ribbon, was once locked up in Victoria Barracks, Sydney, for a weekend on a rather silly AWL charge. He did not think much of the way the MPs treated him, but on the other hand he was 'not much impressed by many of their guests, either'. E. L. Chesson, tough and rough, from the Adelaide slums, 'used to get drunk and fight MPs . . . stand-over merchants. I picked on a couple whilst under the influence. Took three to subdue me. They broke my nose, beat me up next day whilst suffering from a wild hangover. No charges were laid, as officers wanted their cook back'. Then Chesson added a post-script: 'I thoroughly deserved all I got.'

Some men said nothing about MPs, and others said they had no contact, but the weight of opinion did not tip clearly against the provosts, in spite of the lurking resentment of men being kept within limits when the idea was to make whoopee. The loyal Baptist F. J. Bennell believed that a greater part of the MPs were 'good men doing an unpopular job in a reason-able manner'. The wild 'Lofty' was 'arrested by them a few times for drunkenness in various cities, but never charged', and had 'great respect for the 6th Divisional Provost Corps', remembering particularly one MP who remained under fire at his post in Greece and, after capture, was punished by the Germans for defiance. V. H. Lloyd, a left-winger, 'half shared the stupid prejudice against the provosts, but had no real

knowledge of them except as traffic men who did a good job'.
He claimed that, despite *Smith's Weekly* tales, not many soldiers would stand up for principles against authority. When
drunk, the sky might be the limit in causing strife, but they
'faced authority with a certain timidity' after they sobered up.
He had found the same to be true of Australian society generally since the war: 'In small ways Australians maintain a
myth of rebellion, but essentially they remain timid before
authority.' His insistent use of the word 'timid' might have
been an exaggeration – or perhaps not. At any rate, he was
determined to offer a corrective to any distortion the other
way.

And respondents on the whole were more likely to see the
MPs as needed than as born out of wedlock. A great many
were at least partly appreciative of them, and often their
appreciation was strong. Of all the words applied by Ward to
Australian attitudes to police, perhaps 'distrust' is the most apt.
At least *suspicion* of the provosts was apparently quite common
among soldiers. Plain dislike was also there to a significant
degree, and yet the bulk of the respondents did not simply
despise the MPs. In so far as this group of ex-soldiers can be
taken as a useful guide, it could be unwise to settle for a claim
that the Australian hates authority, policemen and military
officers. It might be better to say that, for most Australians, it
depends on how that authority is asserted. There will often be
reservations about police and officers until it is seen how they
behave. If they act well – firmly, but decently and appropri-
ately – they and their authority will usually win solid Australian respect.

Other personal opinions

In point of fact, black-marketeers earned a vastly higher negative vote (88 per cent) than the military police did. Civilians
who made illegal profits on items in short supply would naturally tend to be disliked by troops, although the comments of

some respondents were shrewd and subtle. A. W. Webster was more inclined to blame the customers, remarking that 'the greedy who could not do without items were possibly worse'. And D.S.A. knew his average soldier. The black market was 'frowned on if indulged in at home, but for the troops it was fair game if they could get away with it. I sold my beer ration to the local Sultan at an enormous profit'. Yet the black-marketeers were mostly thought of as being unconnected with the army (one or two respondents alleged that there were some very big rackets run by military personnel), and the condemnation lay in black-marketeering that let down the war effort.

Similarly, trade unionists were often described in terms that were negative (32 per cent) or mixed (24 per cent), mainly because soldiers were deeply offended by how some union actions affected the troops.

> Very bitter about union attitudes. In 1943 about a hundred men in my unit had to work on Sydney wharves, on only army pay ['AASC Officer', a United Australia Party voter].
>
> Resentment against wharfies for strikes and pilfering of badly needed supplies such as compasses and field-glasses [C. F. Young, no political preference].
>
> Waterside workers who robbed cargoes supplying the troops deserved shooting as traitors [N.B.McA., Labor voter and member of Amalgamated Engineers Union].
>
> Very crooked on them for striking in wartime. They were lucky we didn't deal with them when we came back [J. J. C. Bridgefoot, Labor voter and member of NSW Operative Stone-masons Society].
>
> In 1943 our home-going convoy of 32 000 men was held up at Massawa, one of the hottest places on earth, because striking wharf labourers in Sydney had held up the *Elizabeth* for five days, and the whole fleet had to await her arrival. We then had to skirt the Antarctic to avoid a Jap ambush that had been able to get into position to destroy us [P. E. Buddee, swinging voter and member of WA Teachers Union].

Finschhafen, Xmas 1943. The battle's won. Bury the dead. Unload that shipment of eggs. Now tip the eggs into the sea, for all went bad in the holds during that strike in Sydney for better working conditions [A.E.H., a supporter of the UAP, who had not joined his Shop Assistants Union because it had proved useless in eradicating below-award conditions then rife].

Those were not the last words of respondents on trade union activities (and wharf labourers were not the only ones criticised), but such resentments were frequent. A large 28 per cent did not answer, but only 16 per cent were completely favourable.

About the other side of commerce and industry – Australian employers and financiers – a full half of the respondents had nothing to say. Soldiers having to load ships themselves, and doing it twice as quickly as usual, easily develop strong opinions on wharfies, but young men bent on survival in desert or jungle may not expend much thought on bosses and bankers. Of all respondents, 20 per cent were positive in their attitude, 13 per cent negative and 17 per cent mixed; so perhaps the capitalists scored better than the militant unionists, although the silence of the other 50 per cent left the picture murky.

The increased participation of women in the workforce, much publicised and seen as vital for the war, was warmly applauded by respondents. Although 24 per cent had no opinion, 69 per cent were approving and the critics insignificant in number. Typical was J. S. Morris's 'Good on them. My cousin took up heavy welding at Kelly and Lewis Engineering, and my fiancée did piece work at Swallow and Ariell's, packing army rations'. W. J. Thompson said that women 'seemed to make a better effort than the men towards the war effort', and D. A. Welch more sourly saw their involvement as 'one excuse less for the blokes who wouldn't enlist'. On the whole, though, respondents regarded male civilians of military age with considerable tolerance. Of those who expressed an opinion, only 24 per cent were contemptuous, compared with

Brisbane tramcar, 1942, with conductress
Gloria and a soldier. World War II
enabled Australian women to take such jobs

30 per cent who admitted to having 'some reservations' and 46 per cent who – in the era of manpower control and conscription – simply accepted that some men had to stay at work. C. M. Walter thought such men 'very lucky'. VX68246 looked at them 'with sympathy', since he himself had been 'forced to remain in a reserved occupation for two years'. E.J. recognised that it took five or six at home to maintain one man at the front, and A.P.D. 'felt more strongly about those who enlisted and then wangled cushy, safe jobs in the army'. S. J. Oldroyd – formerly a partner in a small printery – even refused to condemn civilians for going on strike: 'Some soldiers complained, but I thought they might be looking after my future working conditions.' QX35757 said, 'Those in productive employment were my equals; I was pleased the other types weren't in the forces'. Those others were called 'leeches' by K.B.B., and it was only the 'exploiters' who disgusted R. H. Timperley – although he did not enjoy, while at Milne Bay, losing a girlfriend to a university student.

The continuation of sporting events during the war was fully supported by 68 per cent of the respondents who answered the relevant question, with 16 per cent expressing some reservations and 17 per cent resenting what it suggested to them: the hollowness of the claim that an all-out effort was being made. 'When we were in Tobruk,' wrote VX47914, 'we

Demure Australian infantrymen at a Palestine beach in 1942 include Harry Davis, a full-blood Aborigine

used to hold a minute's silence for the footballers injured in Australia on Saturday afternoons.' But most men did not see it that way. Those who had reservations sometimes objected particularly to the races, perhaps because they could be midweek interruptions; or they wondered about some of the sporting 'heroes'; but most respondents simply saw the big matches as necessary relaxation such as they enjoyed themselves in their own breaks, and as actually being good for morale. A. A. J. Vane, who only had one home leave in over four years, came out very strongly for keeping sport going: 'People at home or on leave needed these events. They prevented national insanity and an obsessive paranoia over the war.'

Among the most troubled in 1939–45 might have been the conscientious objectors to any war, but soldiers could take a poor view of fit young men who refused to serve even in the non-combatant roles chosen as a compromise by some pacifists. Even Vane 'really felt the conscientious objectors were hypocrites – most *soldiers* did not kill'. The tendency among respondents to condemn conscientious objectors was fairly strong, but not utterly overwhelming. No answer was given by 25 per cent. A totally negative attitude was expressed by 37 per cent, and 17 per cent had mixed views that were usually more critical than sympathetic. 'Some have to witness against evil,' wrote Edwin Badger, 'yet it is hard to see conscience in enjoying a community life you let others risk their lives for.' Deep down, his opinion might not be far removed from that of NX68418, who thought pacifists 'should have been given unsavoury jobs such as the burial parties behind the fighting men'. A resentful F. W. Staggs said, 'They should have been interned, locked up at night and made to work on a soldier's pay in an arms factory by day'. R. R. Kirkwood reckoned that they 'should have had their objections surgically removed'.

Yet 21 per cent of the respondents admired the pacifists for their 'special brand of personal courage', as NX28127 put it. (He also recalled a lull in the fighting at El Alamein when 'Happy' seemed more solemn than usual and finally said it didn't seem right for millions of people to be dying all over the world because politicians couldn't work things out, and he was going to be a real pacifist if he got out of this. He started to go back to his hole and an odd shell killed him instantly.) M. J. Radel respected principled objectors more than cowards who hid in protected industries or base jobs in the army, and R.B.Y.'s summing up was, 'It took guts to buck the system. Look what they did to Jesus'.

There is one other point: the politically conservative were most likely to condemn the conscientious objector. From United Australia and Country Party supporters came 53 per cent of the negative votes and 38 per cent of the positive. Labor, Communist and Social Credit men provided only 30 per cent of the negative votes, but 45 per cent of the positive. Swinging voters or those uninterested in politics spread themselves evenly over positive, negative and mixed. The result doubtless reflected a difference between those who basically thought in terms of loyalty to the establishment and those who valued the establishment's critics.

Body and soul

Conscience, service, sacrifice ... Thou shalt not kill ... Greater love hath no man than this, that a man lay down his life for his friends ...

How did men see those who served in the army as priests and ministers of religion – officially known as chaplains, commonly called padres? A. E. E. Bottrell, who was one of them, explained how chaplains were selected:

The number of members in the major denominations determined the places allotted, so Anglican and Catholic chaplains predominated, followed by Methodists, Presbyterians and Other Protestant Denominations (mainly Baptists, Congregationalists, Churches of Christ and Salvation Army). The total number of appointments from OPD would have been very few.

Then came the real test, and many chaplains passed it, for respondents mostly remembered them with respect. Some 9 per cent did not answer and another 9 per cent damned the padres. A mixed response – which was often, of course, the most realistic for chaplains as for others – was made by 20 per cent; but uncritical appreciation was expressed by 63 per cent, a proportion well exceeding the personally devout and conventional churchgoers among the men.

The diversity, although not the balance, of opinion is readily illustrated:

In the main a sanctimonious lot, full of platitudes and concerned for their own safety [D.R.S.].
Parasites. If there was a God, like they said, he would never permit war [C. W. ('Bing') Crosbie].
Our bloke was an officers' chaplain; most of us found him a creep [WX642].
Our chaplain was called the invisible man [VX4300].
Two types. One talked down to you, the other talked to you [WX35961].
Did not affect me, but for the troops with religion in their veins chaplains were very important [K. G. Wilson].
They seemed to be either very good or very bad [I. L. Duncan].
They were a good bunch of fellows, no matter what denomination, and did a lot for the men [L.P.H.].

In the 1980s M.N.K. belonged to the Revival Centres of Australia, spoke in tongues and knew the Bible as 'an open book' prophesying World War III 'and all that it entails'. Even in the 1940s, when he was a Methodist, ' the second return of Jesus was of paramount importance' to him, so he found most chaplains 'wishy washy, and not on the right track'. K. A. Patterson, a keen Baptist who served on the Australian mainland only, was inclined to see the fault as lying on the other side. Chaplains were 'tryers, but had little scope to do effective work. The war had to be won before we could think of anything else, so they were reduced mainly to welfare work'.

The padres were appreciated from diverse angles. A.B. found them 'good, always helpful; in one staging camp the RC padre was the SP bookie'. T.A.D. thought them 'dedicated and helpful'; he saw one 'bare-headed, in a white surplice, reading from the Bible, at the head of a battalion advancing into Bardia in column of three'. And, while J.H.B. thought that chaplains were like MPs in that both were 'a necessary evil', P. R. Garrett made the kind of distinction between chaplains that was often applied to MPs. Those (especially the Protestants) in Australian base units were not highly regarded, he thought, but the 'combat padres' had deep respect; when crippled by a machine-gun bullet and behind Japanese lines, he was rescued by a group commanded by a chaplain. In the experience of 'NSW Teacher', 'most chaplains were more than priests; several became amongst the most highly respected officers'. B. G. D. Tongs and K. J. Irwin recalled chaplains who died in New Guinea, essentially in the front line.

NX3993 could not understand how 'men of God' could condone war, and sometimes chaplains came near to breaking under war's horror. E. V. Nottridge, a Baptist with mixed views on padres, was moved by a Catholic priest kneeling beside the 'mere remnants' of some fifty soldiers after a Tobruk battle, and then coming to Nottridge's group, weeping and asking, 'Why do we have to go to war to kill each other?' But 'Charlie' thought he could see another aspect of it. At the battle of Slaters Knoll in Bougainville, he witnessed 'the need for padres (a Catholic and a Salvationist) to take rifles and join battle. When survival is at stake even the most dedicated Christians must fight. Both these men killed Japanese, but the Japanese had no respect for Christian ministers anyway'. As NX147794 commented with regard to conscientious objectors, 'the enemy won't go away just because you don't agree with war'.

'Junior' – only 5 ft 4 in tall – served in infantry battalions in the Pacific, and he wrote:

Our chaplain so often said 'Call me Digger' that we *did* call him 'The Digger'. And we had a Red Shield (Salvation Army) representative as a welfare officer whom we called 'The Professor'. The battalion was getting a bit on the nose because we were without soap of any kind, so Digger and Professor somehow acquired a gross of Palmolive shaving sticks and worked into the early hours cutting them up to give each man from colonel to cook's offsider an equal ration. I always thought Digger was the best soldier in the battalion, though he was not of my belief, and I can't speak too highly of the old Professor, with his pencils and paper and 'Write to your Mum, soldier'. When the main force of the battalion landed at Rabaul, I was in the first barge and one of the first ashore. Out of the bush came a voice, 'Coffee, mate – with or without?' It was the Professor. He'd landed the night before, hadn't he? And the Digger: 'You're looking tired, soldier. Give us your shovel. I need some exercise.' Are there still *men* like these around?

The numerical smallness of the Salvation Army among the Australian population meant that there were very few Salvationist chaplains, but there were large numbers of them in welfare work: setting up recreational huts, supplying writing materials, providing men with a cuppa, a block of chocolate, cigarettes . . . right up to the front line. VX66345 thought they were 'sometimes too keen, and didn't realise that we couldn't afford passengers'. But was the Professor a passenger? In fact

'The enemy won't go away just because you don't agree with war.' The enemy came to Victoria, capital of Labuan Island. Among the debris Private M. J. Brincat found a photograph of a little girl. Its source – Rembrandt Studios, Adelaide – had no record of the customer. But the soldier treasured his 'portrait of an unknown girl', and has guarded it ever since, just in case it might be restored to someone who knew her. The offer still stands

the Salvation Army was paid the finest possible tribute by the
enormous number of respondents who said something like:

> Salvos forever. Mad as hatters. Moved out on dangerous patrol
> one New Guinea morning and found a Salvo one mile out with
> hot coffee. Drank his coffee and, with words General Booth
> would not have appreciated, sent him home. Shot our first Jap
> 200 yards on [R. A. Aitken].
>
> Truly God's gentlemen. I think they had an agreement with the
> Japs to let them set up their coffee stalls. Can't speak too highly
> of them [VX136491].

W. T. Dedman believed that all welfare personnel 'tried to do
a good job against red tape'. VX59612 thought the Salvation
Army had an inflated image, and that the Young Men's Christian Association representatives were okay. J. G. Manning
certainly agreed. He *was* a YMCA representative. The YMCA
and the Salvation Army served different units, and Manning
thought that men often confused the YMCA's Red Triangle
with the Salvationists' Red Shield and attributed YMCA service to the Salvos – who were very good at publicising their
work. Nevertheless the respondents, whether justly or not,
were far and away more impressed by the Salvation Army
than by any other body.

F. N. T. Brewer thought that he did see a range of welfare
men early in the war, but after that 'only the Salvos, who were
always popping up in unexpected places'. VX9702 put 'the
Salvos first, the rest far behind'. NX14409 also declared 'Salvos to the fore; hardly saw the Australian Comforts Fund or
their hampers'. C. J. Hughes 'never met a welfare officer until
after the war; he stole my wife, which turned out to be
wonderful for me'. D.B.H. said that 'the Sallies excepted, the
welfare boys were conspicuous by their absence. The junket-
ing of Lady Blamey and her ilk was deplorable'. Warming to
that theme, Roland Marsh wrote:

Don't speak to me of the Red Cross; it was a fraud, a social group. I

remember with resentment Lady Blamey coming to my bedside at
1st Australian General Hospital, Gaza. She actually gave me one pkt
of cigarette papers, one pkt of PKs and a face-washer. How did it
happen that I could *buy* Red Cross cigarettes, meant to be *given* to
soldiers, at a canteen? I never saw a Red Cross official closer to the
front than divisional level, but the Salvo would actually meet us
coming in from patrol with a slice of cake and hot tea. I told my
mother to contribute *only* to the Salvation Army.

Such comments hardly do justice to the work of welfare
organisations other than the Salvation Army. Red Cross parcels saved many POW lives, and E. C. Fancote contrasted the
good fortune of German POWs in receiving those parcels
with the ill fortune of Japanese POWs, who were usually
denied them although the Japanese received them. Yet if the
Salvation Army was sometimes given credit for what others
had done, there seems no doubt that its effort went into the
realm of the superlative – on, perhaps, into the realm of God,
although the Salvos were not there to preach. Here's a cup of
coffee, soldier.

The bodies and minds of men were also cared for by medical personnel – stretcher-bearers, ambulance drivers, orderlies,
doctors, and the women of the Australian Army Nursing Service (the latter being full members of the army, with an 'X' in
their numbers, and always commissioned officers). They had
their critics, but not many among the respondents. With 8 per
cent not answering and 13 per cent expressing mixed views,
there were only 3 per cent against the medical staff and 77 per
cent strongly for them during war service. So high an
approval rating largely speaks for itself, although illustrative
material could spill over page after page.

Jack Hutchison remembers the nursing sister who flung
her body over an already dying man to shield him as a plane
machine-gunned the *Empire Star* out of Singapore. On a hospital ship from New Guinea, hardened soldiers vomited as a
vile stench filled the confined space in which they lay
wounded. It was worse even than the 'peculiarly offensive'

The 4th Australian General Hospital, Tobruk, 1941; pitted with shrapnel but avoided as much as possible by the German planes

odour of decomposing Japanese bodies, and it came from one man's groin-wound that had been patched up with leaves and mud. SX4065 watched as a young sister, sweat and tears pouring down her face inches above the revolting mess, cleaned the wound gently and steadily, piece by piece. 'We soon found out', he added, 'what a terrific job medical personnel did whenever we didn't have them.'

Howard Stone – a draper before the war – was attached at El Alamein to a surgical team, a field unit to do amputations and dress other wounds on the spot: 'The night the push started we lost twenty-two stretcher-bearers bringing in the wounded, but many other lives were saved.' More than one respondent made a simple statement similar to this one from a New South Wales infantryman: 'I owe my life to their untiring efforts, especially at the camp hospital in the Owen Stanley Ranges.' More could hardly be said, unless perhaps the man happend to be a POW on the Burma railway, like M.R.L., and was not only grateful but also amazed at what the doctors achieved with 'nothing to help them'.

Medical personnel, Salvos, padres . . . At the front, caring for the flesh, ministering to the spirit . . . They were deeply appreciated.

The dark underside of Australia

Sometimes a respondent emerged who wrote much on the black and ugly aspects of Australian society and its soldiers. The balance in his commentary might be questionable and need adjustment, yet his point had to be well taken: plenty of Australians and, accordingly, plenty of Australian soldiers could be ripe bastards. Individuals could behave both well and badly in different circumstances, and army life did nothing to help some of them. One of the most negative respondents was SX4065, but his concentration on the dark side was a valuable reminder of its grim reality.

SX4065 was an Australian only by adoption, and he realised that he might be dismissed as 'a whingeing Pom' even after nearly sixty years in the land. He arrived as a lone young man in time to go wandering the jobless roads for several years in the depression, 'hating the sunburnt country and finding the great hospitality of the north to be a myth'. He became 'a dirty unwanted derelict at 24 years of age, hunted out of towns and shunned by all except *some* other hoboes – a humiliating, degrading experience'. Life had improved for him by 1939, but he still joined the 2/27th Battalion because it offered the first secure job he had ever had – and also a chance to see his Cornish home again. But the army disgusted him in many ways.

You will get various replies and my answer might come as a shock, but you asked for *my* version. In the early training days the powers-that-be got discipline from other ranks by veiled threats and innuendos, so successfully instilling fear into us that we were brought to the point of servility. Weekend leave was paramount in men's minds, and it was never a sure thing – it could be refused if we hadn't behaved. So they achieved 'discipline'. Perhaps the men in 'The Charge of the Light Brigade' were battling for a spot of leave; they were certainly disciplined.

And perhaps camp 'discipline' caused chaps to behave badly on leave; they were for a time free. And what were country boys supposed to do with 'home' leave from 5 p.m. Saturday to midnight Sunday? So kids of 19 or 20 – often away from home for the first time – roamed the city with no place to sleep, and learnt the sordid side of life from old drinkers and carousers. The establishment should have arranged billets for all, not just for officers. See the gap that existed? The great camaraderie between officers and men in the AIF is just another exploded myth, a load of crap. I don't blame the new officers, but the establishment that brainwashed them into accepting a system that went against the better nature of some of them (others lapped it up); but it did no good for morale in the lower ranks.

Then the troops went overseas and had leaves in far-off cities where vice was blatantly commercialised in ways most of them had never known. On the other hand, too many Australians already had well-developed vices of their own. SX4065 went on:

I concede that the barrel is not to be judged by one rotten apple, but there were far too many rotten apples. I'm not going to quote hearsay, only happenings I actually saw: hiring a taxi, not paying fare, beating up the driver and over-turning his car; robbing cigarette street-vendors of their wares and upsetting their trays; accosting ordinary women in main thoroughfares with, 'How about a fuck?'; refusing to pay prostitutes for services rendered, smashing the furnishings, shitting in the bath tub and even bashing the women . . . Put a uniform on some men and they think it gives them a licence to create anarchy and worse. Again I blame the higher echelons for not stamping these things out but excusing them as 'letting off steam'. So long as other ranks saluted and did not rock the army boat, everything was rosy.

SX4065 was very guarded in his comments on military policemen, but he did say, 'They did a good job policing brothels'. Without the MPs and the picquets, what would some Australians have been like? And what were some like after the war, when they got home? SX4065 reported on that too.

I am writing of my own platoon, twenty-two men who returned to civilian life with me. They had mostly been in their very early twenties when they joined up. Within two years of demobilisation, three of them were imprisoned. In later life, two were in a home for alcoholics, one was burnt to death while drunk, one committed suicide and one was gaoled for raping his daughter. I knew these blokes inside out, and feel that the 'war', 'army' – call it what you like – was the basic cause of their behaviour. There are only two of us left from that platoon, strangely enough the oldest in it. Maybe it proves that the young chaps' lives were moulded in the wrong direction; not many turned out to be good husbands or fathers. This might not be general, I hope not; but that's what happened to many of my mates.

Nor is there any need to rely on one man for evidence, either of postwar trauma or the fleshpots of Egypt. A three-figure infantryman had maintained close contact with his unit association, and was struck by how few of its wartime officers achieved much in peacetime. He, a corporal during the war, had far outstripped his officers in civilian life, and he wondered why. (He did not think, incidentally, that the same was true of ex-officers from units like artillery or engineers.) Were they men who had to have the badges of rank to function at their best? (Some had done well in the permanent army.) Had army life spoilt them for settling down to study and being under a boss? Were these frontline infantry leaders early achievers who were just burnt out by the time the war was over? And there were others, mostly from the ranks, who became complete no-hopers: 'It used to break my heart to see John ——, a young soldier of good standing in Tobruk, sitting on a seat in a city street, drinking "plonk" until he died.'

Another witness for the prosecution, SX9054, described the 'Can Can' in an old house in Alexandria, to which a small party of curious young Australians – actually AWL – had been guided:

Two very young RAF boys were there, and a very drunk 6th Divvy

engineer, lying on a sofa still with his hat on. Eventually two dis-
robed girls began a poor type of belly dance. They approached each
of us in turn, the large dark girl pushing her pubis (adorned with a
luxuriant growth of hair) as close to us as she could. Most of us
backed off, one or two lifting a chair in the manner of a lion-tamer,
but the drunken Aussie made futile grabs at her buttocks. Finally, she
draped her legs around his neck. Feeling that fur collar, he got very
excited, only to fall to the floor with the girl on top of him. His
hands went everywhere, but she was too quick for him and, after
tweaking him in the groin and making some lewd remark, went on
with the dance. Two of us picked him up and put him back on the
sofa – and then saw horror and disbelief on the RAF boys' faces.
Turning, we found that the girl had lit a cigarette, placed it in her
vagina and was circling and jiggling towards them with it burning in
the forest. They drew back; she laughed and approached the Aussie,
who groped at her and then noticed the fag. He lunged, she pushed
him backwards, but he had the cigarette. As he slumped on the sofa,
he put it in his mouth and began to smoke it . . .

Soon afterwards, though not before seeing 'worse', SX9054
and his little group hurriedly left, two of them – field ambu-
lancemen – to be sick in the gutter.

Every war, and every nation, spews up its vomit.

Social customs? Social vices?

Having mostly been very young in the 1930s, respondents
went into the army as 92 per cent virtual non-gamblers, 79 per
cent virtual non-drinkers and 43 per cent non-smokers (with
another 31 per cent smoking only very lightly). They often
changed. Some people's favourites might be those who went
in as non-smokers, non-gamblers and non-drinkers, came out
as heavy indulgers in all three pastimes, and then went on to
say that the army did them more good than harm. Others
might prefer WX36884, who perhaps improved in one respect. He came out of the army a non-gambler, whereas before

Top: *To please a photographer in a training camp, soldiers stage a two-up game, in which two coins are spun and bets laid on both coins landing with the same face uppermost*

Above: *A real game among members of the 2/10th Battalion and their British driver (left) in the Jordan Valley in 1941. Second from right is 'Stormy Normy' Foster, later a federal and South Australian politician*

he went in he 'had an occasional flutter on cards – couldn't shuffle horses'.

On the whole, gambling increased among the men. Those who never gambled dropped to 26 per cent, and 59 per cent gambled a little. Moderate gamblers doubled (but only from 6 per cent to 12), and heavy gamblers more than quadrupled, although the numbers were always small (from 0.4 per cent to 1.8).

Smoking was what increased most. Heavy smoking rose from 3 per cent to 19, and moderate from 23 to 34 per cent. Light smokers fell from 31 per cent to 19, and non-smokers from 43 to 28 per cent. Drinking was also more common, with the teetotallers falling off to 13 per cent (instead of 32), and light drinkers to 38 (instead of 47) per cent. Certainly half of the respondents thus emerged from the army not much – if at all – interested in drinking, but teetotalism became rarer, and there was the other half: 40 per cent were moderate drinkers, instead of 20 per cent; and 8 per cent were heavy drinkers, instead of 0.7 per cent.

The survey produced 'Infantry Colonel' – an excellent one, his men said – who maintained that the smoker was the worst frontline soldier: he wasted space carrying the makings, and endangered his mates by his cough and glow. The colonel's claims would, of course, be heard with incredulity by many respondents who increasingly smoked while effective front-line troops. There was quite another side to *that* story – and not merely the medical officers' encouragement of POWs to smoke what could be got to allay the pangs of terrible hunger. Yet, whatever the argument on the score of smoking, the gravest problem was resort to drink.

It was not just a matter of the respondent who triumphantly completed the questionnaire only to knock over it a bottle of red, leaving a stained and soggy mess his wife insisted on throwing away. He paid the dreadful penalty of having to fill out another one. Nor was it merely the fact that, as B.F.A. remarked, 'there were few serious disciplinary troubles unless those involved were drunk at the time, or at least a bit under the weather'. The real problem lay with men like some already mentioned – the infantry corporal's John ——, drinking plonk until he died, and the alcoholic mates of SX4065.

J. Arthurson was a schoolteacher who 'liked a few beers', and served in the Middle East and South-east Asia before returning to civilian life as a surveyor. He was one of the respondents who wrote of men who

died surprisingly soon after the war. In quite a few cases they couldn't adjust to the ordered life of office, factory or whatever confined them. Many couldn't face the thought of domesticity. So they drank themselves to death. A lot of us, who had known wild times in the army, were luckier. We were able to leave the booze alone, find the job we wanted and try to make up the civilian years we'd missed.

A number of respondents replied as ex-alcoholics who had rescued themselves with the aid of Alcoholics Anonymous (and thus represented the missing many). They included NX42618: 'Twenty-eight years is a long time between drinks.' He had become totally disillusioned by the lies told to brainwash people into wars, and was anti-imperialist. He had lived rough in both depression and war, and saw no hope for Australia's future. On lonely medical patrols to isolated outposts with the Australian New Guinea Administrative Unit, he was unusual in that he averaged sex with native women two or three times a month, and preferred them to white women; yet he was glad he would not live to see the inevitable completion of the process that was turning Australia into a foreign and coloured land: 'Stop the world. I want to get off.' In their different ways, many ex-soldiers had known the same feeling and had desperately hit the bottle.

Respondents, without being expansive, frequently spoke of men they knew having been psychologically damaged by the war, and often resorting to alcohol. Even with some 40 per cent not commenting at all, about 30 per cent referred to that

Donkey races at an army camp in the Middle East; and the bookmakers

kind of psychological hurt, while others spoke of 'moral decline' or 'social and marital' problems among men they knew. It used to worry the late Professor R. B. Joyce, for it seemed to him that respondents 'so often referred to the other fellows' that some might well be playing down their own trauma. There was even a piece of hard evidence. One respondent wrote that the war had little permanent effect on him, but – through another source – he was known to have become an alcoholic, and to have been admitted to a psychiatric hospital at one time, no doubt due in part to the stress of war.

Anyway, it is abundantly clear that for too many ex-service-men the legacy of war was not that they grew up and adopted the social custom of civilised drinking, but that they tried to ease intolerable strains by depending on alcohol, and so died as they had enlisted – very young.

Going on leave

NX69487 remarked ironically that home leave was 'not granted by Japs to POWs'. But men not quite so inconveniently placed sometimes fared little if any better, and fairly often those who managed to get a few days home failed to enjoy them. Only one-third of the respondents spoke with thorough appreciation of home leave. Some 19 per cent had neutral reactions; 10 per cent recalled very mixed feelings; and for 13 per cent home leave was almost completely distressing. One-quarter of the men either offered no comment or had no home leave worth speaking of. As always, men differed and so did their experiences.

J. A. G. Betts appreciated home more than he had previously realised, but VX56723 mainly felt anxious to return to duty. On his one home leave in Hobart, between the Middle East and New Guinea, TX—— rejoiced in 'the sights and sounds of old surroundings, quiet and calm'; but NX95078 found home difficult: his values had changed, but the family's had not. Having enlisted very young, 'Ex-42nd' enjoyed leave and felt proud of his uniform; but going home just made M.E.E. envious of civilians. With his parents dead and his brothers on active service, SX33439 found 'home' lonely; and NX51603 drank too much (as on leaves anywhere) because there was nothing to do, and it could be the last leave. The experiences of 'Bars' were in striking contrast to that. Although he never left Australia, he was given high regard and royal treatment in his home town and elsewhere. It was 'something to treasure' all his life, and he never regretted having taken no advantage of the daughters of people who

The services mixing cheerfully on leave at Mornington (Vic.) in 1944: a commando, a WAAAF sergeant who should have been wearing her uniform but preferred to look feminine, and a RAAF flying officer

Back from the Middle East in 1943, and right back home in Western Australia for all too brief a time: Paddy Alford with his mother and sister took him into their homes and looked after him like a son.

S. L. Carroll won the Military Medal in Crete for keeping enemy armoured cars at bay. On home leave in 1942 he married, but thereafter could not keep at bay his American allies. His wife played up with them, and when he got later leave he heard conflicting stories but could not find her. Entirely different were Roy Gould and his wife, who used home leave to such good effect that two children were born as a result, and their love and appreciation of each other deepened despite their separations. Yet there were many like NX170955: having been at home, they 'never wanted to go back to camp'.

Leave in Australia without a chance of getting home produced comparatively little comment among the respondents. They had none, or it was an unmemorable break in routine, or the question was ignored. Some men recalled much pleasure in such leaves, and some found them educational – those like R. G. Wilson, who discovered that 'life in Clements Gap was not the only way of life'. Leave elsewhere in Australia caused much less distress than did home leave, although some men were disturbed by civilians:

> I could see how the civvies were enjoying life [S. V. All-chin].
> Many Australians gave us second-class status behind the Yanks [NX145540].
> Apart from mothers, some wives and girlfriends, no one seemed to really care. The AIF seemed to be looked down on by many civilians, and (unless officers) were refused service at flash hotels ['Tom'].
> People were not behind the war as they should have been. The hypocrisy of flag-waving patriots sickened me. If the Japs had landed there would have been plenty of collaborators [W. G. Smith].

Overseas leave was different. Although a large 55 per cent

Top: *Four smart Australians in Alexandria. What lies ahead – in battle, and in a foreign city where respectable locals usually want nothing to do with them, and the leave might be their last?*

Above: *Leave in Colombo, 1941: 'Shorty' Casement, Albert Bannear, 'Star' Hennessey and – as the driver – 'Kiwi' James. The picture was taken with Bannear's camera, probably by a Ceylonese bystander*

either had none or made no comment, the great emphasis among the others was on its educational value – 22 per cent of the respondents made that point. 'I was able', wrote R. C. Beilby, 'to see the Acropolis in Athens and the pyramids of Egypt, both enlightening experiences.' R.W.B. thought that it improved his 'tolerance of other races, customs and religions'. Nor did he forget to add, 'and general larrikinism', thus linking himself with the 9 per cent who spoke only of having fun. Perhaps the locals also found their tolerance enlarged by Australian larrikinism, and perhaps not. At any rate, with 11 per cent of the respondents being neutral about these breaks from service, and only 3 per cent stressing the disturbing effects, overseas leave was much less likely than leave in Australia to produce grief and resentment among servicemen.

Sex: focus on restraint

To ex-service activities 'Larry the Bat' eventually devoted much of his time, but during the war he welcomed any leave from his unit as a chance to 'get away from the bastards for a while'. Leave meant freedom – and sexual freedom for some men, including 'Larry' who, despite his deep hatred of Japanese troops, enjoyed many Japanese women as a member of the occupation force. For numbers of men there were clear priorities: food first, drink next, women third. Sometimes the order varied, and there could be more biological function than anything else in the womanising. 'Sex was often a small part of the soldier's leave', wrote SX4065. 'He simply said, well, I got that over with, let's get down to some steady drinking. In the Middle East I once saw a mate having sex with his hat on, plus uniform boots – which explains why there was always a bit of oil cloth at the bottom of the bed. Perhaps it's the origin of the saying, boots and all.'

For many of the respondents, however, there was no casual sex on leave. They did not want it, or not what was offering;

or there was nothing available at all. They were desperately shy, or had moral scruples, or were afraid of disease. Whatever the reason, there were a lot of virgin or abstaining soldiers – and much suspicion that comrades' loudly boasted conquests were impure figments of fevered imaginations. Over half of the respondents emphasised one or more of those points in their answers; they simply did not find army life an open door to sexual experience.

No man, of course, *had* to answer, and 13 per cent said nothing about sex, while 5 per cent declared it to be a private matter: as WX36884 put it, 'Sex is for the bedroom, not for sick minds to paw over'. When men answered along the lines of 'little or no sex', there was a ring of truth to what they had to say, and their subtle shifts in perspective only added to the realism.

> Many books are so far-fetched that they turn the Australian soldier into a sex-maniac, second only to the Yank. In Palestine, leave came only every couple of months and we naturally longed for female company, but no girl would go out with us or she'd be branded a prostitute. The widow of Captain Moriarty (killed on Crete) opened a tea room at her own expense in Tel Aviv, and it was packed every day purely because we could there talk to women, with sex far from our minds. In Egypt it was worse – no women to talk to, although there were plenty of brothels for those so inclined. In Greece and Crete we were too busy to think about women, to talk to or otherwise [NX3700; single; nominal Presbyterian; middle-class; served from the first possible day of enlistment in 1939 to 1945, in Middle East and Pacific; signaller; sergeant].
>
> Sex? Are you serious? Apart from commercial contact with waitresses and prostitutes, we were totally ignored by females in Israel, Egypt and Ceylon. The army liked to concentrate in one spot, and back in Queensland there were three divisions plus corps troops on the Atherton Tableland; even Errol Flynn would have been battling under those circumstances. When not

concentrated, we were usually in some God-forsaken and woman-forsaken spot [A.J.B.; single; nominal C. of E.; working-class; Middle East and Pacific; artillery; lieutenant].

For me, sex was a non-event, and I can't even recall a lot of talk about it. Perhaps this is more applicable to the Pacific, where opportunity was more restricted than in, say, the Middle East with its large towns for leave [J. P. Cook; single; indifferent Presbyterian; middle-class; Pacific; infantry; private].

I joined up as a virgin and received my discharge five years later still the same. I was no orphan, though the regular rams continued as such. Admittedly, for 3½ years as POWs we were more interested in food than anything else, and we were not enjoying *anything* much [SX10941; single; passive Methodist; not class-conscious; South-east Asia; transport; driver].

If you liked to believe everything, we had a country full of Romeos, and there could not have been any virgins left for mugs like me [E.K.; single; casual Catholic; working-class; Middle East and POW; infantry; private].

Among other influences, specific ideals or moral standards sometimes clearly emerged.

I was not interested in sex outside my marriage. The army provided visual aids to warn those who might indulge – and I did not suffer fools gladly [NX99513; married; sceptical Methodist; middle-class; Pacific; anti-aircraft; gunner].

According to mates there was plenty of sex offering but, when introduced to girls, I always told them I was married and we became nothing but friends. Unfortunately, my wife carried on with more than one man, and left the children and me when I was demobbed ['Life Assurance'; married with two children; serious Congregationalist; ambivalent on class; served in Australia; ordnance; corporal].

Sex came up in almost every conversation. Certain types used brothels, and others tried to meet up with ordinary girls and hoped for luck there. But, to me, love and sex went together.

Without love, sex was nothing [J. N. Barter; single; devout
C. of E.; working-class; Pacific; commandos/infantry; cor-
poral].

Intercourse was readily available in Australia and places like
Ambon. Contraception was not – and using army-issue condoms was said to be like washing your feet with your socks on.
Anyhow, I was not prepared to have a child (known or
unknown) whom I could not bring up, so petting stopped just
short of intercourse [William John; engaged; dutiful C. of E.;
not class-conscious; Pacific; service corps; acting WO II].

Prostitutes were used to good effect, of course, but you might
be interested in our attitude to servicewomen. At a recent reunion of a special wireless group, one ex-AWAS asked, 'What
was wrong with you b——s? I went in a virgin and was still one
when discharged.' I guess we considered them as 'family', okay
for a kiss and cuddle, but warranted our protection [C. K. Hart;
single; sceptical Presbyterian but stong believer in the Christian
ethic; middle-class; Middle East and Australia; signals;
WO II].

Women were scarce except in Middle East, and there were bad
stories about black pox in brothels. Some chaps went for the
women, but a lot of us were brought up strict [Frank Lyons;
single; conventional Catholic; working-class; Middle East and
Pacific; infantry; private].

The social attitudes of the time and the inexperience of youth
were strong determinants of some men's restrained behaviour
– and of some women's discouragement of less inhibited
approaches. From the perspective of the 1980s, it could be seen
as a different world.

Too young, alas, to understand beyond puppy-love. Girls and
most servicemen at that time were influenced by almost Victorian attitudes to sex [J. A. Henderson; single; nominal Congregationalist; not class-conscious; Pacific; signaller].

I was a nervous virgin, and most of my immediate contempor-
aries were similar: uneducated idealists. All women were put on

By superimposing personal photographs, Jean and Jim become very important people. Sometimes the Jeans and Jims were so important to each other that they remained faithful; sometimes it was not so

a pedestal, *and* we didn't wish to take VD home with us. We boasted a lot and did little. The older men probably did better, but growing up was bloody agony. After talking to old mates, the conclusion is that we regret what we might have missed in that way more than all the deprivations of war [A. R. Forder; engaged; contempt for religion; not class-conscious; Middle East and Pacific; transport; lance-sergeant].

Sex in New Guinea or the Solomon Islands? Anyway, in the 1940s it didn't have the same importance as it has now [S.W.B.; single; habitual Methodist; working-class; Pacific; infantry; staff sergeant].

It all depended on the type of soldier and the society he mixed in. Sex is much more to the forefront now than it was then [L. G. Allen; single; C. of E. under family pressure; working-class; Pacific; signaller].

We talked a lot about it, and there were a few brief unsatisfactory encounters, but sexual licence was limited by many factors – fear of disease, religious taboos, being raised in an *un*permissive society ... [NX42488; single; convinced Catholic; unemployed for one year, but not class-conscious; Singapore and Australia; parachute battalion; private].

Like, I'd say, half of my regiment I'd not made love to a girl. On leave in Australia we'd get a skinful of grog and go looking for girls, but they wouldn't be in it. Looking back, you couldn't blame them. The Yanks had first priority, anyway [K. G. Wilson; single; nominal Methodist; working-class; Pacific; artillery/commando; lance-bombardier].

'Hasn't seen a woman for eleven months', ran the caption in Soldiering On *(1942)*

My father's advice was, 'There are good and bad women. If you go out with a girl, make sure she's a good woman – like your Mum. Hell, you know what I'm talking about. Also, when you go over the top be the last over, and fall down every few yards. Don't try to be a bloody hero'. My most hilarious experience was the medical officer's short-arm parades [inspection of penises]. What an assortment of shapes, sizes and deplorable states! Seriously, sex is the most over-rated aspect of service life. We knew who would always look around for women, but they were a minority. Most Diggers (and not only the married ones) preferred to stay together. The ethos in those days leant towards courtesy, hat-doffing, door-opening. Obscene language was restricted to camp. The brothel-visitors were not the bulk of the troops, and average girls were not submissive: the social consequences of pregnancy were daunting. I came close to slipping a couple of times, but remained a virgin. I can't speak for the Middle East, but in the Pacific we were too busy or isolated. In any case, we were more likely to contemplate the 'bottle' than the 'bird' ['Rusty'; single; devout Catholic; working-class; Pacific; pioneer; private].

Then a respondent introduced another aspect; after much hesitation he spoke of masturbation.

Shy, or afraid of trapping myself with a pregnant girl, I was a virgin. A number of my fellow soldiers were always looking out for the 'easy mark' and, according to them, scored a few times in Australia. But three of us – one married, one engaged and I with no attachment initially – were more interested in movies and the odd beer. Then came New Guinea. I don't know of any of our blokes playing around with women there, but the Japs did so. The medical officer warned us that the Japs were there before us, so there would be disease as well as other problems. His solution was: 'If you can stand no more, go behind a tree and whack yourself off.' I had married by that time and, to protect my wife, I did sometimes masturbate. I didn't think too highly of myself, but at least I touched no native woman and endangered my wife. I don't know about other soldiers, but many of them *must* have been like me in the dead of night. So my dark secret is out, in confidence ['New Guinea'; single/married; non-believing C. of E.; middle-class; Pacific; artillery; gunner/signaller].

It might be a mark of his generation that 'New Guinea' remained so furtive about self-relief. He need not have felt guilty, and his guess about others was not wildly astray.

> Girls were scarce, and not many of my mates used brothels when they were available. Old army saying: if you told your mates you masturbated, you were a fool; if you told them you did not, you were a liar ['Bocky'; single; nominal Methodist; unskilled worker; not class-conscious; Australia; service corps; private].
>
> When sex was dammed up there was a good deal of masturbation, and some disguised sexual horseplay. Others sweated it out [WX11470; single; atheist; socialist, but not class-conscious (?); Middle East and Pacific; infantry; private].
>
> With native villages out of bounds in the islands, and the women closely guarded, the main outlet was masturbation (and a few poofters). It was better than nothing [VX69733; married with one child; casual Catholic; working-class; Pacific; artillery; sergeant].

The element of women being guarded was not unimportant. P.G.H. (who insisted on only his initials being used, since he had to maintain his reputation of being an illiterate old bastard) confessed that, in Papua New Guinea, the young bare-breasted girls were attractive, but 'their men were skilled with bush-knives, and we hoped to finish the war in one piece'. Some other soldiers were put off in other ways: TX479 used to 'wish the New Guinea women would turn white and not smell'.

Avoidance of intercourse was solidly linked with dread of venereal disease.

> I once inspected the women in a Celebes brothel, but didn't fancy the wares. Had they been as attractive as some of the women in the street, it might have been another story – but I don't think so; it was against my upbringing. And none of us would have forced ourselves on a woman. My headmaster had alerted us to nature taking its course in 'wet dreams', and I'd say that they were the extent of the sexual experiences of the larger number of soldiers away from home [G. C. Youlden; single; habitual C. of E.; not class-conscious; Pacific; commandos; trooper].
>
> In places like Sarawak and Labuan at the end of the war you could get sex for a cigarette or an atebrine tablet. A decent Malay father offered me his virgin daughter for 47 Straits Settlement dollars. She would always be there for me. Any children would be cared for by nuns on the mainland. I told them I was married, but they said it didn't matter, it wasn't right for a man to be so long without a woman. I refused, but I'm sure they were insulted. Anyway, there were virulent strains of VD in plague proportions – their own and the Japs' – and most of us played safe with 'Do it Yourself' kits [VX59811; single; rare attender at Presbyterian churches; working-class; Pacific; workshop; staff sergeant].

Venereal disease was, in fact, one of the sternest moral guardians. 'Some of it', wrote L. W. Wood, 'was more dangerous than the enemy.' D.S.A. said that the failure to open an army-controlled brothel in Borneo resulted in some shocking cases of VD being flown out ahead of battle casualties. For R. J. Anson, his medical officer's lectures and films on VD as they were going to the Middle East *stifled* all urge to visit the 'houses' when he and his mates arrived there. C. W. Waters, like SX9054 and his mates, watched the 'Can Can' in Cairo; he was put off sex for twelve months.

Marriage vows kept many men in line. 'Most of my friends had sound marriages', wrote the middle-class engineer E. B. Bawden, a sincere Methodist, 'and did not seek sexual adventures.' But this was far from universal, and other respondents were shocked at the behaviour of some married men – those who SX33109 thought were 'the not so happily married'. Husbands, and wives, slipped in the estimation of the working-class Catholic VX86093 when he noticed them playing around during his service in Australia. It was all right for him to play: he was single.

Christian purity was the motive of some men. To those who have already emerged could be added such men as the Presbyterian R. H. Best (who broadened, but did not 'fall', during war service) and another Presbyterian, G. J. Bell (who was soundly converted by some 'Bible-bashing' army mates, and became more pious than ever). Both men were essentially middle-class; both served in the Pacific, and one briefly in Palestine. Yet it is noticeable that profound religious convictions were *not* characteristic of the respondents randomly chosen to illustrate sexual restraint. What persuaded them was usually a more general ethic (as well as disease and lack of opportunity). R.G.W., in fact, offered a salutory comment on some of the pious young recruits. He himself was not one of them, but a nominal Anglican, working-class and single – and a corporal in the Middle East, reduced to the ranks for insubordination on the return trip. His comment about sex was: 'It was mainly the protected and the very good guys who came to grief.' J. P. O'Brien recalled a married and well-respected Salvationist who contracted VD in Greece.

A. S. Tait was a middle-class university student, single and a lapsed Presbyterian, who served in the Pacific as a private soldier with the infantry and commandos. He represented some of the 'protected' types and seemed to a large extent to agree with R.G.W.'s opinion. Tait said, 'I remained sexually naive and inexperienced throughout, and was amazed at the experience and know-how of those from less-privileged sections of society'. R. A. Aitken – a teacher, not class-conscious, and a casual Presbyterian – thought that the very young men and those from an urban working-class background were most likely to be attracted to Timorese women. Countrymen seemed to him to have been 'classless' and too colour-conscious to sexually cohabit with the Timorese, although they had good general relations with them.

So was it the case that the poorer urban classes often came earlier to sexual consummation that did those who were better off or from the country? It is a good question, although one that this study cannot answer because its source material is inadequate. For what it may be worth, it can be seen – by looking back at the biographical notes – that the randomly selected witnesses to restrained sexual relations do not indicate clear and significant class differences. If anything, the working class (the less privileged?) was the prominent one among them – and it may now be added that half of them were completely *urban* working-class. A general attempt was made to correlate respondents' self-perceptions of class with their answers on sex. It was a hazardous venture, and not very reliable, but the result is given in the accompanying table.

What the table mainly suggests is that there was little difference between the 'class' categories, and that at least half of each of them had little or no extra-marital sex while in the army. Perhaps the working-class respondents were a little less ready to discuss sex, but there is no suggestion of gross differences between their general behaviour and attitudes and those of other groups. However, there is here no solid proof one way or the other; too much was hidden by the form of the men's answers ('what I did' was one kind, but 'speaking gen-

Percentage of each 'class' group (except upper-class*)
commenting in various ways on sexual behaviour (N=3634)

Answer on sex	No answer on class	Working-class	Middle-class	Not class-conscious
No answer or 'private'	24	20	13	17
No sexual experiences	15	15	19	18
Very little; unimportant; not available; too much VD; more talk than action	33	35	33	34
General comments, e.g. 'cross-section of society', 'normal men in abnormal circumstances'	15	12	17	16
Sex available and enjoyed – often or occasionally	11	12	13	10
Shock at others; personal shame; moral decline etc.	3	6	6	5
	101	100	101	100

*Too small to be significant

erally of the men' was quite another), and the sample was
doubtless least successful in including enough of the least
privileged.

Nevertheless the respondents' material should be sufficiently strong to suggest that, whatever the tendencies of

different classes to take different attitudes to sex, there were always many exceptions, qualifications and influences that cut across class lines. There were all those urban workers who declared themselves chaste. And it was not hard to find country workers among the sexually active – 'Lofty' and L. A. Hintz, for instance. R. A. Aitken's suggestion that there was something about bushmen that made them classless is worth pondering; perhaps the country could cut across class lines.

It is difficult, also, to classify respondent VX44293. Some would say he was working-class, and others would deny it. Some would put him among the townsmen, and others would lump him in with the countrymen. He *described* himself *only* as working-class. It did not matter to him that his father had progressed to being a country carrier (owner-driver, with an employee or two). VX44293 had been forced by financial need to leave school earlier than he wished. In his small home town, working as a porter, he was a member of the Australian Railways Union and a Labor sympathiser. He could not be put in the notably privileged class, but how *was* he to be described in class terms, or in rural or urban categories? Both could be hard to determine. What is easy to do is to place him firmly among the dedicated members of the Methodist Church, and it was that which gave him his standards on sex – and on drink. His teetotalism caused him initial problems, some men taking it to mean that he thought himself too good to drink with them. But when they realised that he was in earnest, and had never set foot in a hotel, his mates protected him from others who were trying to force him to drink. So he ended up putting more drunks to bed than other men had to, and was the most popular man in the platoon on beer-issue days – for he never drank any of his share. The time came when he would take a soft drink in a bar, but brothels he would not even enter. They seemed to be 'the going thing' for most men on leave, but he feared his 'own weakness' and steadfastly set his face towards 'places of historical interest, Biblical or otherwise'. Thus there was certainly something other than class that determined *his* attitudes.

A good many respondents agreed with the argument of J. S. Falla, DCM, that the behaviour of soldiers was mainly a reflection of their civilian background: 'Putting on a uniform doesn't necessarily change a man. The section of the civilian population that had been promiscuous naturally continued as such.' He thought it likely that more men 'didn't' than 'did'. Having to *inspect* Syrian brothels was enough to put him off, quite apart from his being a religious man who finally married the rector's daughter. A lot of other respondents, however, commented otherwise. Even in Australia, N246397 believed that 'the anonymity of a uniform and absence from the "home sphere of influence" increased the likelihood of casual sex'. K. T. Barrett was sure that many married men found 'greater opportunities for extra-marital sex, and took advantage of them'. After service in the Middle East, the young Baptist J. W. Quinn returned to Australia and sensed its atmosphere. He wrote: 'The men were the same, the circumstances additionally stressful – especially for older and married men. The number of women with men away, and the number of men away from home, produced an explosive situation.'

L.C.N. – solidly middle-class and married – possibly summed up the matter as well as it can be done: 'The complex reactions seemed to depend on factors like degree of maturity, upbringing, strength of the marital bond, personality, religious convictions, etc. Many reactions were predictable; others were surprising.'

Sex: focus on release

Respondents, uninvolved themselves, testified to the other side of the coin, the large number of soldiers who sought release in sexual intercourse.

> Arriving in Perth by train, I found everybody suddenly trying to look out of the windows on one side. When I managed to get

my head out, I saw on the verandahs of several houses girls standing only in their knickers. My first sight of a brothel . . . There was a mad rush by about 60 per cent of the men to get there. In the Middle East, a brothel was the first port of call for quite a lot of men, and I thought it odd because a lot were married just before leaving Australia. But – beer and women because next time into action could be the last? I settled for a few beers and seeing as much as I could of the Holy Land [C. W. Barker; married with one child; serious C. of E.; working-class; Middle East and Pacific; infantry; corporal].

One of the vehicles used by the officers was known as the 'shagging buggy'. Quite a number of men went to the brothels in Perth. I was once in a large dormitory when four or five of the men near me were terrified that they had contracted VD because they had all had intercourse with the same young girl. I was horrified. The lass was in her middle teens, and they had all followed one another [C. J. Bell; single; devout Presbyterian; not class-conscious (but middle-class?); Pacific; various units; bombardier].

I was appalled by the visits of soldiers to brothels (e.g., in Ceylon) so soon after we had left Australia for the Middle East [VFX38754; a nursing sister – hence the 'F' number – who in one way had no right to do the questionnaire, but in other ways had every right (she was even mentioned in despatches); single and aged 25; a dubious Anglican and clearly middle-class].

Probably 80 per cent used brothels when on leave ['Invalided Out'; single; agnostic; middle-class; Middle East; infantry; corporal].

To each his own. I recall a lengthy queue of soldiers outside a Middle East brothel . . . I remember waiting for a senior officer in a brothel until he got his money's worth [S.T.B.; single; negative C. of E.; working-class; Middle East and Pacific; anti-aircraft; captain].

I was on picquet duty at a brothel in Tripoli. (Some MPs were also there, but we wouldn't associate with them.) I took over at 5 p.m. from a chap who'd been counting the visitors to one girl; she'd had twenty. It was a boring job, so I kept counting until the place closed at 9 p.m. She'd had another twenty, and after a while didn't even bother to shut the door. At the end, she offered me one free. I declined ['Finn'; single; unenthusiastic C. of E.; working-class; Middle East; infantry; private].

Another respondent would not indulge, either, and he took a different view of the MPs.

I'd watch the 'dances' in brothels, and I'd mind my mates' paybooks while they had sex. A girl threw my hat under the bed once, but I soon got it back when I told her I had VD. I was older than my mates, and the provosts would listen to me and advise on the safest places to take the boys [VX12335; aged 33; engaged; turned-off Presbyterian; not class-conscious (land valuer); Middle East; artillery; sergeant].

More than mere witnesses, other respondents rejoiced in their sexual activity.

Whenever, wherever, however. The Aussie soldier liked sex and drink; difficult to determine in which order [NX53708; single; conventional C. of E.; middle-class; Pacific and POW; artillery; gunner].

Had sex with a Polish girl while a POW, and in most brothels, including Jaffa, Haifa, Athens, the famous 'Burka' in Cairo, Sister Street in Alexandria . . . Saw it in the raw in places. Never contracted VD ['Lofty'; single; uninterested C. of E.; working-class; Middle East and Greece; artillery; gunner].

I was not very experienced before the war, but had adequate experience by the end. Brothels of the better class played a small but necessary part in my experience [N. P. Batters; single; nominal C. of E.; middle-class; Middle East and Pacific; artillery; lieutenant].

It was necessary and I loved it all. Healthy, and release from battle, etc. I and my section had three objectives: a girl; get rotten drunk; tucker – good stuff, not army slop. As a result of postwar army service in Asia, have several foster-daughters and probably a few natural [kids] I don't know about [L. A. Hintz;

single; nominal C. of E.; working-class; Middle East and Greece
(POW); infantry; private].

Matter-of-fact comment on brothels was quite common.

There was never any hope of 'winning' a sex-partner, so it had
to be brothels or masturbation for sex-relief (and, in retrospect,
army life gave little opportunity for masturbation). In the
Middle East even better-class brothels were affordable for a
private soldier, and were good fun with a few mates [NX15724;
engaged; middle-class; disillusioned C. of E.; Middle East and
Pacific; anti-aircraft; corporal].
If available, you had it. Once fined £5 for taking Italian POWs
to brothel in Benghazi [E. G. Charles; married with one child
(after enlistment); regular Catholic; working-class; Middle East
and Crete (POW); engineers; sapper].
When overseas most of us patronised the regimental brothels.
When we came back to Australia we returned to our wives and
girlfriends [NX11128; single; occasional C. of E.; not class-
conscious (agricultural college student); Middle East and
Pacific; infantry plus others; acting sergeant].
Sex played a big part for the young and virile out to make the
most of their leaves. It was harder to obtain in those days than
now, which is how prostitutes unwittingly made their war
effort. Without them, many men would have become seriously
unsettled [D.D.F.; single; occasional C. of E.; middle-class;
Pacific; artillery; sergeant].

The absolute necessity of well-run brothels was strongly
emphasised by some respondents.

The ready availability of sex outside Australia was appreciated.
In Australia troops were not catered for properly, leaving a big
gap [V. W. Forbes; single; serious Catholic; working-class;
Middle East and Pacific; infantry; sergeant].
Brothels in Palestine were licensed and strictly policed, with
the 'blue light' service as back-up, and photo albums of all

Left: *Women from a Damascus brothel in 1942 – a different breed from others who gave 'feelthy exabeesh' elsewhere – with two Australian soldiers*

Right: *And just what's in the tin in this small street Arab's pocket? At any rate, the serviceman photographer writes, 'Ain't he beautiful?'*

prostitutes in case men came to grief [VX58741; single; nominal Presbyterian; not class-conscious (farmer's son and rural worker); Middle East and Pacific; infantry; corporal].

Army-supervised brothels in the Middle East worked well, lowered disease-rate, etc. On this matter, the church, press and politicians should keep quiet in wartime [J. W. Burnett; single; nominal C. of E.; middle-class; Middle East and Pacific; infantry/war graves; lieutenant].

Regimental brothels were provided in the Middle East to protect personnel from VD. Also, troops were discouraged from close association with local people because of the danger of loose tongues giving information to spies. In Haifa two mates and I were having a few drinks with three girls (we'd arranged to go somewhere with them later), and we were getting a little drunk, but they didn't seem to show any signs of change. They did not want me to taste their drink but, when I did so, I found it was cold tea. We became suspicious and left their company

[R. J. Adams; single; nominal Presbyterian; working-class; Middle East and Pacific; infantry; acting corporal].

Attempts to protect men did not, of course, always work. J. S. Falla remarked that 'some men paid the penalty and were sent to special hospitals, with loss of pay'. Nor was he sympathetic: 'Men at war are there for fighting, not wenching, and the logistic cost of VD to the war effort could be considerable.' Dr Allan S. Walker agreed about the cost. As official medical historian he wrote, in *Clinical Problems of War* (Chapter 22), that 'a good deal of uneasiness' was caused by the loss of men, if only for a month or so, due to VD. Its incidence in the Middle East in 1940–41 was 'too high'. An average of just over 4 per cent of Australian soldiers were confirmed sufferers, with possibly almost as many again contracting some form of it. The 'non-specific' urethritis was excluded from VD statistics, yet during part of 1941 it was roughly in the ratio of two cases to three of officially proven VD, and it was 'usually no less of venereal origin than proven gonorrhea'. Syria in 1942 produced a VD rate of 4.7 per cent. Combatant units were, naturally, the least affected and base and depot units the most, but 'even in Crete . . . during the early lull considerable numbers of men were found to require attention'. In Malaya and the south-west Pacific the rate of infection was usually under 0.5 per cent, although in 1945, often an idle time of occupation, it rose sharply to 0.8 per cent. In Australia itself the VD rate in the army was always under 2 per cent, but the incidence of syphilis came close to doubling from 1941 to 1942. VD was 'unknown' among army nurses, and the infection rate among AWAS always 'very small'. Education in personal hygiene was the best prophylactic, and the increased risks associated with alcohol were fully recognised as 'considerable'.

It is necessary to keep such figures in perspective. The rates of infection might have been high, and the problem very real. The rates were also understated, and the number of men who ran the risk of infection, but escaped it, was doubtless considerably larger than the number of 'specific' and 'non-specific' cases combined. Even so, it was almost certainly a fact that a majority of Australian soldiers ran no such risk. Those respondents who declared that there was more talk about sex than sexual activity were probably right.

There certainly 'wasn't enough sex', according to W. W. McKay. He was single, a nominal Methodist and a rural worker who was not class-conscious. As an artilleryman with service in both the Middle East and the Pacific, and the final rank of sergeant, McKay was one of those who tried to explain why 'visits to brothels were commonplace'. In foreign parts 'a soldier is a very lowly animal, and brothels were the only places where he was well received'.

Other respondents made similar comments on the resort to brothels.

> Lack of sex makes men lonely, especially if married, so many went to brothels. No harm came of this in my experience [R. J. Berry; married; nominal C. of E.; unemployed ex-foundry worker; not class-conscious; Middle East and Pacific; anti-aircraft; WO II].
> Many fit men – isolated from home and thinking, 'So what? Tomorrow I might be dead' – were led into relationships that would not otherwise have occurred. Many men also resisted the temptation. Perhaps there was even more talk than action [SX22714; married with two children; Congregational chaplain; not class-conscious; Pacific; various units; major].
> Queues used to form at the sleazy brothels in the Middle East, partly because the ordinary soldier was banned from the best night clubs. Some said they did not want to die virgins [H. W. Adeney; single; agnostic; middle-class; Middle East; artillery; lieutenant].
> The great and unnatural deficiency was the absence of women. Each individual sought redress in his own way as opportunity presented itself. For the uninitiated there was always the fear of being a virgin under a white cross [C. E. Lemaire; single; neutral

Presbyterian; middle-class; Middle East and Pacific; infantry;
sergeant].

There *was* something psychologically disturbing about facing
death as a man, and yet virginal. It affected many soldiers,
whatever they did or did not do about it.

> I had the sense not to imitate others in going to brothels, but
> when going into battle I was extremely conscious of being a
> virgin [A. G. Bell; single; nominal Presbyterian; middle-class;
> Middle East; machine gun/armoured; corporal].
> I tried in a brothel in Palestine, but couldn't go through with it
> ['Anon. 20'; single; conventional Methodist; working-class;
> Middle East and Pacific; infantry; private].
> I lost my virginity with a nice fat old prostitute at the Burka,
> Cairo, and felt that at last I had become a man [NX20917; single;
> indifferent Methodist; middle-class; Middle East and Pacific;
> infantry; private].

In this matter did servicewomen help just by being sisterly, or
by being more than that? It depended on the women and men
concerned. 'Kyogi' did not think of platonic relations when he
saw 'the numerous attendances of males (mostly married) at
the quarters of nurses and AWAS – although involving only a
tiny minority of the total males in large base areas'. John
Bruce, however, declared that 'even when AWAS arrived in
New Guinea, there was little interest taken in them'. And
VFX47777 – another nurse who inveigled her way into an
all-male questionnaire – said, 'They were damn good blokes.
The boys liked us girls, but *rarely* did we have to fight them
off'.

   For the respondents and, in their view, the army as a whole
there was virtually no question of rape. Instances were excep-
tional rather than common. Although R. A. Burke knew an
officer who boasted of sharing in a pack-rape, 'Kyogi' said that
'at worst, we only heard of pack-rape at fifth-hand'. A.J.B.
could recall only one case of rape throughout a military ser-

vice that extended from 1939 to the end of 1945 in Australia, the Middle East, Ceylon and New Guinea. And, in their varied tones, many respondents rejected sweeping charges of rape against the Australian soldiers.

> As for howling packs of rapists, as depicted by ratbag females these days – rape was so rare as to be practically non-existent ['Rusty'].
> Some Australian behaviour in brothels was very degraded, and seemed more loud-mouthed and exhibitionist than that of men from other armies. It would be hard to say what proportion of our men behaved like that; I'd guess at 25 per cent. But I only knew of one attempted rape. It was in Libya, and an Arab girl was involved, but she was saved by the timely arrival of the sergeant [W.G.B.].
> The Aussie liked his sex at the brothels. Didn't cost much in them days. Your mates were lined up at them everywhere and were a bloody nuisance sometimes. You'd be on the job with a sheila and some smart bugger like Griffo or Shorty or the Lion Tamer would say, 'Look at Davo, going for his life'. You'd look up and see all the grinning faces urging you on. Then some bloke would threaten to throw a sheila over the balcony, but only for conning him. The Australian paid, not as a lot say. Rape was never heard of in Palestine, Cairo or anywhere that I heard of [VX5416].

T. J. Barker was one who thought that soldiers were no different from the male population in general, except that army programmes so 'scared the daylights' out of him and many others, with pictures of children deformed through the effects of VD, that 'it just about froze out any impulse to experiment with prostitutes'. The use of brothels overseas was still 'fairly common', but the army and particularly the medical corps 'deserve credit and the thanks of all Australian soldiers for the great care taken to provide prophylactic services and effective controls over red-light districts'. Nor did Barker know or hear of Australians being involved in rape. 'One of the things that distress me', he wrote, 'is the unfairness of the women against rape, who protest on Anzac Day. They seem to liken the Second AIF to the armies of Attila the Hun, which regarded rape and massacre as a matter of course, whereas rape was just about unknown from the AIF.'

Numbers of respondents attempted some overview of the range of attitudes taken by the troops to sex. Very good jobs they did of it too, although only three snippets can be reproduced. 'Infantry Colonel' remained personally chaste for various reasons, but above all to avoid the risk of lowering the high standard expected of him in all things. Of his younger friends, officers and others, 'many sought a first or further sexual experience before a campaign that might bring death'. And then he spoke of the rifle company he commanded in the Middle East before he was promoted to command a battalion: 'No member of that company in the two years 1939–1941 contracted VD. Their pride as soldiers ensured precautions [not necessarily chastity] to keep them with their company.'

T. N. Binney was never more than a lieutenant. To the best of his recollection, when his 2/3rd Battalion went to the Middle East early in 1940, they had no leave for the first three months, so there was no sex except for the few who went AWL.

Imagine the discipline necessary to hold back 800 mostly young men. When leave was given, I think it fair to say that the troops sought sex whenever and wherever available. Later, with more frequent leave, the rush was not so great. A fortunate few were able to make social contact with women of higher standard. I had a platonic relationship with a sister in the 1st Australian General Hospital; I always felt great after speaking with her. [Binney was then only a corporal, while the sister would have been a commissioned officer.] Sex was short, so it was sought. In Australia the troops were at least a little more restrained.

VX66642 said that a friend told him this story. It *could* be true. A well-meaning chaplain was addressing his unit on the virtues of womanhood – and imagine the discipline necessary to listen to it!

Chaplain: 'Sex is a very beautiful thing.'

Unidentified soldier: 'You're telling me.'

The reading of the preceding pages would have been a waste of time if anyone were to think that such an incident was unlikely to happen among Australian troops. Time would have been equally wasted if someone still thought that such an interjection was typical of the Australian soldier.

An even less typical attribute of those troops was any thought that homosexuality was beautiful. It was so rare, or unrecognised, that only 8 per cent of the respondents mentioned it. Half of that tiny minority declared that it did not exist, and the other half were almost evenly divided between 'neutral' and 'disapproving' when they spoke of rare cases. Only 0.2 per cent of all respondents spoke approvingly of homosexuality: 'I was gay but did not realise it until after my release as a Japanese POW' (R.W.C.). There were mentions of incipient homosexuality, naivete that did not recognise it, the occasional officer or chaplain known to be homosexual or suspected of it, homosexual tendencies 'suppressed by the group in the tent' (as G. R. Bloomfield noted), and occasional couples sometimes isolated and sometimes discharged. But the accent was on 'no homosexuality'. By necessity, men were frequently paired up in foxholes and elsewhere – 'but I did not see or hear of any homosexuality, thank God' (K.G.B.). The vast collective judgement of the respondents would lean to the opinion of T. P. G. Bladen: 'If there is anything in this world better than an understanding and friendly woman, then I haven't met up with it, *and I don't want to meet up with it.*'

Yet the homosexual, of course, could be as effective a soldier as anyone else. The heterosexual C. Y. Hales was in an escape party of POWs who managed to get away in Austria and join the Russians. In the course of the escape 'a queen strangled a German guard with a piece of phone cable'.

Nevertheless, almost to a man, what the respondents were overwhelmingly interested in was a wife.

Marriage and children

QX29419 was 31 years of age at enlistment, and so was 'Dad'
to his mates. He was also 'Daddy' to two young children,
having been married for seven years. Whenever his home
leave ended he was tempted to go AWL, with a wife unable to
hold back the tears and two children clinging to his legs. It
always took a couple of weeks with the battalion before he
could settle down. Yet his wife acknowledged that Australia
was in grave danger, and he had everything to fight for. And,
as it happened, it all came right in the end.

But 'The Babbling Brook' was a born loser, literally so. He
never knew either father or mother, and was a ward of the
state. When he joined up in 1940, from work in the rubber
trade, he was married with one child, eighteen months old. He
was only 21 himself, and it is not hard to guess why he might
have got married at 19 or 20. He had found some peace in
attending the Church of England, but life was still hard and
financial problems were among his motives for going to war.
He went off to serve in the Middle East, New Guinea and
Borneo as a cook (he disliked the idea of killing the enemy). It
was not that he wanted to go. Having a family of his own for
the first time, it was always upsetting to leave them. Lonely in
Jerusalem, he got gonorrhea. He did not know how to spell it
(and who could blame him?), and he thought VD was something different, but he contracted it. He had one stroke of
luck: he was completely cured. Back in Australia, though, his
wife had a baby that was not his. They got together after the
war and patched things up, and he tried to bring and keep the
family together – yet the marriage failed and the war-service
home had to be sold, half to him and half to her. He seemed,
from his answers, to be a nice bloke – but born to trouble. Yet,
taken along with QX29419, he did help to illustrate the
extremes of these soldiers' marriages.

When the respondents went into the army, 14 per cent were
married, and 1 per cent had been once. Not quite 10 per cent
were fathers – mostly of one child or perhaps two children.

Lois and Mick. Marriages were sometimes helped by husband and wife both being in uniform

While serving, two out of three of the men already married had at least one child by their wives, and one respondent in ten had issue from a marriage celebrated during the war but after enlistment. One way or another, about one-fifth of the respondents served as fathers, and over one-third as husbands before war's end.

Were these marriages affected by war service? No, said 53 per cent. 'The gods themselves know why not', wrote R.K.F., but R.H.S. knew why he and his wife survived unscathed: 'We were happily married.' SX3034's marriage was okay because both partners were serving in uniform. Yet some (6 per cent) said that the war had mixed effects on their marriage, and some (also 6 per cent) claimed that the war actually helped. Douglas McPherson was strengthened in his marriage and personal life both because his wife was 'completely loyal and supportive', and also because he wanted his baby daughter 'always to admire him'. J. D. Butler thought that, in the end, the war brought his wife and him closer together. For R. C. Beilby, although married after the war, it was the experiences of war that helped his family life: he knew when he was well off, and he realised that his sons had to be treated as 'men' and 'friends to be won'.

But there were the mixed effects. 'Since we were married in

The late wartime marriage of Max and Merle Brown in 1945. For them, normal married life is not so far away

December 1939, and I was not at home for more than a total of three months in the first six years,' wrote NX4613, 'there must have been some effect, yet the marriage survived.' 'It was very lonely, and I used to drink a fair bit', recalled J. R. Davies. 'I was deprived of seeing my son from the age of three months to nearly five years. For six months my unit was camped in WA not fifty miles from my home, yet we were given no home leave – for security reasons, although everybody knew we had been brought back in case the Japs landed. But we were lucky; there was no infidelity on either side.'

Not so lucky were the 34 per cent who had war-damaged or war-wrecked marriages. VX1552 came back 'with a very chauvinistic outlook'. World War II finished off A. J. Moreno's first marriage, as the Korean War did his second. J. F. Kreckler's engagement was broken while he was a POW, and his subsequent marriage lasted only a few years because of the state of his nerves, and his impatience with his children. TX5429 and his wife did not ever become really compatible, and were divorced. The marriage of VX3390 was saved only for the sake of a daughter and his postwar occupation as a clergyman; he was sure that the long separation after the 1942 marriage had made his wife and him indifferent to each other and too independent. Although W. J. Shallvy had one child, ten months old at his enlistment, his marriage broke up because his wife wanted to 'enjoy her life', not to wait for a soldier to return. VX40721 was divorced when he discovered, on his return, that 'the best man was still the best man'.

Peeping through the comments were the children. Some-times war absences influenced their relations with the father they seldom or never saw. Harm was seen to have been done by about 8 per cent of the respondents – which is uncomfor-tably close to half of those who were fathers in wartime, although some would have been also speaking of children born after the war. The night R.H.S. left Adelaide, his first son took his first steps . . . There was to be 'a kind of four-year gap not known in relations with the younger boy'. That was one sort of problem, temporary or never quite overcome, of which many respondents spoke. 'My eldest daughter was 2 years old before I saw her', wrote J.R., 'it took years before we became close.' Somehow C. L. Barnard 'never quite made it' with his first-born, 18 months old when he set eyes on him.

Male relatives took the place of fathers, not always with bad effects, yet still being rather hard on father-and-son rela-tions. 'In my absence, my eldest son was mainly influenced by a wonderful uncle, a World War I veteran', VX25106 reported; but C. L. Truscott came home on leave from time to time to find that the little boy he left behind preferred his uncles. Strange fathers were seen by children as a threat to their relations with their mothers. The daughter of J. D. Butler, 3½ years old at his enlistment, objected to his sudden intrusion into her dominant position in her mother's affec-tions. T. D. Cross returned with dermatitis and his daughter, aged 4, said, 'Don't let that man my father touch me.' When asked who he was, she replied with considerable distaste, 'That's the man who sleeps with Mummy.'

Discipline could be a problem, not only because fathers were 'new' but also because they were straight from the army. H. E. Conley wrote, 'Shirley was nearly ready for school, and resented me and, perhaps, my inbuilt sense of discipline. I suppose I expected her to "pick up her feet" too much . . .' After two years away, R.E.R. faced rebellion from his 3-year-old boy: 'You're not my boss. You can't tell me what to do.' SX15351 faced another version of that problem; with his marriage came a 4½-year-old stepson, whose father had been killed at El Alamein.

Loss took its various forms. H. S. McKay's son would have nothing to do with him just because he was a stranger, but the children (and wife) of R. F. D. Owen finally could not take 'the changing moods and unsettled behaviour of an ex-POW'. H. E. Wiltshire gave up his child to his divorced wife, and A. J. Kilner lost all trace of his family when he and his wife were divorced during his absence overseas because she gave birth to children who were not his.

Strain follows any war. S.R.C. served in both world wars and had his family after the first. He was distressed by his boys 'always wanting him to tell them about the war', and he refused to do so. How could he talk about the many men ruined by VD in the Middle East in that war (when the rate of contraction was much higher than in the second), of men committing suicide, some of them throwing themselves over- board, and of thousands possibly bringing disease back to Australia? How could he talk of what still gave him night- mares in the 1980s – not World War II, but the battered bodies of his mates lying there on the field of battle in World War I?

Probably many of the respondents would say, if pressed, that they were better fathers because of the lessons war service taught them. For some it was true of their relations with children born before or during the war; but for most it would apply to children who came later. D.S.A., for instance, was glad of his service in World War II when his son was called up for service in Vietnam; it helped him to appreciate the fam- ily's feelings, and enabled him to advise his boy.

But that was long afterwards, at a time when the respon- dents' war was behind them and they were civilians, and family men, and middle-aged. Old soldiers.

OLD SOLDIERS

A 1983 photograph of a New Guinea and Borneo veteran. A champion athlete in his youth, he clearly maintains healthy habits. And yet – after a jungle patrol what was better than a beer and a fag, if available?

13 • 'A STRANGE SENSATION'

When R. H. Byrnes walked out of the barracks gate on his discharge he could have kissed the footpath. The 'incompetent sods' hadn't killed him. It was the turn of D.D.F. a couple of months later. Told unceremoniously by bored discharge personnel that the army had finished with him at last, he felt he had been 'chucked out the back door'. It was all 'a strange sensation'; he had thought, for one thing, that a senior officer might have shaken each man by the hand, thanked him and wished him luck.

The great bulk of the respondents left the army in 1945–46 because the war had ended, although there was a dribble of men who were discharged throughout the war for transfer to other services, to meet manpower requirements on the home front, or on compassionate or similar grounds. (Some 10 per cent of them were released because of wounds or sickness.) Before and after the end of the war a tiny few were dishonourably discharged for reasons unstated or given as – for example – being under age (R. F. Emonson) or committing a robbery while a member of the British Commonwealth Occupation Force in 1949 (M. J. Hurley). Harry Rogers went AWL after the atomic bombs had been dropped, but it did not get him the expedited release he hoped for. Instead, it resulted in a charge of desertion, twelve months in detention and the loss of all his Middle East and Pacific campaign medals. Yet, whenever and on whatever grounds men were discharged, they faced a reorientation that might be wonderful or just a return

Back to the same work as before the war, at Roy Hill Station (WA) in 1947 – with 135 bales of wool loaded

to normality, a bit hard or difficult to the point of disaster. Always it must have been a strange sensation.

Still, a striking number of the men took up virtually where they had left off in the kind of work they did. Some three-quarters of them resumed much the same occupation and most of them remained in similar jobs for the rest of their working lives. Greater interest, perhaps, lies in men such as NX8872. Before the war he was a battler who did anything available, and during the war he became a POW in Germany. At the end of it he took a course under the Commonwealth Reconstruction Training Scheme and became an optician. For A. R. Weetman the big difference between prewar and postwar years was that, instead of having to work as a carpenter to finance his medical studies, he was granted throughout the rest of his course an adequate allowance for books, instruments and living expenses – even enough to marry on. The ill-educated C. L. Barnard, a country worker and farmhand from the age of 13 years, was given rehabilitation training as a welder, which led him into the engineering industry, accountancy studies, and eventually the establishing of his own business. WX26817 went at it more directly. A drifter before the war, he used up his four months of accumulated leave, then bought a vehicle and equipment and built up a lawn-mowing business. 'Maitland Boy' – coalminer's son, poorly educated, untrained and unemployed – had so much experience in the army as a motor mechanic and diesel fitter that he was never out of work after his discharge. Yet disappointment in civilian life was the fate of one man who made a long and successful career of the army. F.J.A., copy-boy and clerk in 1939, remained a soldier until 1974 and retired with the rank of lieutenant-colonel to take up a civilian administrative job that was not much more than clerking – at any rate, 'a good sergeant could do it'.

Just over half of the respondents received no rehabilitation assistance in the way of training or allowances, but the rest got at least a little help – mainly in trade training, commercial or other financial assistance, and educational opportunities. Under 2 per cent were helped to go onto the land. VX66642 was rightly impressed by the total result of the rehabilitation programme. He had been better educated than most before he joined the army, and sorry for the many able lads forced by economic circumstances to leave school early. He believed that 'one of the great investments Australia made after the war was the training given to many of the returned men'. Although unmeasurable, the consequences must have been enormous, he thought, and there was the added advantage that 'education was not so much the privilege of the wealthy'.

Many men did not seek assistance – 'the most important thing was to get out', according to A.J.W., while J.M.N. 'wanted nothing but discharge papers'. Others were ruled in-eligible for aid: SX6482 already had a position in the railways, D. H. E. Massey's job at the Broken Hill mines was judged to be adequate (although it was not what he wanted), and G. H. Warr, who got free training in the Postmaster-General's Department, 'could not have the best of both worlds'. VX35821 said that there was no assistance at the time for country chaps like him (only those in a trade got help), and VX22875 applied to do a veterinary course with merely primary schooling behind him – and was rejected. He did get £10 for tools when he went farming, which was 'not much for four years of army service'. D.R.S. was discouraged from taking a course by his government department, where he was required to do shift work.

A raw house, bought in 1956 with a war-service loan, has a well-established garden by the 1980s

There were also cases of intolerable slowness, misinformation, and even a total lack of information. A.E.H. thought he was too old and poorly educated to undertake training; he applied for a business loan, but delays in approval made it finally impractical. K. M. P. Niland had the idea that all courses were closed by the time he was discharged in July 1946, so he went rabbit-trapping. No advice was given to L.E.V., on either occupational rehabilitation or the further medical treatment he required. Without doubt there were many failures to inform men properly, and much strangling bureaucracy, but it must also have been true that a lot of men did not do enough – or were not in a fit state – to find out all that was possible.

Those who did receive assistance were not a discontented group. Respondents voted by three to one that the assistance was satisfactory. Their continuing treatment over the years was also voluntarily remarked on by 7 per cent of the respondents and, from that perspective and in that group, the balance tilted the other way: the Department of Veterans' Affairs was praised by only two men for every five complainants. Nevertheless the comments came from too few men to be significant, and those with burning grievances might be more likely to air their complaints anyway.

Handling civilian life

What was it *like* to be demobilised? How did men feel? How did they cope? For some of them their return was pure trauma. Discharged at the age of 21, twice wounded, ill and never to recover full health, J. W. Quinn had a sense of unreality, 'almost of bereavement'. The former German prisoner VX5175 was 'completely out of touch' with society, family and women, and could barely handle his freedom to choose and the need to plan his daily life. SX1840 too found it extraordinarily hard to move from everything being organised for him to having to make his own decisions. Men like P. L. Bladen felt that civilians had very little understanding of them. H. E. Y. Bell, who won the Military Cross but lost a leg, learnt that 'employers soon tired of those who lost time through war injuries'.

QX35534 came home to find that his 'old friends did not exist any more'. A. S. Goodliffe so missed the close support of the army that he nearly re-enlisted, and A. A. Ely often wished he had stayed there. NX42488 did re-enlist – after four troubled civilian years – for service in Korea, and he remained in the army to serve also in Vietnam; but a major part of his

difficulties had been that, in five years with the AIF, he had
seen no action. It was no fault of his, yet it had preyed on his
mind.

Ex-sergeants felt their loss of identity and prestige. J.H.B.
was suddenly back as an apprentice plumber, and VX44293
was a porter at Melbourne's huge Spencer Street Station,
where 'practically everyone' was his boss and he had to sweep
the platform, pick up papers, and take over from the lavatory
attendant. Used to responsibility, the former captain TX1158
was unhappy as a lowly bank clerk again, and R. K. Chapman's 'unchallenged authority' as a warrant officer in a 'big
brother' army took a sad tumble in his post of mercantile
clerk. VX43031 could not face an office again after five years
in the open, but he was driven back to it, in a 'somewhat
shattering' return to civilian life, at the end of a year as an
inexperienced and under-capitalised dairy farmer.

VX28988, an ex-POW in Germany, had not only lost contact with normal people but also with ordinary things like
money. The former Japanese prisoner J. T. Haig found the
family circle difficult to fit into; his mother had died while he
was away, and he hankered restlessly after the company of his
own kind, his fellow ex-prisoners. One of those prisoners,
after an appalling run of illnesses, returned with badly
impaired vision and to a wife who felt she no longer loved
him: she had become withdrawn from him after hearing
nothing in three years, except that he was almost certainly
dead. Their marital problem was finally overcome, but the
damage to his sight was permanent.

A. W. Bruce's nickname was 'Lucky'. Did it fit? Son of a
blue-collar worker, he had only primary schooling before
becoming a seasonal rural worker and managing, after a time,
to buy some land, clear it and plant a small orchard and vine-
yard, which he left to enlist in 1939. In the Middle East he was
wounded badly enough to make any return to the land impossible, so he accepted training as a loom tuner and went to
work in a textile factory. It was a strange and difficult world
for him.

Getting hold of themselves was often the trouble. L.E.V. tried to cope with the effects of a severe wound, with much less physiotherapy than he should have had, and also to hide the mental stress he was constantly under. SX10675 came out of a Japanese prison camp with bad nerves made worse by a sense that he had failed and disgraced his family in being a POW. From a German prison camp came R. W. E. Werry, with a temporary loss of powers of communication, a personality crisis brought on by nervous disorders, and nightmares of being caught on the barbed wire. R.L.D. almost did not return from Borneo; his nerves were so frayed during the voyage home that for days he had to resist an impulse to throw himself overboard – just why, he never did understand. Back in Australia, he spent several weeks camping – sometimes alone, sometimes with friends – until he quietened down enough to start adjusting.

W. G. Smith was very near a nervous breakdown after the New Guinea campaign. Memories of the dead revived in him, and he was disturbed at the thought of relatives being reminded of their loss by the sight of other men returning. He loved and lost, and the experience left him in deep depression for years. He saw many alcoholics and ruined marriages, and he broke with friends and relatives. In an attempt to 'overcome the strangle-hold of the conservatives', he helped form an RSL sub-branch, but had to leave the organisation after a couple of years because he was at that time a communist. He had enlisted in the belief that he was fighting for humanity, and had emerged a cynic. It was a long time before he overcame the worst of it.

On moonlit nights H.R.J.M. was unable to sleep. He did not know why. One night a noisy aircraft passed low over his house. Air raid! Yet it could not be; the war had ended three years before. And that was it – the Japanese had always bombed on the bright nights. One neurosis was uncovered and cured, but it had taken three years. One by one, very slowly, his other neuroses weakened and died.

'What do you do', VX59612 worried, 'now that the war is

over, and you enlisted as a 19-year-old bank clerk, and you are trained to kill, and it is assumed that you will kill, and you keep on thinking about the killing, and you have to take the responsibility for your own decisions?' In his case the answer was university education under the Commonwealth Reconstruction Training Scheme, followed by preparation for the Anglican ministry. But there were other men for whom the way was less clear.

H. C. Halligan came back with a head injury worse than was suspected at the time, and found himself among people with whom he had nothing in common – whingeing about all the things they had to go without, claiming that the Americans had saved Australia and the British had won North Africa, and suggesting that the AIF had just had a Cook's tour. 'So I was having runs in with everyone, friends and strangers', he wrote. 'It was at that time I shut up and said nothing, and now – through this questionnaire – I've been conned into opening up a bit. Thanks for the therapy treatment, but is anyone going to believe what you've been told by a lot of "ex-AIF boozers"?'

After nearly four years as a prisoner of the Germans, WX1042 tried to return to structural engineering as a boilermaker but was nonplussed by the grudging attitudes of former workmates and the union. He had not been engaged in that type of work during war service, they argued. But he had been assisting welders while a POW, he protested. Well, he could be trained as a welder, but only as that. So he was obliged to accept an inferior status within the trade. It was a bewildering and disturbing experience that completely changed his attitude to his fellow Australians. Keith Hart also found the transition hard. It had been disgusting enough to contrast the panic in Australia in March 1942 with the courage – especially of the women – he had witnessed in Greece and Crete, but it was even harder to stomach Australia at the end of 1945. Having had all his needs met for five years, and having been given interesting work in the security service towards the end, he came back to cope with 'a very pregnant wife, no home, boring work as a packer, and hostile workmates' – the antagonism having been born of his replacing one employee under regulations that gave preference to ex-servicemen.

Wounded at Tobruk and again at El Alamein, with badly affected nerves and service with RAAF aircrew after 1943, O.W. came out of the war with a drink problem and was 'unable to adjust to civilian life for over twenty-five years'. He felt that civilians were suspicious of ex-servicemen, while returned men were critical of civilians, so in order 'to join a school in the local pub' he used to take off his RSL badge.

Another respondent, H.M.W., did not find the initial return hard, but over the years he steadily turned into a 'nervous, miserable recluse' – on a TPI pension, finally separated from his wife of many years (who had taken enough), and finding the Department of Veterans' Affairs less helpful than he thought it should have been. He commented, 'I think now that a "typical Digger" is an ex-soldier who is treated like dirt by the governments and people who have forgotten what he did'. Enlisting at 19, he had seen service in the Middle East, New Guinea and Tarakan. He had been in vicious hand-to-hand fighting. A wound and illness had been his lot, and his best mate died in his arms in the last week of the war. Doubtless there were other sides to what he complained about, and he was partly to blame for his own difficulties, but war's horror had made its vast contribution to the wrecking of his life. Had he no grounds for complaint as he struggled to cope, and people could not care enough? He did not complete the first questionnaire sent him, but replied to a follow-up letter: 'I will try again. Last time things got out of hand. I could talk the answers easily but to write them seemed harder' – as hard as lying wounded among dead mates while, only yards away, the *Afrika Korps* relieved the Italians and dug in before attacking hours later, an incident that involved H.M.W. in another fight for his life, battered but unattended leg and all . . .

The marriage of WX10675 was doomed from the start. One of those early wartime marriages that was not going to work, and was made worse by the death of a child that

An ex-POW hut housed a soldier-settler and his family in 1947. By the 1960s they had developed a flourishing dairy farm in the same spot

resulted, it was soon on the rocks when WX10675 came home. Thereafter he had no home, only a series of lodgings near the various jobs he took. C.H.L. was one of those who found it hard to mix with women. W. H. Harding was irritated by the very sound of their voices – and not only because his mother was upset by his occasional bouts of drinking. But brothers were the problem for R. V. Evans. He had enlisted at 18 to protect his family, yet returned to find that 'big brother had taken over the family farm with little brother', so he had to go elsewhere. QX7964 was another young farmer who found that there was no place for him because others had moved in during his war service.

A life on the land was what Ray Murphy determined on, but first it had been a case of 'where do I go from here? There seemed a great vacuum in my life. I had left as a single man and now I was a family man with no job, no rehabilitation training, no real skills and all my mates of nearly five years gone elsewhere'. Still, he had done many kinds of practical work before the war, he had a desire to make a home somewhere on the land he had fought for, his wife and relatives were encouraging and, under the Soldier Settlement scheme, he was eventually allotted an irrigated dairy farm of 104 acres, with an ex-POW hut as a first home. They battled successfully through, yet Murphy recalled that initially he had 'a bewildering feeling. The whole world had changed, and I don't think I was mentally equipped to cope with the situation that I suddenly found myself in'.

The quirks of rehabilitation selection and the dire shortage of housing both gave trouble to NX25055. He had been with the army service corps in the Middle East and then a member of the RAAF in the Pacific, but was refused assistance to matriculate: he had not been decorated or wounded, among other 'funny' reasons. So he started again as a stores clerk. There was no house to be rented, and he and his wife had to 'live and love' in one room, paying 45s a week for it from wages of 95s. When his wife became pregnant, his landlord said that babies were not allowed. 'Is it any wonder', asked NX25055, 'that I knocked him out on the spot?'

Yet it was 'Tom' who painted the worst picture of postwar housing. He and his wife first rented two attic rooms from a widow in Manly, but they had to leave when a baby was on the way. The next step was a room in an ex-serviceman's house, taken on condition that as well as paying a steep rent they fed the landlord and washed his clothes – although 'Tom' bucked at the last requirement, and successfully. Then the landlord's estranged wife wanted the house and by cruel persecution managed to drive the couple and their baby out. Their third 'home' was an open balcony sheltered only by two canvas blinds. It was cold and wet, and the baby developed

*An ex-serviceman's first car –
a Ford Prefect – in the backyard
of his first house. His first
daughter prefers her own means
of transport*

bronchitis. Persistent application for help at the State Housing
Department resulted in information that a fiver slipped to the
boys behind the counter might help. In the end, and without
the lubrication of any fiver, they were placed in a hut of
unlined 'fibro', which was actually preferable to the swelter-
ing galvanised iron of most huts, in a former American-negro
camp that had 'obviously not been built for white troops'. And
at least they had their place to themselves; all the *iron* huts
were divided into three by plywood partitions about 7 ft high,
and a family was allotted to each section, so that 'every word,
every breath could be heard by the whole shed'. In this state-
created slum there was a large criminal population – perverts,
child-molesters, wife-bashers . . . The resident social worker,
so called, was 'a lady of much muscle and few manners' who
carried a pistol in a holster, years before the police were
allowed to do so. With all that to cap his neuroses, injuries and
struggle to become a commercial artist, is it surprising that
'Tom' became an alcoholic? That happened in spite of his
delicate wife's determined survival, or perhaps partly because
her strength underlined the weakness in himself. All sorts of
things may help to break a man.

The shock of return to civilian life must be fully allowed
for, yet it was not too bad for most ex-servicemen. Only 13 per
cent of respondents found it extremely hard to adjust to their
new life. Some real difficulties were recalled by another
30 per cent, and that was only to be expected. But a majority

(54 per cent) said that they made the transition very readily – and they included 16 per cent for whom the return home was simply 'wonderful'. They were alive and well. They could return to wife and family – even to a house, if lucky. They were regaining independence and privacy. They had chances to study, train, take up new work or their interrupted old careers ... Some individuals adjusted easily to change, anyway. Just as lots of men had adapted to the army without fretting, so also many of them re-adapted to civvy street with comparative ease.

In postwar years C. L. Barnard had seen most of his friends from the 2/43rd Battalion and the 2/28th Canteen Services do 'very well, particularly the Aboriginal boys'. The odd few had taken to drink, but they 'probably would have, anyway'. Over many years SX20848 noted that, in his small rural community, the 'active part played by ex-servicemen in local affairs was outstanding'. He put it down to most of them returning with 'a much broader, more tolerant and less class-conscious outlook, and being far better equipped to take their place in society and carry out their responsibilities'.

'Jab' said that to come home was 'both very difficult and wonderful, I'd lost so much and gained so much – I can't explain'. 'Mick' remarked, 'The war was over and I returned to my job as a linotype operator. I'd tried to be the best soldier in the AIF, but my wife and children were more important to me than the army'. With the number QX361, and over a period of six years, W. G. Gaulton had been transported to the United Kingdom, the Middle East, Greece, Syria, Palestine, New Guinea and New Britain; at discharge he felt like a released convict.

Attitudes at discharge

Appreciation of Australia, always strong among respondents, nevertheless increased over the course of the war. There were men with serious reservations, and there was some disillusionment yet to come, but Australia was home and there was no place like it. Empire loyalty, about as strong for this group on enlistment as Australian nationalism had been, seemed to decline during the war. At least half of the men were still very positive about the empire at the end, but there had been an increase in uncertain or disappointed feelings. 'It could never be the same,' thought F. K. Wallace, 'its infallibility had been shattered.' 'I was no longer so madly British', wrote 'Artilleryman'. 'Britain's failure to fight a long hard war on the Malay Peninsula had a profound effect on my thinking.' About the new United Nations Organisation soldiers were often ignorant, or naturally uncertain and divided. Some optimistically shared in a widespread hope for a better world order, while others were dubious even then.

In general the war had done little to interest respondents in political questions; if anything, they might have been even more sceptical about 'politics'. On education they were often positive: it was a desirable acquisition, and more was needed. Many liked the idea of getting back to real work, especially those like 'Artilleryman', whose regiment had done little since returning from the Middle East, and who thought that many gunners would have done more back in the factories and on the farms than they did in the islands. Of family – to get back to, or begin – many were eagerly aware. 'I *liked* the army until I met my wife-to-be in 1944', declared VX100383, 'but she wouldn't marry me before discharge, and after that I despised every facet of army life. Marvellous the power of a girl.'

Was there a decline in religious belief among these young men caught up in war? It is impossible to be sure about the group as a whole, since so many men (49 per cent) gave no answer to the question, at the end of a wearisome questionnaire. Of all respondents, 25 per cent reported that, when they were discharged, they had a favourable view of religion. This means that, of those who supplied an answer, about half were positive, compared with about half who had been that way when they enlisted. So there may have been no overall decline

in religious certitude or sympathy. Those who were negative
or ambivalent on religion declared themselves in about equal
proportions, and for some of them the war had produced those
negative attitudes. For others, however, war had simply confirmed their trust or had even brought them to religious
faith.

The 'very religious' Catholic QX1358 emerged from the
war as 'definitely atheistic', and the previously churchgoing
Anglican nicknamed 'Killer' lost interest after the 'horror and
suffering' of war. Equally good churchmen, like the Baptist
J. W. Quinn, remained as they always had been. Two nominal
Presbyterians went in quite opposite directions: A. S. Goodliffe became religious, while VX100383 was led to the bitter
conclusion that religion 'would not restore one soldier to life'.
The Middle East was the turning point for pro-communist
'Anon. 24': the war took him 'to the cradle of Jews, Moslems
and Christians', and he embraced a religious outlook. M. G.
Elliston, conventional Anglican and Japanese POW, found
that his war brought him closer to God. It would have been
hard to predict the effect of war on a man's religion.

Life was daunting or quite soured for some men, but all the
more appreciated by others. Only the love of wife and family
made it still worth living for D. G. Armstrong, and it was not
truly worth it at all for K. E. Hayden: 'If I stood on the
threshold of life, knowing what I know now, I would decline
the offer.' Yet, as NX4320 remarked, 'I used to say, while an
infantryman, if you don't like life you only have to stand up.
Life is worth the effort'. A lot wondered at their survival.
'Why was I alive and so many better men dead?' mused Ken
Knox. 'But it was bloody wonderful to be alive.' QX16129
reckoned that 'the greatest ecstasy was not sex but the real-
isation that you've been fired at and missed'. All was borrowed
time from then on for A.E.H., who would try to be thankful
for every day. Often the word 'precious' was applied to life:
'How short, how precious' ('Bertie'); 'It is very precious – I
saw too many mates die' (R. F. Wenham). Life lay ahead for a
grateful 'Tobruk Rat', his wife and son, yet it was ghastly to

think of the millions done to death, and it gave rise to vague
thoughts of building a better world. E. O. Bloomfield, a Japanese POW, said it was generally agreed that they had not
properly valued life until they had come close to losing it:
'You don't appreciate a good feed until you've lived on
mouldy rice for three years.'

On the Burma railway, Bloomfield said, he lost the fear of
death as such; it was the manner of it that bothered him –
'being slowly eaten away by dreadful tropical ulcers'. The
manner of dying . . . VX105172 came home to go, later, to
friends' funerals and think how lucky they were to have
known graves, or any grave at all. Very few respondents were
like NX68718 in claiming not to have been affected by violent deaths at the time. There were those like R. F. Burton (a
Japanese POW) and QX62751 (a member of a war graves unit
in Borneo) who saw so much death that they were afraid they
had grown callous. Others, such as SX6977, just became
increasingly fatalistic; death had not deeply worried M.G.R.,
who had read Omar Khayyam. Some men were embittered;
death to Charles McCausland had become 'a lottery that made
no sense of any divine providence'. J.W.B. – who claimed to
have seen three hundred youths die on the Kokoda Trail – was
quite sure that 'behind the face of death there is *only* death'.
VX1959 learnt to accept death gracefully: 'Having seen it
come to some of the finest men, I felt I could welcome it so
long as I went with a clear conscience.'

There were religious men like R.H., who might fear the
manner of going, but looked confidently forward to eternal
life. T. B. McDonald, an Anglican chaplain, found grief
mounting to a distressing level as he continually buried the
young and informed their relatives. Yet a soldier who had
helped at a burial would often say something like, 'I had a
funny feeling that old Bert was still with us, saying "Thanks,
fellas", for doing for him what he couldn't do for himself'. At
any rate, it remained McDonald's firm belief that death was 'a
radical entry into more life'. But many men never forgot the
threat that had been around them on all sides for so long. The

1939 enlistee QX297 wrote in 1983: 'I have cribbed forty-four years.'

Death in the course of duty is what a soldier's discipline conditions him to face. And in discipline and duty most respondents continued to believe strongly. Of those who gave an answer, 83 per cent were positive on discipline, and 85 per cent positive about duty. Discipline might be 'a very ugly word for intelligent teamwork', but it was essential, said F.J.A. It should be 'sane rather than harsh', a matter of 'leading rather than driving' (H.N.G.), and based on a 'self-imposed determination not to let others down' (W. R. J. Shields). Without their discipline, 'many more Australians would have died as POWs' (R. C. Tompson). At first disliking strict discipline, T. D. Cross came back from New Guinea convinced of its fundamental importance. Among a small minority, W.S.H.M. thought that the Australian soldier 'would have been better if more highly disciplined'. Many more believed with C. E. Lemaire that 'the Australian battle discipline was superb' – and such a comment could be a matter of observation rather than of boasting.

On 8 July 1942 the 9th Division went into position by night near the North African coast and before dawn began the 5 mile advance to Tel el Eisa. With the forward infantry company went A. J. Guy, who was travelling in a Bren-gun carrier as an artillery radio operator. In the dawn light he watched the infantrymen, all loaded with 90 lb of gear, moving slowly forward amid shellfire, occasionally going down on one knee, then getting up to go steadily on – as if they were out picking mushrooms. There was no safe place, due to the 'air burst' mixed with the shells, but the infantry stopped only to clean up some enemy resistance here and there. 'They were just ordinary blokes – and they say the Australian is not disciplined. It called for discipline to keep going under those conditions for 5 miles.'

Discipline might be 'irksome' and, in fighting units out of action, might often have been 'casual, to say the least', according to C. E. Edwards of the 2/22nd Battalion. But there was no casualness of approach when action was joined. Units would operate towards the general objective despite fatigue and fear, casualties and loss of leaders. The ranks always seemed to be working out ways of obtaining the objective – and that's 'battle discipline'. On leave the so-called unruliness of the AIF was usually exaggerated. I knew how necessary discipline was – in the army and in my civilian future. Esprit de corps is an old-fashioned phrase, but it's the only one I can find to describe it.

The deeply resentful also emerged from the army. To R. F. Emonson 'the ones with the least to lose had made the biggest sacrifice', so he had changed his ideas about duty. Some felt that they were entitled to rest on their laurels, or at any rate be well looked after: 'I had done my duty', reckoned A.E.H. 'Now society had a duty to provide opportunity for me.' (Joseph Compton shared a sense of duty done, but reacted less demandingly: 'I felt that I'd done mine. Bit proud, really – but keep it quiet.') A suspicion of the notion of duty was expressed by K. L. Lewtas; he had enlisted partly from a sense of duty – to family, Australia and the empire – but at the end believed duty to be 'a dangerous idea. Many atrocities were carried out in the name of duty'.

Yet most respondents continued to hold to the concept of duty to self and others. Going into the army very young, D.K. emerged with a 'deeper sense of duty', as well as being more aware of the need for discipline from without and within. For QX29419 his guide to the future was the same as that which had led him, a married man with children, into the army after the Japanese attack: 'My duty was to Australia, my family and fellow citizens.' Men like R.J.F. went further still:

Your questions have reminded me that I had been thinking at the time that if we all did our duty always, there would perhaps be less war. When the nation was threatened then, a spirit of unselfishness permeated it. Is it not a pity that a similar spirit could not sweep through us now? If strong and orderly ourselves, and less materialistic and pleasure-seeking, we could do more for our underprivileged neighbouring nations, and they would more readily consult us, confident in our integrity.

A duty to discipline ourselves, and be good neighbours . . . As a bonus, war would be less likely.

War and conscription

Warmongers these men were not. Even although 22 per cent gave no answer when asked their attitude to war, 50 per cent of the whole group were entirely negative about war as a means of settling disputes.

> War, I had decided, was a terrible insult to man's intelligence [NX17715].
> Hoped the UNO would end the stupidity [E. L. J. Berry].
> Cruel, senseless, hell. Pray it's the last [VX37431].
> I hated war since hearing my parents read from the newspapers in World War I. I loathed World War II, and would do anything possible to prevent another [Keith Faux, who served – and had three brothers who also served – because his parents and early teachers instilled into him 'duty and patriotism'].
> Sorrow, mutilation and death. I hated it – and the vermin on both sides who caused it [N.B.McA.].
> One of the hardest moments in my life was to see my eldest son leave for Vietnam. I knew only too well what was involved in war, and I knew no word bad enough to describe it [J. A. G. Betts].
> On return to civilian life I never marched in parades. No reunions. Just paid subs to RSL. When my youngest son was about 7 he asked me if I would take him to a Dawn Service on Anzac Day, as his friends' fathers did. It was dark when I parked the car, took his hand and meandered over to the Shrine. Men were urinating in the bushes, vomiting from premarch reunions . . . The ceremony was first-class, but we walked back in the breaking dawn through the drunks, groups reliving it, men

Left: *Off to a 1953 reunion – a 2/32nd Battalion dinner – in Western Australia. From left: 'Shorty' Graham, Jim Bowman, 'Tich' Wilson and Paddy Alford at Sawyers Valley*

Right: *Anzac Day 1967 at the Shrine in Melbourne – mainly ex-members of the 2/32nd Battalion with their wives*

asleep on seats. As we drove home he slipped his hand in mine. I looked down. 'Daddy, was the war really as bad as that?' Twenty-five years later he is in Europe on exchange duties to do with guided missiles. He is deeply religious, but he can talk about 'clean' bombs blithely. Blast about a mile up, no damage to cities, only dead people. 'Dad,' he says, 'you're not with it anymore.' But I am [VX9785].

It has hurt me to be branded a warmonger and accused of glorifying war because we march on Anzac Day and have reunions to share a past we can't share with others, and to ease our present problems. I honestly believed that our cause was just, but I learnt in my first five minutes of action, as my mates fell killed or wounded, that war was no joke. As it blundered on I became quite convinced that mankind must find another way of solving its differences. I had to see that job through, but now I *hate* war [C. E. Edwards].

War is the ultimate obscenity [David Cambridge].

Another 22 per cent were caught on the horns of the old dilemma.

War is evil, but sometimes the lesser evil [J. W. Quinn].
I hated it, yet you have to fight when threatened [B. B. Bennett].
If it happened, a necessary evil. But it shouldn't happen [VX85129].

About 7 per cent of respondents were anxious, above all, to stress the rightness of *their* war.

Is anyone suggesting we should not have resisted Hitler or Tojo? [K. M. Esau – an Australian-born nominal Presbyterian, in spite of his name].
A nuclear war of the future must raise different moral issues, but I was convinced that, in defending my family and way of life in World War II, I was engaged in a just war, as defined by St Thomas Aquinas [R. A. Burke].

Such opinions did not make those men warmongers, either. The futility of expecting permanent peace emerged in the comment 'war is inevitable' from 'South African Immigrant', but even that respondent could have written 'volumes on the tragic and frightening' sides of his war.

Nevertheless only about 20 per cent of respondents expressed opposition to conscription (or national service), with 20 per cent saying nothing, 20 per cent having mixed views, and 40 per cent favouring it. This postwar response was not really contradictory, but reflected ideas about unavoidable war, the lesser of two evils, preparedness as a deterrent, and the discipline and community spirit that national service might help develop. Of the anti-conscriptionists, 61 per cent had been AIF members through their entire war service, so that the old AIF prejudice against the Militia was still showing. Overall it was not as simple as that.

I would hate to have to depend on someone who did not want to be there [M.J.K., taken prisoner on Crete].
Conscription is to be avoided like the plague. The best soldier is

always the volunteer. At the RSL I voted against involving national servicemen in Vietnam, but was heavily outvoted of course [Lloyd Armstrong, 18-year-old volunteer in 1940].

Conscription is an indictment of our own principles [SX6977, AIF 1940].

No man should be forced to war [NX86844, conscripted in 1942, subsequently in AIF].

Definitely against conscription. There can only be wars if people are sent to them [A.P.D., AIF 1940].

Definitely out. Let the bludgers be seen. But compulsory training should be done by all, and even conscientious objectors could do nursing [R. J. Weston, 19-year-old volunteer in 1940].

If a nation cannot get all the volunteers it needs, its cause is not just or its leaders are incompetent [C. W. T. Kyngdon, regular army, Duntroon graduate and lieutenant-colonel in 1942].

No conscription. The ones conscripted are those without influence who own the least and contribute the most [R.A.P., prewar regular army, AIF 1939, WO I].

No war is worth conscripting men – but at least it is fair for all classes [G.F.T., 1941 volunteer militiaman, AIF 1942].

Yes, conscript. Why should only some take full responsibility for the sacrifice, but all enjoy the benefits? [NX8116, 17-year-old volunteer for AIF in 1939].

Volunteering is an unfair way of sharing the national burden [J.V.A., medical officer, AIF from 1942, previous Militia service].

Conscript. We are a sitting duck ... We must have national service [VX148129, volunteer in 1941].

If volunteers were insufficient, conscription was better than Japanese domination [M. A. Bishop, volunteer militiaman 1941, AIF 1941, to colonel in postwar regular army].

Conscript if the country is in danger, but support the genuine objector [Bryan Cowling, rejected by RAAF, conscripted to Militia 1941, transferred to AIF 1943].

Compulsory service, not for overseas wars, but for Australia's defence. Service life is broadening and developing, and gives a sense of belonging ['Rusty', a volunteer militiaman 1941, AIF 1942].

No conscription for war, but have national service training for all [QX48193, rejected by RAAF, conscripted to Militia 1942, transferred to AIF 1943].

We must have national service training. An untrained man is like a player in a top sports team who has never seen a game [A.G.M., into Militia under age (16 years) 1943, AIF 1943].

In peacetime *everyone* should spend one or two years in military or other national service after leaving school [Peter Bowen, AIF 1940].

National service for all males and females, to produce a patriotic and positive community [C. C. Eling, rejected by RAAF, volunteered for Militia 1939, AIF 1942].

Either all volunteers or all conscripts, but not both [W. R. Tapscott, AIF 1940].

Ex-service organisations

A continuing association with other ex-servicemen was deeply valued by most respondents. Only 6 per cent had never belonged to a veterans' organisation, and at least 70 per cent held current membership of one or more. They mostly included the Returned Services League, and 86 per cent of respondents were RSL members or had been at one time. It was therefore only a small proportion (8 per cent) that had been members solely of such groups as a unit association or the Australian Legion of Ex-servicemen and Women – the latter originally formed to cater for those who were then excluded from the RSL by, for instance, not having seen active service as defined by the League. The representativeness of the respondents was weakened by this bias towards RSL membership: too few other ex-army types were among them.

Some respondents had given up membership of the RSL because they did not fit happily into their local sub-branch, and some had left – perhaps temporarily – over disagreements with national RSL policy. (Roughly 10 per cent came into each category.) A few had simply been casual and intermittent members. There was some tendency to drift out after joining immediately the war ended – although VX116572 (and others, he thought) had at first wanted to forget it all and not be in the RSL, but later joined to help mates and sustain values in the community. There were similarly contrary trends to pick up membership or just let it go in old age. Nevertheless, about two-thirds of respondents had maintained a connection with some ex-service association throughout most of the years since the war.

The comradeship of the survivors, their pride and mutual support, were paramount in joining. Many called it mateship, and it was much more than a purely social activity for most of them. The strengthening of ex-service groups was a signifi-cant motive, as also were the giving and getting of help. Quite often men said that they joined because it was their right to do so; it was something that they were proud to assert, and which could have advantages for them.

Some men did not quite know why they remained mem-bers, but again the common suggestions were mateship, adding to the strength of the ex-service lobby, and the possi-bilities of aid – given or received. About 7 per cent of respon-dents were actively involved in groups like Legacy and the Limbless Soldiers' Association, which were specifically formed for welfare work (in addition to that done by the general associations).

As with many other things, it was hard to predict who would be members of the RSL and who would not. A. J. Koorey was too opposed to war and 'hypocritical cant' to have ever been a member of even a unit association; but J. N. Barter, although hoping that the world could live in peace forever, had become a life member of the RSL ('it does good work') and was still a member of his Commando Association ('close friends after forty years'). S.R.C., with service in two world wars, had joined the RSL in 1919 and was still a member in 1982. Unable to equal that, K.G.B. had nevertheless clocked

In 1951 the 1/10th and 2/10th Battalions 'married' into one association. Third from right is Lieutenant-Colonel Miles Beevor, who led 'A' Company of the 10th Battalion ashore at Ari Burnu knoll (Gallipoli) at dawn on 25 April 1915

up thirty-seven years membership of the 24th Battalion Association and the RSL. He thought that there were no winners in a war, and he wanted no more of it, yet he considered the RSL to be 'a great organisation' because of both its fellowship and its aid to the distressed.

R. F. Emonson might have been expected to have given the RSL away. He had been brought up hard, had become embittered by the war, and was disappointed by much in his subsequent life – even as a boxer he had 'never made the big time'. Yet he was an RSL stalwart, finding in it 'an oasis from life . . . kindred souls, a select club, and strength'. He had been a member for thirty-six years. With a less difficult childhood and a higher niche in society (though he was not of the really privileged classes), 'Jeweller' did not like the RSL. He found it 'cliquey' and gave it away in favour of long involvement with the Rats of Tobruk Association, 'an exclusive organisation open only to those who served in Tobruk between April and November 1941'. So much for cliques? That was not of course what 'Jeweller' meant; he thought the one organisation to be riddled with class and status, the other classless.

'Ex-42nd' had kept in touch with friends through unit associations, but he rejected the RSL as 'going hand-in-hand with the profit-takers' in a corrupt Australian establishment. J. B. Begg, on the other hand, was a long-term member of the RSL since he believed that the servicemen of his World

War II generation had received better treatment because of the efforts of the World War I members.

VX19853 thought of the RSL as the ex-servicemen's union – something they needed, in all fairness, to protect their rights. L. G. Hall belonged to the RSL, Ex-POW Association, TPI Association, Partially Blinded Ex-service Association and 2/30th Battalion Association. He was proud to be a member of the last, but he belonged to the others from a sense of unity and a duty to help. He would cease to belong only when he became 'a memory'. The RSL was defended by T. K. Burke against the charge of sabre-rattling; he said that it was from bitter experience that the League urged defence preparedness and the need for training. And the bond between his RSL friends was placed by W. J. Goodall above any other link he knew, greater than church fellowship and beyond that of blood brothers. If Goodall could feel so strong a tie without service farther afield than Darwin, what might men not feel after Tobruk, Greece, Thailand, New Guinea, Borneo?

The odd man here and there found it not so. Occasionally they spoke of the ex-service thing being overdone, and of old cobbers at reunions pretending to be the same, and trying to be politely interested in each other, yet actually having lost what once was so strong a bond. They were the exception on the unit level, but in the case of the RSL the rifts were more often apparent. The League's policies and statements sometimes undercut the common ground on which all could stand together, although disaffected ex-members could be won back, and it always retained some loyal dissenters, cynical opportunists and many merely habitual members.

V280259 was a militiaman because his father, a returned man from World War I, had stood in the way of his enlisting and, anyway, after being conscripted in 1941 he was found to be not quite up to AIF physical standards. He did not serve in a designated war zone, so he could only join the Legion of Ex-servicemen, and he considered the RSL unfair in its attitudes: a soldier could only serve where he was sent. N.B. left the RSL because of its arrogance towards other ex-service associations. A.C.B. left it after ten years when 'a senior RSL character', unfriendly to A.C.B.'s family, told him that his service in Australia had not made him eligible. WX10736 left when refused help with a medical problem. SX5222 had joined in 1943 simply to get a drink in dry Adelaide after hours; after that single year of membership he had not rejoined until 1982, when he was grateful for RSL advocacy of his case before a medical tribunal. QX12612 was a member early and much later, but had been told to hand in his badge in the middle period, at a time when he could not afford the subscription. A.T.F. joined in 1943, but left after a few years because the members were still fighting World War I; by 1974 time had changed that, and he rejoined. Malcolm Bingham did not renew his membership; at his sub-branch there was too much drinking for a teetotaller and, at 22, he had not fitted in with the older men anyway.

Politics often spoilt the RSL, in the view of some men. T. D. Cross resigned over Vietnam, because he was opposed to that war and the League was in favour of it; but he rejoined after the death of his hard-line state president and, in the 1980s, headed his local RSL youth club. William Drysdale joined the RSL, but was soon barred for being a communist. 'Burke'n' left the RSL between 1959 and 1966 because of its anti-communist stance. He had friends of that political persuasion when he was in the army, and he believed that the 'no politics or religion' rule should apply to communists as much as to any others. VX150307 refused to join the League both because it banned communists and also because, at the sub-branch level, it showed distinct male chauvinism towards potential female members. He himself was not a communist, but he objected to any exclusion on political grounds, and he happened to be married to a former member of the Australian Women's Army Service who had been in Papua from May 1945.

VX26672 had considered it mandatory to join the RSL in 1945, but had gradually eased himself out as he became 'less chauvinistic' than many in the League. It was the RSL's 'meddling' in politics, its 'witch-hunts' and, finally, the advocacy by a couple of its leading lights of children being brought up to be war-minded, which convinced C. J. Duncan that he had no place in the organisation. 'Smiler' had belonged to the RSL only for the odd year here and there: 'Too many Royalists, too much anti-socialism, too many bullshit artists claiming to have served in every theatre, too much shrapnel, too few below the rank of sergeant . . . [The prominent RSL leaders] do not represent the real Digger, thank goodness.'

Sidney Buckley let his RSL membership go as poker machines took over the clubs, non-service members were admitted, and 'political discrimination' was practised. A.J.B., a Labor man, said that 'RSL policies and mine are poles apart'. He had been a member early and again later, but only for the benefits he was entitled to. QX13154 was president of his sub-branch, but he disagreed with so much the RSL did that he expected to be 'thrown out'. Many RSL members, many respondents, would resent some of those comments and would want to make reply. But they were the sorts of things said by other respondents – and any reply should be addressed to them!

Gains and losses

Most of these men could be expected to keep in touch with some ex-service group. After all, four out of every five of them declared that army service had done them good or, in most cases, more good than harm. Many said it in spite of war's terrible legacies for them. It ruined the health of H.G.H., and put a barrier between him and civilians, yet the humiliations of being a prisoner of the Japanese developed in him the strength to cope. There was a wide range of gains, but two stood out above all else: coming to terms with other types of men and points of view, and developing self-confidence. Respondents also thought that others had mostly gained in the same ways, growing in confidence and tolerance – although

the latter sat poorly with the charges that the RSL was in-
tolerant.

The army and promotion to field rank so developed the
leadership qualities of N.G.T. that he felt restricted when he
returned to his job of process-engraving on a newspaper. He
therefore obtained commercial marketing experience and
ended his working life as state manager of an international oil
company. In the army VX150307 'developed mentally in
ways that would have been unlikely in civilian life'. He learnt
the value of what he called 'good housekeeping' in making
life more pleasant among a large group. He found that he was
an effective organiser, and that university graduates – common in a forestry unit and the Army Education Service –
'were no smarter than many who had not had the same opportunities, and some were short on common sense'. The army
jolted him out of the prewar rut he had been following as a
clerk, and helped him into postwar journalism. It also introduced him to the woman who was to be his wife. She was then
with the AWAS and, he said, 'She had served as long as I, and
that cut down the bullshit in our household'.

'Rural Labourer' had lost his mother as an infant, and
acquiring a stepmother to go with his war-pensioner father
did little for him. In fact, until he was about 13, he lived on the
farm of an elder brother who dominated him and jeered
whenever he asked a question. It was utterly different in the
army: 'I received knowledge from other soldiers. The friends I
made were only too happy to help.' And when the war was
over, he was trained as a carpenter and set on a path that led to
his becoming a builder in his own right. Another man who
was put on his feet was David Cambridge. Living from hand
to mouth as he wandered the country as a youth had developed
in him strength and the cunning to grasp opportunities, but he
was still 'an uneducated larrikin' when the army took him and
gave him real 'opportunities to learn'. He gained in 'self-
respect and confidence' and was 'shaped by service into a responsible citizen'. He had to give much credit for his refor-
mation to the influence of his wife, yet 'it was army life that

first kindled and nurtured an ambition' to make something of his abilities. Cambridge probably attributed too much to the army itself; what he had really responded to was the change from being a youth not much wanted by his country, to being a young man his country badly needed, and so would feed, clothe and train.

NX68275, a 'superior' bank clerk, gained immensely by finding that 'uncouth' types from Sydney slums could be caring mates, and his whole attitude to people changed permanently for the better. H. J. Tolhurst, a young professional, thanked the army for showing him that he was a snob – indeed 'a prejudiced, insufferable little prick' – and that a man should be judged for what he was, not on the school he had attended or the social class he belonged to.

There were other respondents who thought the army had little permanent effect on them, or who said that it harmed rather than helped them. (Each group came out at around 7 per cent of the whole.) Even some of those who stressed the army's benefits had also to point to the damage it had done to them and to others. Between harm to self and harm to others there was a different balance. Whereas only 11 per cent of respondents admitted to psychological problems for themselves, 30 per cent spoke of psychological difficulties produced in others. Was this a case of the more balanced objectively reporting on the men who had gone to pieces? Or did it suggest that it was easier to see trauma in others than fully to recognise one's own? Probably there was a lot of the latter in it, although final proof is impossible, and respondents had at least ridden out the storm: many other men had not.

Some preoccupation with self emerged in 17 per cent who claimed that their own careers had been badly interrupted by war, compared with only 8 per cent saying the same of others. But two other categories were claimed about equally for self and others: damaged social and family relations (13 per cent) and physical hurt (approximately 20 per cent). On the latter, there were respondents who wryly commented, 'Some men died'.

And some sensitive men, as A. H. Skene wrote, 'never recovered. Some became extremists, and some finished on skid row'. As an infantryman and German POW, Skene learnt compassion – but not for himself. Through the years he carried a sense of guilt over two incidents that involved three deaths. When convoys were dive-bombed during the Greece retreat, they stopped to allow troops to scatter, but two men always ran so far that they held the convoy up for anxious minutes every time movement was to be resumed. Skene finally made these two men stay near the truck and, as it happened, they were killed there. Then on Crete, when Skene and a lieutenant were searching for stray Germans, one stood up behind them and aimed his rifle at the lieutenant's back. Skene's Tommy gun jammed. He tried a hand grenade, but its pin stuck. So he could not save his officer. One part of his mind had called both of those happenings bad luck; but another, irrational part had kept relentlessly crying for over forty years, 'Skene, guilty Skene, for those deaths you are to blame'.

It was as an engineer that E.J.M. found his cross to carry for the rest of his life. At Balikpapan, in Borneo, he was assigned to the 2/12th Battalion to demolish Japanese bunkers. Some were strongly defended, but one tunnel appeared to be empty.

Still, I was told to blow it, because the Japs could return at night and hide behind our lines, so I laid the charge, blew the entrance and forgot about it. A fortnight later I was told that it had been opened and a number of Japanese found in it. They had died of suffocation, trying to dig their way out. What a way to die ... I have felt bad about it ever since. I used to have nightmares, and my conscience bothers me every time I look at a Japanese. I don't know why it affects me so. It was only a job to do. I usually never speak about it, and have only ever told a couple of doctors because of the effects it had on me. And now I have told you because, as stupid as it may

A welcome pause for part of the 2/8th Field Ambulance during the battle of El Alamein. Even more welcome was the cessation of all hostilities some three years later. Yet peace could be as hard to adjust to as war was

sound, I can only be sorry for what happened, and never proud.

The sensitive do what they have to do, and sometimes burden themselves with a guilt that is not theirs at all.

F. M. Paget put up his age to join the AIF. 'When we returned to Australia from the Middle East in 1943,' he wrote, 'I was surprised at the number committing suicide on the ship home. But at the end of 1945, when I was coming home from Borneo, I contemplated doing just that myself. You just felt you weren't a fit person to live in a decent, clean society.' Then his wife took up the pen – and who had a better right? On the back of a page she wrote:

I am pleased that at last some recognition is being given to these men who went overseas more than once, suffered their traumas, and then were expected to settle back into civilian life with little help. Mick was plain scared to get close to anyone in case he lost their love, as he had with mates who died beside him. It wasn't easy being married to him. He couldn't show affection to me or his children, and we all suffered. He seemed hard, yet underneath was soft as butter. It's taken many years of heartbreak, but we've weathered it, although it was harder for the children, who didn't understand.

Yet Paget thought that the army had done more good than harm to him, an ignorant country boy who needed experience and broadening.

For such emotional wounds men were often reluctant to seek help. There was a stigma attached to them, said Clyde Cook, and attempts to hide them only made the problem worse. But sheer physical damage also left its terrible legacies. C. C. Campbell had no doubt about the harm his service had done him: 'Having been 122 times in hospital since the war, and had 38 operations, there is not much to say about my postwar life except that the Repat. has been very good.' Campbell had suffered three wounds and various illnesses in the Middle East and Pacific, and had seen service from 1939 to 1945 before he virtually collapsed and normal life ended for him.

Past, present and future

Hear a strong complaint from 'Rusty':

The youthful generations regard us as old warmongers and agents of imperialism and the Right. If they only knew how much more understanding of evil we really are . . . Nor do they seem to realise just how they might have lived in servile drudgery and subjugation, but for the willingness and courage of youth two generations ago. Those who died and were maimed have been cheated, although I suppose it was naive to think it would be different. But the political and amoral ideologue has won the day, along with the capitalist money-grubbing class. Never mind, there's still Anzac Day.

'Rusty' of course did mind, and so did many another returned man. One of their strangest and most bitter experiences had been that sense of becoming despised by later generations.

Respondents tried to explain themselves and their point of view. They varied in their hope or dismay, their impatience or sympathy with later attitudes, and their feelings about the youth of the 1980s. But they all wished to be understood for what they had been and done in their own youth, and some of them tried hard to relate it to the present and the future. J. W. Quinn put his case this way:

The attitude of the community in general, and of my Baptist Church in particular, has changed. These days the church sometimes makes me feel isolated because of my war service, and young people do not seem to understand that *we* were young in 1940 and that putting on a uniform was our way of *protesting*. Against what? For what? I believed I was fighting for freedom, and I believed I should do my *own* fighting. I believed that 'truth', 'right' and 'freedom' were religious values. I believed that the empire was worth fighting for, and had been taught that at school. But I joined up against my will. When I decided to do so, I was so frightened I was gastric for a week, but I went on with it because I knew it had to be done. In the desert, after evening stand-down, we used to yarn and confide in each other, and many said that, basically, they were there because a job had to be done and 'some bastard had to do it'. Community rejection tends to push ex-servicemen back onto each other. Who else shows that they understand what we were about?

For QX1060 most surviving ex-service personnel were just members of the community who had served their community in war, and had continued to serve it in peace. Remembrance of those who had not survived that service was the essence of Anzac Day. He wrote: 'Many people have an unreal image of ex-service men and women, thinking that they all received a pension or compensation, and are all drunks and warmongering exhibitionists who meet on Anzac Day to booze, chant patriotic platitudes and criticise everyone else.' Some were like that, he granted, but even as late as the 1980s the ex-servicemen were still often active, successful and respected in many walks of life.

When one looks about, even at this late stage, one sees a Lord Mayor (ex-commando), a manager of a large firm (ex-artilleryman), headmasters, heads of government departments, engineers, professors, successful farmers . . . I remember the state manager of a bank – he'd been a sergeant; and his predecessor, incidentally, had been a returned man from World War I.

The services were mainly composed of civilians in uniform, who became civilians once more when the war was over, and who succeeded in life, frequently with little help and often with war disabilities to overcome. Some never made it, but many did. There were also the dead – approximately 30 000 – who asked for nothing, but there was 'a huge family circle' that never forgot them. So there was still Anzac Day, and still sufficient remembrance for it to be a force in the community. Rightly so, thought QX1060. What was wrong were the strange ideas about ex-service civilians that had grown up among too many other Australians.

Caricatures of the ex-serviceman were blamed by VX29041 partly on his own RSL. He remained a member of the League because of 'comradeship and the need to protect ex-service interests', but it did not always project the right image. That was all the more to be regretted because it played into the hands of 'present-day pseudo-intellectuals who totally misrepresented the meaning of World War II (cause and effect) and the attitude of the *real* returned soldier'. He himself had been able to approach postwar life with confidence because that was what he had learnt in the trained, disciplined, seasoned 9th Division. Life for him had been 'wonderful', but it had not been handed to him on a plate at discharge. He had no rehabilitation assistance because he did not satisfy the criteria of having been under 21 at enlistment, or partly through a course of training. So it had been under his own steam that he attained a satisfying occupation as a dairy supervisor in a department of agriculture. He had married, raised a family and 'retired to growl about taxation on superannuation'. Life? In the end, to a great extent, it was what you made it. War?

That was more difficult: 'No person with experience of war wishes to glorify it – and anyone who can think that an Anzac Day march and ceremony are for the glorification of war either has a twisted mind or suspect intentions. On the other hand, as undesirable as war is, pacifism only helps those who are not pacifists.' So VX29041 spoke for life and confidence, and they did not go with oppression. He spoke for peace, but not at any price.

For peace or war? Where have the Copemans stood? Son of an Anzac, and wanting to be 'as good as Dad', young James Copeman joined the AIF in 1939 with simple loyalties to country and empire, friends, and freedom as he saw it. On the Damascus–Beirut road he won the Military Medal for repelling a tank with small-arms fire. In New Guinea he earned the Military Cross for skilful and cool leadership in an attack by a platoon from the 2/3rd Battalion. He thought he had done with the army in 1945 but, when real peace had not come to the world by 1953, he rejoined the CMF. In the next dozen years he was seconded several times for service with United Nations military-observer and armistice missions in India, Pakistan and the Middle East, and his efforts as a CMF officer were recognised by the award of an MBE. He was at least as good as his father; what of his own son? Russell Copeman joined the regular army in 1965; two years later he died of wounds received on a long-range SAS patrol in Vietnam.

A warrior family, these Copemans? Or peacemakers? James Copeman was not quite sure himself. Yet he maintained that, while war may be profitable industrially and beneficial in scientific and medical developments, it was 'wasteful of lives and, on that ground, wrong'. It is reasonable to see Copeman service – in three wars, two AIFs, the citizen and permanent forces, and with the United Nations – as attempts to end war, restrict or prevent it. James Copeman spoke of brain-washing on both sides in World War II, and he deplored the then world leaders' readiness to sacrifice millions of lives for victory. His beliefs – 'so different from those formed by a 19-year-old boy forty-four years earlier' – had led him to one conclusion: 'If people generally could accept the need for high taxation to ensure peace in peacetime, as they do endure high taxes in time of war, there would be no need for war.' His argument rested on the deterrent effect of defence preparedness. The latter was necessary but costly, and Australians begrudged the money. This reluctance was dangerous, shortsighted, greedy – and greed caused war, one way or another. Copeman claimed that in the Pacific campaigns (and in Vietnam) most casualties occurred among the scouts, and that such losses would be greatly reduced by replacing manned patrols with electronic surveillance; but this equipment and training in its use were expensive – hence the need for citizens willingly to sacrifice money to save lives. Furthermore, servicemen thus trained could use their technological skills in civil life, whereas an army manual on employment used to say that there was *no* civilian equivalent to a rifleman's duties. These were elementary examples of what Copeman thought could be developed all along the line, at every level. Readiness for war increased the chance of peace. As an experienced military observer he had been able to interpret Indian or Pakistani commanders' movements, and so he saved many lives by forestalling imminent acts of aggression. He found more satisfaction in that than he had ever found in war.

NX31016 declared his faith in the younger generation of Australians. He still marched on Anzac Day, and if any of his three sons, their wives and children were in the vicinity they would come to watch the few men who paraded in the small township of Kootingal (NSW):

When I go by I hear them say, 'Good on yer, Dad'. And that makes it worthwhile because I reckon that, if ever a similar need arises again, they will remember me as I remembered my Dad (who never fully recovered his health after World War I, and died young). They will rise to the occasion and do as I did, and my Dad did, and all our love and pride in this country will be expressed by a new generation.

They will put on the slouch hat. I could not bear to think otherwise.

He was not wishing war on them, but expressing belief in
them. Deep down they retained the ideal of service, and in a
crisis the young would still be aware that 'the heart of the
nation lay in its people who were prepared to stand and be
counted'.

R.F.D. veered the other way, but not against youth. His
hope lay in the younger generation being 'better educated and
more ready to question authority' than his own had been. His
heart had gone out to those of a new generation involved in
the 'greater horrors' of Vietnam, and at that time he had come
to realise just how young had been those victims of the Japanese war he had nursed in the 2/14th Australian General
Hospital. His delayed reaction was to damn war as a futile
waste of life and to trust that the young would refuse to participate in it. It had been different in his day:

Far away from other countries, living at the end of a depression and
few of us having much schooling after the age of 14, we were ignorant and not politically minded. We thought that ours was the war
to end wars. Because it wasn't, have people become more hardened to
it? Or will the better-informed younger people refuse to be led into
slaughter? I have respect for Anzac Day and the old Diggers who
march, but I never do. It is a sad day for me, and it brings back bad
memories of war. I don't feel like boozing and renewing old friendships. War is hell.

So is unemployment, and that was why W.K. was deeply
concerned for many young Australians in the 1980s. He knew
about that from hard experience long ago. At an early age he
was placed in an orphanage where love and tenderness were
sissy, and canings by staff and bullying by older inmates ruled
day and night. At 14 he went to work on farms where hours
were long and pay short. Three years later came the depression, through which W.K. carried his swag, desperate for

work, always lonely and wondering if life was to be like that forever. In fact, things looked up in the good years of 1936 to 1939, with work and high pay on the Western Australian goldfields, but he joined the army at the outbreak of war, 'hoping to travel overseas and swagger around England or the Middle East like we were led to believe the original Diggers had'. Then came action, exhilarating in North Africa but soon ending in the disasters of Greece and Crete. Four humiliating, hungry and sometimes cruel years as a POW followed before W.K. found himself back in Australia – out of touch, withdrawn, and unhappy with the way society was changing. He adjusted after a year or two and, working and saving hard, finally took a horticultural course that gave him a better career. He married, and found love and security at last. In retirement, although on a TPI pension, W.K. was 'living comfortable' in a way he could never have envisaged in his young days. Since the war he had become 'strongly pacifist' – although 'someone had to stop Hitler' – and he had left the RSL because he thought its leaders were 'too far to the Right'. What had not been shaken was his belief in Australian youth:

I have great faith in young people; they are really us at a later stage in history. I like all nationalities, and it is good to see the young marrying all kinds of New Australians. I am sad that so many start life on the dole. They are not all bludgers – the system has made them disillusioned, and after that comes crime and no will to work. We had social injustice and depression before the war and, for some strange reason, the oldies I know now have a feeling of pride that we went through it. But one thing – it's strange because I was always impatient of authority myself – is my feeling that there is not enough discipline and respect for authority in our civil life today.

In their role of young person's guide, the respondents began to get confusing, and somewhat confused themselves. Where had the stereotype of the Digger and ex-Digger gone? Respondents took different attitudes to war and peace, Anzac Day and the RSL, resisting or accepting authority . . . But at least some of them were champions of the young. Respondent A. V. Aldham was something of a rough diamond. What he wrote in connection with the questionnaire was 'only the second or third letter' he had written since his army days. He mistrusted his spelling and his ability to put down the facts, but he had full confidence in Australian youth: 'Our young is as good as it ever was. Give them a chance to prove themselves. We have many needs in this country – get all your wise men together, give the young the training to do what's needed and they will prove themselves beyond any doubt.'

But schoolteacher Douglas Pyle was similar to W.K. in his worries. Despite having spent his working life with young people, he had finally found himself inadequate to advise them in an era of permissiveness and shortage of employment. What he had learnt as a corporal in the army had been 'to take an order and give one', and to value personal integrity and mutual trust. He remained committed to those values, but he seemed to be atypical in his profession. He claimed that there were too few ex-service teachers, due to exemption from the forces (it was more likely due to servicemen not returning to teaching). There were bad effects. He himself had not talked about the army to his pupils; in fact, he had 'rigidly and deliberately' avoided doing so; but the values and attitudes he had developed in his early life just did not seem to be widely shared any more. And was that the trouble – along with unemployment?

Edgar Chisholm was inclined to think so. He protested that he was not a whinger, although he was going to sound like one:

I only want everyone to enjoy to the fullest what we have got, and it will only come by sharing things more and not allowing a minority of greedy people to manipulate things for their own ends. The present situation is not the fault of the young because, when all is said and done, we older ones set the standards. But it would be hard to explain to our war dead why we are expected to turn our backs on previous allies, and how old values such as honesty, respect and good manners have broken down. To ride rough shod over others is just the opposite of democracy in my book, and if the drug scene and much that is condoned by authority to avoid treading on the toes of people in high places is progress, then the war was a terrible waste of young lives, our beloved country is in danger of going into decay, and our war dead have been badly let down.

QX29419 was not at all sure how he would feel if he were young now. Nor was he sure that the young soldiers of World War II had felt well used, or thought that their world was being put to rights. Perhaps many of them, much of the time, had just felt that they were being used up – and far too soon. It was not that QX29419 himself had been regarded as young by his wartime mates – he was the one whom they had called 'Dad' because he was 31 when he enlisted. Some three years later he and a very young signaller were attached to infantry detailed for an extended fighting patrol towards Madang to 'show the flag' to the retreating Japanese. Their signals equipment was a single wireless set powered by one small battery. It was not of much use, being 'built like a butter box and as heavy as lead', but it was all they had. On the morning of their departure 'Dad' found young Bill, with both headphones clamped over his big head, joyously listening on short-wave to the ABC's popular Mike Connors. Angrily 'Dad' pulled the earphone plugs and told Bill, in good army language, that he was using up the only available battery. They weren't next to Woolworths and, although the wireless wasn't much good, they were dependent on it. Bill looked up, hurt, with tears in his eyes. 'It's all right for you, Dad,' he said. 'You've lived your life. But what about me? I'm only 19.' Forty years later, 'Dad' wondered if history were not repeating itself with the 'hopelessness and despair of youth', and their dismissive attitude towards the oldies. 'Yes,' he mused, 'today I *have* lived my life . . . But what if I was only 19?'

So there was no easy way through, not then and not two generations later. Yet respondents tried to make some points

'Some bastard had to
stop Hitler and Tojo.'
A few of those
'bastards' just in from
patrol on Canning's
Saddle (NG) in 1944,
with the strain still in
their faces, and the
Japanese forward
position only about
350 yards away

and fumble out some clues to a future. Australia had in a real
sense been saved during World War II, and to cold-shoulder
those who had thus served it was unrealistic and ungrateful. In
their generation they had stood up to be counted – and shot at
– in making their protest against those who seemed to be out to
deprive free peoples of their rights and liberties. Willing
enough though some of them had been to go to war, hardly
any of them returned wanting any more of it. The average
ex-soldier was no warmonger, but was more likely to be the
respected departmental head just about to retire, or the decent
old bloke next door. Perhaps both of them marched on Anzac
Day; if so, it was not to glorify war. Yet ambivalence
remained: some bastard had once had to stop Hitler and Tojo.
There was a mistrust of pacifism, as well as some turning
towards it. Peace might still demand war, or at least defence
preparedness, or the active support of the UNO. Peace certainly had to be worked at and paid for. The tradition of
service had to be maintained; the argument really began over
whether that might involve the equivalent of 'the slouch hat',
or could – paradoxically – become an informed and principled
refusal to take part in slaughter.

And Australia should not be spoilt, although there were
many danger signs. So much unemployment among youth
was destructive. It might be possible to battle through it, as
many Australians had done in the past, but a better chance was

every young person's right. Older and influential members of
the community had much to answer for, and Australians
should not be manipulated by cynics, exploited by million-
aires, brain-washed by slick but shallow trendies, made to feel
unwanted – or, for that matter, made to feel free to do anything they wished. The eagerly grasped permissiveness was
damaging. There were other values that seemed important to
respondents: reasonable discipline, personal integrity, mutual
trust, honesty, caring, sharing . . . In the army, many men had
seen such qualities develop. 'Among new recruits in training
camps', C. C. Lee recalled, 'there was a lot of theft, and
nothing of value could be left around. When these same men
became part of a unit, all that changed. I've seen large sums of
money lying around – both overseas and back in Australia –
and nothing was taken.' It was for that sort of reason that
respondents thought it a pity that so much of the best of the
army spirit had been lost in peacetime Australia.

That was part of R.J.F.'s meaning when he held up the
ideals of less materialism and more unselfishness, and a
greater sense of duty to each other – our neighbours at home
and abroad – as the way to peace. And it was the essence of a
lament by VX59612 about the contrast between Australia at
war and what had happened afterwards:

Now that my generation, caught up in the war, is passing out of
leadership in the community, I regret that no way was found to
harness the great fund of learning and co-operation we developed
through our war experience. What was lacking was a failure to find
what William James called the 'moral equivalent of war' – a chal-
lenging style of life that called forth the admirable qualities of
mateship, unselfishness, resourcefulness, perseverance, quiet en-
durance and readiness to take the responsibility and face danger.
Where did all this go? It vanished on discharge like water in the
desert. So many fine young men; so many inflexible, reactionary,
prejudiced old men in the RSL. Deep reflection (I believe theological
reflection) on the experiences of war is needed. The servicemen's
contribution to the common good is lost so long as this area is

neglected – difficult though it is to work on without narrowness, moralism or bias.

Some people – respondents among them – will think that such a view idealises the Australian soldier and glorifies beyond reality the spirit of the World War II army. Some will argue that even that war failed to produce in the nation as a whole a true unity or high ideals, so that peace just meant more of the same selfishness and shallowness. Some will feel that VX59612's reflection was too negative about postwar achievements. Others, however, may agree that World War II produced at least an unusual degree of dedication, and set some precedents that might have been adapted to the years ahead but were allowed to slip away.

It is no new vision, no new lament. In the black year of 1942, when Australia's future hung in the balance in New Guinea, there appeared C. E. W. Bean's *The AIF in France during the Allied Offensive, 1918*. On the last page, Bean pondered on the fate of that *First* AIF and *its* postwar world – on the failure 'to save their children from having to fight out the contest again'. Bean wrote: 'The need for a postwar effort, as sustained and urgent as that of the war itself, to make the settlement effective was then realised by few even of the world's brightest minds. The tired victors simply sank into peace . . .'

There will be people who remain deeply suspicious of any panacea rooted in a military effort, a 'spirit of the army'. It will smack to them of a warrior caste, military juntas and simplistic thinking. Indeed, it *is* always easier to find a common purpose in a fight for sheer survival than in a peacetime community with diverse goals and conflicting 'solutions'. In some ways a true democracy and an efficient army must be contradictions in terms. But no respondent had anything like a military dictatorship in mind – rather the reverse; and it *is* possible for appropriate values and real inspiration to be carried over from a democracy to an army, and vice versa. One *can* serve the other.

Most respondents would have asserted without apology that, in 1942, the failure of the Japanese to take Papua New Guinea, and the Nazis the Middle East, led to happier lives for most Australians. It was better for them to import Volkswagens in the 1950s, and the products of Mitsubishi in the 1980s, than to have had enemy tanks in Australian streets in the 1940s. Even respondent Keith Hart, who was sorry that Australians had not been brought to their senses by actual invasion, had never wished final defeat on his people. At any rate, the country was then in deep trouble, but it survived. Why?

For reasons far beyond Australia and its forces, of course; yet *in part* because of what Australian soldiers did. And the respondents have provided glimpses of the real people behind that amorphous term. Mainly they were just young men in the street, from office or farm, industry or unemployment. Some of them were straight from school. Few had much education, or real training for war. Some were religious; others were not. Few of them were politically informed or could even begin to comprehend the incompetence and perfidy – on *all* sides – that had led to war. They mostly knew only that bad things were happening, and their side was in danger. Adventure and travel appealed to many, though some were desperately afraid. The image of the Anzacs helped a lot of them, and pride in the British Empire. Most of them had at least a gut feeling about freedom and duty. They felt that they belonged to Australia, though it had often treated them badly, and that Australia belonged to them, although few of them owned much of it. They reckoned that they should do something for it, and for those other places where liberty seemed threatened. Some were more willing that others, and there were higher and lower motives, better and worse performers. But mostly they settled down into a team, a series of co-operating teams. They became disciplined. They learnt to live together, tolerate one another, depend on each other. In action they adjusted for themselves what had been wrong in their training. Failure showed them how to succeed. They accepted risk and endured monotony. They knew that victory would not come tomorrow, and were prepared to wait, though they did not stop struggling towards it. They sacrificed years, and some their health and mental peace. Many died. Most were young then, and the victims of older men's decisions, but they saw the job through.

A mass army and a total war had brought out the best in many Australians. Why can't a comparative democracy and a precarious peace do the same? The question bothered some respondents, and must trouble us all. Even the men most directly involved sometimes failed among themselves to carry over into peace their wartime comradeship. A.J.B. described what could happen.

I had some very close army mates. We would still help each other in distress, but we are no longer close. In war we shared a common aim and similar interests, and we had the same amount of money to spend. In peace we have no common aim, and our interests often oppose each other. One of my former close mates is a wealthy grazier, who is a Country Party voter. Another has a large printing business, and is a Liberal Party stalwart, who hates trade unions and detests public servants. I am a retired public servant and a Labor supporter. On Anzac Day you get a wave and a raised glass. 'How's things?' 'Mum and the kids okay?' And off you go to find someone else with your own problems and outlook, even though he *wasn't* a wartime mate.

V. H. Lloyd ran a car rental and parking business with another returned soldier for twenty-one years. He was a newsagent for the next nine years, and then enrolled as a university student and went as far as postgraduate study for the degree of Master of Arts in English literature. He had already written a couple of novels in the 1950s, so enterprise and achievement were notable in his postwar life; yet he had also unhappily watched old comrades coping with their civilian life.

The most disturbing aspect has been the steady elimination from the

The young soldier and the old – Ray Murphy, of Shepparton (Vic.)

ex-soldier of the quite noticeable idealism of the war years. Whenever the long and desultory conversations then touched on the shape
of the postwar world it was always suggested that, when we returned,
we would never let things settle back to the same old spectres of
unemployment, poverty, class distinction – all the problems that had
dogged the prewar years. However, the end of the war and the dis-
integration of units left all of us facing a need to find some kind of
niche, so all of those unformed ideas were lost in the battle to become
established with some security. With each passing year the oldtimers
have become a little more conservative and highly critical of youthful activities which are but a pale shadow of some of their own
exploits. The RSL is controlled by political conservatives, guilty of
racism and intolerance, and while many old mates are unquestioning
members, I feel they tend to be exploited politically while enjoying
the social amenities. As they get older they are less concerned about
the implications.

Old myths are enshrined in clouds of sentimentality. It may well be that this is a universal trend, and – if so – revolutions aimed at social reforms are doomed forever to founder on the rocks of their own myths and a natural resistance to change. If anything, today's youth seems more susceptible to advertising pressure and to propaganda than even my generation, despite better education, which was once thought to give the equipment to think logically. The only challenge to this conclusion might have been the resistance to Vietnam, but that kind of radicalism died without any legacy of idealism, just as World War II idealism did.

So Lloyd was disappointed, close to despair. In making his comments, was he being unfair to his old mates and letting them down? Or was he standing with them still, and standing with all mankind to remark on a common failure? He stood to the left among them, but men on the right saw a grim outlook too: old spectres still haunting Australia and the world.

Yet most respondents also saw old gains, partial victories. As soldiers they had helped to preserve rights, including the liberty of Australians to combine in the writing of such a book as this, and to express their opinions of it openly. Respondents watched their grandchildren around them, and usually dared some hope for the kids. But they encouraged no pretence about all being right with the world, then or now. In their patient answers they have lapped us with their humanity, their strengths and weaknesses, and revealed to us their private thoughts. They have shown us their world and their war, and – as respondent W. N. D. Bow suggested – both could often be described as SNAFU. More politely rendered than in Bow's version, it means 'Situation normal. All fouled up'.

It has still to be reckoned with. A distressed world is a normal situation. It has long been thus, or little different. World War II was not abnormal so much as an aspect of the ordinary. What many Australians did about it was to respond positively, do what they had to do, bear what they had to bear, and hope for the best. Some did not come through, and none broke through into a new world; but many survived, and much good survived with them. If the present time is still SNAFU, each generation must rise to its own challenge. Peace, however, may be even harder to wage than war.

14 • SNAPSHOTS

Things I remember? At this late stage I mainly recall the thrill of enlisting, and the pleasure of discharge in one piece [Atholl Wright].

I suppose that sailing for the Middle East and arriving home for final discharge would each be memorable in themselves, but my mother made them more so. In 1941 we left Northam camp at midnight to go by train to Fremantle and board the *Queen Elizabeth*. At the wharf I was told that a lady was calling my name. It was my mother. I'll never know how she knew I was on that train, or how she negotiated the barbed wire. Then a military policeman abused her for being in a restricted area, but he left when she laid into him with her umbrella. She was only 5 ft tall. At the other end of the war, in December 1945, I arrived in Fremantle on the *Aquitania* and got ashore to find the family lined up: wife, mother-in-law, grandparents, uncles, aunts – and my mother. History more or less repeated itself. A bombastic military policeman ordered me straight onto the train – admittedly I'd been on the last lighter to leave the ship, and the train was ready to pull out. But little 'Five-foot' took to *him* with her umbrella. The moral is obvious: never underestimate a mother with an umbrella when her son goes to and returns from a war [J. R. Ferguson].

Our home in 1932 had neither telephone nor wireless, and to set our clocks my mother used to look at the hospital clock through a telescope. When I was about 12 years old I asked

her, 'How do you know that clock's right?' Quick as a flash
she replied, 'Because it's a Government clock.' I accepted that
without question, and only tell this little tale to illustrate how
our whole upbringing was that the government was always
right, and so was the British Empire. So we went to war, to the
first permanent job many of us had ever known, and we got
our teeth at last into something that really meant something.
A lot of us survived, but of course nothing was quite the same
ever again. Nothing ever is. My old wartime gang never meet
up, or wear medals in a march. Perhaps we had seen too much
and yet found nothing. Perhaps we were weak enough to
believe that we would be thanked for what we had endured
. . . Perhaps it was all best forgotten. We were just little grains
of sand on a big beach, as it always has been and always will be.
But I still sometimes see a movement from the corner of my
eye, and start to crouch. I see a few birds fly up from the
ground in the distance – disturbed by what? ['The Gink']

Where will I begin? I have hundreds of memorable experiences . . . The day another soldier and I 'captured' five
hundred Italian troops. The day I demonstrated how to use an
Italian carbine, and blew a hole in the roof of the signals
office. The day I said I could drive an army truck, but did not
say that I had no previous driving experience. My first Good
Friday in Palestine, April 1940, when there were three cere-
monies going on simultaneously about twenty yards from
each other, and all well attended: a church service in the Salvation Army Cheer Up Hut, a two-up school, and an Arab
fornicating with a female donkey. My first brush with a German patrol at night, or how to do a mile in under four
minutes. The day Brigadier 'Old George' Vasey nearly blew
the pips off a lieutenant in language that would have put a
bullocky's in the shade (I had *told* the lieutenant that he was
issuing wrong orders, but that was because I – an ordinary
signaller – was entrusted with despatches that nobody but a
brigade liaison officer should ever have handled; which shows
how wrong things were). The day Brigadier 'Red Robbie'

Robertson got mad because somebody pinched the Derna mosque clock. The day the Hurricane fighter above Derna shot down three Italian biplane fighters (CR42s) in about the time it would take to say one, two, three. The days the German Stukas dive-bombed us from Yugoslavia to Crete. The Greek wine, women and song, and Greece itself – a lovely country. The day we had Lewis gun practice at Liverpool (NSW); no one hit the bull's eyes, but the flagpole fell down. The flies, the dust, the monotony of doing nothing, and our meeting with conscripts in Northern Australia. All those things and much more I could talk about – and they were all experienced for what? Millions died for what? So that we who survive may stand at 2100 hours in any RSL club and recite, 'Lest we forget'? [NX5872]

My war diary [wrote R. J. Anson] shows that on 30 October 1941 half a dozen of us walked to the Tobruk War Cemetery and wandered up and down its long rows of graves, pausing at those of men we had known in the battalion. They included Jack Edmondson, VC. All the while the gun-fire rumbled along the Bardia road. Over a year later my diary notes that it is 11 November, the Armistice Day of 1914–18, the war in which my father fought and my uncle died, at Gallipoli. But Dick and I were trudging through sand thinking of the mates we had just lost at El Alamein, and talking of the fellows who had been in our last prewar stock camp – Jim shot down over Europe, Paddy killed on Crete, John in Syria, Tip at Tel el Eisa, Fletch taken POW in Malaya. Would *we* ever ride our horses in the outback again? My diary for 1944 contains the name of Eric Vincent, badly wounded alongside me at El Alamein, but rejoining the battalion at last, only to be killed in New Guinea. Now, on every Remembrance Day, I see how unconcerned our population is, and I think of W. H. Auden's lines:

> To save your world you asked this man to die;
> Would this man, could he see you now, ask why?

I joined the 2/10th Battalion well after the battle of Milne Bay in which the battalion was overrun by the Japs and lost many men, but I was with the battalion at the memorial church parade on the first anniversary of that battle. I watched the survivors, standing erect, chins thrust forward, tears running down their faces as the Last Post was sounded. And I was with the battalion at the Balikpapan landing, as were three great mates, only 19 years old – Dave Crawford, Alan Creighton and Frank Churchill of 15 Platoon, 'D' Company. In the assault on Hill 87, Crawford died from a machine-gun burst to the stomach. Near the top of the objective, Churchill was killed by a bullet in the forehead. Creighton was one of nine men, out of thirty-two, who gained the top. He had bullet holes in the collar of his shirt, and a mirror smashed in his haversack. Later I saw him a dazed, trembling pack of nerves, an old man so young, with the horror of war etched into his face. Being a NSW boy, I lost contact with this SA battalion, but I have often wondered how Creighton survived the return to civilian life [J.A.L.].

Even after forty years many things stay vivid. Watching Sydney drop out of sight from the deck of the *Queen Mary*, and wondering if I would return. The excitement of finding at El Alamein, in my first action, that my beholders didn't see me as a coward, even though I was at times terrified. The day I left a command post seconds before a direct hit killed all inside it. Walking in the path of the Lord in the old city of Jerusalem. Seeing Sydney again on a sunny day, with crowds going wild. The introduction to New Guinea jungles – the filth, desolation, rotting dead bodies, the tremendous contrast with the desert where we could *see* our adversary. The issue of condoms before the assault landing on Labuan, giving some troops the idea that they were in for a great time, until the order came to put the condoms over our rifle muzzles to keep the water out of the barrels. (The sight of them dolefully dangling must have been a bit much for the Japanese.) Tending a dying soldier alone, not knowing if the Jap would have another go, and not knowing where he was; he could see us, but for some reason did not kill again. General Morshead's compassion when appealed to about a number of critically wounded men who could not be evacuated; he had them put into his Catalina flying boat and sent to an American hospital in the Philippines. The day we heard that the war was over, and the dreadful fear of the following days while the Japs in our area fought on and the dying continued. The bitterness towards the Japanese guards and executioners when we went into the Sandakan POW camp in North Borneo and found that no prisoners had survived. The thrill and *strangeness* of my return to civilian life after having spent 20 per cent of my life in uniform. Oh, that's enough writing, but there's so much more I remember [A.N.M.].

My most upsetting memory is of driving through a burning town in Greece in 1941 and having to remove a middle-aged Greek couple from the running board of my vehicle and leave them by the road. Fifth columnists were active, and we were forbidden to pick up civilians, but I have never lost the image of that event [F. H. Wood].

Grant Road, Bombay, was strictly out of bounds. Therefore someone in our group on a day's leave suggested that we have a look at it. It was a brothel street where women were caged, and I found myself looking into a pair of liquid brown eyes set in the face of an old-young woman. Once she had been beautiful. With desperation she held up three fingers on a delicate hand and called out, 'Three annas.' She would have given me her body for the price of a newspaper. Between us were bars like those on the cage of the chimpanzee at the zoo. I was young, full of hopes and ideals. What could I do to help her? Nothing I could think of, short of becoming a client – and at that thought my good lunch heaved in my stomach. She was one of the girls whose parents could not support her and who had sold her to those who put many like her into the cages of

Grant Road. Hurt in my insides, I turned quickly away. We saw many things that day, and when the evening entertainment ended we rode back to the ship, paid off our guide and became soldiers again. Yet I was haunted by a pair of dark eyes, and a graceful hand holding up three fingers. Sometimes in the desert, breathing the clean night air, I would look up at the stars and think of brown eyes gazing through bars. After battle came, and they told us that we had 'won a great victory', 'set the pattern', 'made military history', all six of us who teamed up that day in Bombay were dead or wounded. And the girl? What did it matter for her that armies were gathering? What did the many words of politicians mean to her? She would not know. She would not remember us. Her slender hand would wave in no celebration of victory. I still wonder what became of her [J. W. Quinn].

You can believe this story or not, but I know it's true. Three of us were 'sightseeing' the Alexandrian brothels. In one of the 'rooms of choice' we noticed a young girl on her own, crying. We went and sat with her. She had some English and we found that she was a Greek, 16 years old, who had lost all her family in the German advance and had been brought out of Crete by some Australian and English lads who had managed to pinch a small boat. Dumped in Alexandria, this pretty child was a 'natural' to be picked up for the trade, but we found her before she was 'used'. With some quick decisions and diversionary tactics we got her out of the brothel under the madam's nose, and took her to the Toc H Hostel where they undertook to look after her. Some months later, when on leave from the Western Desert, we stayed at the Toc H and the girl was happily there on the staff of the hostel. I've forgotten her name [NX34070].

For a time I was stationed at Army Command, a building opposite the public library in Melbourne, but I was only too pleased to leave it and return to the Middle East. That building was known as Coward's Castle or Zebra House, because all 'other ranks' there had stripes. It was said that a telegram boy (in those days wearing a uniform) got lost in the building for two days and emerged as a major with a row of ribbons [F. P. Melrose].

I thought I should answer as one who served in a base – petrol – unit. It was formed in Sydney when we were under threat of invasion, the officers being oil company personnel who were given two weeks army training. Petrol dumps of approximately 6000 drums were established in towns in the mountains, but it was then found that the octane rating was too low and would have to be lifted by an additive. We became the ethyliser squad, and toured the state for about nine months. Dressed in overalls, cap, knee-length boots, rubber apron, elbow-length gloves and a respirator, we decanted the additive into 4 gallon drums, measured a quantity into the 44 gallon petrol drums and agitated it with a handpump. At the end the whole squad volunteered for overseas service, but we were kept back in the 'Bulk Issue: Petrol and Oil Depot' as its 'backbone'. Perhaps one can be too good [K. T. Barrack].

Everybody raced out into the street, thinking that American planes had come, but instead they found Japanese bombs falling on them. That was the first raid on Darwin, on 19 February 1942, when I was there as a civilian fireman still. My superior officer and I witnessed panic at the very top, and heard advice given to get out of town fast because the Japanese would land that day. We were disgusted, and tried to do what we could on our own. At the RAAF station the water storage tank was in two levels, the bottom one being kept as an emergency. This was an emergency – the bombs had broken many water pipes – but who had the key to the bottom tank? By the time the padlocked chain on its valve had been chopped through with an axe, aircraft in a hangar had been destroyed by fire. That's a positive fact. Another is that the hospital ship *Manunda* was breaking the conventions of war by being anchored amid merchantmen and men-of-war, but a Japanese dive bomber – coming in to attack her – veered off when the pilot saw the red cross on her side. I was taken into the army very soon after that first raid, and remained in Darwin for something like sixty-six more, but the defence was a shambles. A few hundred of us were left to protect the peninsula, but we were to fall back to the water, if necessary, and make our way across the harbour. How, I didn't know; there were no boats. My equipment was a Lewis gun, fifty rounds of ammunition and three hand grenades ['Hawk Eye'].

At about 9.45 a.m. on 19 February 1942 we were on parade when a flight of planes came over Darwin. We did not realise that they were not ours until bombs dropped. We manned our guns and went into action – and it was good to see the results of years of training paying off [A.R.K.].

During the first raid on Darwin we were engaging the Jap bombers when out of the dust came a wallaby closely followed by an American serviceman. 'Come on, Aussies,' he said, 'let's get out of here.' Our CO immediately threatened to shoot any man who tried it [N279537].

Slowly steaming down Darwin harbour was HMAS *Swan*, all guns blazing and being repeatedly lifted out of the water by near-misses. And there was the US destroyer *Peary*, practically awash but with her guns still firing as she exploded [C. R. Pearce].

I was in Darwin during the first raid – not camped near it, but *in* it. In one hour I saw twelve large ships sink. I was wounded lightly, burnt a little, covered in black oil. By midnight I had pulled the living and the dead from the water, and had assisted in burying the pathetic little bundles of post office personnel – I had known three of them. That night I was on duty in one of two coastal defence forts, knowing that the army and hospitals were pulling out for eighty miles south. It may have been a wise military decision, but to be one of a few hundred to stay was not heartening. We had little food and no fresh clothing except what we had looted from the town. After the second raid I had seven rounds of ammunition left, and it remained that way for two months. To this day, blowflies and hot oil sicken me. The dead seamen were Lascars, Chinese, Indians, Britons, Australians, Americans – and far more in number than is admitted. I suppose the dead were also Catholic, Anglican, Gentile, Jew, Moslem, Hindu. They all looked and smelt the same. Until someone can explain *why* these things happened, I prefer to be agnostic [VX——].

Isolated on Timor as a small group of commandos, we ambushed a Japanese truck one night. In the morning we watched the enemy arrive in force and interrogate the villagers. Allan Hollow, who later proved his courage and determination beyond all doubt, was taking a somewhat jaundiced view of the situation. He said, 'Singapore's gone. Java's gone. We don't even know if Australia's still there. The unit is running round the hills like rabbits. Here we are, 18 men, sitting on a ridge waiting for 126 Japanese to come and eat us. We've counted those little bastards. They're the only concrete thing we know. What do we do now?' Paddy Knight, his 21 st bulk reduced to 18 by malaria, was trying to make himself still smaller by digging a shallow hole next to a boulder. He rested, and offered his views. 'I think it's about time we were writing to *Smith's Weekly*. They say that they're the Digger's friend.' For the record, Paddy was too big a target. When we finally left, he and Mitch the Bren-gunner remained behind, dead [R. A. Aitken].

The beauty of Tarakan Island remains clear in my mind even while the trauma of the islands campaign has faded. Monkeys abounded in the treetops, and one of our sentries accidentally shot a rare proboscis monkey in mistake for an infiltrating Jap. The impact on wildlife of the din and devastation of battle is apt to pass unnoticed [G. T. Nowland].

We returned from the Middle East early in 1943 and disembarked in Sydney. All SXs entrained for Adelaide and at last our steam train shuffled through the hills on the western side of the Mount Lofty Ranges just as the sun was rising on a beautiful fine day. Finally we cleared a cutting and there, between us and the sea, lay Adelaide in all its clean glory. After two years abroad and two campaigns in the desert, it was the most beautiful sight I had ever seen. Someone close to me said with reverence, 'Christ, just take a look at that' [A.A.J.].

On the rail trip from Adelaide to Alice Springs the 'Ghan' would stop at Quorn, where the townspeople would serve a fine meal of roast beef to all the troops. I believe they met every northbound troop train to give them their last good meal for many months. I have not read anywhere of this splendid service by a few people who were not endowed with wealth [K.R.G.].

Did you ever hear of the division that barked? The transports were crowded when the 9th Division returned from the Middle East, and the troops were so herded about that they started baaing like sheep and barking like dogs. Concentrated on the Atherton Tableland, doing route marches (to harden up!), the men got browned off again at being driven around like mobs of sheep. So, when individuals met or companies passed, they would bark and 'Ho Ho Ho' at each other to such an extent that the new divisional commander issued an order for it to stop forthwith. More powerful than that divisional order, though, was the latrine telegraph. At 'Lights Out' on an agreed night the barking started up. From unit to unit and back again, barking, yapping, howling, ho-ho-hoing, rising to a crescendo from Ravenshoe to Atherton. It was fantastic, and it had a sequel. In the close and vicious fighting around the approaches to Sattelberg, our troops and the enemy became so intermingled that nobody knew who surrounded whom. So the barking was resurrected and positive identifications made. The Japs could not understand it at first, and by the time they began to catch on and make hopeless attempts to imitate, it was too late for them [TX——].

In June 1941 a signaller poked his head above ground in Tobruk and yelled, 'Company has just rung to say that Russia is in the war.' Mindful of the non-aggression pact between Russia and Germany, I asked him which side they were on. He looked puzzled for a moment. 'They didn't say,' he replied, 'I'll give them a tinkle and find out' [F.A.J.].

We had a lieutenant – a good one too – who was at times afflicted with a bad stammer. On one famous day he was trying to give the order for a section to start marching. 'Quick m-m-m-m . . .' Pause. 'Qu-quick m-m-m-m-m . . .' Longer pause. 'Wh-when I can g-get the w-word out, we'll f-f-fuck off' [NX72561].

By the time we got to the Middle East the language used by the men in my company seemed to be a bit over the fence, and I tried to do something about it. I paraded them and pointed out that their swearing mostly involved either bodily parts or bodily functions, and I suggested that they might tone things down by substituting the words 'parts' or 'functions'. Somehow the idea caught on, and when I left the unit some twelve months later it was not at all unusual to hear some man under stress burst out with '*Parts* and *functions!*' ['Two Pips']

There was an organisation called the Rockhampton Soldiers and Sailors Help Society that used to send regular parcels to our unit. Each was accompanied by a small ticket from the donor, and one came to me with the name of a miss on it. So Don Juan took up pen and poured reams of bull to the address. Back came a typewritten answer, and Lover Boy was into it again. The next reply enclosed a photo of a gorgeous doll. I paraded it around the 'playground', boasting that 'Some's got it. Some haven't. And I've got it'. So it went on until my tent mate took pity on me and revealed that the photo was one of our Loot's birds, and the letters had been typed in the Orderly Room. I took some rubbish over that, I can tell you; however, it enhanced my standing with the fellows. If you use this story, may I say 'Bugger you, Harry and Bob' ['Chesty'].

Part of a consignment of grog for the officers' mess went missing. There was hell to pay. At RC church parade the padre (himself an officer, of course) informed us that stealing was a sin – even pinching from officers was a sin – and, if his congregation included the offenders, the beer should be returned immediately. We didn't much fancy putting ourselves in, and the booze was hidden in a tricky spot, but my mate 'Blue' found the perfect solution: 'How about I tell Father in confession? That way he's bound by the seal of the confessional and can't spill on us.' I said, 'Bloody ingenious, cobber.' And that's what he did.
  'I stole the beer, Father.'
  'You did? You must return it, now. Where is it?'
  'Under the floorboards in your tent, Father.'
  '*Get it out of there!*'
  Some we drank, some we returned, and only three of us ever knew ['Rusty'].

When that American Liberator crash in 1943 wiped out the 2/33rd Battalion's 'D' Company, a replacement company was immediately lent by the 2/2nd Pioneer Battalion for the attack on Lae. But that was only temporary. A new 'D' Company had to be created somehow, and the way it came about was once described by Reg Harris, who served with the 2/33rd before becoming a war correspondent. Captain Kevin Power sought volunteers from men in the Port Moresby area. He had only non-infantrymen to draw on because all infantry units were committed to planned operations, and he was not at all hopeful. But he appealed to the 7th Division Carrier Group – an armoured unit – and was overwhelmed by volunteers for a hard campaign in a role for which they were not trained. They said that it didn't seem that their unit was going to be committed to action. They felt they were loafing on their mates. So they came forward in such numbers that Power was able to handpick the most suitable of them. And when the selection had been made and the company was at full strength, some of the rejected volunteers tried to bribe their way in [QX6794].

I have watched an infantry battalion – I think it was the 2/16th – advance steadily under heavy fire in Syria, keeping their line and interval, and no one breaking. It was brave. I know how artillery units relied on the telephone lines laid between forward observation posts and the guns, and between the guns and headquarters. Those lines depended on the maintenance signaller, a particular breed of soldier whose cold-blooded courage never failed to amaze me. But the bravest thing I ever saw was done by a party formed in an emergency under an orderly room sergeant, M. M. Johnson. They were clerks, batmen, cooks. And they went out from regimental headquarters to go up a cliff to stop the fire from a section of the French Foreign Legion. None had been trained for that sort of thing. Few, if any, were even competent shots. They were all terrified, but they went – and it doesn't matter a scrap that the Foreign Legion had pulled out before they could be engaged [E. J. King].

I entered into army service at a fortunate time. The major battles had been fought; I was well trained by experienced NCOs; and I joined a battalion as a member of a platoon containing ten or twelve men who were veterans. They were kind to me – I think they regarded me as still a schoolboy – as I served through one campaign with them: Aitape-Wewak. By that time (1945) there was talk of a 5 × 2 plan of discharge, by which men who had served five years, including two years overseas, were the first eligible. It was a very hard situation for the veterans in my platoon, those dozen or so men and our

senior NCOs. Discharge was in their sights, but they still did
their share of the patrolling – and the fighting patrols. Other
members offered to take their places on these dangerous jobs,
which made their chances of survival so much slimmer, but I
don't know of one of those men ever accepting any such offer.
That I thought was the real gutsy 'Digger' at his quiet best
[W. A. Newton].

When our khakis were handed in at Townsville to be dyed
green [wrote C.H.L.] we soon had unintended green singlets
and underpants as well, and very green bodies. There was a
poem written by Rebecca Morton that was very dear to us,
and spelt out the situation very clearly. It was called 'Faded
Suits of Green', and it described how they had gone into the
dye-pots in a hurry, when there was 'no time for fuss or finish'. If they 'came out in patches of pale yellow, green and
brown, They were fashioned for the jungle, not for touring
round the town'. And on through the jungles Rebecca Morton
imagined them going: 'Torn and tattered, splashed with crim-
son, Glorious faded suits of green.' She thought of the waiting
POWs and assured them that rescue was coming dressed in
shabby green. Then she looked further into the future:

> When the bells of peace are ringing
> As they did in days of yore,
> When the hated sounds of war drums
> Shall have ceased for evermore;
> When we live in love and laughter
> And happiness serene,
> Oh, Australia! Please remember
> Those faded suits of green.

After six or seven weeks as a prisoner of the Germans on
Crete, I escaped and joined the local partisans for some
months. I returned to Crete in 1981 and found some old
friends who hadn't forgotten me. They all seemed to have
remembered, while Australians have not. The Cretan children

knew more about our military history than most of ours do. While we were there a ceremony was held to open a new shopping square, and it was named 'The Square of the Australian Fighter'. I hope that the wars and suffering of Australian servicemen will come back into our schoolrooms once again [T. C. Birch].

I haven't any great tale to tell. I was just one of thousands who thought Australia was imperilled and were glad to assist her. I knew some brave men. I enjoyed their company, and was often very frightened. I made some great mates who are still mates. However, in the years since the war we were used up in some way, I think, and I certainly would not like any son of mine to go to so useless a thing as war. The Japanese told us, as we locked them into compounds, that the war wasn't ended but would last a hundred years . . . [D. J. Doran].

As a POW I suffered from malaria, beri beri, dysentery, typhoid, pneumonia, kidney abscesses, hookworm, osteomyelitis and a few other things. (You did *ask* to be told.) The most memorable of all my experiences is of lying sick in a prison camp in Japan and seeing through a window the 'poached egg' flag hauled down and the Union Jack hoisted [E. O. Bloomfield].

Stalag VIIIB in Poland was a large camp, well supplied by the Red Cross, packed with all kinds of 'British' troops, humming with activity, including much of an educational character. We put on weight, and there were no suicides there. Then came the big freeze of January 1945 and, with it, the Russian advance. The Germans marched all POWs away from the camp and the approaching Red Army. It was so cold that anyone who spent the night outside was likely to die, and what food we had was sometimes frozen into uselessness. There was no organised food supply anyway; Germany was in a state of collapse. We were still shambling along in March, getting weaker daily, bags of bones plagued by dysentery and vampire lice. Each day men died. A gang of skeletons slowly passed, with eyes as dead as a cod's on a marble slab. For some reason they were pulling a World War I army cooker along by fencing wire. It was polished to perfection but quite empty; the skeletons were asking in German for food . . . Then the sweet music of a thousand Flying Fortresses seen in the sky, and a call one morning, 'The Yanks are here.' A horde of filthy, unkempt, screaming scarecrows descended on a poor tank commander to slap him on the back. I went to a stream to wash for the first time in months, and startled a prison guard, one leg in a pair of civilian pants. Who was the captor and who the captive I did not know. I walked past him, and smiled. He smiled, and we had declared our own peace [N. W. Pritchard].

I saw Lord Mountbatten take the surrender of the Imperial Japanese Army in Singapore. I hitch-hiked from Changi gaol to the city, some sixteen miles, to watch the ceremony, and was then entertained (afternoon tea – 'tiffin') on a Royal Navy aircraft carrier. Tea and scones and butter, and the butter happened to have been made in my home town of Bairnsdale. I'm afraid I became most emotional, and made a fool of myself [F. W. Jackson].

Thank you for the opportunity of being involved in your exercise. It was quite a trip. You see, I had never gone back over my life much, and now that I have I wish I had done more of it earlier. There were lots of things we did which would be hard to describe. Once a patrol of ours found one of our mates, who had been missing. He'd been tied to a tree by the Japs, with a length of bamboo forced into his backside. He was still alive, but died soon after. I went a little insane for a while, and when we cornered some Japs later on, the things we did to them now seem horrifying – but I guess that's war [VX66349].

The little Jap prisoner stood between a sergeant and a private from one of the infantry battalions on Scarlet Beach, Finsch-hafen, in October 1943. With his thumbs tied behind his back and his trousers removed, he reminded me of a small terrified animal. A barge was due to pick up a number of wounded men and the prisoner, but after some time word passed around that the barge wasn't coming. The two infanteers moved off the beach and into the jungle with their prisoner. Shortly afterwards I heard the unmistakable crack of a .303 rifle. Later I passed one of those men and asked, 'What happened to the little Jap?' He looked at me steadily for some seconds, and then replied, 'The Nip? Ah, he shot through, mate. Yair, he got away' [R. J. Berry].

On pre-embarkation leave my uncles and aunts asked me, in an amused fashion, what I would do if I came face to face with a German soldier. Mentally I said that I'd make signs for him to go his way while I went mine. I never did meet a German in quite that situation, but I met a Japanese. He was lying on his face, seemingly to avoid detection, and I was some distance from my nearest mate. I said something to the Jap, then plucked at a tag on his uniform. He rolled over. I saw his eyes, but no weapon. Nevertheless I jumped back and pumped five shots into him. It was a single-shot rifle, which meant that I had to cock it each time. We found that he had no weapon and was possibly sick from malaria. I was very upset at the time by my nervous reaction and, while I can't say that I'm actually haunted by it still, on Anzac Day (which I spend at home) that 'unknown soldier' gets into line with others of my own kind that I might think about [M.G.R.].

The army must have done me some harm. It turned me from a fairly harmless extrovert into a dedicated, legalised murderer. When I shot my first enemy soldier, I was actually ill. Within six weeks I was tallying them up like rifle scores – and being ill later [R. A. Aitken].

One night a Dyak warrior joined us, apparently from nowhere, and he attached himself to me because I had a piece of great magic – something on my back that spoke when I spoke to it. In the morning we were held up by small-arms fire, and my Iban friend disappeared to reappear shortly and present me with a bloody, dripping Japanese head, *still wearing its spectacles*. Somehow it brought home to me as nothing else had that the enemy were fellow humans. I was very grateful that the war ended soon afterwards [W.S.].

The really big thing overlooked is the length of time it takes to really return to civilian life; it would average seven to ten years to get back to some sort of normal behaviour. The army trains you to hate the enemy and be a killer; and, having no help, hundreds of our best men, who distinguished themselves in the service of their country, were said to be rotters because they never made it back to civvies. It affects all in different ways. Some relive their army life forever (one friend wore his army driver's cap until he retired), and others try to forget. For some ten years I could not attend an Anzac parade or see a war film without ill effects for days. It's the same for my son, who served twice in Vietnam. It cost him his marriage and children, and almost cost his life. He can't get psychological help; his only help is work up to sixteen hours a day. How can wives and family understand what torments go on in the ex-serviceman? I feel very strongly about the need for more and longer rehabilitation after *active* service, although I was one of the lucky ones, having married a Christian girl who has stood by me and helped me grow in faith [C. C. Lee].

As man is the only animal on earth that continually kills its own kind, he will eventually be his own destroyer. But one has to try to survive in a time of war, and I still had the most precious thing in the world – life – after duty done to king, country and family. I was married by the end of the war, and I had a job to go to. Even so, it was a bit hard to return to civilian life. How can you just walk away from your battalion after nearly five years of mateship and hell, laughter and tears? [J. R. Ferguson]

• THANKS

Like many books, this one owes about as much to others as to its author. The role of the late Professor Roger Joyce is explained in the dedication, and there were many other substantial contributors. Mostly they were female – the author's 'monstrous regiment of women', as some of them dubbed themselves. The respondent who said, 'Don't let the ladies see this bit' would have been deeply shocked at what they saw.

Cheerfully and reliably, Mrs Audrey Morris handled and recorded the vast two-way flow of letters, queries and questionnaires, methodically filing mountains of material for many months, and often going home to mutter the alphabet in her dreams ... McCay, MacKay, McKee, Mackie ... Mrs Brenda Joyce, no relation of Roger but his secretary, undertook jobs ranging from sealing envelopes to computer operating, and did it all with enthusiasm on top of her natural speed and efficiency.

Mr R. M. Gallagher, Assistant Registrar (Information Management) at La Trobe University, generously devoted his skill and many hours of time to the questionnaire, its voluminous results and their subsequent computer processing. As he once asked, 'What is a problem but something to be solved?' In the end it always was.

Mrs Barbara Joyce, as Roger's wife and widow, was a staunch supporter of the work from the beginning, interested in its possibilities and predicaments, and sharing in the coding and computerising. She richly deserves whatever satisfaction she finds in the book. Dr Leonie Foster squeezed a good deal of coding into days she might have devoted to completing her doctoral thesis. But her motto was, 'I want to be where the action is' – and she managed to materially assist this work *and* bring her own to a triumphant conclusion.

Margaret Barrett, the author's wife and a professional editor, combined both roles in the making of this book. Marital relations and editing a writer can each be tricky, but Margaret managed them together – carefully, skilfully and lovingly. As our kids say, 'Thanks, Mag'.

Many other people earned the writer's gratitude: those who made essential money available through the Australian Research Grants Scheme; Mr R. J. Pinkerton, as Dean of Humanities at La Trobe University, with his back-up research fund; the leaders of the Returned Services League, who were well aware that some respondents would be critical of them, yet still gave every assistance to the project; the various other groups and individuals who gave free and vital publicity to the call for respondents; Messrs Michael Piggott and Paul Macpherson of the Australian War Memorial, for conducting searches; Mr Richard Glenister, a postgraduate in history at La Trobe University, for key material on a court martial and on Japanese treatment of POWs; various other members of the university (among them Mrs Kim Reynolds, who put the manuscript finally onto the word processor; the staff of the Reprography Section, who handled the photographs; people in the mail room, who risked hernias for the sake of the army project); and helpful people elsewhere, not least those involved in all the processes of book-publishing (Mr Jim Anderson of Abbtype was splendid). Mr Greg Dunnett drew the maps, and Mr Elmar Zalums (once a Latvian conscript in the German army) produced the index.

There still remains one very special individual: long-term research assistant Dr Nancy Renfree. Together with Roger Joyce, she did the lion's share of the coding, and then she did much more. Sensitive to what the project was intended to do, she spent months combing through the answers to find those

that best illustrated the various points and, when computer
lists were disappointing, she never minded searching man-
ually for that reply known to be there somewhere. It even
came about that a sign once went up in the 'army room': 'Just
remember. On 25 November, 3664 questionnaires were gone
through before the wanted one was found. Ponder on that and
take heart.' Nancy was an excellent sounding-board for all
ideas bounced her way. As an ex-WAAAF sergeant she stood
no nonsense, but as a research assistant she excelled even
among that remarkable breed.

Above all – and that is to go very high indeed – thanks are
due to the men who provided the rich material. It was brief or
extensive, barbed or gentle, enthusiastic or sceptical – and
often an interesting mixture. But overwhelmingly it was
honest; biased perhaps, but straight from the shoulder. Taken
together, the replies could not help but illuminate a nation's
understanding of the men who formed one of its wartime
armies. If this book has merit, it is because of the respondents.
They made it possible, set its tone and endowed it with their
own qualities.

Their material will be preserved – almost certainly to be
lodged finally with the Australian War Memorial, Canberra –
for use by approved researchers for as long as the nation
retains any interest in who these soldiers were, what they
fought for, and what they found in the end.

Illustration credits

Only a few of the illustrations are in any sense official.
Mostly they came from the collections of respondents and
other friends of the project. Grateful acknowledgement is
made to: J. M. Akhurst; H. P. Alford; R. J. Anson; Australian
War Memorial; A. E. Bannear; Gwyn Bates; Keith Battye;
Dennis Bird; M. J. Brincat; William Butler; G. R. W. Carter;
F. C. Cheal; G. D. Combe; C. R. Criddle; T. A. Crosbie; A. M.
Dean; Education History Services, Vic., and Brian McKinlay;

T. H. Fardy; E. N. H. Fletcher; Barbara Joyce; Ken Knox; D. J. Lee; Leunig and the *Age*; Vane Lindesay; Maurice Melvaine; E. L. Milgate; Ray Murphy; T. E. Musgrave; David Potts; Nancy Renfree; Kevin Sherry; H. C. Simmons; *Soldiering On*; D. L. Whittington; and R. K. Whittle.

A Note to the Penguin edition

The appearance of this book as a Penguin provided the opportunity to correct a few errors and remove some infelicities that were in the original Viking edition. The *Costa Rica* incident remains as V. H. Lloyd described it on p. 9, but Keith Hooper has pointed out that her drifting hulk was finally sunk by HMS *Hero*, which survived the war. The passage describing the formation of the 9th Division has been tidied up on p. 40, and the 6th Division's role in the Syrian campaign is now acknowledged on pp. 40-1. The 2/10th Battalion's fighting was done in Tobruk, not Syria (p. 45); and, while no change has been made to the claim that the 2/10th 'rather came to grief at Milne Bay', it is freely granted that the full battalion was not committed to battle, that those members of it who were engaged had to try to counter tanks without any anti-tank weapons, and that they succeeded in delaying the Japanese for long enough to improve the chances of the Australian defenders further back. QX5170 was naturally indignant at being described as an artilleryman when he was an engineer (p. 202), and the former members of the 2/3rd Anti-aircraft Regiment were outraged by having a mutiny attributed to them that actually occurred in a battery of the 2/3rd Anti-tank Regiment (p. 215). To all such ill-used men and units the guilty author offers his sincere apologies, while taking great comfort in many other men's expressions of satisfaction with 'our' book. As for infelicities of expression, they were better changed quietly without attention being drawn to them. Like every good military unit, all writers have their pride.

• INDEX

Compiled by Elmar Zalums

307, 309, 313–15, 317, 382; *see
also* Royal Air Force
Bromfield, E. L., 155
brothels, 6–7, 265–7, 334–5, 346–9,
351–3, 356–61, 363–5, 428–9;
see also sexual conduct
Brown, B. A., 275
Browne, R. A., 290–1
Bruce, A. W. ('Lucky'), 380
Bruce, John, 364
Bruton, S. J., 293, 297
Buckland, L. D., 65
Buckley, Sidney, 202, 402
Budd, G., 173
Buddee, P. E., 180
Budden, F. M., 43
Bullwinkel episode, 57
Burke, R. A., 179–80, 195–6, 364,
395
Burke, T. K., 400
'Burke'n', 401
Burma–Thailand (Siam) railway:
Burma railway, 77, 96, 237,
253, 255–6, 265, 268, 332, 390;
'H' Force, 254–5; *see also*
prisoner-of-war camps
Burnett, J. W., 361
Burns, J. H., 229–30, 234
Burr, G. C., 99
Burridge, 'Bluey', 222
Burton, H., 172
Burton, R. F., 390
Butler, J. D., 369, 371
Butt, W. E., 305
Butterworth, T. S., 66
Butwell, C. J., 68, 104, 305
Byrne, Father, 9–10, 78
Byrnes, R. H., 213, 222, 375

C.A.B., 188, 241, 243
C.B.P., 75
C.E.S., 112–13, 155, 284
C.G., 284
C.H.F., 133, 288

C.H.L., 384, 437
C.P.C., 132–3
C.R.B., 120, 143
C.R.T., 315
Cade, D. B., 222, 305
Caffrey, W. H., 200
Callaghan, D. W., 59
Callinan, J. M., 305, 307–8
Cambridge, David, 57, 79, 394,
403–4
Cameron, W. J., 70
Campbell, C. C., 407
Campbell, L. M., 156
Canadian troops, 304
cannibalism, 219, 222, 251, 260
Carlson, R. H., 132
Carroll, S. L., 343
Cassidy, John, 179
Catholic Weekly, 152
Catton, W. A., 207
Chamberlain, Neville, 149
Chambers, E. W., 207–8
chaplains, 435; attitudes to sex,
363, 367; criticism of, 75, 79,
206, 326–7; Mass under air raid,
9–10; respect and praise, 78,
211, 267–8, 326–8, 332;
selection of, 326; as SP bookie,
327; welfare work, 95
Chapman, O., 172
Chapman, R. K., 380
Chard, Frank, 245
charity work, 66, 71, 112, 346
Charles, E. G., 360
'Charlie', 30, 87, 291, 328
'Chas', 229
Chauvel, Harry, 148
Cheal, F. C., 158–9
Chesson, E. L., 319
'Chesty', 434–5
Chew, Alec, 249–50
Chifley, Joseph B., 214
Chinese bandits, 243
Chisholm, Captain, 263

D.C., 159
D.D.F., 360, 375
D.K., 392
D.R.S., 309, 326, 377
D.R.W., 74
D.S.A., 179, 321, 353, 372
Daily, 'Stew', 172
Daniels, J. D. T., 59
D'Aran, F. G. V., 156, 199
Darwin, Charles, 70
Darwin air raids, 430-2
Davies, J. R., 313, 370
Davies, N. E., 141
Day, H. E., 98, 102
Day, L. A., 87
Dedman, W. T., 132, 330
Defender (ship), 9
Denny, A. E., 60-1
depression, commercial, 4, 61, 66,
    92-3, 107, 111, 119, 124, 137,
    216, 412-13
Derrick, T. C. ('Diver'), 222,
    227-9
'Desert Head', see Rouvray, K. M.
'Dick', 24, 52, 76
Dick, A. N., 225-6
Digger, 93, 223, 228-9; old
    Diggers, 67-8, 158, 412;
    original Diggers, 413; qualities,
    297-302; real Digger, 402, 437;
    typical Digger, 86, 163-4, 169,
    203, 298, 383; word little used,
    298; see also Anzacs; subjects
    pertaining to Digger
discipline, see authority
divorce, 57, 164, 370-2, 383-4
Dobson family, 61
Donohue, J. D., 314
Doran, D. J., 310, 438
drifters and larrikins, 59-60,
    178-9, 264, 274, 276, 279, 284,
    286, 333-5, 376, 386, 403-4
drinking: drunkenness, 24, 61,
    115-16, 145, 190-1, 211-13,

236, 269, 279, 286, 298, 304,
    319-87 *passim*, 401, 412; light
    drinking, 63, 69, 159, 338-9,
    341, 350-1, 358-9; teetotallers,
    63, 336, 338, 356, 401; 'wet'
    canteens, 37
drug-taking, 415
Drummond, A. H., 284
Drysdale, William, 401
Duckworth, Padre, 268
Duncan, C. J., 402
Duncan, I. L., 14, 326
Dunlop, Edward ('Weary'),
    205-6
Dwight, G. R., 218, 245
Dwyer, Mick, 251
DX33, see Wignall, G. E.
DX100, 284

E.J., 104-5, 323
E.J.D., 154
E.J.M., 405-6
E.K., 250-1, 253, 318, 347
E.R.W., 298-9
Eather, K. W., 213
Eddy, J. M., 77, 268
Edmonds, A. 172
Edmondson, Jack, 426
education: attitudes to, postwar,
    377, 388; attitudes to, prewar,
    84-7, 89-97, 274, 281-2, 284;
    formal, 20-1, 23-5, 51-114
    passim, 147, 157, 187, 211,
    283-4, 356, 376-7, 380, 412;
    further education efforts, 63,
    68-9, 71, 82, 86, 94, 96, 376-7,
    382, 420; promotions and, 66,
    69, 85-6, 93-4; schools
    attended, 52, 67, 75, 78, 84-6,
    111-12, 115, 142, 147-8, 177,
    184, 276, 285; secondary, 25,
    85-7, 92, 94-5, 107, 111-12,
    142, 183; tertiary, 67, 69, 84,
    110-11, 118-20, 148, 156, 159,